I may not write, as there
is an amount of strong
disapproval of them in
some quarters which may
under them abortive
My address is to the
care of

J. R. Preece Esq
Ispahan
where I should be de
lighted to have news
of you.

I am most sincerely

Isabella L. Bishop

A CURIOUS LIFE
FOR A LADY

The Story of
ISABELLA BIRD

By Pat Barr

The Coming of the Barbarians
A story of western settlement in Japan 1853–1870

The Deer Cry Pavilion
A story of Westerners in Japan 1868–1905

A CURIOUS LIFE
FOR A LADY

The Story of

ISABELLA BIRD

❧❧❧❧❧❧❧❧

PAT BARR

MACMILLAN
JOHN MURRAY

First published in 1970 by

Macmillan & Company Limited
Little Essex Street
London w.c.2

and

John Murray (Publishers) Limited
50 Albemarle Street
London

and distributed by
MACMILLAN AND CO LTD
London and Basingstoke
Associated companies in New York Toronto
Dublin Melbourne Johannesburg and Madras

Printed in Great Britain by
ROBERT MACLEHOSE AND CO LTD
The University Press, Glasgow

Why has no poet offered a dithyramb in favour of Curiosity as a receipt for happiness, a stimulus to life?

To discover how and why a thing was done, to learn the real motive or meaning of some action, to put facts to facts and make them tell a story – this is the detective itch that keeps men young.

A. J. A. Symons in 'The Tennants of Glenconner', *Essays and Biographies*

To Margot,
who broadened many early horizons

Contents

Contents

List of Illustrations

Kashmir and Tibet

Persia

Korea

China

Endpapers: A letter from Isabella Bird to her publisher John Murray describing her terrible journey from Baghdad to Tehran during the winter of 1890.

ACKNOWLEDGEMENTS

Acknowledgement is due to the following: to John Murray for 1, 2, 4, 5, 6, 7, 9, 10, 11, 15, 16, 17, 24, 26, 28, 29, 30, 32, 33, 34 (reproduced from books by or about Isabella Bird), for 12, 31, 35 and 36 which are from original photographs taken by Isabella Bird, and for 18, of which the original hangs in 50 Albemarle Street; to the Rev G. E. Wood, rector of Houghton and Wyton, Huntingdonshire for 19, the original of which hangs in Wyton Church; to Mr Duncan McQuarrie of Salen, Isle of Mull for 20; to the Radio Times Hulton Picture Library for 25; and to Mr Tsuneo Tamba for 13, reproduced from an original in the Tamba collection of the Kanagawa Prefectural Museum, Japan.

Acknowledgements

FIRST of all my grateful thanks are due to Mr John Murray, who kindly allowed me access to Isabella Bird's original letters and photographs, and to my editor at Macmillan, Caroline Hobhouse, for her unfailingly generous help and encouragement.

I have corresponded with several people in an endeavour to learn more about Isabella's personality, and I would particularly like to thank Mrs Dorothy Middleton, whose admirably perceptive essay on Isabella in her book *Victorian Lady Travellers* was my original starting-point. Additional valuable guidance on the American section of the book was kindly given by Professor Alfons L. Korn, formerly of the English Department of the University of Hawaii; by Mrs Alys Freeze of the Western History Department of the Public Library in Denver, Colorado; by Mrs G. Vloyantes of Fort Collins, Colorado, and by Mr Marshall Sprague, whose book *A Gallery of Dudes* contains an entertaining account of Isabella's meeting with Jim Nugent. Leads on the Malayan section were given me by Professor J. Kennedy and Mr James Pope-Hennessy, whose excellent work *Verandah* contains much fascinating material on the early career of Hugh Low.

It proved very difficult to find much in the way of unpublished material on Isabella's immediate family or any surviving impressions of the life of the Bird sisters in Scotland. I am, however, indebted to Mr Godfrey Bird of Headley, Hants, Mrs M. Abercrombie of Edinburgh and Mr Duncan McQuarrie of Salen, Isle of Mull, for help in these directions.

Pat Barr

Preface

THE buoyant name of Isabella Bird is an apt identification of that
reckless lady with 'the up-to-anything and free-legged air', as she
herself described it, who went breezing about the remote parts
of the Asian and American continents for thirty years and became one of the most popular, respected and celebrated travellers
of the later nineteenth century. It was equally fitting that she
should marry a man with the name of Bishop, with its overtones
of an earnest and pious respectability, its settled-down and no-
nonsense air. For the lesser-known, home-grown Isabella was the
devout elder daughter of a clergyman, philanthropic gentlewoman of Edinburgh, wife and soon widow of a worthy physician
in that city. The 'Bird' and the 'Bishop' journeyed in uneasy
tandem for most of Isabella's days; the former was often irritable,
impatient and bored with the latter, the latter often anxious, dis-
approving and a little guilty about the former.

It is Isabella Bird as traveller, writer and adventurer extraordinary who commands the limelight and is the inspiration of this
tale; yet this Isabella did not really take off until she was forty years
old – a classic case, if ever there was one, of life beginning at that
climactic juncture. And so I make no apology for beginning there;
I merely give two assurances. First, that had I chosen to start
the story in 1831 when Isabella was born, and then plod step by
step through her early years – as ailing young lady lying on the
sofa of a country parsonage, as student of hymnology and religion, as diligent worker in various charitable causes – it would
have been a rather wearisome and spiritless introduction to such a
resolute and zestful person. Secondly, that as it is, nevertheless,
quite unwarranted to dismiss the first half of anybody's life simply
because it makes for a less spirited read than the second, I have
in Part Two outlined the essential patterns of Isabella's early

13

years. And those years, though they lacked the thrill of adventure, were nonetheless fruitful and valiant in their quieter fashion.

But I intend to start when Isabella found her vocation: 'Miss Bird is the ideal traveller', announced the *Spectator's* critic of her second major book, *A Lady's Life in the Rocky Mountains*. 'She can see and she can use the words that place what she sees before the reader. . . . There never was anybody who had adventures so well as Miss Bird.' And re-reading the eight ponderous-looking volumes that she wrote, I am convinced that the reviewer spoke no more than the truth. For, in each one, the lands and the people she saw and her experiences of them still live, vividly, freshly, with the bloom still on – and now with the added patina of interest and nostalgia for times past.

In my attempt to recreate the worlds she visited, I have drawn most extensively, of course, on Isabella's own books and letters, and all the quotations not otherwise attributed are hers. I have supplemented and I hope enriched these with other contemporary writings about the same scene which provide a change of pace, a different viewpoint, and with additional chat, information, forewords, postscripts about the people and places that came her way. I have also presented the material, mostly from the unpublished letters, which gives some indication of her complex and deeply riven personality, and I have hazarded a few interpretative suggestions on this theme, which can only be regarded as informed guesses.

Many of Isabella's moral, social and political attitudes were staunchy typical of the Victorian age in which she lived, and she retained throughout her life a confident and, by modern standards, rather dismaying admiration for the conventional and respectable. She did not attempt to provide herself with any broad-based philosophical justification for the way in which she quietly and serenely side-stepped the conventions of her time and yet, as a Victorian gentlewoman, the extent of her departure from those conventions was quite astonishing.

It was, of course, an energetic age, and many English ladies travelled immense distances. Frequently they went as reluctant 'dependants' of their husbands to the farflung outposts of Empire, and sometimes, in pleasurable pursuit of health, spectacular scenery, exotic trophies, they travelled the fairly well-beaten globetrotters' routes which, by the 1870s, covered a great deal of the world. Miss Bird, however, sedulously avoided these beaten tracks and fled in horror from tourist meccas such as Yokohama, Singapore or Shanghai; she tended to avoid the Empire altogether, in fact, and it is significant that the only large eastern country she neither explored nor wrote about was India.

Isabella Bird belonged, in short, to that colourful band of travelling individualists of the late nineteenth century who, for all their eccentricities, had one feature in common – an innate, abiding, intensely emotional distaste for the constraints imposed by their own highly civilised society. Like others among them, Isabella tried to explain her most unconventional journeys in conventional terms by stressing the worth of 'the rich cargoes of knowledge' she brought back from them. But it cannot, and indeed need not, be claimed that her efforts in this direction were of very lasting significance. Rather, the story of her life is valuable and pleasurable today simply because she used it to journey far and tell her tales well. The life was the work; the work was going to various parts of the globe and having adventures better than anyone else; the first adventure begins here.

Part One

❧ ❧ ❧ ❧ ❧ ❧

A LADY'S LIFE ON HORSEBACK

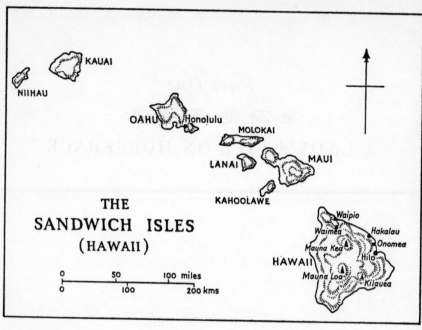

THE
SANDWICH ISLES
(HAWAII)

NIIHAU

KAUAI

OAHU   Honolulu

MOLOKAI

LANAI   MAUI

KAHOOLAWE

Waipio

Waimea   Hakalau

Mauna Kea   Onomea

HAWAII   Hilo

Mauna Loa   Kilauea

0   50   100 miles

0   100   200 kms

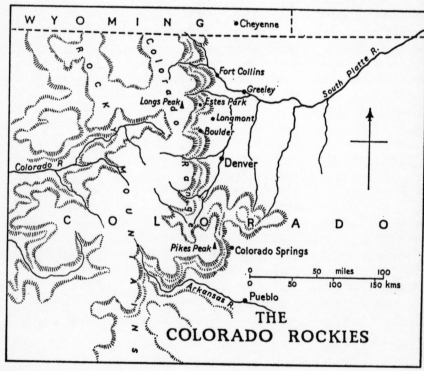

W Y O M I N G   • Cheyenne

Fort Collins

Greeley

R O C K   Longs Peak

Estes Park

Longmont

Boulder

Colorado R.   Denver

C O L O R A D O

M O U N T A I N S

Pikes Peak   Colorado Springs

Arkansas R.   Pueblo

0   50   miles   100

0   50   100   150 kms

THE
COLORADO ROCKIES

CHAPTER I
The Sandwich Isles

I N midsummer 1872 a quiet, intelligent-looking dumpy English spinster sailed to Australia in a desperate search for physical and mental health. Up to that time, Isabella Bird's life had developed in appropriate conformity with her position as the dutiful daughter of a middle-class Victorian clergyman. During her early years, she had studied diligently, learned needlework and music, organised Sunday School classes, and also suffered the onset of a chronic spinal disease, which was to recur throughout her life. As a young woman, she had promoted various charitable schemes to help the poor, studied metaphysical poetry, and written articles on hymnology and moral duty while laid up on a sofa convalescing after the removal of a fibrous tumour from the base of her spine. She had also travelled in Europe and America and these early, fairly conventional journeys had benefited her health temporarily – suggesting that, for her, travelling was indeed an elixir. During her thirties, Isabella, still sickly and plagued with backache, lived with her maiden sister, Henrietta, in a dignified square in the city of Edinburgh and had a circle of high-minded, intelligent friends. But because Isabella was an extraordinary woman, all these fairly ordinary endeavours provided few outlets for the immense reserves of energy, enthusiasm and enterprise she possessed. Now she was forty, and added recently to her woes were debilitating attacks of insomnia and nervous prostration. She felt herself growing old, unused, unfulfilled; she was fretful, depressed, frustrated and near mental collapse. On the day she sailed she wrote in her diary, 'All his days he eateth in darkness and he hath much sorrow and wrath with his sickness.'

At first the whole enterprise seemed a ghastly failure, and the letters she wrote home from Australia show a mind numbed with ever more harrowing melancholy, shadowed with an ever more consuming sickness. She was suffering, it seemed, from 'neuralgia, pain in my bones, pricking like pins and needles in my limbs, excruciating nervousness, exhaustion, inflamed eyes, sore throat, swelling of the glands behind each ear, stupidity'. She took three bromides a day and still 'felt shaking all over and oppressed with undefined terror . . . I am such a miserable being,' she groaned. 'My back is better but my head remains so bad and I always feel so tired that I never wish to speak . . . I wish I cared for people and did not feel used up by them, for people one can always have. I like toil with occasional spurts of recreation. This is such an aimless life.'

Recipient of these distressing and unhappy letters, as of all the bubbling happy ones soon to follow, was Henrietta – Hennie, as she was usually called. Hennie was a gentle, worthy soul whose function in life was that of lodestar to Isabella's wanderings, fire-keeper for Isabella's return and inspiration for Isabella's best writing; it was Isabella's whole-hearted effort to make her younger sister see what she had seen, share what she was doing, that made her letters so alive. These long, discursive, personal, discerning epistles were written more or less on the spot like war-reports and then sent to Hennie, who shared their contents with a small circle of intimate women friends. On returning home, it was Isabella's habit to 'excise a mass of personal detail' from the letters, edit them, add chunks of historical and political information and then publish them in book form. When Isabella was care-free and enthralled, as she invariably was when travelling, her letters romp; on the few occasions when she was oppressed, they sag, snarl and whine – as did those from Australia, a continent that could do nothing right in Isabella's eyes.

It was a 'prosaic, hideous country' with 'hideous leafage' and 'a golden calf its one deity', she decided. Its acacias stank like drains; its bluebottles battered her like an Egyptian plague; its gum-trees depressed her, for their colour was 'that of town-grown willows smothered with dust'; its heat was so torrid that she came out in a rash all over and some of her hair fell out. The people of this unfortunate land did little to raise her spirits. Its 'colonial born young ladies all seem afflicted with hysteria', its dressmakers ruined her clothes, its clergymen indulged in petty wrangles and gossip and most of its remaining denizens were 'lumpish and heavy'. Even its photographers were quite without talent and the 'portraits' they produced of her – with sparse hair, clothes that had 'gone crooked' and those numerous afflictions – made her look 'completely insane and suicidal'. Better to go home again herself, she thought, than to send photographs like that!

But home to what? That was the rub. She loathed the '*constant murk* of Scottish skies', she told Hennie – but what was the alternative to their Edinburgh home? For: 'Houses and situations are so perfectly dismal and with this tendency to depression it is dangerous to put oneself in depressing circumstances. We have not money to get a house in a good situation and the w.c.'s of flats are so objectionable.' Perhaps a small house then? – though they hadn't the money for anything 'too elaborate'. But it must be *cheerful* with a sunny drawing-room. Or perhaps she should relinquish the role of gentlewoman altogether? 'If my back gets well enough I seriously think that a servant's place would be the best thing. Manual labour, a rough life and freedom from conventionalities added to novelty would be a good thing.' And so Isabella travelled hopefully, desperately on, in search of freedom, novelty, some different mode of experience with a rough, real, challenging edge to it. And at the tail-end of the drear year she found herself wilting beneath the 'white, unwinking, scintillating sun' that 'blazed down upon Auckland, New Zealand. Along the white glaring road from Onehunga, dusty trees and calla lilies drooped with the heat. Dusty thickets sheltered the cicada, whose triumphant din grated and rasped through the palpitating atmosphere. In dusty enclosures, supposed to be gardens, shrivelled geraniums, scattered sparsely, alone defied the heat. Flags drooped in the stifling air. Men on the verge of sunstroke plied their tasks mechanically. Dogs, with flabby and protruding tongues, hid themselves away under archway shadows. The stones of the sidewalks and the bricks of the houses radiated a furnace heat. All nature was limp, dusty, groaning, gasping. The day was the climax of a burning fortnight of heat, drought and dust, of baked, cracked, dewless land, and oily, breezeless seas, of glaring days, passing through fiery sunsets into stifling nights.'

In Auckland harbour, Isabella boarded the *Nevada*, an ancient, lumbering paddle-steamer with ailing boilers, leaking seams and listing masts. It was bound for California, where, she had been told, the air of the mountains was brittle and zestful, and the tough realities of pioneer life jerked one into health. The voyage proved eventful: a shrieking hurricane nearly wrecked them on the second day out; Mr Dexter, a young male passenger, became critically ill and was nursed by his mother and Isabella in the deck-house; there was constant threat of permanent engine failure as mysterious internal 'tubes' gave way 'at the rate of ten to twenty daily'. The cabins were alive with rats, food squirmed with ants and weevils and was served in a dining-room usually awash with spray from the leaking deck above.

But this bright-eyed tension of true danger, this drama of tropical sunrise and storm, this irresponsible, rolling rollicking life on the ocean wave was most enlivening. Suddenly Isabella felt much much better, her spirits flowered. 'At last', she wrote home, 'I am in love and the old sea-god has so stolen my heart and penetrated my soul that I seriously feel that hereafter, though I must be elsewhere in body, I shall be with him in spirit! . . . It is so like living in a new world, so free, so fresh, so vital, so careless, so unfettered, so full of interest that one grudges being asleep; and instead of carrying cares and worries and thoughts of the morrow to bed with one to keep one awake, one falls asleep at once to wake to another day in which one knows that there can be nothing to annoy one – no door-bells, no "please mems", no dirt, no bills, no demands of any kind, no vain attempts to overtake all one knows one should do. Above all, no nervousness, and no conventionalities, no dressing. If my clothes drop into rags they can be pinned together . . . I am often in tempestuous spirits. It seems a sort of brief resurrection of a girl of twenty-one.'

In this carefree and fledgling mood, destinations scarcely seemed important any more. Thus, when her shipboard friend Mrs Dexter, whose son was so ill, begged her to disembark at the Sandwich Isles instead of going straight to California, Isabella agreed, explaining, 'The only hope for the young man's life is that he should be landed at Honolulu, and she has urged me so strongly to land with her there, where she will be a complete stranger, that I have consented to do so, and consequently shall see the Sandwich Islands.'

II

The Sandwich Isles (now the American State of Hawaii) were then the nearest approach to Paradise, the 'Blessed Isles', the 'Isles of Eden', the 'peacefullest, restfullest, sunniest, balmiest, dreamiest haven of refuge for the worn and weary spirit the surface of the earth can offer', as Mark Twain described them in 1866. And so they still proved for Miss Isabella Bird, who reached them in January 1873. She looked a quaint and buttoned-up little figure in that flamboyant landscape, but beneath her sedate exterior bounded all the energy of a twenty-one-year-old, newly-resurrected and in tempestuous spirits.

As the *Nevada* trundled toward Honolulu harbour, canoes came bouncing over the surf to greet it; natives floating naked in the blue water and fishermen poking about the coral reefs flapped an easy welcome; and from the steamer's high decks the passengers, relaxed and jolly after their marine ordeals, yearned towards the solid green hills and smiled down at the crowds on the quay who were laughing and called up at them 'in a language that seemed without backbone'. 'Such rich brown men and women they were, with wavy, shining black hair, large, brown lustrous eyes, and rows of perfect teeth like ivory.' Such an exuberance of colour they made – the women in floppy robes of primrose, scarlet, lilac; the men with jaunty bandanas at the throat and, like the women, positively blossoming with tropical flowers, festoons and swathes of them, looped upon their heads, their straw hats, their necks and wrists and swinging in garlands to their waists. At just a small distance, stood a cluster of 'foreign ladies' in sprigged muslins and pretty hats, looking, Isabella noticed, 'so un-burdened and innocent of the humpings and bunchings, the monstrosities and deformities of ultra-fashionable bad taste', and beaming, as the whole world beamed on her that day, 'with cheer-fulness, friendliness and kindliness'.

The warmth of that arrival was happily typical. As Isabella several times remarked, there could have been few places on earth where hospitality was so unstintingly given, the needs of strangers so joyously assuaged, cordial friendship so spontane-ously offered as on the Sandwich Isles during the mid-nineteenth century. When Isabella arrived there, she was simply an unknown

English lady unarmed with any of those official introductions to high places that would smooth many of her later journeys, and ungirded with the rather formidable reputation for influential comment and disquieting perspicacity that, in years to come, would bring her much flattering attention from some who hoped for an eulogy. The island settlers liked her simply for herself; they opened their homes and sometimes their hearts to her; they planned her excursions and provided her with horses, mules and guides; they admired her energy, sincerity and eager receptive interest. 'There is something soothing and gratifying in being so much liked,' she confessed to Hennie. 'It makes me such a nice, genial and pleasant person!' And so this softened, newly-genial Isabella who had planned to stay about three weeks on the Islands to help her friends, the Dexters, actually remained for seven months and left mainly because she felt herself succumbing to the temptation to stay for ever.

Apart from the occasional ship such as the *Nevada* come up from the Antipodes, communications with the independent kingdom of the Sandwich Islands were scant. One Pacific Mail steamer ploughed back and forth between them and San Francisco about once a month, a small number of whaling and naval vessels nosed in and out and there were a few large sailing vessels that zipped along nicely when the trade winds were favourable.

On the archipelago there was but one hotel, the Hawaiian, opened the year before. Light and shade from feathery tamarinds quivered across the dining-room tables that were piled high with guavas, bananas, melons, strawberries, limes, mangoes, pineapples plucked fresh for every meal. On the verandahs one could sit for hours watching the blue-green light deepen over the Nuuanu valley and listen, perhaps, to the distant music from a ship's band in the harbour and the closer chatter of the guests – naval officers from Connecticut or Liverpool, sheep-farmers, sugar-planters and their families, retired whaling captains.

It was comfortable, sociable, respectable and held few charms for Isabella, once she had settled in and helped Mrs Dexter to arrange medical attention for her son. 'I dislike health resorts and abhor this kind of life,' she states abruptly, in personal rejection not only of the Hawaiian, but of all the luxurious hostelries, international menus, bedrooms-with-hot-and-cold,

cocktail lounges and guided tours that were developing to satisfy
the expectations of that increasingly familiar figure on the world
scene – the middle-class, middlingly affluent, western globe-
trotter. Isabella's prejudice was a fortunate one. As a future
result of it she would spend many a night in log-cabins in the
Rocky Mountains, in palm-leaf shanties in the Malayan jungles,
in Tibetan tents, Persian caravanserais, Japanese country inns,
Kurdish stables, Korean monasteries, Chinese sampans; as an
immediate result of it, she was soon out of her comfortable rattan
chair on the hotel's verandah and aboard a steamer bound for the
lesser-known island of Hawaii, where she would soon spend her
first night in a native hut with grass roof, mud floor and a pillow
of tree-fern down.

The occasional perils of voyages to the Sandwich Islands were
minor afflictions compared with the uncertainties of going from
one island to another. The 400-ton screw steamer *Kilauea* that
forged the tenuous link looked like 'a second rate coasting collier'
or 'an old American tug-boat' and her past history was as full
of ups and downs as any vessel's could possibly be. Local legend
said that she had scraped her doughty bottom on every coral
reef in the archipelago; nevertheless, in 1873 she was still wobbling
along and Isabella gained first-hand experience of her many
vicissitudes. The *Kilauea* took some three days to amble over the
two hundred miles between Honolulu on Oahu and Hilo on
Hawaii, lurching remorselessly in the windward swells most of
the way. Frequently her machinery ground to a total halt; in the
blue tropic afternoons she seemed to fall quite asleep, her rudder
drowsily creaking and awnings flipping listlessly against the deck-
poles; during storms, water cascaded through the dining-room
skylights, while those who could stomach it were served with a
good curry by a sweetly-apologetic Malay steward wearing gum-
boots who waded in from the kitchen. 'A grand feature of the
voyage on the *Kilauea*', trumpeted one of the earliest Hawaiian
guide-books, 'consists in the licensed observation of Hawaiian
home-life at first hand.' This was possible, indeed unavoidable,
because the native passengers, as the guide continued, 'are not
infrequently so thickly congregated forward of the privileged
quarter-deck – reserved for foreigners who pay for the privilege –
that they are unable to lie down but remain wedged up in a

tangled mess of men, women, children' and, in addition, as
Isabella soon discovered, of 'dogs, cats, mats, calabashes of *poi*,
coconuts, breadfruit, dried fish'.

By day, the natives scooped up the *poi* with their fingers,
smelled fiercely of the dried fish and rancid coconut oil, giggled
and crooned to their pets, mostly 'odious, weak-eyed pink-nosed
Maltese terriers'; at night, they lay on their mats, if they could
find room, and gazed up at the rolling stars. Isabella curiously
observed the native home-life during the day, and at night was
allotted a berth in a cabin where 'sex, race and colour are included in a promiscuous arrangement'. She numbered among her
sleeping companions the Hawaiian Governor, Mr Lyman; a
female American tourist; one Afong, Chinaman; and Governor
Nahaolelua of Maui Island whose head, she was told in the
morning, she had used as a footstool all night. Other occupants
included cockroaches as big as mice 'of an evil dark red with eyes
like lobsters and two-inch-long antennae'. On the second night
Isabella joined the natives on the deck.

And on the third morning they floated into Hilo Bay – a
crescent of pearly sand fringed with palm-trees that was gold
under the sun, pink at sunset, silver by moonlight, that was
perfumed with oleander, jasmine, passion-flowers, that was lulled
with the rhythms of surf on sand, patter of gay feet, soft chatter
of sugar-canes and banana-groves. Hawaii, in short, embodied
that seductive dream of the South Seas, the enchanted isles of
the lotos-eaters that, in 1873, was almost as provocative and beguiling as it is today. But, at that time, the gulf between the
sweet dream and the reality was much smaller.

Hilo, the 'administrative capital of the island' (to use words
that sound grotesque and abrasive in the context) was a large
village with a few open stores facing the beach, three churches, a
courthouse, a number of white clapboard houses and bunches of
native huts that seemed to be growing amid the glossy breadfruit
and candlenut trees. The stores sold kerosene lamps, stirrups,
peppermints, fish-hooks, wooden tubs and twine; the most imposing church, horned with bell-towers, was for the Catholics;
the two smaller, wooden-spired in the thrifty New England
manner, were for the Protestants (foreign and native respectively);
on the lawn before the court-house, the Sheriff, the Judge, the

Governor and other leisured gentlemen played interminable games of croquet. They and other foreign settlers (about thirty in all) lived in white-wood houses, each with a trim parlour adorned with sea-shells, water-colours, vines, manila matting on the floor, net curtains puffing at the open verandahs. Most of the foreigners were Americans who had settled on the Islands and, as Isabella soon discovered, 'American influence and customs' were prevalent and 'Americans "run" the Government and fill the Chief Justiceship and other high offices of State'.

Nevertheless, at that period it was still the natives who set the tone of Hawaii. The natives, said the foreigners, were like spoiled children – feckless, merry, lackadaisical, innocent, unreliable and picturesque. When they were hungry they had but to shake a pineapple or coconut from a tree or suck a calabash of *poi* (that glutinous lilac-coloured mush made from baked fermented *taro* root which tasted, Isabella said, like 'sour bookbinder's paste'). When they were hot, they simply scooped off their single garment and cavorted in the nearest pool. When they felt energetic, they jumped on their surfboards and rode shorewards on breakers that bucked like wild horses, or they saddled steeds of a fleshier kind and galloped over the sand. When they were tired, they simply rolled into a green shade and slept. Their music was a lilt of skin-drum, nose-flute and pipe, their language was a soft song of words composed of only twelve letters, and their dance, the notorious hula, was the most provocative and openly sexual invitation in the world. And so the Sandwich Islanders innocently and charmingly embodied an absolute antithesis to that Anglo-Saxon Puritan-Christian ethic which was the harsh guiding light of the American pioneer missionaries who had landed on their shores in the year 1820.

Later, Isabella learned the details of that dramatic, explosive encounter; for the moment it was sufficient to land at Hilo herself, amid a chorusing of *alohas*, a bestowing of kisses, a garlanding of *leis*, and then to be swept warmly away to the home of the American Sheriff, Luther Severance. As there were no hotels on Hawaii, respectable foreign residents received respectable foreign visitors into their homes, and Isabella was soon friendly with everyone. Her hosts, the Severances, were among her favourites. When he was not playing croquet, Luther Severance trotted off on horseback to the sugar-plantations, kept an eye on the few whalers and the sale of liquor, and, wearing his postmaster's hat, supervised the distribution of mails. Mrs Severance, like other foreign ladies on Hawaii, was busier than her husband. This was partly because having no servants, except perhaps a Chinese cook, the ladies themselves 'in their fresh pretty wrappers and ruffled white aprons, sweep the rooms', and enjoyed doing it. 'The nuisance of morning calls' was thus unknown, and people visited after supper, taking their lanterns and just dropping in at the verandah windows for a chat. 'There are no doorbells [For which Isabella had a peculiarly strong aversion] or solemn announcements by servants of visitors' names, or "not-at-homes".' There were no dressmakers and so no 'high fashions'; 'the ladies don't have to bother with stockings either,' she told Hennie, and that saved a lot of tiresome mending; there were no carriage roads and so no carriages and no need to keep up with the Joneses with the smartest turn-out; no thieves, and so not a locked door on the island; and 'no carpets, no dust, no hot water needed'. Freed of so much, the settlers had abundant leisure 'for reading, music, choir practising, drawing, fernprinting, fancy work, picnics, riding parties'. While the natives, similarly deprived of over-strenuous employment, spent hours making *leis* and lounging on the sand while their dishes of sweet potato and chicken roasted in outdoor ovens.

This idyllic picture had its meaner, grosser elements, as Isabella soon realised, but in the first surge of uncritical enthusiasm she just wanted 'to become Hawaiianised' in every way – and so made a discovery that was greatly to facilitate her future journeying. Isabella passionately adored horses. One of the few engaging memories of her childhood preserved by her early biographer, Anna Stoddart, is that of a five-year-old Isabella in a simple smock riding a full-size carriage horse through the lanes of Cheshire. Nevertheless she was a frail child, and her activity was cramped by that spinal complaint which continued to afflict her whenever she walked a long distance or rode – in the ladylike side-saddle fashion. Thus, after a short ride out of Hilo, Isabella returned with excruciating backache and the despondent conviction that she would be unable to ride as far as the famous Kilauea volcano which she longed to see.

Surely what she needed then, said Luther Severance, was a Mexican saddle. A Mexican saddle was a very masculine affair, ornamented and brass-bossed, with a great horn in front and large wooden stirrups with long leathern flaps and guards of tough hide – a seat made for the jaunty bottoms of cow-punchers, bullock-hunters and other wild men of the open prairie. But on the precipitous bridle-tracks of Hawaii everyone used them, even the ladies, who had created for the purpose special straddle-proof 'riding costumes' of 'full Turkish trousers and jauntily made dresses reaching to the ankles'. It was just the job, and Isabella's friends soon ran one up for her in tartan flannel. In it, she straddled her first horse and discovered that she could gallop comfortably at last – at one with the steed, instead of perched inflexibly on its side. 'It was only my strong desire to see the volcano which made me consent to a mode of riding against which I have so strong a prejudice,' she assured her readers hastily. But that prejudice once conquered, Isabella rode many a mile astride many an animal – Arab stallions, Japanese packhorses, Persian mules, Tibetan yaks. She also wore variations of the 'Hawaiian riding-dress' theme for years, but the trousers were always utterly concealed beneath the skirts, and when she came to a town of any size she always rode a ladylike side-saddle through its streets. That was Isabella's way; she was not an iconoclast and confined her comfortable unconventionalities to foreign parts where they were not necessarily judged as such.

On Hawaii then, where no eye was censorious, Isabella supplemented her riding costume with 'great rusty New Zealand boots', a pair of jangling Mexican spurs, a *lei* of orange pandanus seeds and a 'coarse broad-brimmed Australian hat which served the double purpose of sunshade and umbrella'. Thus accoutred and securely mounted on the native policeman's horse with a blue blanket strapped behind her Mexican saddle, Isabella began her explorations. She jogged along under canopies of monkey-pod and mango leaves and loops of flame hibiscus and convolvulus, blue as the sky; she splashed through gulches laced over with ferns and vines; and came to temporary rest below the palms, those muttering, haughty palms, providers of milk, oil, food, matting, with 'curved, wrinkled perfectly cylindrical stems bulging near the ground like an apothecary's pestle' and leaves rearing amber-yellow and aged above the lower greenery. She jogged along, for a start, to a sugar-plantation owned by relatives of Mrs Severance.

The growing of sugar on the Islands was still a fairly speculative proposition. 'Christian missions and whaling have had their day,' Isabella noted, 'and now people talk sugar. Hawaii thrills to the news of a cent up or down on the American market.' When Mark Twain was in Hawaii he had discovered that as there was never any frost, there was no sugar 'close season' and the plantations which then existed could produce up to '13,000 pounds of sugar an acre on unmanured soil'. Twain found out the price of everything (as he always did), totted up his arithmetic in good old Yankee greenbacks and announced that, with a little effort and know-how, Hawaii could be 'the king of the sugar world'. He had it all worked out: the importation of cheap coolie labour from China to work the plantations, so that the whites could drop their shovels and become overseers; the chartering of cargo vessels to carry the sugar to San Francisco; the distillation of 'inferior molasses' (then fed to hogs) for the brewing of whisky as a profitable side-line. This all came to pass, more or less, in due season, but less rapidly than Twain had hoped, owing to the natural lethargy of the islanders and the continuing heavy import duties levied by the United States. A new reciprocal trade treaty between American and the Islands was signed three years after Isabella was there, and later sweet fortunes were made in sugar. But in 1873 there were only thirty-five plantations and, in Isabella's view, 'few of the planters at present do more than keep their heads above water'.

However, the blissful picture she draws of the Onomea plantation where she stayed suggests that its owners, at least, were comfortably afloat in their well-ordered semi-feudal world. Judge Austin and his wife of Onomea lived in a roomy frame-house on a slope, a grass-hut village dozed in the valley below and the land behind swept high to a belt of forest whose shades 'threw into greater brightness the upward glades of grass and the fields of sugar cane' in the foreground. Little houses for the overseers, bookkeepers, sugar-boilers and machinists dotted the compound, there was a store run, inevitably, by a Chinaman and the mill itself where the cane-juice poured 'as a pale green cataract' into the troughs and later burbled reddish-brown, oily and seething at a temperature of 150°.

When Isabella strolled upon the verandah of the main house, she could hear the distant cadence of breakers on the shore and the cheery rustle of cane that had never known a frost; she could smell the passion-flowers on the trellis, the grittiness of dust kicked by horses' hooves, the over-ripeness of molasses; and she could watch the satisfactory bustle in the compound, 'overseers, white and coloured, natives riding up at full gallop and people coming on all sorts of errands, the hum of the crushing mill, the rush of water in the flumes and the grind of the waggons carrying cane'. Sometimes a procession of mules plodded by loaded with iron-banded wooden kegs of sugar to be piled in the sandy cove below for shipment by schooner to Honolulu when the wind was favourable. Six hundred tons of sugar a year jolted away from the mill in this fashion, its cane leaves were chewed by the baggage animals, its 'trash' (dried stalks from which the juice had been pressed) was dried in the sun and re-used for fuel, its silvery tassels were woven into sunhats worn by the workers. The crop was beautiful at every stage; its patterns were perfect.

And here, at the pattern's centre, lived the Austins and their four merry barefoot sons – typical settlers, Isabella thought, with 'faces not soured by the east wind or wrinkled by the worrying effort to "keep up appearances" '; with leisure enough to be 'kind, cultured and agreeable', with honesty enough to ask any congenial traveller 'to occupy the simple guest chamber or share the simple meal'. At the meals, the food was wholesome and un-pretentious – sweet potatoes, sliced guavas, griddle cakes with (of course) molasses; and the talk was the sort that Isabella enjoyed – gossipy, homely but full of interest and surprise to a stranger. She heard about a scheme for introducing mongooses from India to battle with the increasing number of rats, about the habits of the industrious Chinese coolies, some of whom gambled half their wages away and bought opium with the rest, and about the much less industrious natives who, lengthening their jolly faces into lugubriousness, would complain of multi-farious minor afflictions in order to get off work for a day. One lunch-time, Mr Austin suggested that Isabella should visit the famously beautiful Waipio Valley and he arranged for a native girl, Deborah, to guide her and lent her his favourite mule, a creature adept at putting its feet together and sliding over rough places.

The trip took five days and proved quite adventurous. En route they were joined by a young man called Kaluna, Deborah's cousin and a zany addition to the party. 'His movements are impulsive and uncontrolled and his handsome face looks as if it belonged to a half-tamed creature out of the woods. He talks loud, laughs incessantly, croons a monotonous chant, which sounds almost as heathenish as tom-toms, throws himself out of his saddle, hanging by one foot, lingers behind to gather fruits and then comes tearing up, beating his horse over the ears and nose, with a fearful yell and a prolonged sound like *har-r-rouche*, striking my mule and threatening to overturn me as he passes on the narrow track. . . . His manner is familiar. He rides up to me, pokes his head under my hat, and says interrogatively, "Cold!" by which I understand that the poor boy is shivering himself. In eating he plunges his hand into my bowl of fowl or snatches half my biscuit.' He was the 'most thoroughly careless and irresponsible being' the maiden lady from Edinburgh had ever met, but 'I daresay he means well', she concludes placidly and found most of his antics amusing. Though an emotional and highly-strung woman who responded tensely to the stresses of modern society, Isabella was quite unflappable when faced with untoward behaviour such as this. She realised that she often cut quite a ludicrous figure on the foreign scene and that the natives often poked fun at her. But she never displayed any irritation or alarm and she put up a front of imperturbable good humour that blunted all mockery. She needed her reserves of equanimity that night – her first in entirely native surroundings.

There were drenched by a slapping rain long before they reached 'the house of a native called Bola-Bola' where they planned to stay. Squelching across a pig-ridden yard, they found Bola-Bola's house to be a derelict and dirty one-room shack that already contained 'mats, boxes, bamboos, saddles, blankets, lassoes, coconuts, *taro* roots, bananas, quilts, pans, calabashes, bundles of hard *poi* in *ti* leaves, bones, cats, fowls, clothes' together with a frightful, shrivelled nude old woman tattooed all over, a girl of twelve 'with torrents of shining hair', two other young women 'in rose-coloured chemises' cradling a baby, and Bola-Bola himself, who hospitably killed a fowl for their dinner. When darkness fell, a piece of beef fat was lit in a hollow stone, and by its sputtering gleam the women stared remorselessly at their weird visitor. At last, to Isabella's relief, a curtain was pulled to shield her from those brown, inert eyes and a *pulu* shakedown was produced. *Pulu* was a silky fibre that grew on the fronds of the Hawaiian tree-fern. Before the foreigners came and introduced the word 'export' to the islanders, they used *pulu* to stuff quilts and the cavities of their dead, as part of a traditional embalming process; between the 1850s and 70s, having learned the meaning of 'export', they gathered bumper bundles of the fibre from the forests and sent it overseas to stuff the pillows and eiderdowns of the merely sleeping. So a *pulu* shakedown must have been comfortable, but Isabella couldn't sleep on hers. She was lying directly below a broken window through which jumped and landed on her, one after the other, five large wild wet cats, and 'had there been a sixth,' Isabella concluded, 'I think I could not have borne the infliction quietly'. Each cat stole a strip of the jerked beef that hung stiffly from the rafters, but one let a piece fall which wakened everyone, and so the natives all got up again and smoked and ate more *poi* and laughed together until a pallid watery dawn crept through the thatch.

Starting early, Isabella, Deborah and Kaluna trotted past herds of semi-wild bullocks with crooked horns that were being driven to Hilo market by yelling cowhands, past villages, each with its glitter of goldfish ponds, *taro* patch, grove of orange and coffee in blossom, and alongside streams where native women were shrimping, up to their ample bosoms in the water, pushing trumpet-shaped baskets before them. Shrimps were a delicacy to be eaten raw and so very very fresh that, as the people chewed their juicy heads, their pink tails were still threshing against the chewers' white teeth. It was, Isabella remarked, a repulsive sight.

The next day they reached the grandiose falls that plummeted down the Waipio Valley, and Isabella left her companions to wade along the river until the tepid water was up to her throat and 'the scene became real' to her. The thunder of many waters was always close on Hawaii – the high white surf pounding sand, tinkling village streams and cascades that poured down the beautiful, dangerous *palis*, precipitous chasms of volcanic rock, often measuring some 4,000 feet from cliff-top to valley floor, which gashed the coastline. There were no bridges across the *palis* then and travellers slithered down steep zigzag paths, forded the waters, clambered up the far side. Isabella and her companions crossed several of these, but as the rains continued, each torrent surged deeper and faster than the last, till, on the return journey, they reached the mightiest of all, the Hakalau gulch. 'The roar was deafening and the sight terrific. Where there were two shallow streams a week ago, with a house and a good-sized piece of ground above their confluence, there was now one spinning, rushing, chafing, foaming river, twice as wide as the Clyde at Glasgow.' Kaluna was off on some acrobatic exercise of his own and Isabella begged Deborah to turn back. But the girl wanted to get home and simply ploughed in, calling 'Spur, spur all the time.' Deborah was mounted on a strong large horse, Isabella on an unshod, untried mare called Bessie Twinker that she had bought the day before. Thinking this might be Bessie's and her last ride, Isabella cut loose a bunch of coconuts from her saddle and plunged. Bessie, knocked off her feet by the brawling waters, swam, struggled and snorted, Deborah shrieked as she was carried out towards the vast breakers on the nearby shore, Isabella, battered, dizzy and deafened, spurred landwards and at last Bessie's floundering hooves clawed the opposite bank. Ahead of them, Deborah's burly steed had also touched ground and they were safe. It was a foolhardy exploit, but one that excited Isabella with its authentic smell of danger, its promise of how well she could perform under physical stress. Some other travellers reached the gulch soon afterwards and, she records smugly, 'suffered a two-day detention rather than incur a similar risk'.

Having dried out and rested, Isabella returned to the unruffled, claustrophobic, amiable Severance home in Hilo and 'the pleasant little gatherings for sewing, while some gentlemen read aloud, fern-printing in the verandah, microscopic and musical evenings, little social luncheons and on Sunday evenings what is colloquially termed "a sing"'. Clearly, the prevailing social tone of the respectable settlers' life was prescribed by the American missionary contingent, and patriarch among them in Hilo was the Rev. Titus Coan, whose company Isabella enjoyed.

Coan was a pioneer missionary who had reached the Sandwich Isles in 1835 – accompanied by his wife who had borne the delicious maiden name of Fidelia Church. Now he was a courtly venerable pastor of his native flock who liked to relax in the shade of his latticed verandah and tell visitors about his early adventures during month-long 'missionings' into the Hawaiian interior. In those days there were few tamed horses, so Coan travelled on foot armed with nothing other than two calabashes (one for food, one for Bibles), but fierce and potent with the word of the Lord. He scrambled down *pali* sides on a rope, swam the foaming torrents, preached up to thirty sermons a week in as many villages. As Mark Twain put it, rather brutally, 'The missionaries braved a thousand privations' to come and make the islanders 'permanently miserable by telling them how beautiful and blissful a place heaven is and how nearly impossible it is to get there; and showed the poor natives how dreary a place perdition is and what unnecessarily liberal facilities there are for going to it; showed him what rapture it is to work all day long for fifty cents to buy food for the next day as compared with fishing for a pastime and lolling in the shade through the eternal summer and eating of the bounty that nobody laboured to provide but Nature.'

Needless to say, this was not how Titus Coan described his evangelistic endeavours to Isabella, nor would she have regarded them thus. In the course of her journeys, she met – and enjoyed meeting – numbers of the 'unconverted heathen' and she certainly did not unconditionally consign them to damnation. But she ardently believed that Christianity was a beneficent and civilising creed that spread a salutary moral influence and was infinitely preferable to, for instance, the amoral, crude, sometimes savage code by which the Sandwich Islanders had lived before the white men arrived. So she listened with enthusiastic sympathy as Coan told her about the Presbyterian pioneers who broke the spiritual trail and of their glorious heydays – the 'Great Revival' of the late 1830s and 40s when the message of the Gospel seemed to sweep across the islands like spring rain and converts sprouted thick as rice seedlings in the valleys. That this revival began on Hawaii was largely due to the zeal and open-heartedness of Coan himself. Most of the evangelists before him had followed an exclusive and doctrinaire line, as typified in this report from a missionary on Hawaii to his Church Board in New England: 'The attention to religion here continues and pressure to get into the church is very great; and if an entrance into the visible church was a guarantee of salvation we should do wrong to hold the people back. But we find so little of the deep feeling of sinfulness and unworthiness which a correct knowledge of the human heart and a clear discovery of the character of God always produces, that we feel justified in putting off almost all applications for admittance to the Church.'

Such painful and stringent entry requirements naturally disqualified many, but Coan introduced what a later historian terms 'a more wholesale policy' towards conversion. His sermons were highly emotional, rhetorical and revivalist in tone and the people responded to them: 'I wish you could have heard Mr Coan . . . tell of that stirring time,' Isabella wrote to Hennie, 'when nearly all the large population of the Hilo and Puna districts turned out to hear the Gospel and how the young people went up into the mountains and carried the news of the love of God and the good life to come to the sick and old, who were afterwards baptised, when often the only water which could be obtained for the rite was that which dripped sparingly from the roof of caves.' The people accepted Christianity wholeheartedly, its new promises and its new taboos. They pulled up their tobacco plants and cast them in the sea, they threw their pipes on the fire, they poured away their fermented liquors and, in Coan's words, 'The nation became a great Temperance Society with the King at its head.'

Sexual licence was less easy to eliminate. Many of the native huts were like Bola-Bola's with but a single room, and at night, as Miss Constance Cummings (a Scottish traveller, there a few years after Isabella) carefully puts it: 'Men and women, lads and lasses are all herded together promiscuously with one large sheet of woven grass acting as a household blanket.' This custom had not resulted in any problem of over-population, however. If a baby, perhaps one born on the wrong side of the blanket, was unwanted or was inconveniently noisy, the parents had a simple remedy, as Miss Cummings explained: 'A hole was dug in the earthen floor of the house and the wailing baby was therein deposited, a bit of cloth thrust into its mouth to still its cries, the earth and mats replaced and quiet being thus restored, domestic life continued peaceful as before.'

Nakedness was another new sin, and Isabella records that the missionary wives 'daily assembled the women and children and taught them the habits and industries of civilisation, to attend to their persons, to braid hats and to wear and make clothes'. And soon, at the white man's approach, the natives obligingly donned short shirts and old top-hats so as not to offend his sensibilities. During this dramatic period, hundreds of islanders flocked to Hilo where they were taught, watched over and examined by the missionaries. Then the 'accepted candidates' assembled for mass baptism, one of which Coan described to Isabella: 'On the first Sunday in July 1838, 1705 persons, formerly heathens, were baptised. They were seated close together on the earth-floor in rows, with just space between for one to walk and Mr Lyman [another venerable missionary] and Mr Coan passing through them, sprinkled every bowed head, after which Mr C. admitted the weeping hundreds into the fellowship of the Universal Church by pronouncing the words, "I baptise you all in the name of the Father and of the Son and of the Holy Ghost." '

But while the new life offered by Christianity may have been more wholesome and charitable, it brought new complexities and dissensions. In 1840 some French Catholics built a mission in Honolulu, and they informed the natives that there was no necessity for them to give up tobacco or liquor or wear clothes after all – as long as they attended the right services and learned the right prayers they would be saved. Later the Mormons came and, in Coan's words, 'spread themselves in squads all over the islands like frogs on Egypt'. Then, in 1862, as a result of active encouragement from the Hawaiian royal family, who corresponded with Queen Victoria on the subject, an Episcopalian Church was founded with Dr Staley, self-styled 'Lord Bishop of Honolulu', at its head. This church was distinctly Anglican–Establishment in style and, inevitably, sharp controversy flared between it and the unadorned fundamentalism of the New England missions.

But Coan's bitterest ire was reserved for the Catholics who, he felt, actively encouraged the natives to break the new taboos that he and his colleagues had framed. This hostility intensified as the

Catholics gained ground and Coan frequently came upon 'many confident Romanists' in villages where, formerly, he alone had held the key to salvation. 'I asked some of them if they read the Bible,' he writes, 'and they answered "Yes", showing me their little catechism with more prayers to Mary than to God. I asked one who claimed to be a teacher how many commandments there were in the Decalogue. He answered "Ten"; but on going through them in order I found that he omitted the second and divided the tenth in two parts to make good the number.' One evening, as he was riding home from a 'missioning', Coan met the local Catholic priest and some converts who started shouting insults at him. 'Peter is the Head of the Church,' thundered the priest; 'No, it is Jesus', roared back Coan, and the altercation continued for a considerable period. It was a sorry spectacle in that island sunset: the two black-robed men of God shaking their fists at each other and positively quivering in their saddles with hatred, while their native converts stood silently by in open-mouthed bewilderment.

And so the voice of the ageing patriarch on his verandah grew fretful as he lamented that the schisms in the church had brought dissension to the Islands. And Isabella, who often deplored the fruitless arrogance of sectarian strife, heartily agreed, though it probably occurred to her that holding impromptu examinations in the Decalogue and engaging in public slanging matches did little to mend matters. She did not say so; it would have been no use; and besides she was easy and happy in the sun. It was pleasanter and kinder to divert Coan's thoughts elsewhere – to the alarming behaviour of the island's turbulent volcanoes for instance, on which he was something of an expert, or the preparations for the impending visit to Hawaii of the King of the Sandwich Isles.

The Hawaiian monarchy, as Isabella explained, was 'no longer an old-time chieftaincy made up of calabashes and *poi* and feather-cloaks' but had a proper 'civilised constitutional king, the equal of Queen Victoria', who commanded a great deal of loyalty. And so, 'the good people of Hilo have been decorating their houses anew with ferns and flowers, furbishing up their clothes, and holding mysterious consultations regarding etiquette and entertainments, just as if royalty were about to drop down in similar fashion on Bude or Tobermory. There were amusing attempts to bring about a practical reconciliation between the free-and-easiness of Republican notions and the respect due to a sovereign who reigns by "the will of the people" as well as by "the grace of God", but eventually the tact of the King made everything go smoothly.'

Early one morning, an American ironclad with the King and several high-ranking American officers aboard came chugging into Hilo Bay. Bunting bloomed amid the palms and the long tattered banana-leaves with their heavy whorls of golden fruit shining in the sun; every balcony and stair in town was packed with people in their smartest hats and bonnets; the beach was a jostle of garlanded natives on horseback who waved brilliant bandanas when the King disembarked and whose children ran ahead of him in a joyous riot of colour, while a huge chuckling native called Upa beat a big drum. The King, whose lilting name was Lunalilo, had been on the throne only three months when he went to Hilo and would be dead in about a year. He was a genial, tolerant man of thirty-eight who believed in a liberal constitutional monarchy and was therefore a great improvement on the old-time chieftains, whose rule a historian wrote, had been one of 'despotism tempered by assassination'. Lunalilo was 'above all', 'the well beloved', 'the darling of the people' and formally elected by them when the previous King, Kamehameha V, died without a successor. Unfortunately Lunalilo, like several past members of the royal family, 'was witty when drunk and wise when sober', as Miss Cummings put it – and he often preferred being witty.

But on that day in Hilo the King, who was trying to reform, behaved impeccably. His muscular brown frame was carefully stuffed inside 'a sort of shooting suit, a short brown cutaway coat, an ash-coloured waistcoat and ash-coloured trousers with a blue stripe'. It was a dreadful rig-out, Isabella added for Hennie's benefit, but was fortunately concealed beneath welcoming festoons of light-lemon amaranth, spiky rose *ohia* blooms, purple and cream passion-flowers. His Highness paid a courtesy call on Mr Coan, patiently listened to the Flute Band of Father Lyman's Mission School and graciously received bounteous loads of offerings from his subjects. This present-giving, an old Hawaiian custom called *hookupu*, was both touching and gay. It took place at the court-house the next morning, and 'long before ten, crowds had gathered outside the low walls of the lawn, natives and foreigners galloped in all directions, boats and canoes enlivened the bay, bands played, and the foreigners, on this occasion rather a disregarded minority, assembled in holiday dress in the upper verandah . . . Hawaiian flags on tall bamboos decorated the little gateways which gave admission to the lawn, an enormous standard on the government flagstaff could be seen for miles, and the stars and stripes waved from the neighbouring plantations. . . .' At ten, the King, his suite and the foreign administrators of Hawaii appeared on the lower verandah and the people trooped by in their thousands, not a one empty-handed. 'Many of the women presented live fowls tied by the legs, which were deposited, one upon another, till they formed a fainting palpitating heap under the hot sun. Some of the men brought hogs decorated with *leis* of orange blossom, which squealed so persistently in the presence of royalty that they were removed to the rear. Hundreds carried nets of sweet potatoes, eggs and *taro* artistically arranged. Men staggered along in couples with bamboos between them, supporting clusters of bananas weighing nearly a hundredweight. Others brought yams, coconuts, oranges, onions, pumpkins, early pineapples and even the great delicious fruit of the large passion-flower. A few maidens presented the king with bouquets of choice flowers and costly *leis* of the yellow feathers of the *Melithreptes pacifica.*' (*Melithreptes pacifica,* popularly known as the Royal Bird, was a glossy black songster with the misfortune of having one beautiful gold feather under each wing. The feathers were collected, usually at the expense of their owners' lives, and woven into lustrous *leis* or cloaks fit for kings. The gold-feather cloak buried with Lunalilo a year later was said to be worth a hundred thousand dollars.)

From the court-house balcony, overlooking his hill-high heaps of gifts, Lunalilo expressed his gratitude and told his people, 'You must persevere in your search of wisdom and in habits of morality.' (Cheers from the crowd). And, he concluded significantly, 'At the present time I have four foreigners as my ministerial advisers. But, if among these young men now standing before me, and under this flag, there are any who shall qualify to fill these positions, then I will select them to fill their places.' The loudest cheers of all greeted this overt suggestion that foreign influence in the Island's affairs was predominant, but not necessarily desirable. It was of course logical. Foreigners had introduced the whole western-style apparatus of constitutional government and then had to provide trained officials to make it function. Most members of the Hawaiian Cabinet therefore, were American lawyers, missionaries, business men, and teachers; foreigners headed the new ministerial departments at pleasantly adequate salaries, for those days, of four thousand dollars a year each.

The flummery of western-style public life had been introduced along with its institutions: there were royal garden-parties where sombre-suited Cabinet Ministers with starchy wives nibbled meringues in company with former tribal chiefs resplendent in military uniforms encrusted with flourishes of epaulettes and gold lace. Later, in Honolulu, Isabella attended such a party, at which 'tea and ices were handed round on Sèvres china by footmen and pages in appropriate liveries'. The islanders had, of course, gained much more than footmen and Sèvres. An effective system of education had been initiated by the missionaries, there were a supreme court, a police force, numerous hospitals, not to mention more dubious benefits such as all those competing churches, a civil list, a regiment of household troops and a national debt (the latter recently doubled by government financing of the Hawaiian Hotel). Naturally enough, some opposition to all this had developed, and when Isabella attended a meeting where one American settler openly advocated the immediate annexation of the Islands by America, she heard faint dissenting cries of 'Hawaii for the Hawaiians'. It was to this latent undertow of anti-foreign nationalism that Lunalilo appealed when he made his speech from the court-house balcony.

But at that time the theme was not pursued. It scarcely *could* be when Lunalilo had been brought to Hilo on an American naval vessel and had been burdened with an official programme that seemed designed principally by and for the foreign residents. It included, for instance, a 'social evening' at Father Lyman's where Isabella was officially presented to the King. Unofficially, she had met him the day before when, on a fern-gathering expedition, she had trotted round a corner of a bridle-path and there he was –

slap-bang in front of her, with members of his suite about him. 'When I saw these strangers and their wild stares,' she told Hennie, 'I remembered that I was in my Bloomer Suit and astride a horse and that probably they had never seen such a thing before. And I wished I were anywhere else!' So she turned and cantered away into a grove of breadfruit trees. The King chose to ignore this episode, or perhaps he did not even recognise the small lady in rustling black silks who was presented to him at what she terms 'the Lymans' horribly stiff and dull party'. The King was handsome, with large, dark, melancholy eyes, whiskers 'cut in the English fashion' that concealed a soft full mouth. He questioned Isabella intently about the powers of the British monarchy and its possession of a parliamentary veto, while 'Father Lymans' boys' serenaded interminably on the verandah. 'The Lymans are trying to make the King good,' she told Hennie, 'and I fear the result will be a reaction into a most outrageous spree when he gets out of their hands.'

But the King was not yet out of the foreigners' hands; there was a supper party at the Sheriff's to attend first. And Isabella gladly joined in the turmoil of preparation and cooked for thirty-six hours at a stretch, along with Mrs Severance, a Chinese chef and 'a Chinese prisoner' who was a dab hand at grating coconut. They made sponges, 'drops', custards, and Isabella's special was a huge trifle into which she surreptitiously poured some sherry (the Severances, like most of the Americans there, were Good Templars). The trifle was an astonishing success and after-supper jollity included 'a refined kind of blind man's buff' and dancing under swinging Chinese lanterns, when 'the King insisted on teaching me to dance the polka on the verandah'.

Everyone enjoyed it, Isabella decided, even the King and the docile round-eyed islanders who stood outside the whole evening, peering over the garden fence. Certainly the King must have enjoyed meeting Isabella, for he called the next afternoon bearing a verse he had composed to wish her God-speed on a journey she was about to take to nearby Waimea, and when she left Hilo he escorted her to the steamer and 'helped with the luggage'! As for Isabella, 'I found him peculiarly interesting and attractive,' she wrote home, 'but sadly irresolute about the mouth and I saw from little things that he could be persuaded into anything.' Lunalilo was, unfortunately, persuaded into many things that were detrimental to his own good, and when he died the next year of tuberculosis aggravated by alcoholism, he was, according to the missionaries, a victim of the unscrupulous 'reprobate whites' who had led him astray.

III

Until she visited the 2,500-foot-high tableland of Waimea that stretched along the leeward side of Hawaii, Isabella knew little about that numerous body of settlers, often classed as 'reprobate whites', who were not missionaries, teachers, lawyers or business men and who had little in common with those who were. But now she had arrived in rough-and-ready cattle-raising country; cool airs ruffled the pastures and 'there are few hours of day or night in which the tremulous thud of shoeless horses galloping on grass is not heard in Waimea'. From the green roots of the plains the great bulks of two volcanoes – Mauna Kea and, beyond it, Mauna Loa – swept skyward; between the pasture and the sea burned a bald desert 'unwatered and unfruitful, red and desolate under the sun'; from the beach where the steamer called a rutted mule-track stretched ten miles up and away across the torrid zone to the farming settlements and Mr Spencer's sheep-station where Isabella stayed.

Compared to the trim, slightly starchy homes of the Hilo residents, Spencer's house was a slapdash sort of place where you were quite likely to find a hen underfoot or a baby helping himself to your bowl of *poi* or a few fleas snuggled in your *pulu* shakedown. Spencer was a Tasmanian with a half-white wife, a bluff, outdoor fellow and one of the many settlers who, she said, 'admire courage, perseverance and jollity above all'. Isabella made herself easily at home and particularly liked Spencer's mother-in-law, a roly-poly old party who spoke excellent English and loved to tease the whites, who were 'a sour, morose, worrying, forlorn race' in her view. And Isabella, watching the carefree routines of the household's women – making quilts, collecting flowers, weaving sunhats, 'talking, bathing, riding, visiting' – could see her point.

The life at Waimea made Isabella realise that though the New

England Christian ethic had been successfully screwed upon some of the natives, there was a reverse trend in operation – other settlers had gaily and unashamedly 'gone Hawaiian'. Most of these were men, whalers, bullock-hunters, sheep-shearers, plantation overseers, and their talents were lassoing the one calf from the herd, shooting, curing hides, breaking the wildest stallions. Often they had floated on to the island's romantic shores by chance and, liking what they saw, had shacked up with native women and stayed. There were ex-cabin boys from Liverpool, steamboat-men from the Mississippi, gold-rushers who hadn't 'seen the colour' in '49, farmboys from the mid-West, itinerant printers from London, ex-trappers from the Canadian Rockies, ex-sailors from just about everywhere. As a result, Isabella felt, 'the moral atmosphere of Waimea had never been a wholesome one'. The 'flagrant immorality and outrageous licence of former years' had been curbed by the imposition of legal penalties handed down by the new courts, but still ' "the Waimea crowd" is not considered up to the mark'. And, Isabella adds, 'it was in such quarters that the great antagonistic influence to the complete Christianisation of the natives was created and it is from such suspicious sources that the aspersions on missionaries are usually derived'.

As Isabella suggests, this 'antagonistic influence' had been stronger in the earlier period when a flourishing whaling trade had centred on the Islands. As recently as '66, when Twain was around, all the talk was still of whaling, and he gives a graphic account of what racy, rumbustious talk it was. There were heated disputes over 'long lays' and 'short lays', which were the proportions of profit to which each sailor and officer was entitled. Whaling was a risky business: crews were not paid fixed wages but simply took a percentage of the net profits when all the oil from the sperm-whales and bone from the Ochotsk and Arctic whales has been sold. As Twain pointed out, the sailors often got a raw deal as numerous deductions were made for freight, leakage and 'slops' (items bought by the crew on board) before the proportion of gold coin payable to each man was calculated.

Now most of the whalers had gone elsewhere, but the fundamental antagonisms between those who had revelled in the pagan, amoral, 'innocent' Islands of the recent past and those who wanted to christianise and 'civilise' them for a progressive future still remained. The Islanders were now a wretched and dwindling race because the missionaries had forced them to wear clothes and go to school and thus ruined their constitutions, said the 'reprobate whites'. The islanders were decreasing in numbers because of the venereal disease and ruinous addiction to bad whisky introduced by immoral foreigners, said the missionaries. Indubitably there were fewer islanders since the white men arrived, and among the principal causes were emigration (mostly of young men gone a-whaling), the inroads of smallpox and, increasingly, of leprosy, and the notorious carelessness with which the native mothers treated their children. A noisy baby was no longer buried under the living-room floor, but a family would cheerfully give one away, if there were any takers.

As a result of all these factors there were fewer than 52,000 natives left on the Islands by 1873 (as compared to some 85,000 twenty years earlier) and Isabella often came upon deserted hamlets, fields that were no longer tilled, churches and schools much too large for their present flocks. 'Whites,' she concluded, 'have conveyed to these shores slow but infallible destruction on the one hand and on the other the knowledge and skills of civilisation and the hope of a life to come; and the rival influences of blessing and cursing have now been fifty years at work.'

But on the plains of Waimea that were so airy and vast, flecked only with cattle and the sailing shadows of clouds, it was easy to forget that other people were necessary and to 'be' simply, just where she was. On the first morning after leaving Spencer's sheep station, she *was*, by eight o'clock, again atop the precipice of the Waipio Valley, looking down its enchanted length, 'full of infinite depths of blue – blue smoke in lazy spirals curled upwards; it was eloquent in a morning silence that I felt reluctant to break. Against its dewy greenness the beach shone like coarse gold, and its slow silver river lingered lovingly, as though loath to leave it and be merged in the reckless, loud-tongued Pacific.'

For the next few days she meandered about the remote coast-line. She came to a river that acted as highway for the nearby hamlets and rode up it in triumphant procession, the water lapping over her horse's belly, she with her feet on the animal's neck, while two canoes and all the children and dogs for miles around paddled along behind her. She rode up the shelving sides of a 2,500-foot-high *pali*, the track so narrow that she had to take her left foot out of the stirrup to prevent crushing it against the cliff-wall, while her right dangled over the precipice, and dislodged stones bounced sickeningly off into the void. At one place the track completely disintegrated and she had to dismount, an alarming manoeuvre when there was no ground to dismount upon. 'I somehow slid under him,' she explains, 'being careful not to turn the saddle, and getting hold of his hind leg, screwed myself round behind him' and went the rest of the way up hanging for dear life on to his tail.

Isabella describes her excursions in the Waimea region gaily and with seeming completeness, but something else happened during that time which, in its very different way, probably made her feel as giddy as the *pali*-climbing. It is not mentioned in her book, but she told Hennie about it. Among the men of the 'Waimea crowd' whom she met at Spencer's station was a certain Mr Wilson, a hunter of bullocks, maker of roads, jack-of-all-trades, 'a fine pleasant backwoodsman', Isabella says. Wilson got into the habit of calling at Spencer's constantly when Isabella was there (and she was there for several weeks, on and off). They went riding together and talked about wool prices, the raising of bullocks, the uncertain future of the Islands. He liked her earnest commonsense, her demure sense of humour, her utter fearlessness; he liked to watch her at the Spencers' where, because she had few clothes, she sometimes wore her 'black silk with the low front' which, she candidly admits, 'looked grotesque' in the room she shared with 'magpies, ducks, fowls and a carpenter's bench'.

Anyway, Wilson liked this little English lady so much that one day she received a note: 'My friend Mr Wilson is most anxious to propose to you but dare not after so short an acquaintance. I can only say that his character is excellent, that he is about the best-hearted fellow on the island – Spencer.' Wilson may have experienced initial shyness, but he had the blunt persistence that sometimes accompanies it, and soon appeared to plead his suit. He told Isabella that he had felt 'stronger all over' the first time she spoke to him, and that he 'had never felt so good and happy as the night before when he was talking with me, and that the sight of my knitting needles had affected him so by reminding him of his mother in Canada'. Isabella felt inclined to laugh, for she did not believe his affections were seriously engaged and, probably, did not find the comparison to his mother particularly warming. 'He was so perfectly respectful and yet so perfectly *assured*,' she marvelled. And this very assurance made Wilson determined that she should see him plain. 'He told me that he could not deceive me, that he had been what women call very wild. And *what* this means in Waimea,' Isabella added, 'it is fearful to think of!' All in all, she told him, there were fifty reasons why it would not do, and he leaned over her smiling and said that if she'd stay and tell them, he would dispose of every one. 'He was a splendid-looking fellow,' she explained to Hennie, 'and what I might have said if it had not been for *you* I don't know.' She considered mentioning the difference in their social backgrounds 'or some such stereotyped thing' but she charitably refrained, evading him with the excuse that she had to return to England 'to earn a living' (which was not strictly true), and promising to write to him when she got to Honolulu. 'Oh now don't go, stay and try if you can't like me,' he concluded rather pathetically.

But she didn't stay. Throughout her life, her instinct was to fly from the threat of any intimate personal entanglement, as she herself partly recognised, for she sometimes complained (rather guiltily) that the very presence of people exhausted her emotional reserves. So to escape Mr Wilson she went to Honolulu, intending to leave the Islands forthwith and return directly to 'the hard prosaic north' which would be warmed only by the securely familiar and beloved face of her sister. But Honolulu only served as a sharp, unwelcome reminder of all the civilised trappings of her homeland. It was, even then, something of 'a metropolis, gay, hospitable and restless'. Along the dusty palm- and banana-shaded streets you could buy almost anything – 'good black silks' for ladies, milk-pails, chandeliers, topsail chains, photographic volcanic 'views', 'souvenir Polynesian war-implements' and melon-flavoured ice-cream. Four newspapers circulated every crumb of local gossip, and a frantic social whirl kept the journalists off the breadline. 'Visiting begins at breakfast-time, when it ends I know not, and receiving and making visits, court festivities . . . entertainments given by the commissioners of the great powers, riding parties, picnics, verandah parties, "sociables" and luncheon

47

and evening parties on board the ships of war succeed each other with frightening rapidity.'

Isabella's reaction to all this was a return of her nervous attacks and headaches. Her face, that had been reddened, freckled, opened by the sun and wind, began again to look drawn and aged. While she was conscientiously finding out about the Islands' constitutional framework, attending social functions and lectures on the country's economic future, a part of her was aching for a return to 'the congenial life of the wilds' where she had 'rioted most luxuriantly'. 'The uncertain future and the disappointment which it always is to me to break down when I am among people and ordinary ways make me feel depressed,' she explained. 'I like congenial, informal cultivated people, yet I feel that, however much I may recover, I shall never be able to enjoy more than the very quietest society.' While she was in that rebellious, nostalgic, self-punishing mood, a packet of letters arrived from Hennie saying that she was well and happy. The lifeline was secure, and Isabella, grabbing at the leeway offered her, decided at once to stay four months longer on the Islands. So she boarded the sixty-ton schooner *Jenny* which was scheduled to carry an overload of natives, cattle, hides, sugar and molasses to the little round island of Kauai. Mrs Dexter, who was still stranded on Honolulu with her ailing son, saw her friend off and, Isabella says, 'pitied me heartily, for it made her quite ill to look down the cabin hatch; but I convinced her that no inconveniences are legitimate subjects for sympathy which are endured in the pursuit of pleasure'. It was another of her lifelong Travelling Principles, though in later years she occasionally forgot it.

Kauai, the 'Garden Isle', was a distant, lonely, gentle place with none of the fiery volcanic dramas of Hawaii or the sophistication of Oahu's Honolulu. Some five thousand natives, accounted rustics by the inhabitants of the other islands, were scattered about its wooded, fertile terrain which, at that time of year, was cooled by a riotous trade wind and warmed by a mild sun. Very few foreigners lived on Kauai, but among them Isabella discovered the Sinclairs, the most attractive and original family she met anywhere on the archipelago. Her book indicates that they interested her; her letters make it clear that, for a time, she found them absolutely fascinating.

The Sinclairs had been among the early pioneer settlers on Kauai, and matriarch of the clan was a seventy-two-year-old widow, 'a lady of the old Scotch type, very talented, bright, humourous, charming, with a definite character which impresses its force upon everybody; beautiful in her old age, disdaining that servile conformity to prevailing fashion which makes many old people at once ugly and contemptible'. Mrs Sinclair and her husband had originally settled in New Zealand and had brought up a large family there on a large sheep-farm. After her husband's death, the widow decided that, instead of declining into a placid old age, she wanted to see more of the world and persuaded the whole family to join her. So they sold their property, bought a clipper barque and simply set sail over the Pacific on a voyage of discovery. Thus it was that there appeared at the Honolulu wharf one day during the early 60s a 'trim barque with this large family on board, with a beautiful and brilliant old lady at its head, books, pictures, work and all that could add refinement to a floating home, about them, and cattle and sheep of valuable breeds in pens on deck'. The family, who undoubtedly had a good deal of ancestral canniness about them, bought the whole off-shore island of Niihau from the then king for a very low price, and there settled. By the time Isabella met them, Mrs Sinclair and most of the family were living on nearby Kauai, in an airy, isolated house on a cool green plateau fringed with orange-groves. From the front verandah, one looked over a steep ravine to a golden empty sea on which the island of Niihau floated 'like amethyst'. There, one of the Sinclair sons reigned 'like a prince' over 350 natives and some 20,000 sheep. In the main house too, the life-style was unabashedly feudal and conducted with an old-fashioned, independent grace that appealed to Isabella enormously, so that her letters on the subject gush in an uncharacteristic way.

She had been there a few days when Mrs Sinclair appeared, a quaint figure on horseback 'in a large drawn silk bonnet which she rarely lays aside, as light in her figure and step as a young girl, looking as if she had walked out of an old picture'. The formidable lady reigned over the household of a bachelor son, two widowed daughters and three grandsons, dashing moustachioed princelings in scarlet shirts, tight leather trousers, boots and spurs. Their lithe bodies were masters of the surf-board, the lasso, the galloping stallion, and when they thudded back from a late herding, winding their horns as they came, the women rushed to the verandah to greet them 'just as in olden days'. Proficient too in more formal arts, the boys learned Greek and German from one Mr Müller, a Prussian who had been with Maximilian in Mexico, and of him, at first, Isabella could not find enough kind things to say. He was 'brilliant, sparking, exquisitely refined', a 'converted Christian', the Bible never far from his sensitive hand, 'his prayers are so wonderful, . . . but I dislike his ideas'. Prayers, ideas and all were enunciated by Mr Müller in the most beautiful English, for 'his refined instincts make him avoid all Americanisms'. During the cool of the evening, Müller played the piano 'exquisitely' in the elegant drawing-room, and then, as the notes died away, he 'turned his radiant face to one with the query, "What does that say to you?"' (But there was, as one might guess, something suspicious about Mr Müller. All praise of his ' "spirituelle" character' ceases abruptly in the letters. In the book, Isabella comments briefly that he was 'still suffering from Mexican barbarities'.)

The late evening talk was of politics, theology, current books – a refreshing change from the webs of Hilo gossip. The family were thoroughly conversant with the language and culture of their adopted homeland and from them Isabella learned much about the Island's history – that sweet dream of indolence and plenty which was sometimes barbed and mutilated to a nightmare by the savage, senseless tyranny of the *tabu*. The *tabu* system had been operated by, and for, the priests and chiefs, whose catalogue of 'thou shalt not' was longer than any Presbyterian missionary's. Not only were women forbidden to eat with men (a common restriction among primitives) but any woman entering a room where men were eating was killed. Now and then the priests proclaimed a period of general *tabu*, an orgy of masochism that was, perhaps, a psychological necessity in a land of such natural ease and bounty. During it, canoeing, swimming, fishing, dancing were prohibited; no fire could be lit, no noise could be made. This latter injunction was so strictly enforced that, according to Miss Cumming, even the mouths of the priests' dogs were tied to prevent them barking and fowls were swathed in cloth and penned under calabashes lest they should venture to cackle!

In contrast to the earnest discussions of the Sinclair family evenings, the days seemed simply for fun, more 'sybaritic' fun than Isabella had ever experienced. Isabella was fond of the word 'sybarite' and often protests that she was not one, as indeed she was not; but for a while she indulged herself in the general frolics. A party of them rode to the mountains where they 'played at living' for three days, eating wild roast pig and mangoes, bathing in 'fern shrouded streams that brawled among wild bananas', sleeping in a forest 'bird-house'. This enchanted dwelling was shaded with candlenut trees, wreathed in morning-glories and orange star-blossom, and its roof was hung about with wasps' nests – but even the wasps didn't sting.

The sting, for Isabella, came when amid that riot of colour and plenty she pictured dear Hennie, pallid in a lacklustre land which was then crouched grey under the slashing rains and winds of March. Writing home in a mood of guilt-ridden love and mad optimism, Isabella suggested that they should perhaps move to the Islands? They could have a ranch with lots of horses, and they could 'help the natives'; Hennie could pay visits easily; no one would mind if their furniture was a bit shabby; they wouldn't be made miserable by poor servants, for few were employed here; you could buy two sirloins of beef for what a pound of chops cost in Edinburgh. And she was so fitted for island life now, she could cook, wash, mend clothes, saddle and bridle horses and felt so much more at ease 'with manual than intellectual matters'. Then Isabella imagined Hennie reading the letter and being happy and excited with it and showing it to a dear friend Bessie – but shrewd Bessie 'will toss her head and say, "She better stay where she is, for she'll only come back to grumble at everything and hate us all!" ' And so Isabella, on lush Kauai, sighed and smiled at the thought of Bessie's home-truths, and her romantic castle-in-the-air probably tumbled even before she sealed the envelope. It was the only time that she allowed herself to be briefly seduced by the dream that she could make one entity of her two divided lives – the adventurer-traveller and the English gentlewoman. But poor Hennie, who lost most from the division, took the dream rather seriously and sat down at once in her dreary little drawing-room and wrote to say that, yes, perhaps she *should* join dear Isa in Hawaii, for it all sounded so wonderful.

Isabella received this proposal just as she was finally leaving the Islands about three months later – and in a hastily-written reply, squashed it very flat. Hennie's role was the traditionally female one of waiting and watching; ranching and riding would be most unsuitable for her delicate constitution. Hennie had to be the stay-at-home to whom all happy wanderers return, trailing their bright tales behind them.

IV

And so, while Hennie waited, Isabella accumulated more tales for the telling. She tore herself away from the sybaritic Sinclairs and cantered back to the other side of Kauai alone. The aloneness was intoxicating. 'I liked it, oh how I liked it,' she told her sister. 'I did wild things which I can't do with white people, such as galloping wildly up and down hill, hallooing a horse to make it go, twisting my knee for a few minutes around the horn of the saddle, riding without stirrups and other free and easy ways. I thought of nothing all that day.' And natives who saw her madcap capers laughed and waved and threw flowers after her and shouted '*paniola, paniola*' and she laughed back, liking its sound. The word meant 'cowboy', she learned later, 'lassoing cattle and all that kind of thing', and secretly Isabella hugged it as a compliment, though it was not generally used as such about a foreign lady.

She was thoroughly a fully-fledged *paniola* by now and continued to island-hop alone until May, when she returned to Hilo. From there she made a short expedition to the southern Puna district with Luther Severance and his wife, whose company she preferred 'even to solitude'. They jogged over grasslands dotted with pandanus and clumps of eugenia hung with crimson 'native apples' crammed with tart juicy pulp. The sea stirred close and 'surf kept bursting up behind the trees in great snowy drifts'; birds, crimson as apples, bounced among the palms and below, in their fan-tailed shadows, coconuts tumbled in tawny heaps and were chewed open by dogs, cats, hogs. They visited the 'sight' of the region – a natural pool cradled in basalt. The water, bluer than any Italian grotto, glazed coconut shells and rocks on the pool's floor with frosted azure and changed to blue-tinged marble the limbs of the foreigners as they floated about in it, gazing up at golden balls of guava fruit that swung overhead. Lulled in all this beauty, Isabella realised that she had 'developed a capacity for doing nothing which horrified me and except when we energised ourselves to go to the hot spring, my companions and I were content to dream in the verandah and watch the lengthening shadows and drink coconut milk till the abrupt exit of the sun startled us and we saw the young moon carrying the old one tenderly and a fitful glare sixty miles away, where the solemn fires of Mauna Loa are burning at a height of nearly 14,000 feet'.

Mauna Loa, there at least was a challenge, a brute fact to stiffen the indolent will, and every time she looked towards it, the biblical question of Hazael to Elisha thrummed in her mind: 'Is thy servant a dog, that he should do this great thing?' The query seems a little high-flown in the context, but to Isabella it apparently suggested a 'cowardly' protest against the reckless self-punishing compulsion of the explorer that was tempting her with the summit of Mauna Loa. Isabella's awe, admiration, fear of Mauna Loa was not groundless; she was not making a mountain out of a molehill. This 'Matterhorn of the Pacific', largest volcano in the world, sweeps to a height of 13,650 feet; the circumference of its base is some 180 miles; from the height of 7,000 feet it rises as a harsh desert of tossed and twisted lava, riven into crevasses and blown into gigantic bubbles of rock by frequent earthquakes. The few men who had climbed it invariably returned shaken, bruised, their eyebrows burnt off, reeling with exhaustion and the effects of altitude sickness; as far as people knew, only one foreign woman had ever reached the top – so far.

Knowing all this, Isabella might have submitted to her cowardly doubts had it not been for Mr William Green, shipping agent, acting British consul and amateur expert on volcanic phenomena. But Mr Green, as it happened, was planning an ascent of Mauna Loa, and it was soon the hottest news of the day in Hilo that the English lady Miss Bird was going up with him. When she went to the beach-stores to buy camp supplies of potted meat, chocolate and oats for the horses, everyone said, 'So you're going up the mountain with Mr Green,' and they all wished her luck and thought she was mad. No one, however, seems to have thought it in the least 'improper' that Isabella should be going off unchaperoned with Mr Green, a man of about her own age. On several future occasions too, she was to travel in the company of a male with whom she would share the inevitable proximities of camp life. For, once she had fixed on some particular goal, she quite ruthlessly made use of men and animals in order to reach it. But she must have gone about it in such a straightforward, single-minded, matter-of-fact way that not an eyebrow was raised. 'Travellers are privileged to do the most improper things with perfect propriety, that is one charm of travelling,' she later declared. It was a strategy which liberated her and she first began to practise it with success on the Sandwich Islands. So, in this instance, the residents of Hilo, far from being scandalised by the proposed expedition, were most helpful and lent her a camp-kettle, a peaked cap and an enormous Mexican poncho. Mrs Severance rustled up some thick chemises, and an aged Scotswoman produced from the bottom of an old trunk 'a stout flannel shirt and a pair of venerable worsted stockings'. Offering them, the old woman said, with a mixture of awe and disapproval, 'Oh my, what some people will do!' Isabella rather liked that.

She liked starting off too, early one morning on mule-back, shaking with excitement, 'for everything is happening that could happen. . . . I had on my usual red suit, my little brown hat, the long white scarf wound several times round my neck, a handkerchief tied over my face. A bag with six pounds of oats tied to the horn of my saddle, your shawl with ends hanging down in front of me, some strips of rawhide and a lasso which I have been obliged to borrow of Mr Wilson for a tether, rope hung to one side of the rings and immense saddlebags behind. Several of the Hilo people came to their garden gates as we went by.'

As an apéritif, she and Mr Green climbed 4,000 feet to the crater of Kilauea, and stood dazed above its lakes of molten fire as the blasted ground reeled and rumbled beneath them. 'The motion was as violent as that of a large ship in a mid-Atlantic storm,' she decided, and added, 'I am glad to have felt such good earthquakes.' Between this journey and the big ascent, they spent a night in a flea-ridden, desolate grass house among a number of cross-grained, lugubrious ranch-hands who were full of fearful prophecies about their forthcoming adventure, and 'entertained us with the misfortunes of our predecessors on which they seem to gloat with ill-omened satisfaction.' Outside too the landscape had become ominous – a cracked tableland of volcanic waste, blotched with clumps of sow-thistle, wintry trees, dense cold fog. But inside, huddled round a wood-fire, Isabella was happy in spite of the omens, having 'volcanic talk' with William Green, eating doughnuts and stewed chicken, making cruppers for the pack-horse out of goats' hair and old stockings. Isabella had taken her travelling companion's measure by now and, while she liked him, she did not feel as totally in his debt as she had at the outset. She told Hennie that Green, 'like many thinking and scientific men who have good wives, is quite in a dream about practical things . . . I have to remind him of everything and suggest plans'. Still, it was a mutually satisfactory arrangement: he had gained a valuable travelling housekeeper and she so far 'had led him with a thread of silk, and often think how much better it is to travel with a man than almost any woman'.

They rose at dawn and Isabella crowded upon her short thick body all the clothes she had, 'which gave me the squat, padded look of a puffin or Esquimo'. Two natives, one of them a goat-hunter by trade, led the way, and by mid-morning, when they stopped to tighten the animals' girths, the sterile land had taken on the cruel tense glitter of an empty mountain world. The ground, weird as a moonscape, was contorted and crushed into *a-a* and *pahoehoe*, bizarre formations of igneous rock. *A-a*, the cruellest kind, was vindictively jagged; *pahoehoe*, 'satin rock' by comparison, lay in smooth whorls, with 'the likeness, on a magnificent scale, of a thick coat of cream drawn in wrinkling folds to the side of a milk-pan'. Over such terrain, progress was slow: 'Horrid streams of *a-a*, which after rushing remorselessly over the kindlier lava, have heaped rugged pinnacles of brown scoriae into impassable walls, have to be cautiously skirted. Winding round the bases of tossed up fissured hummocks of *pahoehoe*, leaping from one broken hummock to another, clambering up acclivities so steep that the packhorse rolled backwards once and my cat-like mule fell twice, moving cautiously over crusts which rang hollow to the tread; stepping over deep cracks, which, perhaps, led down to the burning fathomless sea, traversing hilly lakes ruptured by earthquakes and split in cooling into a thousand fissures, painfully toiling up the sides of mounds of scoriae frothed with pumice-stone, and again for miles surmounting rolling surfaces of billowy ropy lava – so passed the long day, under the tropic sun, the deep blue sky.'

At one point they had to cross a stream of *a-a*, a slowly moving mass of 'upright rugged adamantine points . . . wide as the Ouse at Huntingdon Bridge' and the animals 'shrank back, cowered, trembled, breathed hard and heavily, and stumbled and plunged painfully. It was sickening to see their terror and suffering, the struggling and slipping into cracks, the blood and torture. The mules, with their small legs and wonderful agility, were more frightened than hurt, but the horses were splashed with blood up to their knees and their poor eyes looked piteous.' Eventually, when they were sick and silent with exhaustion, their pulses racing, they reached a fissure of frozen snow. They jumped it, and there, eight hundred feet below, yawned the crater. It was six miles round, its infinite blackness intermittently shattered to incandescent gold by the famous 'fire fountains' of Mauna Loa, whose jets of pure flame roared some 300 feet high. These fountains erupted with volcanic unpredictability, and Isabella was lucky to see them, to feast her eyes on their terrible and glorious certainty.

They pitched their tent precariously near the crater; the natives got a fire going and a cheery kettle was put to boil – at which 'Mr Green discovered that he had forgotten to bring the tea of which I had reminded him over and over again.' So she brewed up a brandy toddy instead to wash down the tinned salmon and more doughnuts, and then William Green and Isabella Bird 'huddled up in blankets, sat on the outer ledge in solemn silence to devote ourselves to the volcano'.

It was an awesome spectacle, as if all the firework displays the world had ever produced were pitched into one terrifying, violent celebration of nature's energy. Fires were everywhere, 'burning in rows like blast-furnaces,' lone and 'unwinking like planets,' tossing skyward 'like golden wheatsheaves'; the light from them was molten red, sunset amber, blue-white as frozen spray. Reluctant to tear her eyes away, but yearning to share the exaltation of it all, Isabella got out her writing materials and, in a quavery script, penned a triumphant heading: 'Edge of Crater of Mauna Loa, Mokuaweoweo, 6 pm. June 6th, 1873, 13,650 ft.

above the sea. Great mountain of fire below. . . . My Pet,' she began, 'Probably you are the only person in the world who has ever had a line from this wonderful place . . .' And only a few lines it was, for her hands and the ink were freezing, her head was reeling with vertigo, and she was forced to seek rest inside the tent – for pillow a wooden saddle, for mattress the spiked ridges of lava, for lullaby the crash, boom, rattle of volcanic detonations, the 'ebb and flow of the thunder-music' from the fiery fountains.

Before dawn she woke, and unable to resist the unearthly *son et lumière* outside, climbed over the sleeping forms of Mr Green and the natives, and stepped into a world of light – vivid, broad, rose-coloured, that stained to a deep ruby the white tent-walls, the grey humps of lava, the silvery index of her thermometer, which stood at 23° F. She sat on the ledge alone, overwhelmed by the sublimity and power of the scene. It was, for her, an apocalyptic vision, prodigal, infinitely mysterious. The whole world fell away, the moon faded wan and dull and, in the intensity of her passionate devotion to this fiery miracle, 'all lighted homes, and sea and ships and cities and faces of friends, and all familiar things, and the day before, and the years before, were as things in dreams, coming up out of a vanished past.' She was elevated, ecstatic: 'How far it was from all the world, uplifted above love, hate and storms of passion and war and wreck of thrones, and dissonant clash of human thought, serene in the eternal solitudes.'

After that experience, the nearest she ever comes to describing her semi-mystical adoration of nature's grandest dramas, the rest was inevitable anti-climax. In the morning, the climbers' limbs were heavy with extreme lassitude, they felt too ill to eat, the water in the canteen was frozen, one of the natives was writhing on the ground with altitude sickness. Wearily they stumbled down towards the mundane earth, and about ten hours later rode triumphantly into the corral of the grass hut, where the ranch-hands 'seemed rather grumpy at our successful ascent, which involved the failure of all their prophecies, and indeed, we were thoroughly unsatisfactory travellers, arriving fresh and complacent, with neither adventures nor disasters to gladden people's hearts'. And the last day of the exploit, being a Sunday, they luxuriated in the 'sybaritic' comforts of a wealthy ranch-house down in the valley, where she and William Green sat on the verandah and contemplated with considerable complacency the conquered summit rearing above them, and Isabella, finishing the next instalment of the letter home, told Hennie, 'I read a great deal of *Paradise Lost* with new admiration today, though I dislike the helpless idiotic jellyfish style of Eve's speeches to Adam.'

Back on the rolling Waimea plains, she found her particular Adam, in the shape of blunt hopeful Mr Wilson, still waiting; from her he received not one 'idiotic jellyfish style speech'. They sat together in a tree one sunny afternoon and she told him that 'he was mistaking liking for deeper feeling,' and that 'he had never succeeded in making me feel that he loved me', to which Mr Wilson mumbled that he thought he did. On their ride together the next day however, perhaps realising that his suit was hopeless and needing to salvage his wounded pride, he affirmed that she was right – he had 'the greatest liking and respect' for her instead. To which she sternly replied (rubbing salt, perhaps unconsciously) that she 'hoped he would never again propose to anyone till he was quite sure of the state of his own heart'. And then he laughed, she concludes, 'and we took a tremendous gallop back again'.

So the remote contingency of Mr Wilson was firmly put away, and Isabella, in a mood of reaction, went on to complain about the predominating 'low American influence' on the Islands, the insular, shallow, hybrid atmosphere, and the surprising – undoubtedly true – fact that she had met scarcely any intellectual equals there. 'You can hardly imagine,' she explains, 'what an unpleasant feeling the lack of large public interests gives . . . You hardly feel the beat of the great pulses of the world.' The fretful note continues. She suddenly felt 'out of her element' at Waimea; and yet even the Hilo missionaries were 'of the coldest, driest, hardest, shrewdest type of American piety and have not the manner or tone of American gentlemen, with the single exception of Mr Coan'. When 'stationary', (that is, out of her saddle) she was assailed by lassitude and nervousness 'as if everything were a drag'; she worried about Hennie who was 'going about in England incurring the perils of trains' – and peril was Isabella's preserve. She realised it really was time to leave, though she refers again and again to the soft pull of the deep banana shades where she could lie lax as a lotos-eater and 'no longer roam'.

But roaming, as she had just discovered, was her vocation, the talent and passion for the rest of her life when so much else would fall away. And roamers, as she knew in her bones, were doomed to leave even the fairest anchorage. So 'better a finger off than aye wagging', she told herself as she prepared to leave Hawaii for the last time. Cannily she re-trimmed her brown travelling hat, and, upon investigating her finances, discovered that life in the Sandwich Isles had cost her only ten pounds a month. To her many friends who saw her off she gave presents of fern-prints and spatterwork; for Mrs Severance was reserved the blue parasol she had used but once 'when Prince Albert came to Edinburgh'; Mr Wilson received her big gentle horse for consolation. In the bottom of her trunk she packed her 'bloomer dress' and spurs that jangled nostalgically, doubting that she would ever have occasion to wear them again. She did not know that before she reached home, she would experience new intensities of physical ordeal and emotional involvement compared with which the climbing of Mauna Loa and the relationship with Mr Wilson were mere trail-blazers.

That lay ahead; for the present, returned to Honolulu, she was torn with the thought of departure: 'I am glad that I am so sorry to go'. She boarded the Pacific Mail steamer *Costa Rica* on the afternoon of 7 August and sailed for San Francisco. 'Everything looked the same as when I landed in January except . . . that I know nearly everyone by sight and that the pathos of farewell blended with laughter and *alohas*, and the rippling music of the Hawaiian tongue; bananas and pineapples were still piled in fragrant heaps; the drifts of surf rolled in, as then, over the barrier reef, canoes with outriggers still poised themselves on the blue water; the coral divers still plied their graceful trade, and the lazy ripples still flashed in light along the palm-fringed shore. . . .'

CHAPTER II

The Rocky Mountains

THE colours simplified and then dimmed. When she reached San Francisco, the gaudy heaps of cantaloupes, peaches, tomatoes, squashes piled on the sidewalks were the only reminders of the bounty she had left. The Californian coastal towns blazed and clanged in the dusty midsummer heat, and she boarded the first train east. Its two jaunty engines, named *The Grizzly Bear* and *The White Fox*, pulled seven hundred feet of rolling stock that included a truck filled with grapes, a smoking-car filled with Chinamen, a Wells Fargo express car filled with bullion and several platforms filled with Digger Indians, filthy, ragged and sullen, their hair plastered with pitch, who, according to other derisive passengers, subsisted on a diet of grasshoppers. Isabella was en route to the Rocky Mountains, 'where, people say, the elixir of life can be drunk,' she had written to Hennie from Australia when only the joyless dregs of existence seemed hers. At that time she also hoped to find 'the elixir of life' in the Rockies and in a sense she *did* find the elixir of life there – more freedom than she had ever known, more delight than she had ever expected, and passion, if that was the word for it, the one romantic passion she ever experienced.

The adventure began in Greeley, Colorado, where Isabella left the train and stepped into a world that seemed full of prairie dogs, flies and pioneer waggons. The prairie dogs lived in underground honeycombs on the plains, furry, reddish-brown little beasts that yelped like pups, looked like baby seals and sat on the rims of their burrows 'begging with their paws down and all turned sunward'. The flies, of a peculiarly noxious kind, spun drowned and drowning in the greasy gravy of the dinner she ate in Greeley's only tavern, a wooden shack on the edge of beyond where 'nobody was speaking to nobody'. The waggons, junks of the plains with their white tilts flapping and filled with bone-weary, dusty, gaunt pioneers, creaked alongside the cart she rode the next day from Greeley to Fort Collins.

During the journey, Isabella's three male companions argued politics the whole way, for it was election time and most able-bodied white men 'were galloping over the prairie to register their votes'. At this date, Colorado was still a territory outside the Union, a brash, unproven, improvised land many of whose settlers had put down still-tentative stakes more recently than, say, those in Honolulu. Its laws, like its railroads, were in the process of being laid down and one of the questions that much fretted the three men in the cart was 'to drink or not to drink'. Greeley, the settlement she had just left, was a Temperance Colony – its inhabitants a sprinkle of teetotallers in a soke of whisky addicts. Greeley throve as a result, Isabella thought, for there was no violence there and people worked harder. 'A thousand songs and fifty fights' were stoppered inside each whisky barrel, said the Indians, and many of Colorado's inhabitants certainly spent a lot of time singing and fighting. And so, understandably, did the Indians themselves who, when inflamed with the white man's 'fire-water' and armed with his guns, sometimes resorted to carousals, robbery, violence and were thus the sooner reduced to the only role offered them – that of bogeymen, scapegoats and incubi of the territory. ' "To get rid of the Injun", is the phrase used everywhere,' Isabella remarked. 'The white man has come to take the place of the red and is stamping the superscription of his kingship on the face of the land,' blared the editor of an early Colorado magazine, whom Isabella later met. 'And the screaming of his locomotive wakes the echoes which a while ago multiplied to the war-whoops of the savage.' There had been much 'Injun trouble' in the area before Isabella came and it was not quite over yet. Raids and equally brutal massacres of reprisal had been an uncomfortable feature of pioneer life there in the previous decades, and isolated outbreaks occurred in the 1870s, though, by that time, the Indians were cowed with defeat and loss.

But Isabella evinced little interest in these grim scraps; her eyes were not on the plains – where the deer and the antelope roamed and everyone carried rifles to shoot them with – but on the

61

Rockies beyond. There, she had been told, lay a remote and beautiful valley called Estes Park, and she could feel the place in her bones, a cool promise of peace. Owing to a shortage of reliable horses, helpful information and roads, the first problem was how to get there. From Fort Collins, a place as 'altogether revolting' as Greeley, 'given up to talk of dollars, as well as to making them, with coarse speech, coarse food, coarse everything', she took a buggy into the foothills and there gained first-hand experience of settler life as it often was, but is seldom depicted.

She stayed with the Chalmerses, a family from Illinois who had taken up a 160-acre 'squatter's claim' nine years before. They were in all ways hard: their faces were granite-set with ill-humour and disillusion; their thoughts were mean, suspicious and clenched like little fists ready for instant disagreement; their habits were comfortless, laborious, unlovely and monotonous, bound to a treadmill of stark survival. They were frugal and sober, yet shiftless and simply incompetent. They owned a patched waggon, a few animals, a sawmill, a cabin and some cooking-pots. The sawmill kept going wrong, the pots were rusty, the cabin partly in ruins and bits of its roof fell on the table when it rained. The oxen-harnesses kept breaking, the horses were ill-shod, their saddles held together with twine, and the poultry was gaunt. Mrs Chalmers, who always wore the traditional dusty-black sun-bonnet, was 'lean, clean, toothless' and spoke 'in a piping discontented voice which seems to convey personal reproach'. Her husband was a pig-headed, glum, Reformed Presbyterian who loathed 'England with a bitter personal hatred and regards any allusions . . . to the progress of Victoria as a personal insult'. Their children were lumpish, unmannerly and 'unchild-like'.

Like many of the settlers, Chalmers had been a consumptive and had gone to the territory in search of health; that he found, but the hardships of pioneer life were so great that he lost, if indeed he ever had, all capacity for joy, charity and love. It was a common pattern, Isabella felt, typical of the 'unornamented existence with which I came almost universally in contact'. She stayed with this doleful *ménage* for a week or so, making herself useful by showing the women how to knit, and improvising an Hawaiian-style lamp with a wisp of rag in a tin of fat. At length, Chalmers was sufficiently won over to agree to guide her to Estes

Park, some fifty miles away, and even 'to make a frolic out of it', as
he put it, by taking his cheerless wife. It would be hard to
imagine a less frolicsome trio than the three who set off early one
September morning in quest of Estes: 'I had a very old iron-grey
horse, whose lower lip hung down feebly, showing his few teeth,
while his fore-legs stuck out forwards, and matter ran from both
his eyes. It is a kindness to bring him up to abundant pasture.
My saddle is an old McLellan cavalry saddle, with a battered
brass peak, and the bridle is a rotten leather strap on one side
and a strand of rope on the other . . . Mrs C. wore an old print
skirt, an old short-gown, a print apron, and a sun-bonnet with
the flap coming down to her waist, and looked as care-worn and
clean as she always does. The inside horn of her saddle was broken;
to the outside one hung a saucepan and a bundle of clothes. The
one girth was near breaking point when we started.

'My pack with my well-worn umbrella upon it, was behind my
saddle. I wore my Hawaiian riding-dress, with a handkerchief
tied over my face and the sun-cover of my umbrella folded and
tied over my hat, for the sun was very fierce. The queerest figure
of all was the would-be guide. With his one eye, his gaunt, lean
form, and his torn clothes, he looked more like a strolling tinker
than the honest worthy settler he is. He bestrode rather than
rode a gaunt mule, whose tail hair had all been shaven off,
except a tuft for a tassel at the end. Two flour bags which leaked
were tied on behind the saddle, two quilts were under it, and my
canvas bag, a battered canteen, a frying pan, and two lariats hung
from the horn. On one foot Chalmers wore an old high boot, into
which his trouser was tucked, and on the other an old brogue,
through which his toes protruded.'

Their surroundings, however, became increasingly enchanting
as they climbed higher. Heavy-headed elks gazed shyly from the
cottonwood trees, crested blue-jays jabbered in the pines and
beavers flipped about in the rivers. The forests were fringed with
sloping glades, the streams with cherry-trees; 'dwarf-clumps of
scarlet poison oak like beds of geraniums' flared in the grassy
dells and there was a tangle of plants whose local names, though
unknown to her, were homely and pleasing – wild-hog peanut, for
instance, red baneberry, beard-tongue, staghorn sumach and
buffalo currant. Above all this, cynosure and crown, 'the splintered,

pinnacled, lovely, ghastly, imposing, double-peaked summit of
Long's Peak, the Mont Blanc of Colorado', reared into the blue.
She felt a shiver of expectation as she looked at that dramatic
height and knew that, at its base, waited the deep hollow of
Estes Park.

But she was not to get there yet. With his characteristic
bumptious ineptitude, Chalmers led them into a steep ravine
along which, he thought, was a man-made trail, but this, as it
turned out, was one padded down by bears in search of cherries.
That night they slept in the open, and when they woke the horses
had disappeared because Chalmers had forgotten to bring
picketing pins to tether them. While the squabbling pair went off
in search of the steeds, Isabella got so hungry that, she says, she
ate the kernels of some cherry-stones she found in the stomach
of a dead bear! After Chalmers returned with the horses, he again
searched for a trail, but by mid-afternoon he had to confess that
not only had he failed to find one, but he couldn't find the way
home either. At this, his 'wife sat down on the ground and cried
bitterly. We ate some dry bread, and then I said I had had much
experience in travelling, and would take the control of the party,
which was agreed to and we began the long descent. Soon after
his wife was thrown from her horse, and cried bitterly again from
fright and mortification. Soon after that the girth of the mule's
saddle broke, and having no crupper, saddle and addenda went
over his head and the flour was dispersed. Next the girth of the
woman's saddle broke, and she went over her horse's head. Then
Chalmers began to fumble helplessly at it, railing against England
the whole time, while I secured the saddle and guided the route back
to an outlet of the park. There a fire was built, and we had some
bread and bacon; and then a search for water occupied nearly
two hours, and resulted in the finding of a mud-hole, trodden and
defiled by hundreds of feet of elk, bears, cats, deer and other
beasts, and containing only a few gallons of water as thick as
pea-soup, with which we watered our animals and made some
strong tea.' Late that night they got back 'home', Estes unfound,
the 'frolic' a disastrous failure.

Soon after this, Isabella went to stay with the Hutchinsons,
vastly more agreeable settlers who found the going equally tough.
They were idealists of a different sort, a young doctor and his wife

Isabella L Bird

'*Hawaiian Ladies' Holiday Riding Dress*' – *one of the engravings from* Six Months in the Sandwich Islands

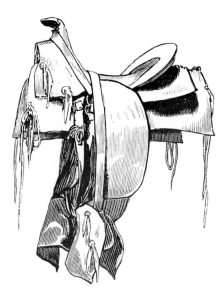

The Mexican saddle – 'a seat made for the jaunty bottoms of cow-punchers, bullock hunters and other wild men of the open prairie'

A group of Hawaiians on horseback

Night scene in the crater of Kilauea

'*My home in the Rocky Mountains*' *The cabin on Griff Evans's ranch in Estes Park where Isabella lodged*

Lava beds on Long's Peak, which Isabella and Jim Nugent climbed. 'One of the mightiest of the vertebrae of the backbone of the North American Continent'

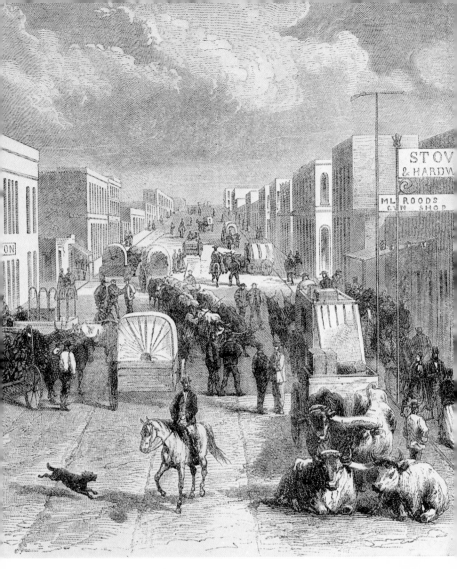

This engraving of a street in Denver illustrated Isabella's account of the town which delighted readers of The Leisure Hour *in 1878*

A dramatic view of Fujisan. It was, Isabella admits, 'altogether exceptional' owing to 'exceptional atmospheric conditions'

Left: *Isabella's straw rain-cloak. 'The cloak, hat and figure are from a sketch of myself, but the face is the likeness of a young Japanese woman'*

Right: *An old Ainu man of 'a truly patriarchal and venerable aspect'*

Kanaya, Isabella's host in Nikko, with his family. She had no camera in Japan on her first visit so this group must have been taken on a subsequent trip

Japan when Isabella first arrived there in 1878 was at the height of the social and economic revolution that followed the arrival of the western powers. This contemporary woodcut shows a Tokyo street scene

Hugh Low

Isabella on an elephant 'This mode of riding is not comfortable'

who, shaking the dust of materialistic Britain from their feet sought the beautiful, the simple and the good in Colorado. The first they found; the simple was complex at first because they had no farming or domestic skills: Hutchinson didn't know how to saddle a horse or his wife how to boil an egg. The good never materialised because, Isabella says, they were shamelessly cheated by other settlers who regarded people with such refined manners and high ideals as 'fair game'. Hutchinson taught himself to yoke oxen, milk cows, raise crops, saddle horses; his wife learned to patch clothes, churn butter, raise the hens as well as boil their eggs. But it was a harsh, careworn, monochrome existence and basically 'against the grain'. Isabella felt sad and anxious for the Hutchinsons' welfare, and one day urged them to take a brief respite together while she did all the chores: 'After baking the bread and thoroughly cleaning the churns and pails, I began upon the tins and pans . . . and was hard at work, very greasy and grimy, when a man came to know where to ford the river with his ox-team, and as I was showing him, he looked pityingly at me, saying, "Be you the new hired girl? Bless me, you're awful small!"'

That was one of Isabella's favourite stories, for it highlighted so sharply the gulf between Miss Bird, seemly gentlewoman of Edinburgh, and the travelling Isabella who could actually be taken for a hired girl! The story had the additional point that she enjoyed vigorous physical work when it was basic and open-air: 'It is all hollow and sickly that idea at home of degradation in manual labour. I am sure all women – except weaklings like you,' she added hastily for Hennie's benefit, 'would be better for stirring about their own homes.' But though she was stirring about and feeling marvellously fit doing it, Isabella still had not reached Estes Park. So she went down to Longmont, (then Longmount) another recent settlement of 'dust-coloured frame-houses set down at intervals on the dusty buff plain, each with its dusty wheat or barley field adjacent, the crop not the product of the rains of heaven, but of the muddy overflow of "Irrigation Ditch No. 2". Then comes a road made up of many converging waggon tracks, which stiffen into a wide straggling street, in which glaring frame-houses and a few shops stand opposite to each other. A two-storey house, one of the whitest and most glaring, and without a verandah like all the others, is the "St Vrain

Hotel", called after the St Vrain river, out of which the ditch is taken which enables Longmount to exist. Everything was broiling in the heat of the slanting sun, which all day long had been beating on the unshaded wooden rooms. The heat within was more sickening than outside, and black flies covered everything, one's face included.'

The hotel's landlord was an amiable fellow in spite of his establishment, and it was he who finally facilitated her passage to Estes by arranging that she be guided thither by two young men going that way, who, he said, 'seemed very innocent'. Their names were S. Downer and Platt Rogers, and the latter, who later became a Mayor of Denver, mentioned the incident in his recollections of some Colorado worthies. When he and Downer were asked by the landlord to 'escort a lady' to Estes they agreed eagerly, he says, hoping for some young and pretty lass to beguile the way. But when Isabella appeared 'wearing bloomers, riding cowboy fashion, with a face and figure not corresponding to our ideals' they were quite huffy and wished they had never agreed to it. Apparently they never recovered from their sulks, for Isabella mentions once or twice that the pair, though 'innocent' enough, were most unmannerly and sullen – though she did not, presumably, know why.

Anyway, the next morning the three of them left together, bound for the Park. The parks of Colorado, as she explains, had nothing in common with the type of decorous demesne that graced the Home Counties with ' "park palings" well-lichened, a lodge with a curtseying woman, fallow-deer and a Queen Anne mansion'. Colorado parks were high-lying wild grassy valleys, famous for hot-springs, minerals, wild flowers, juicy pasture. Red-waistcoated trout teemed in their rapid rivers, busy beavers built dams across their bright streams and, upon their meadows, hundreds of elk cast their magnificent branches of horn.

The parks were well away from such beaten tracks as Colorado had, and to reach Estes, Isabella and the innocents followed a devious trail over the prairie, across the rushing St Vrain, through canyons and gulches – a glorious day-long ride. Isabella's horse was 'all spring and spirit, elastic in his motion . . . a blithe joyous animal to whom a day among the mountains seemed a pleasant frolic'. He carried her past aspens shivering gold over

66

silver streams, higher until the gritty plains fell away and the air tightened till it was as 'elastic' as his movements. The enchantment of the mountains cloaked her; as the sun set, water rushed blood-red through the purple canyons; they came to an open stretch and she cantered across it, the evening air stinging her cheeks. She reined, and there was a 'trim-looking log-cabin, with a flat mud roof, with four smaller ones; picturesquely dotted about near it, two corrals, a long shed, in front of which a steer was being killed, a log-dairy with a water-wheel, some hay-piles, and various evidences of comfort; and two men, on serviceable horses, were just bringing in some tolerable cows to be milked'. It was as if she had come home: 'Estes Park!!!' she begins her next triumphant letter.

Estes Park, Isabella's own, she says, 'by right of love, appropriation and appreciation', was an irregular narrow valley, about eighteen miles long, for 'park palings there are mountains, forest skirted, 9000, 11,000, 14,000 feet high; for a lodge, two sentinel peaks of granite guarding the only feasible entrance; and for a Queen Anne mansion an unchinked log cabin with a vault of sunny blue overhead.' Its moods, all grand and sublime, ranged through the fury of a hurricane, the promise of a winter sunrise mirrored in its lake, the sizzle of white-hot noon, the menacing quiet of long-lying snow. Its most numerous inhabitants were beavers, deer, both 'black-tailed' and 'big-horned', skunks and skulking mountain lions, gruff grizzlies, coyotes, lynxes that spat like wild-cats and 'all the lesser fry of mink, marten, hare, fox, squirrel and chipmunk', and the names of its parts were thus fitting – Bear River, Fish Creek and Rabbit Ears Mountain.

Apart from this casual dubbing, man had as yet made scant impression on the park scene. Indians had cantered through from time to time and felled a few of its denizens with bow and arrow; some twenty years ago, the 'mountain men' had arrived – fur trappers in search of beaver who caught their prey in steel traps using the sex gland of a dead victim for bait. These 'whites' were renowned for gambling, drinking, cohabiting with squaws, and one of their number was Joel Estes, who gave the park its name. There were a few pioneer families now, who bred cattle, farmed, hunted and acted as guides to the newest comers of all – the wealthy British sportsmen. These later remarked a scornful journalist, 'know very little at home and do not travel abroad for the purpose of adding to their stock of knowledge; landing at New York, they look neither right nor left but streak across to the West for the sole purpose of slaughter'. People like that would soon despoil Isabella's 'grand, solitary, uplifted, sublime, remote, beast-haunted lair'. There would be dude ranches and phony hunting-lodges with elk-heads over the fireplaces and nervous ladies trotting side-saddle and millionaires in deerstalkers with ghillies in attendance. And one of the first to encourage this trend, who was running a sort of dude ranch years before they were officially recognised as such, was the 'short pleasant-looking' man who gleefully shook hands with Isabella when she arrived that first evening and 'introduced himself as Griffith Evans, a Welshman from the slate quarries near Llanberis'.

Evans helped her to dismount and took her over the main cabin, 'a good-sized log room, unchinked however, with windows of infamous glass, looking two ways; a rough stone fireplace, in which pine logs, half as large as I am, were burning; a boarded floor, a round table, two rocking chairs, a carpet-covered backwoods couch; and skins, Indian bows and arrows, wampum belts, and antlers, fitly decorated the rough walls, and equally fitly, rifles were stuck in the corners. Seven men, smoking, were lying about on the floor, a sick man lay on the couch, and a middle-aged lady sat at the table writing. I went out again and asked Evans if he could take me in, expecting nothing better than a shakedown; but, to my joy, he told me he could give me a cabin to myself, two minutes' walk from his own.' That night, staring from the window of her very own little cabin at the blue-black pines, the blue-black lake nearby, she realised that, at last, she had found 'far more than I ever dared to hope for'.

II

During that day's glorious ride, Isabella had also met a man – one who was in some respects closer to her ideal of manhood than she had ever dared hope for. The meeting had occurred at the Park's entrance where, riding through 'a long gulch with broad swellings of grass belted with pines', she had noticed a pretty hobbled mare feeding, 'a collie dog barked at us, and among the scrub, not far from the track, there was a rude black log cabin, as rough as it could be to be a shelter at all, with smoke coming out of both roof and window. . . . The mud roof was covered with lynx, beaver and other furs laid out to dry, beaver paws were pinned out on the logs, a part of the carcass of a deer hung at one end of the cabin, a skinned beaver lay in front of a heap of peltry just within the door, and antlers of deer, old horseshoes, and offal of many animals, lay about the den. Roused by the growling of the dog, his owner came out, a broad, thickset man, about the middle height, with an old cap on his head, and wearing a grey hunting-suit much the worse for wear (almost falling to pieces, in fact), a digger's scarf knotted round his waist, a knife in his belt, and a "bosom friend", a revolver sticking out of the breast-pocket of his coat; his feet, which were very small, were bare, except for some dilapidated moccasins made of horse hide. The marvel was how his clothes hung together, and on him. The scarf round his waist must have had something to do with it. His face was remarkable. He is a man about forty-five, and must have been strikingly handsome. He has large grey-blue eyes, deeply set, with well-marked eyebrows, a handsome aquiline nose, and a very hand-some mouth. His face was smooth-shaven except for a dense moustache and imperial tawny hair, in thin uncared-for curls, fell from under his hunter's cap and over his collar. One eye was entirely gone, and the loss made one side of the face repulsive, while the other might have been modelled in marble. "Desperado" was written in large letters all over him. I almost repented of having sought his acquaintance. His first impulse was to swear at the dog, but on seeing a lady he contented himself with kicking him, and coming up to me he raised his cap, showing as he did so a magnificently-formed brow and head, and in a cultured tone of voice asked if there were anything he could do for me? I asked for some water, and he brought some in a battered tin, gracefully apologising for not having anything more presentable. We entered into conversation, and as he spoke I forgot both his reputation and appearance, for his manner was that of a chivalrous gentle-man, his accent refined, and his language easy and elegant. I inquired about some beavers' paws which were drying, and in a moment they hung on the horn of my saddle. Apropos of the wild animals of the region, he told me that the loss of his eye was owing to a recent encounter with a grizzly bear, which, after giving him a death hug, tearing him all over, breaking his arm and scratching out his eye, had left him for dead. As we rode away, for the sun was sinking, he said, courteously, "You are not an American. I know from your voice that you are a countrywoman of mine. I hope you will allow me the pleasure of calling on you." '

The man was Jim Nugent, 'known through the Territories and beyond them as "Rocky Mountain Jim"', and known to George Kingsley, who met him the following year, as 'The Mountainous One', 'on account of the extraordinary altitude of his lies'. Some said he was an unfrocked priest or an ex-schoolmaster, some that he was a 'hard-case', a 'wind-bag', a 'four-flusher', and a 'scoundrel'; Jim himself said he came from good Irish-Canadian stock, had run away from home because he couldn't marry his first love and was, all in all, more sinned against than sinning. Certainly he had been a fur-trapper for the Hudson Bay Company and then an Indian Scout in the pay of the Government; in which capacities he had slaughtered first animals and then Indians with little mercy or discrimination. When Isabella met him he had a 'squatter's claim' in Estes Park and forty head of cattle; he earned money by trapping, casual guiding, stock-raising, and spent all he made in orgies of drunkenness and ruffianism during which few men cared to cross his path unarmed. Nevertheless, there was 'a certain dazzle' about him, it haloed him, romantic, picturesque, fascinating as his careless golden curls. He was a legendary figure on the Colorado landscape – celebrated for daring, chivalry, eloquence and pride; notorious for vindictiveness, brutality, bitterness and dissipation. He was a complex man who sought a simple setting: his past crimes prodded him to guilt, his lost chances curdled him to self-pity, his present weaknesses jeered him to shame. So he skulked, lonely, moody, slovenly in his black cabin at the entrance to Estes. When his world looked fair, he wrote poetry and essays; when melancholy returned, he drowned in whisky-wild oblivion; he was as vain as any Dick Turpin about his reputation as both knight-errant and desperado. He loved the natural beauty of his surroundings, and was gentle with the melting charm of the Irish to children, who adored him in return. It had been a long time since Jim Nugent had found any other creatures worthy of his affection.

Isabella, interested in him from their first meeting, heard some of this from Griff Evans, the 'hospitable, careless, reckless, jolly, social, convivial, peppery, good-natured' little Welshman who, in spite of his usual affability, loathed Jim and so regaled her with the less savoury details of his history. Not that Griff could be too self-righteous, for he shared Jim's ruinous love of the bottle, and his money, too, Isabella said, 'went into a "bag with holes" ' and so did little to ease the lot of his overworked wife and children. Into Griff's holey bag, Isabella put eight dollars a week, for which she hired the cabin and was given unlimited food. The cabin had a stone chimney, a hay-bed, a tin basin and a skunk that lived under the floorboards. Each night she fell asleep to the sound of its snorts, scrapes and scuffles, but no one dared dislodge him for fear of the resulting effluvium that would have made the cabin untenable for weeks. In that sharp air, all food was exquisite and 'as much as you could eat' was a lot. Steers were simply hacked apart and devoured from head to tail, hunks of oven-warm bread were gilded with just-churned butter, puddings made with molasses came piping hot and toffee-brown. The company gathered for meals in the main cabin, and when Isabella first arrived it included a 'high-minded and cultured' American couple in search of health, prospectors in search of silver, hunters in search of elk, and an English youth who 'because he rides English saddle and clings to some other insular peculiarities is called the "Earl" '. The permanent residents were Evans and family, including a daughter called Jinny, a lugubrious 'hired man' and Evans's partner, Edwards, 'tall, thin, condemnatory looking, keen, industrious, saving, grave', a teetotaller who 'grieved at Evans's follies' – and probably foretold his ruin with secret zest.

Isabella had scarcely found her feet in this mixed community when Jim Nugent called as he had promised and offered to guide her, Downer and Rogers up Long's Peak, that 14,700 feet of lofty inaccessibility that had tantalised her from afar as had Mauna Loa. She did not like to keep seeing a mountain that she had not climbed, so she asked Mrs Evans to bake a three-day supply of bread, they chopped some steaks off the freshest steer and were away. Jim, Isabella says indulgently, cut 'a shocking figure' in a pair of baggy deer-hide trousers, four ragged unbuttoned waistcoats, 'an old smashed wideawake' and 'with his one eye, his one long spur, his knife in his belt, his revolver in his waistcoat pocket, his saddle covered with an old beaver skin, from which the paws hung down; his camping blankets behind him, his rifle laid across the saddle in front of him and his axe, canteen, and other gear hanging to the horn, he was as awful looking a ruffian as one could see.' First he showed off his equestrian paces on his skittish Arab mare, then pulled up alongside her and, 'with a grace of manner which soon made me forget his appearance, entered into a conversation which lasted for more than three hours, in spite of the manifold checks of fording streams, single file, abrupt ascents and descents and other incidents of mountain travel'.

She was fascinated, engrossed, amused. He was so breezy and clever, so merry, quick and melancholy by turns, above all so refreshingly 'strange altogether', so different from any man she had ever known. He seemed quite outside and extraordinarily irrelevant to those strict codes of moral behaviour which, carefully implanted in her childhood, she had seldom questioned. He was by no means a mere blarneying and shallow flirt, however – Isabella would have seen through that immediately. Several times she refers to his culture, the erudition of his wit and, as she emphasises, 'though his manner was certainly bolder and freer than that of gentlemen generally, no imaginary fault could be found'. With such a delightful rapport established between them – for Isabella responded with wit, charm and intelligence of her own – the ride to Long's Peak passed in a glow of beauty. 'There were dark pines against a lemon sky, grey peaks reddening and etherealising, gorges of deep and infinite blue, floods of golden glory pouring through canyons of enormous depth, an atmosphere of absolute purity, an occasional foreground of cotton-wood and aspen flaunting in red and gold to intensify the blue gloom of the pines, the trickle and murmur of streams fringed with icicles, the strange sough of gusts moving among the pine tops – sights and sounds not of the lower earth, but of the solitary, beast-haunted upper altitudes. From the dry buff grass of Estes Park, we turned off up a trail on the side of a pine-hung gorge, up a steep pine-clothed hill, down to a small valley, rich in fine, sun-cured hay about eighteen inches high, and enclosed by high mountains whose deepest hollow contains a lily-covered lake, fitly named "The Lake of the Lilies". Ah, how magical its beauty was, as it slept in silence, while *there* the dark pines were mirrored motionless in its pale gold, and *here* the great white lily cups and dark green leaves rested on amethyst-coloured water!'

The lemon, gold, amethyst light dwindled; by the time they reached the camping-ground 'a big half-moon hung out of the heavens, shining through the silver blue foliage of the pines on a frigid background of snow, and turning the whole into fairyland.' They built a huge fire and sat near it chewing strips of beef while the moonlight and flames fused together on the edge of the frosted dark. Isabella made friends with Ring, Jim's dog, 'with the body and legs of a collie, but a head approaching that of a mastiff, a noble face with a wistful human expression and the most truthful eyes I ever saw in an animal. His master loves him, if he loves anything, but in his savage moods he ill-treats him.' The two young men, who had 'little idea of showing even ordinary civilities,' did bestir themselves for the general entertainment after supper with student songs and spirituals, and Jim contributed 'one of Moore's melodies in a singular falsetto' and they all joined in *The Star-Spangled Banner.* Then she bedded down in a bower of interlaced branches strewn with pine-shoots, covered with a blanket, a saddle for a pillow and Ring, at his master's bidding, stationed against her back to keep her warm.

But sleep eluded her. Everything was so exciting: ominous gusts of wind howled round the rocky heights she was expected to scale the next day, wolves and lions yowled painfully close, owls hooted, the fire crackled and, in front of the fire, lay the man, 'a desperado, sleeping as quietly as innocence sleeps' with, for sure, the best side of his handsome face turned towards her. What had grown so suddenly between them, she wondered? Surely she had sensed a spark of attraction from him that very evening? She confesses as much to her sister later, and then adds, 'but I put it away as egregious vanity, unpardonable in a woman of forty'. But the attraction was there: Platt Rogers says casually that, during this expedition, 'Jim took quite a fancy to her and she took quite a fancy to Jim.' An extraordinary predilection on both sides, from the young man's point of view!

Dawn was a glory of rose-and-gold; faced with its splendours, Jim 'uncovered his head and exclaimed, "I believe there is a God." ' The gesture, Isabella assures us, and perhaps herself, was involuntary and reverent (but it sounds like a little bit of Irish

theatre notwithstanding). As the sun wheeled up the sky, they
began what was now more than a mere ascent for both of them.
For Isabella it was a test of courage and endurance; it was her
way of proving to Jim that she was the bravest, toughest, and
most extraordinary English lady ever to have come his way; for
Jim, it was a display of his own strength and expertise and an
exercise in chivalry and hope. He really wanted her to live up to
his expectations of her, and she did, though it was by far the most
fearsome mountaineering exploit of her life.

He half-dragged her to that summit, 'like a bale of goods by
sheer force of muscle'. He roped her to him and pulled her up over
great ice-strewn boulders, he bent and she climbed on over his
shoulders, he made steps for her with his hands and feet and she
ascended them, she crawled on hands and knees, swinging by both
arms, and he caught her wrists and hauled her up to join him. It
was a grotesque and cumbersome *pas de deux*, intimate and yet
detached, perilous and yet preposterous. She put her life in his
hands and he was proud to take good care of it. The last five
hundred feet was a perpendicular crawl up a 'smooth cracked face
of pink granite' that made her sick with fear and which even
valiant Ring wouldn't attempt.

And then they were pinnacled triumphant at the top, above a
panorama of 'unrivalled combination'. In one direction the snow-
born River Thompson sparked off towards the Gulf of Mexico
and ice-splintered ranges piled to meet the clouds; nearer, green
valleys still lay in the lap of summer; and to the east stretched the
grey-brown of the endless plains. Isabella was enraptured,
uplifted on 'one of the mightiest of the vertebrae of the backbone
of the North American continent'; she was also giddy, bruised,
exhausted, and one of the young men, who had earlier made
pointed remarks about the encumbrances of female-kind, was now
more seriously incommoded by severe bleeding from the lungs due
to the altitude. On the descent, the youths went ahead and Jim
devoted himself entirely to her. In spite of his efforts she had
'various falls' and 'once hung by my frock, which caught on a
rock, and Jim severed it with his hunting-knife, upon which I fell
into a crevice full of soft snow'!

On their return to the camping-ground, Isabella pitched into
exhausted sleep for several hours and when she awoke it was dark

and Jim was sitting smoking by the fire, where she joined him. As the pine-knots crackled and the wild beasts yowled on the dark margins, Jim told her yarns of his misspent, ungoverned youth, how all his flair and energy had somehow gone the wrong way, how aimless and blighted his present life was. She listened, saddened, her kind heart flooded with sympathy, and yet withal, cautious – shrinking a little suspiciously from so much emotion so candidly and unreservedly offered on such a very short acquaintance. 'His voice trembled, and tears rolled down his cheek. Was it semi-conscious acting, I wondered, or was his dark soul really stirred to its depths by the silence, the beauty, and the memories of youth?'

The return to the ranch the next morning was uneventful and the days that followed were full of zest and happiness. 'I really need *nothing* more than this log cabin offers,' she declared. Each morning began with a thump on her cabin door and Griff's cheery voice shouting, 'I say Miss B. we've got to drive wild cattle today. I wish you'd lend a hand – I'll give you a good horse.' So it was out in the dawn when the lake turned from purplish-lead to orange, and the crested blue-jays 'stepped forth daintily on the jewelled grass'. And it was away over the mountains with the wind biting her face and the dogs barking; she with the stockmen, the hunters and Evans, all 'with light snaffle bridles, leather guards over our feet and broad wooden stirrups and each carried his lunch in a pouch slung on the lassoing horn of his saddle'. It was Hawaii all over again, because the terrain and the air and the company were so invigorating. They cantered madly towards the wild herds feeding in the valleys, and ' "Head them off boys!" our leader shouted; "all aboard; hark away!" and with something of the "High, tally-ho in the morning!" away we all went at a hand-gallop down-hill. . . . The bovine waves were a grand sight: huge bulls, shaped like buffaloes, bellowed and roared, and with great oxen and cows with yearling calves, galloped like racers, and we galloped alongside of them and shortly headed them, and in no time were placed as sentinels across the mouth of the valley. It seemed like infantry awaiting the shock of cavalry as we stood as still as our excited horses would allow. I almost quailed as the surge came on, but when it got close to us my comrades hooted fearfully, and we dashed forward with the dogs, and, with bellowing, roaring, and thunder of hoofs, the wave receded as it came. I rode up to our leader, who received me with much laughter. He said I was a "good cattleman," and that he had forgotten that a lady was of the party till he saw me "come leaping over the timber, and driving with the others." '

Then it was back in the chill dusk, stiff, tired and content, with the owls hooting, the polecats snarling, the pole star hanging just opposite the cabin door, and inside the cabin, the warm smells of fire and food. And as they hugely ate, the talk was all of bear-tracks or the movements of the nearest big-horn herd, the merits of different types of rifle and/or fishing-tackle, the hunting skills of Ring as compared with those of Griff's dog Plunk, the latest blood-curdling rumours of Injuns on the war-path, the arrival of a waggon that brought strange, irrelevant, silly news from the outside world. After the meals, Isabella performed extraordinary sartorial feats ('I have just made a pair of drawers from the relics of a night-gown', she tells Hennie), while the hunters lay on the floor playing euchre and making trout-flies. Mr Power, a young French-Canadian who had a wonderful way with a harmonium, produced an inexhaustible repertoire of 'sonatas, funeral marches, anthems, reels, strathspeys', and Evans led them all in rousing choruses of *D' ye ken John Peel* and *John Brown's Body*. 'A little cask of suspicious appearance was smuggled into the cabin and heightens the hilarity I fear,' she noted one night, in a surprisingly indulgent tone. Even the whisky, winking tawny-gold in the firelight cajoled her into the belief that it wasn't quite so wicked here as elsewhere. Her ethical certainties were slightly blunted: by the strict standards of her upbringing, nearly all this company would stand condemned, of fecklessness, laziness, self-indulgence at the least, and some – with their sporadic drunkenness, violence, fornication – were positively criminal. Yet they were so pleasant and easy to be with, she felt so happy and healthy there, warmed by the fire and the joviality, not thinking much, just being.

And added to all this was the spice of Jim Nugent, whose 'business as a trapper' brought him to the ranch with uncommon frequency of late. She continued to find him 'splendid company', relishing his 'remarkably acute judgment of men and events', his sudden 'graceful railleries', the leaps of his mercurial imagination that seemed to her 'full of the light and fitfulness of genius'. And when communication faltered, or the borders of circumspection were approached, they would change horses for the fun of it and go for a good gallop, 'the fearful-looking ruffian on my heavy waggon horse, and I on his bare wooden saddle, from which beaver, mink, and marten tails and pieces of skin were hanging raggedly, with one spur, and feet not in the stirrups, the mare looking so aristocratic and I so beggarly!' The blossoming friendship, undoubtedly a subject for log-cabin gossip, did not please Griff. He was bitterly envious of Nugent's reputation and social flair and looked upon him as a rival claimant to the territory of Estes Park. As Isabella soon realised, even this remote spot seethed with hatred, pride and greed and 'there is always the unpleasantly exciting risk of an open quarrel with the neighbouring desperado [Jim] whose "I'll shoot you" has more than once been heard in the cabin.' The violence trembled in the future, and would be worse than her worst imagining.

After a few weeks Isabella felt she had to get away for a time. Perhaps the relationship with Jim was intruding too much upon her consciousness; perhaps she was simply and prosaically determined to see more of Colorado, a desire from which even Jim's presence could not deflect her. At any rate, on October 19, she and the musical Mr Power jogged off together towards Longmount. At 'Muggins Gulch' (as it was popularly called) Jim waylaid her, looking as ragamuffin as always, 'with his gentle cosy manner, low musical voice and slight Irish brogue. . . . He leant on my horse and said, "I'm so happy to have met you, so very happy. God bless you." And his poor disfigured face beamed with nice kindly feeling. Mr Power remarked what a thorough gentleman he is and how very much he likes me, both of which things are true.' This incident, told for Hennie's benefit, sent Isabella on her way tremulous, flattered, happy, a little perturbed; probably she pushed it from her mind, to concentrate instead on the comparatively simple business of riding across part of the Rockies, beset only by snow blizzards and sub-zero temperatures.

III

Her companion, comfort, mainstay for the ride was Birdie, a bay Indian pony, 'a little beauty with legs of iron, fast, enduring, gentle and wise'. This intelligent creature, 'always cheerful and hungry', with her 'cunning, lively and pretty face', her 'funny blarneying noise' of greeting and her nuzzling, faithful, willing ways became everybody's favourite. She had but two bad habits: if a stranger led her, she reared up like a wild bronco; when saddled, she swelled herself up to quite abnormal proportions so that later, when she condescended to deflate, all her girths had to be tightened. On Birdie's back, Isabella strapped her carpet-bag full of patched, reconstituted clothes, including the inevitable 'black silk', and the two of them trotted off across the plains towards Denver.

Late that afternoon a wind whirled up, storm-and-dust-laden, grey as the two prairie wolves that loped ahead of her in cowardly flight. Cresting a slope, she saw 'the great braggart city spread out brown and treeless, upon the brown and treeless plain which seemed to nourish nothing but wormwood and the Spanish bayonet'. Isabella sighed, dismounted and, she tells Hennie, reluctantly put on her skirt and 'got on again sideways, using the horn as a pommel. To ride sideways now seems to be as if, having the use of two feet, one was compelled to always hop on one.'

Riding thus, uncomfortably lady-like, she entered the braggart city, capital of the Territory since 1867, whose settlers had first begun to boast of its future ten years before that. In those days, the settlement had suffered its share of disasters: fire and then flood engulfed its makeshift shanties, Indians besieged it one year and grasshoppers besieged it several years, billions of them that clotted the ground and shredded bare the pioneers' precious crops. By 1873 though, Denver was safely on the up and up; it had gaslights, horse-cars, law and order and, above all, trains. The first train had puffed importantly across the plain in the summer of 1870, had ridden magnificently over the solid silver spike that ceremonially nailed the last piece of track in place, had come to triumphant rest in an 'elegant brick depot', the local reporter explained. 'Pretty nearly everybody was wild with enthusiasm,' he continued. 'Old timers who had toiled across the Plains in ox-teams or on foot in the early days, dodging the Indians in season and out of season, and enduring discomforts which tried their souls and bodies too, clasped hands in congratulations that the old order of the overland days was done and Denver was nearer to

New York today than she was to many of the mining camps in the mountains.'

The new railroad carried a diversity of peoples to Denver, so that its streets when Isabella saw them had 'a harlequin appearance'. There were sufficient asthmatics come from the East in search of health to warrant the holding of an 'asthmatic convention', and sufficient consumptives come to try the fashionable 'camp-cure' of living rough in the mountains to ensure a brisk trade in tents, sleeping-bags and portable cooking-stoves. There were the old-timers still: 'hunters and trappers in buckskin clothing; men of the Plains with belts and revolvers, in great blue cloaks, relics of the war; teamsters in leathern suits; horsemen in fur coats and caps and buffalo-hide boots with the hair outside, and camping-blankets behind their huge Mexican saddles'. And there were the newcomers: 'Broadway dandies in light kid gloves; rich English sporting tourists, clean, comely and supercilious-looking'; and the oldest comers of all: 'hundreds of Indians on their small ponies, the men wearing buckskin suits sewn with beads, and red blankets, with faces painted vermilion, and hair hanging lank and straight, and squaws much bundled up, riding astride with furs over their saddles'.

Confused and uneasy in this predominantly masculine throng, Isabella made but two calls in town. Her first was to the editor of the *Rocky Mountain News*, who duly recorded it in his personal column: 'Miss I. Bird . . . a noted traveller in new and strange countries is in Denver . . . She travels almost altogether on horseback and has laid out a pretty good winter's work for herself.' Her second call was to ex-Governor Hunt of Colorado, who assisted her 'winter's work' by giving her a map and introductory letters to settlers en route, for, as in Hawaii, there were no inns, and it was customary for people to receive travellers in their homes. Hunt, incidentally, was a man typical of his time and place: finder of a fortune in the gold rush of '49 and loser of it over a poker-table; blazer of trails to the mines and over the mountains in the past, and now wheeler-dealer in railroads and local politics; governor of the territory during the Indian troubles of the later 60s and now friend of the Ute tribe, one of whom he introduced to Isabella. But she failed to appreciate the picturesque vitality of such men, because she was not really very interested in the grand adventure of 'Opening up the West'. Her cast of mind was essentially conservationist and non-partisan; she took little satisfaction in seeing an iron track tame a hitherto inaccessible pass, or brick-and-stucco burgeoning where there was wood-and-daub before. Men like Hunt with their railways and politics, their paved streets and tourist hotels were pushing back the freelance extemporary loners such as Evans and Nugent with whom she felt a natural kinship of temperament.

So she left the cocky city with its hustlers and hucksters just as soon as possible and headed south for the open spaces. There the snow was marked only by the claw of bird, paw of squirrel, track of solitary rider like herself, and the local names had that homespun ring suggestive of a less pushy age – Horseshoe Gulch, Rattlesnake Divide, Sweetwater Range, Handcart Gulch, Yellow Pine Peak and Bitter Foot Mountain. On the third day out she climbed the Arkansas Divide where 'Everything was buried under a glittering shroud of snow. The babble of the streams was bound by fetters of ice. No branches creaked in the still air. No birds sang. No one passed or met me. There were no cabins near or far. The only sound was the crunch of snow under Birdie's feet.' At the Divide's 7,975-foot-high summit lay an ice-green motionless lake, owls shrieked along its pinewood margins, the solitude was 'unspeakable', palpable as a presence. The next day began 'grey and sour', but brightened as she wended a lonely way among gorges of coloured rock, through cold valleys crouched below ghastly peaks, past a 'decayed-looking cluster of houses bearing the arrogant name of Colorado City' and into Colorado Springs, where she again donned the hated skirt and rode side-saddle, 'though the settlement scarcely looked a place where any deference to prejudices was necessary. A queer embryo-looking place it is . . .!' and to Isabella quite unappealing.

Colorado Springs had been highly recommended to her by Rose Kingsley, eldest daughter of the celebrated Charles, who, with her brother Maurice, had been there two years previously when its condition was positively ovular. When Rose arrived, a plough had only recently furrowed the direction of its main streets, twelve wooden huts and a few tents were scattered about and each night packs of coyotes plunged by in search of sheep, with demoniacal howls that sounded shudderingly like Injuns on the war-path. The plucky little 'Denver and Rio Grande' narrow-gauge railroad ended there then, and the Santa Fe stage took over. Rose, peeping from the railway company's office above Fields & Hill dry-goods store, often watched the transition. Mails and luggage were stowed outside the coach, glum passengers stuffed inside, and then 'when all is ready and not till then' out walked the driver 'in yellow blanket coat and hat securely tied down with a great comforter, he mounts the box, arranges himself leisurely, the messenger is beside him wrapped in buffalo robes, then the reins are put in his hand and as he tightens them away go the horses with a rush that take one's breath away.' Rose, very much an indoor young lady compared with Isabella, spent much time sewing, feeding caged snow-birds, learning how to roast antelope, and her main enterprise was the formation of Colorado Spring's first 'intellectual society – The Fountain Society of Natural Science' – hopefully intended 'to keep young men away from the drinking saloons in Colorado City'.

By the time Isabella rode on the scene, the stage and its drivers were quaint memories, for the railway had plunged on southwards to Pueblo. Now the town, 'laid out as a beautiful residence city', said the hand-outs, boasted rows of houses, the Colorado Springs Hotel, billed as 'the most elegant hostelry between Chicago and San Francisco', and enough 'intellectuals' among its inhabitants to support the publication of the literary magazine *Out West*, whose editor, Mr Liller, entertained Isabella. She slept at a nearby boarding house and there had a rather gruesome experience which epitomised for her the casual callousness of pioneer life. Sitting in the parlour talking to the establishment's landlady that first evening, she noticed a door opposite 'wide open into a bedroom, and on a bed opposite . . . a very sick-looking young man was half lying, half sitting, fully dressed, supported by another, and a very sick-looking young man much resembling him passed in and out occasionally. . . . Soon the door was half-closed and some one came to it, saying "Shields, quick a candle!" . . . All this time the seven or eight people in the room in which I was were talking, laughing and playing backgammon, and none laughed louder than the landlady, who was sitting where she saw that mysterious door as plainly as I did. All this time . . . I saw two large white feet sticking up at the end of the bed. I watched and watched, hoping those feet would move, but they did not; and somehow, to my thinking, they grew stiffer and whiter, and then my horrible suspicion deepened, that while we were sitting there a human spirit untended and desolate had passed forth into the night. Then a man came out with a bundle of clothes, and then the sick young man, groaning and sobbing, and then a third, who said to me with some feeling that the man who had just died was the sick man's only brother. And still the landlady laughed and talked, and afterwards said to me, "It turns the house upside down when they just come here to die; we shall be half the night laying him out." ' 'Colorado for Consumptives' was the battle-cry among local promoters, but it obviously didn't work for some who, coming there only to die, didn't even have enough money left to bury themselves decently, as the Springs' inhabitants grumbled.

Behaving, briefly, like an obedient tourist, Isabella went to the 'Garden of the Gods', in which, she remarks, 'were I a divinity, I certainly should not choose to dwell'. There, according to the guide-book, he should have seen bizarre rock formations featuring 'The Sphinx of Egypt,' 'Elephant attacking Lion' and 'Seal making love to a Nun' (this last was soon bowdlerised to 'Seal and Bear'). She stayed that night at the luxurious Manitou Hotel, whose nearby medicinal springs were guaranteed, in the words of a local enthusiast, Dr Solly, to cure 'increased venosity, gravel, catarrh of the bowels' and promote 'diminution of fat' – a sure sign of the invasion of well-padded easterners on the lean pioneering western scene! But Isabella was not impressed: 'I am now quite sure there is no place in Colorado like my glorious rathole [Estes] with all its comforts, its huge fires, rocking chairs and hot stones and jovial spirits,' she told Hennie. The theme was repeated several times during her ride, but she carried on stubbornly nevertheless.

Westwards first, across the Ute Pass where the Indians used to wait for the buffalo coming down to winter pasture and, occasionally, for whites, six of whom had been scalped there five years before. She followed the course of the Fountain River, a fair stream 'cutting and forcing its way through hard rocks, under arches of alabaster ice, through fringes of crystalline ice, thumping with a hollow sound in cavernous recesses cold and dark, or leaping in foam from heights with rush and swish. . . .' Dwarf oaks, white cedars, juniper, majestic redwood of the Pacific, grand balsam-pine of the Atlantic all crowded the water's edge and above all 'towered the toothy peaks of the glittering mountains'. It was 'Grand! glorious! sublime! but not lovable'.

And she felt roughly the same about many of the pioneers she met; there was a certain grandeur about the very fierceness and perseverance of their enterprise under such arduous circumstances, but only a few were 'lovable'. There was, she diagnosed, that same money-grubbing stinginess of mind and spirit abroad that had characterised the Chalmerses. 'The almighty dollar is the true divinity', and a brash, unprincipled 'smartness is the quality thought most of'. Among the rough-and-ready settlers, the English were specially unpopular, and at one cabin Isabella met a nutty old grandmother with a stentorian voice and a clay pipe who 'raged at English people, derided the courtesy of English manners and considered "Please" and "Thank you" and the like were "all bosh" when life was so short and busy'. The un-popularity was mainly attributable to the number of wealthy British gentlemen travelling in the region, and Isabella's description of one of them is interesting, as evidence of her refreshingly candid contempt for the loving of the English lord (quite a common affliction among her social peers) and as a salutary reminder of just how dreadful members of that species could be. 'This gentleman was lording it in true caricature fashion, with a Lord Dundreary drawl and a general execration of everything; while I sat in the chimney corner, speculating on the reason why many of the upper class of my countrymen – "High Toners", as they are called out here – make themselves so ludicrously absurd. They neither know how to hold their tongues or to carry their personal pretensions. An American is nationally assumptive, an Englishman personally so. He took no notice of me till something passed which showed him I was English, when his manner at once changed into courtesy, and his drawl shortened by half. He took pains to let me know that he was an officer in the Guards, of good family, on four months' leave which he was spending in slaying buffalo and elk, and also that he had a profound contempt for everything American. I cannot think why Englishmen put on these broad mouthing tones and give so many personal details.' Isabella's own accent, incidentally, must have been quite free of affectation, for she was often mistaken for a Swede or an Australian.

Farther away from Colorado Springs, she penetrated higher and deeper into the mountains, where there were no marked tracks and general opinion informed her that the route was impassable. Yet she came to no harm and did not lose her way. 'I have developed the most extraordinary organ of locality,' she told Hennie, and needed it to make sense of such directions as 'Keep along a gulch four or five miles till you get to Pike's Peak on your left, then follow some wheel-marks till you get to some timber, and keep to the north till you come to a creek, where you'll find many elk tracks; then go to your right, cross the creek three times, then you'll see a red rock to your left . . . etc.' Well, she found the way, wheel-marks, elk-tracks and all, and spent that night at the cabin of a hunter called Link. After supper, a vehement argument brewed between Link and other travellers present about which way she should go next. Mrs Link, she tells Hennie, 'wondered that a person like me "who looked so dreadfully delicate" could ride at all. I fear I must look mean, for in spite of my stout figure people often say so – women that is, men usually think I am as strong as themselves!' In this case even the men doubted her capacities: 'The old hunter acrimoniously said he "must speak the truth", the miner was directing me over a track where for twenty-five miles there was not a house, and where, if snow came on, I should never be heard of again. The miner said he "must speak the truth", the hunter was directing me over a pass where there were five feet of snow and no trail. The teamster said that the only road possible for a horse was so-and-so . . . Mr Link said he was the oldest hunter and settler in the district, and he could not cross any of the trails in snow. And so they went on. At last they partially agreed on a route – "the worst road in the Rocky Mountains," the old hunter said, with two feet of snow upon it, but a hunter had hauled an elk over part of it, at any rate.'

However, two more days' ride brought her safely in sight of the glittering ranges of the Great Continental Divide on the far side of South Park, a treeless, high-lying prairie that had been thoroughly 'rushed'. Its chief centre, Fairplay – thus dubbed by miners hopeful of a better deal than they'd had in neighbouring camps – was, nevertheless, pretty lawless and uncompromisingly masculine, and she was probably wise to give it a wide berth.

By so doing, Isabella met one of those picturesque characters so bedaubed with later legend and song that it is hard to believe they ever really existed. But apparently they did, for riding casually though a little larger than life, along the frozen Denver waggon road was a man who wore a big slouch hat, from under which a number of fair curls hung nearly to his waist. His beard was fair, his eyes blue, and his complexion ruddy . . . He was dressed in a hunter's buckskin suit ornamented with beads, and wore a pair of exceptionally big brass spurs. What was unusual was the number of weapons he carried. Besides a rifle laid across his saddle and a pair of pistols in the holsters, he carried two revolvers and a knife in his belt, and a carbine slung behind him.' In spite of his weaponry, his manner to her was 'respectful and frank' and she found him 'good company'. They ate some bread and his venison steaks together and rode up to the crest of the Divide, he beguiling the way with yarns spun around the two great themes of the West: wild animals and wilder Indians. His name, she later learned, was Comanche Bill, a 'notorious desperado' whose family had been massacred by the Cheyennes and whose life since had 'been mainly devoted . . . to killing Indians wherever he can find them'.

She left Bill atop the Divide and turned reluctantly north-east, down through an icy canyon in the pitch darkness, and ended up, perforce, at Hall's Gulch, in a roofless, doorless shed and among a company of whisky-sodden miners whose looks she did not at all like. Jim had made her promise to carry a loaded revolver on her journey; she took it out for the first time that night and slept with its cold metal against her cheek – a flimsy bulwark for, she remarked, 'I cannot conceive of any circumstances in which it could do me any possible good.' When she awoke, the day was cheerful and she ridiculed her fears. But she heard later that a man had been 'strung up' by the Hall's Gulch miners on a tree near the shed just the previous day; presumably the corpse had been swinging in the dark a few yards from where she slept.

Unscathed and pleased with her success, she started back towards Denver, but even before she came within range of the city – symbol of the restraints and complexities of 'civilisation' –

the old frets and problems crowded in upon her. She spent the last night of the adventure lying sleepless on the floor of a grocery store with three families of teamsters, worrying, she told Hennie, about the prospect of returning home 'with nothing fixed to do. I am beginning to be so afraid of breaking down as soon as I leave this life.' She recalled with dread and clarity her state when she had left home some sixteen months before: the sense of frustration, tension, unchannelled energies, the pain, lassitude, insomnia. She tortured herself with the conundrum of her own temperament – how *could* she be so strong, tireless, vital when travelling, so vulnerable, sickly, depressed at home? It was an insoluble enigma, and, back at Denver, she found a foolproof excuse for shelving it. A financial crisis, that had been threatening for weeks, had struck the West, the Denver banks would not cash her circular notes; Griff Evans, to whom she had rashly lent money, could not repay her, for cash was unobtainable. Stranded penniless without a train-fare and pleased to be, she decided that the most, indeed the *only* sensible plan was to return to Estes where she could, in all senses, live free. 'It does not seem a very hard fate,' she confessed, as she and Birdie cantered away to the icy, sublime, beast-haunted solitudes.

IV

And Estes Park was indeed solitary now, most of its 'jovial spirits' driven away by the onset of winter and, at the ranch, only a couple of young men 'batching', that is, looking after themselves and the stock. Their supplies were low and Isabella realised that they would scarcely jump for joy at the unforeseen arrival of an English maiden lady come to stay for 'an indefinite period'. However, unlike the two 'innocents' of her early acquaintance, these two, Kavanagh and Buchan by name, were courteous and friendly and agreed to share the work and the remaining supplies with her. Kavanagh made the best bread, Buchan and he brought in the wood, water, and fed the stock, she got most of the meals and 'did the parlour', that is she swept piles of mud and ash off the floor with a buffalo's tail several times a day. The three of them rubbed along nicely together. 'The men are so easy to live with,' she told Hennie after a week, 'they never fuss or grumble or sigh or make a trouble of anything' – Isabella always enjoyed the simplicities of unconstrained male company.

But with Jim Nugent, waiting for her down at Muggins Gulch, such easy companionship was no longer possible. The story of their emotionally-charged and increasingly complex relationship during the next weeks is partially told in the letters to Hennie – a strange tale of a frangible but powerful attraction between two hopelessly disparate people. Its very incongruity and improbability in that magnificently wild setting gives it a touching air of late romance that borders on fantasy. And it is difficult to imagine how Hennie, and the intimate circle of letter-readers responded to Isabella's latest from Estes Park, dated November 18. 'There is a tragedy about Mr Nugent that has made me too terribly nervous,' she begins. The fact was that while out riding with her on the second day back, Jim confessed that 'as soon as I had gone away he had discovered he was attached to me and it was killing him. It began on Long's Peak, he said. I was terrified, it made me shake all over and even cry. He is a man whom any woman might love but whom no sane woman would marry. Nor' she adds hastily, 'did he ask me to marry him. He knew enough for that. A less ungovernable nature would never have said a word, but his dark proud fierce soul all came out then. I believe for the moment he hated me and scorned himself, though even then he could not be otherwise than a gentleman.'

She clung to that, but he was determined to disabuse her of all illusion and lay bare his tortured soul, as the Victorian novelists might have put it (their influence on Isabella's vocabulary in these particular letters is marked). So, as they rode, he thrust upon her the most harrowing details of his dissolute life, and through his narrative thudded the crack of rifle and whip, the thunder of hooves, the screams of hunter and victim – thrilling and violent as the wild beat of a war-dance. 'Vain, even in his dark mood, he told me that he was idolised by women, and that in his worst hours he was always chivalrous to good women. He described himself as riding through camps in his scout's dress with a red scarf round his waist, and sixteen golden curls, eighteen inches long, hanging over his shoulders. The handsome, even superbly handsome, side of his face was towards me as he spoke.' As he grew older, his periods of reckless ruffianism and dissipation reached new depths, after which, all seed and money spent, he skulked back to his lair 'full of hatred and self-scorn' till the next time. 'My heart dissolved with pity for him and his dark, lost, self-ruined life. He is so lovable and yet so terrible', she wrote.

Guiding her to a shelter out of the snow-laden wind, he reined his horse, faced her and shouted, 'Now you see a man who has made a devil of himself! Lost! Lost! I believe in God. I've given Him no choice but to put me with "the devil and his angels". I'm afraid to die. You've stirred the better nature in me too late. I can't change. If ever a man were a slave, I am. Don't speak to me of repentance and reformation. I can't reform . . . How dare you ride with me? You won't speak to me again, will you?' Pity, awe, warmth, sadness swelled in her throat; 'I told him I could not speak to him, I was so nervous, and he said if I could not speak to him he would not see me again. He would go and camp out on the Snowy Range till I was gone' . . . And then he wheeled his horse and thundered away into the blinding storm. Miserably, Isabella rode back to the ranch alone and 'I could not bear to think of him last night out in the snow, neither eating nor sleeping, mad, lost, wretched, hopeless . . .'

Nor, of course, could she think of anything else. For the first time in her life, as far as we know, and certainly for the last, her whole nature was aroused – her keenly developed instincts of compassion and warmth, her latent, hardly touched sexuality. She blamed herself for her involvement and vulnerability, and blamed him for his lack of reticence. 'It was very wrong of him to speak as he did, he should have let me go without the sorrow of knowing this. It takes peace away,' she complained with prim irritability, feeling the injustice of being trapped in such a distracting situation in this idyllic, remote spot. 'I cannot but think of poor Mr Wilson in Hawaii and his quiet, undemonstrative, unannoying ways, and comparing him with this dark, tempestuous, terrible character, wondering how it is that the last is so fascinating.'

Surely this was a little naïve, for Jim had all the melodramatic attraction of the talented wastrel and a theatrical flair for playing the role to the hilt. So much of his promise crumbled to regret, so much of his energy ground to vindictiveness, so much of his intelligence blown out to idle bluster. He was unconventional, footloose, a true lover of nature and physical activity, the sort of 'manly' man she admired; he was handsome, chivalrous, witty, cultured, to boot, and with, she admits, a real 'gift of the gab' that much appealed to her own unacknowledged yearning for high drama. So really it was not in the least surprising that she found him much more alluring than blunt Mr Wilson, in spite of his manifold sins. More surprising, really, was that a man like Nugent should declare his love for a short, plump, devout, high-minded English spinster of over forty – proof positive of what a gay and original spirit lurked beneath Isabella's rather unexciting exterior.

Shying away from the knowledge of what she had unknowingly started, Isabella sought a typically feminine refuge in vigorous housework. She baked four pounds of biscuits, made rolls raised with six-week-old buttermilk, re-patched a chemise, fed the horses, tended a sick cow, wielded the buffalo tail in every corner. She marshalled her thoughts back to familiar channels: 'I am always thinking of my own darling,' she affirmed to Hennies trenuously. 'I keep its picture always on the table by me and when it [Hennie] says any nice words to me I read them over and over again. I care for it unspeakably.' Her dream life was less easy to direct, and wandered among fantasies whose probable interpretation in modern Freudian terms would have appalled her. 'I dreamt last night that as we were sitting by the fire Mr Nugent came in with his revolver in his hand and shot me . . .'

The next day, Jim arrived carrying a revolver that he laid on the table, and Isabella found her hand veering instinctively towards it. His manner was 'freezing, courteous of course, but the manner of a corpse'. They went for a mute, dismal ride, Jim looking pale, haggard and coughing continuously – determined that she should feel guilty for the cold he had presumably caught while in exile on the bare mountain. Isabella was furious with herself and him; her hearty appetite had quite deserted her; she was tense, fretful, piqued as a love-lorn adolescent, and she wouldn't endure it. Sitting miserably by the fire she was haunted by doubts of his sincerity. How much was all this a pose, a cynical bit of Irish blarney produced for sheer devilment and the slim hope that he might add her to his list of conquests? At last, impatient, she wrote to him: 'Dear Sir, In consequence of the very blameworthy way in which you spoke to me on Monday, there can be nothing but constraint between us . . . It is my wish that our acquaintance should at once terminate. Yours truly, I.L.B.' On the way to his cabin, they met, he took the odd, stilted missive and pocketed it unread, saying that an old arrow-wound was troubling him and he was going to bed. 'He looked so ill and wretched going to his dark lonely lair, and I felt I had stabbed him and not made sufficient allowance for him . . .' She longed to 'make him warm tea and be kind to him', joke and chat with him, instead of playing out this wretched little melodrama of pride, suspicion, sexual tension.

Two days later, a trapper called to say that Jim was very ill; she saddled Birdie at once and galloped towards his cabin – and met him, not so ill or so proud, coming to her. Glad to be together, they sat under a tree and had a muted, honest talk. 'I told him that if all circumstances on both sides had been favourable and I had loved him with my whole heart, I would not dare to trust my happiness to him because of the whisky . . . He said he would never say another word of love.' So love, with its fearful promises and precarious commitments was laid aside in favour of mutually acknowledged affection, and perhaps there was never really anything more to it. Yet Jim must at some point have actually proposed marriage, for she says that 'he had built such castles in the air' of Hennie coming to join them in the mountains, which presumably meant that she would have been living there permanently with him. 'There's a man I could have married,' she tells Hennie, but she was a little too mature for such a preposterously reckless step, and her deep love for her sister pulled her homeward. 'You would like Jim so,' she assures Hennie, but her optimism must have faltered at the vision of pious little Miss Henrietta Bird of Edinburgh actually faced with her dear, ragamuffin desperado. Clearly it had to be one or the other; clearly it couldn't be a man with blood on his hands, lawlessness in his heart and whisky-fumes so often on his breath. Fortified by her strong instinct of self-preservation and a very prudent distrust, she allowed herself only a deep and genuine compassion for this man with two faces – one of them scarred by violence and reck-lessness, the other handsome, sensitive and warm.

At that point, light relief arrived unexpectedly at the ranch in the shape of 'Mr Allan', a callow, brash theology student come to earn his keep. Though both lean and lazy, Allan was blessed with

a gargantuan appetite which was exceedingly inconvenient at the
time, for food supplies were desperately short, and Edwards, who
was supposed to bring replenishments, failed to appear. 'The
boy', as they called Allan, just kept eating willy-nilly, and nothing
was safe from his greed. 'He has eaten two pounds of dried cherries
from the shelf, half of my second four-pound spiced loaf before it
was cold, licked up my custard sauce in the night, and privately
devoured the pudding which was to be for supper. He confesses to
it all, and says, "I suppose you think me a case." ' Each morning,
his first query was, ' "Will Miss B. make us a nice pudding
today?" ' One day Miss B. did bake a nice cake, but added cayenne
pepper instead of ginger. 'During the night we heard a com-
motion in the kitchen and much choking, coughing and groaning,
and at breakfast the boy was unable to swallow food with his
usual ravenousness. After breakfast he came to me whimpering,
and asking for something soothing for his throat, admitting that
he had seen the "ginger-bread" and "felt so starved" in the night
that he got up to eat it. . . . He is a most vexing addition to our
party, yet one cannot help laughing at him.' By this time, the
Park was set fast in the grip of winter, holding the five of them,
Isabella, Jim, Kavanagh, Buchan and the vexing newcomer in
close and interdependent proximity. The lake was rigid enough to
wheel a waggon over, snow blew constantly through the chinks in
the cabin walls and layers of it drifted on to the table, over their
beds at night, and mixed with the mud on the 'parlour' floor.
Water froze as it came from a heated kettle, milk froze in the
churn, ink in the bottle, molasses in the pan, eggs in the shell, and
when Isabella got her hair wet in a storm it froze to her head in plaits.

None of this bothered her, but the bother was still Jim who, after
their last talk, had wrapped himself in 'an ugly fit' as harsh as the
weather itself. She invited him to share the special Thanksgiving
Dinner that she cooked, but 'he said he was not fit for society and
would not come. . . . It is really miserable to see him . . . I believe
he hates himself and me and everyone else . . . I can't do with this
at all.' Poor Isabella! It was true indeed that she had never in her
life before 'had to do' with anyone like Jim. And it was perhaps
just her unsophisticated honesty, her refusal to be quite swept off
her feet by his dramatics, her lack of any sort of affectation or the
flirtatious coquetry of 'having to do' with men that won his heart.

But still he unsettled her, and despite their reconciliation it was apparent that his very presence in the Park precluded peace. 'I am howling frightfully, fearfully, about leaving this place,' she told Hennie. 'It will be better when it is over now . . . I could not prolong my stay here because of him.' Clearly it was another case of 'better a finger off than aye wagging', she told herself firmly.

And yet and yet how she loved the land: the purity of air, earth and water, the snow that snapped and sparkled from the horses' hooves, the intense sunlight glaring on the pearly peaks; the comfortable homely sounds of chopping wood, lowing cows, rattling buckets and men talking about the elks in the forest, the trout under the ice, a horse that bolted, a sick calf in the pen. The life fitted her right and tight; she was so healthy and energetic; she felt 'like a centaur' on horseback; she could lasso cattle, bake bread, drive a waggon. 'It is so sad that you can never see me as I am now,' she told Hennie, 'with an unconstrained manner and an up-to-anything free-legged air.' And yet and yet, they had no tea, flour or sugar left, the venison was going sour, Kavanagh and Buchan wanted to go hunting further afield, Jim was still there.

On 1 December she went to see him, taking young Allan as a sort of chaperon and intending it as a farewell visit. His 'den was dense with smoke, and very dark, littered with hay, old blankets, skins, bones, tins, logs, powder-flasks, magazines, old books, old moccasins, horseshoes and relics of all kinds. He had no better seat to offer me than a log, but offered it with a graceful unconciousness that it was anything less luxurious than an easy-chair.' The very squalor and neglect of his surroundings, indeed, threw into fairer contrast 'the grace of his manner and the genius of his conversation.' The shadow of her impending departure brought a return of their gay companionship. They talked for hours, free in the awareness that Allan's presence would keep a curb on the encounter. She read him her account of the Long's Peak ascent, and he listened with attention and enthusiasm and, as 'a true child of nature', 'tears rolled down his cheek when I read the account of the glory of the sunrise'. Not to be outdone, he read part of his 'very able paper' on Spiritualism to her. With subdued gallantry, he suggested that he would 'guide' her to the plains when she left, and she agreed, though she knew the way perfectly well.

She lingered for another week, during which Evans and Edwards

finally turned up with the supplies and introduced a stern parsi-
mony into the household's regime. Evans (though he repaid
Isabella, to his credit) was in considerable financial difficulties;
Edwards, the lean and cheerless, held the whip hand and served
scraps of dried venison and rationed the milk. Jim came along to
dazzle her that Sunday, arrayed in his 'best', clean, spruce,
looking 'barely forty' and 'with sixteen shining gold curls falling
down his collar'. He stayed to dine, the perfect gentleman, but his
arrival only increased the tension; Evans was 'not himself' and
Jim adopted a 'stiffly-assumed cordiality, significant, I fear, of
lurking hatred on both sides'.

It had come to the crunch with Evans's return, and what could
she do but go? The Park would be closed until the next May, only
the few men would stay with the wolves, the bears, the elk come
down from the heights. 'By May we shall be little better than
brutes in our manners at least,' one of them prophesied, in
reference to her salutary presence among them as the only
woman. And Isabella concurred in the view, explaining that the
'mission' of 'every quiet, refined, self-respecting woman' was to
exert a restraining and civilising influence where she could, and
not to forfeit her traditional role 'by noisy self-assertion, masculinity or fastness'. Even in her wildest moments of 'free-
leggism', she was not a hoyden, and that too greatly attracted
Jim – the piquant combination of utter fearlessness and womanly
sympathy, of spirited dash and capable housewifery. The combination came to her naturally, *was* her nature, and she could
have stayed there indulging it for the whole winter, except for
Jim who took peace away.

On the day of her departure she rose early, and sadly watched
'the red and gold of one of the most glorious winter sunrises and
the slow lighting up of one peak after another'. Evans rode with
her to Jim's cabin where she parted with the faithful pretty
Birdie. When Griff had gone, Jim presented her with his finest
'mouse-coloured kitten beaver's skin', and then they rode from
the Park together, she astride his skittish Arab mare. Soon the
'dismalness of the level land' swamped them; Jim was subdued;
'like all true children of the mountains he pined even when
temporarily absent from them' was her explanation of his silence.
That night they lodged at a queer little inn at St Louis, from

where she would get the waggon-coach for Cheyenne the next day. The landlady, a competent, florid widow 'top heavy with hair', was thrilled to learn that the 'quiet kind gentleman' with Isabella was none other than Rocky Mountain Jim himself; for, she explained, he was the family bogeyman, and if her children were naughty, she told them that 'he would get them, for he came down from the mountains every week and took back a child with him to eat!' In spite of his sinister gastronomic reputation, she was 'as proud of having him in her house as if he had been the President, and I gained a reflected importance'. The children, braving his voracity, crawled on Jim's lap and played with his golden curls and even the local men crowded the doorway to get a glimpse of him.

After supper the kitchen was specially cleared in their honour, and while the music for a local barn-dance thumped and skirled in the background, she shared for the last time the sweet pleasure of his company. Again she 'urged upon him the necessity for a reformation in his life, beginning with the giving up of whisky, going so far as to tell him that I despised a man of his intellect for being a slave to such a vice. Too late, too late! he always answered, for such a change. . . . He shed tears quietly. "It might have been once," he said.' Yes, it might have been; that was the deepest poignancy of their whole encounter.

The next morning was beautiful beyond endurance. There was a 'frost-fall' of frozen moisture-particles floating and glittering in the pure air like feathers, ferns, diamonds, and the violet mountains she had left were 'softened by a veil of the tenderest blue'. When the waggon rolled up, there was aboard one Mr Haigh, an English dandy whom she had briefly met elsewhere. She introduced the men to each other and Haigh 'put out a small hand cased in a perfectly-fitting lemon-coloured kid glove. As the trapper stood there in his grotesque rags and odds and ends of apparel, his gentlemanliness of deportment brought into relief the innate vulgarity of the rich *parvenu*.' That brief moment, when the immaculate, pretentious kid glove was grasped by the large rough paw of her dear desperado, was one she long remembered with distress. It symbolised for her what lay ahead, compared with what she had left behind; more than that, it had dire consequences far beyond her reckoning at the time.

The horses pawed the ground, the driver tightened his grip on the reins and with the crack of a whip, creaking of wheels, flailing of hooves in the mud, they were away. She turned to wave and watch and watch ' "Mountain Jim", with his golden hair yellow in the sunshine, slowly leading the beautiful mare over the snowy plains back to Estes Park, equipped with the saddle on which I had ridden 800 miles!'

V

'On her way home from the Sandwich Islands,' records Miss Anna Stoddart, Isabella's early biographer, 'Miss Bird spent some months at a Sanatorium in the Rocky Mountains, achieved her famous ride and then made her way to New York and stayed with Mr and Mrs Robertson till her steamer sailed for Liverpool.' Thus, with quiet and deadly decorum, the whole bizarre and passionate adventure of Colorado is de-fused and expurgated for the Edinburgh drawing-rooms to which Isabella returned, and Rocky Mountain Jim, shorn of all his volatile and sensual glamour, is relegated to an object fit only for the moral zeal and compassion of a good Christian woman. Miss Stoddart supposes that 'She spoke very gently to him about the influence which redeems from sin and fortifies the repentant sinner, and repeated to him a text to keep ever in his remembrance as a reminder to the unhappy man whom her gentleness had restored to a measure of self-respect'. Truly, Isabella did lecture Jim about his drinking and talked to him of the love of God, and truly Jim himself, in moments of self-abasement, called upon the deity to save his black soul — but it did not, fortunately, happen in quite that squeamish and sanctimonious fashion. There was so much more sheer life, drive, passion in both Jim and Isabella than in trim, bloodless, conventional Miss Anna Stoddart who seldom left her Scottish hearthside and who could only begin to compass Isabella's experiences by cutting them savagely down to her own size.

But Isabella herself of course abetted and encouraged this emasculation process the moment she got off the steamer in Liverpool and hurried home to dear, good, predictable sister Hennie. The two Miss Birds visited friends, heard a fine sermon or two, had a boating holiday on the placid River Ouse; and Isa bella worked on the manuscript for a book about the Sandwich Islands, 'throwing fragments of Hawaiian history' into the concluding chapter and 'excising a mass of personal detail', Anna Stoddart says, so that, naturally, the 'unannoying' and almost unremembered Mr Wilson was mercilessly expunged.

During that summer of 1874, just as Isabella was about to leave for a holiday in Switzerland, a letter came from Colorado: it said that Jim Nugent had been shot in the head by Griff Evans in Estes Park. Isabella says that she received five different versions of that shooting and wisely refused to publicise any of them. The tragedy, she says simply, 'is too painful to dwell upon'. Yet, for a while, she must have dwelt upon it – that beautiful valley, indelibly stained with the blood of an evil deed perpetrated by a man she liked against a man she almost loved.

The fullest published account of the tragedy by someone who was almost on the spot appears, rather improbably, in *Notes on Sport and Travel* by George Kingsley, father of the redoubtable Mary. Kingsley, in his usual capacity of sportsman-medico, was staying at the Evanses' ranch with Lord Dunraven when it occurred. One sunny day in June, according to him, Griff was dozing on his bed, and on the cabin door-stoop sat Mr Haigh, the gentleman with the lemon kid gloves who 'was dawdling about in these parts under the pretence of hunting'. Quite unaccountably, Mountain Jim suddenly lunged upon the scene in the ugliest of his 'ugly fits' and aimed at Haigh with his rifle. Haigh jumped up shouting, 'Jim's on the shoot', Evans reached for his gun, bounced out of the door, peppered the desperado with buckshot, then rode off to the nearest town to take out a warrant against Jim for assault. Jim meanwhile lay under a clump of aspens with a bullet in his head. He was given first aid by the hastily-summoned Kingsley, who expected him to die there and then. But Jim lingered in Fort Collins hospital, even though, Kingsley says, 'he had two halves of a bullet in his brain'.

Obviously there was more to it than that, and two principal motives were proposed for the flaring of such murderous antagonism between the men. The anti-Jim faction maintained that his behaviour for some time had been increasingly eccentric and dangerous, and that he tried to seduce Evans' daughter Jinny, a girl of about sixteen. Jim's penchant in that direction is borne out by Platt Rogers who says that, when playing his local bard role, Jim wrote poetry 'in praise of Jinny's charms and about the deplorable condition in which he found himself because his passion was not returned'. This version, which Isabella undoubtedly heard, must have wounded her most deeply and may well be what she had in mind when she says, in a published footnote, that it was not 'until after his death that I heard the worst points of his character'.

But that may have been malicious gossip, spread to cover up the real, and in some ways more plausible-sounding motive for the murder. For it was a fact that the very Mr Haigh to whom Isabella had first introduced Jim the day the two parted was an agent of Lord Dunraven's come to further the earl's plan for the purchase of Estes Park as a private hunting-ground. According to Jim, who lived long enough to give his own version of the affair, he was shot because he refused to sell out to Dunraven and allow free access to the Park across his land; Evans had become 'Dunraven's creature' and agreed to kill the man whom, as Isabella makes clear, he had loathed for years. The local papers reported the affray in accordance with their own prejudices. One informed its readers that Jim simply 'blazed away' at Griff who shot back in pure self-defence; another, that Jim was shot 'by a creature of the Earl of Dunraven because of the fraudulent transaction regarding the sale of Estes Park' (and if this motive is the right one, then Kingsley's testimony is highly suspect). Jim got his own account published in the *Fort Collins Standard* stating that he was attacked without provocation 'by two English ruffians' with 'well-filled pockets which they are willing to empty into the lap of the man' who could keep them from the court. He concludes with a last bout of his fiery rhetoric: 'Great God! Is this your boasted Colorado? That I, an American citizen, who has trod upon Colorado's soil since 1854 must have my life attempted and deprived of liberty when the deep laid scheme to take my life has failed, and all for British gold!'

Certainly poor Jim got less than justice in the end. Griff was arraigned for assault but allowed bail; Jim, while in hospital, was, he says, in the custody of the sheriff. For a short time, apparently Jim staged a sort of recovery and left the hospital, but seems to have taken no action against Evans. However, his condition soon deteriorated because of the bullet left in his skull and finally, says Kingsley with rather evident satisfaction, 'he keeled over like a well-killed rabbit'. The *Rocky Mountain News* was clearly on Evans's side and, in Jim's obituary, said that he died from 'bad whisky and too much of it'. There was not enough public sympathy for Jim to force the issue to the courts and, though a writ for assault with intent to murder had been filed against Evans, the case was dropped the following year without a hearing, and all witnesses to the deed melted conveniently away.

So, if guilty of premeditated murder, cheery little Griff Evans got away with it, and the Earl of Dunraven got most of his Park for a few years too – although he found it unexpectedly burdensome owing to the difficulties of keeping out the plebs, which gentlemen with game-preserves could do with ease in Britain. For Isabella, there were the painful, upsetting letters each with its own version of the elusive truth, the knowledge that the fascinating Mr Nugent 'lay buried in a dishonoured grave with a rifle bullet in his brain' – and a vision. According to Anna Stoddart, Isabella went on her Swiss holiday after hearing the news 'full of the distressing conviction that Jim had died unrepentant and occupied with the remembrance of their mutual promise' – that they would meet again. As she lay in her hotel bedroom one morning in a state of suggestible melancholy, Jim appeared to her, Anna says, 'in his trapper's dress, just as she had seen him last . . . he bowed to her and vanished'. Later, naturally, the date of the vision was found to be that of his actual death. Whatever the cause of the phenomenon, it does suggest the very powerful hold that Jim had on Isabella's imagination, for she was not in the least subject to visions as a rule. Impossible to say how deeply she grieved at his fate, for it would, even at the time, have remained a partly secret sorrow; impossible to know how intense her passion had been. In a letter to a friend several years later, by which time the Colorado adventure must have seemed a rather unlikely and marvellous fantasy, she wrote, 'Don't let anybody think that I was in love with Mountain Jim . . . but it was pity and yearning to save him that I felt.' So be it; it was over.

The next year gave an early boost to her spirits with the publication by John Murray of *Six Months in the Sandwich*

Islands. It was an instant hit, 'a remarkable, fascinating and beautifully written book,' applauded the *Spectator*; the *Pall Mall Budget* praised her sheer physical energy and enthusiasm in such a clime, where the very 'richness of the soil fosters indolence'; the learned periodical *Nature* expressed gratified astonishment at the accuracy and breadth of her botanical knowledge. The few adverse comments noted a tendency to gush and a 'flux of epithets applied with some lack of discrimination'. This was a fair stricture, as Isabella really knew, though she tried to justify the fault to her publisher by suggesting that 'a redundancy in my style . . . is perhaps more excusable when writing amidst the luxuriousness of a tropical climate' – a dubious analogy which probably amused, but did not convince, the shrewd John Murray. Anyway, she adds, 'I assure you I am beginning to think it rather a nice book . . . there has been nothing but what is pleasant connected with it.'

Buoyed up on this little crest of acclaim, Miss Bird throve for a year or so. She took histology lessons to further her botanical knowledge, she attended the Edinburgh May Assemblies, she involved herself in social work, including the provision of a 'Shelter and Coffee Room' for Edinburgh's cab-drivers, and she spent part of each summer on the Isle of Mull, where her sister had recently leased a cottage. But then the familiar syndrome reasserted itself as she had dreaded it would: she began to suffer from neuralgia, 'intermittent fevers', spinal pain, bouts of listless depression. Again the doctors advised travel and she set her heart upon the Orient – the beginning of a twenty-year passion. Early in the year 1878 she sailed for Japan.

CHAPTER III

Japan

THE Japan that Isabella Bird reached in the late spring of 1878 was, even at that time, Asia's up-and-coming country. It had been just a quarter of a century since the American Commodore Perry had landed on its secluded shores and more or less forced the Tokugawa Shogun then in power to sign a treaty that eventually led to the opening of the country to foreign trade. From then on the Japanese were spurred into activity as if they had been just waiting for the West to blow the starter's whistle – as indeed, some of the more far-sighted and progressive of them had – and their rate of progress had been phenomenal. By the end of the 1850s, three of their ports were open to trade and a few enterprising foreign merchants had set up shop; by the end of the 60s, other ports had opened, trade had greatly expanded, aspiring Japanese politicians had toured the capitals of the western world in order to assimilate everything they possibly could, the Shogun had been overthrown in a relatively bloodless civil war and the country was ruled by a generally forward-looking oligarchy under the sovereignty of the young Emperor Meiji. By the time Isabella was there, Japan had its first railways, banks, newspapers, post-offices, factories. Its peasants sent their children to the newly-enlarged schools to absorb western-style knowledge and sometimes stared at the telegraph wires strung across their paddies in the hope of seeing the messages go by; its urban sophisticates were riding in barouches and landaus, wearing morning suits and top-hats, drinking champagne, eating with knives and forks. In short, everything western, were it functional or frivolous, mechanical or monstrous, unsuitable or unsightly, had to be tried for size by the hustling Japanese of the 1870s.

Isabella admired much of what she saw and was **very much**

JAPAN

miles 0 ... 300

kms 0 ... 500

SEA OF JAPAN

PACIFIC OCEAN

HOKKAIDO

Sapporo

Hakodate

Tsugaru Strait

Aomori

Odate

Akita

Shinjo

Nikko

Minato

Tokyo

Fuji Yama

Yokohama

Kyoto

Inland Sea

SHIKOKU

KYUSHU

interested in it, but she didn't love it. New Japan lacked what she always termed the 'grooviness' (and to Isabella this of course meant unexciting, hidebound) of the irredeemable, backward-looking, essentially immutable Orient that gave her true solace. She deplored, during this and later visits to Korea and China, the 'hopeless darkness' in which the oriental peasant lived; he was, she felt, ignorant, superstitious, bigoted, crafty, cruelly used by those in authority over him and cruelly bound by custom. Yet when she came to any large settlement where conditions for the common people were better – there were a few commercial enterprises perhaps, drains, a railway station, gas-lamps to lighten the darkness – she fled back to the 'savage freedom of the wilds'. Her reason told her that the technology and learning of the West had come to enrich and invigorate the East, and she faithfully describes the developments in this process during her Japenese tour, but it evoked little emotional sympathy. She did not thrill to the sound of a steam-whistle where buffalo-carts used to trundle, or the sight of a store selling tinned meat and bottled beer where only dried fish and rice-wine were sold before. Secretly in a self-contradictory sort of way, she felt that the old was more genuine, honest and sane than the new. 'I long to get away into the *real* Japan,' she wrote after spending just one day in hybrid, thriving Yokohama, with its ponderous western-style buildings, its pavements, lamps and dignified hotels along the Bund with all 'mod. cons.' and rooms full of tourists talking 'in a nasal twang'.

For Japan was already on the edge of the globe-trotters' circuit. It was exotic, people heard, but safe; romantic, but not dangerously wild; beautiful, but not inaccessibly awe-inspiring – and the people were so clean and polite. Such an impeccable list of virtues would entice hordes of western visitors to come and 'do' Japan during the next thirty years, and Isabella was only just ahead of the mob, which made it the more imperative for her to get away quickly into the hinterlands. *Unbeaten Tracks in Japan* she calls her book, feeling the beat of the globe-trotting feet unusually close behind.

The first stage in the escape was to get advice on such indispensables as an interpreter, ponies and 'gear', and for this she was fortunate and celebrated enough to have a letter of introduction to Sir Harry Parkes, British Minister in Japan. 'A young-

looking man, he was,' she wrote after their first meeting, 'scarcely
in middle life, slight, active, fair, blue-eyed, a thorough Saxon
with sunny hair and a sunny smile and a sunny geniality in his
manner.' Clearly she liked him immediately and they became firm
friends, which was lucky because Sir Harry was just about the most
experienced and informed expert on both Chinese and Japanese
affairs then in the British Diplomatic Service. And to sit, as
she did, in the Legation drawing-room after dinner and listen to
his first-hand accounts of the development of modern Japan was a
most pleasant and meaningful introduction to the country.

Sir Harry had first come to Japan thirteen years before when
the Shogun was still in power and foreigners were still very much
the 'red-haired barbarians from without'. While he had learned to
admire the determination and energy the Japanese had displayed
in coming to grips with western encroachment, he was beginning
to feel that they were too often content to imitate modern in-
novations without fully understanding their substance or impli-
cations. His early enthusiasm for the country was tempered by
certain disillusionment and this he undoubtedly voiced to Isabella. And she, in her turn, is cautious when estimating Japan's
material and social progress, emphasising that, while the country
'had done many things well and wisely, much is still undone'. By
her explorations of the remote interiors, Isabella saw much more
than most westerners of what was still to be done if the Japanese
were to achieve their dreams of modernisation; and it is these
accounts, a revelation to many, of the oriental squalor and
ignorance that lay behind the sophisticated westernised facades
of the treaty ports and the capital that gave her book its highly
original and popular appeal.

Unlike many of the cautious foreign residents, who had never
ventured into such dark hinterlands themselves, the Parkeses were
all in favour of Isabella's journey. Lady Parkes contributed two
baskets with oil-paper covers and an invaluable 'india-rubber
bath'; Parkes gave her a passport for practically unrestricted
travel north of Tokyo. This document, required of all foreigners
except diplomats who travelled outside the limits set by the
international treaties, was a relic of the days of Japanese xenophobia, when it was considered dangerous to allow the 'barbarians' any rights of access. So foreigners had to state that they

were moving about 'for reasons of health, botanical research or scientific investigation', and most were squeezed into one category or other – Isabella, presumably, in the elastic first. The passport, of a loquacious and lengthy nature, forbade its bearer to 'light fires in woods, attend fires on horseback, trespass on game preserves, scribble on temple walls, ride fast on narrow roads . . . or shoot, trade or conclude mercantile contracts with the Japanese'. Isabella did not find any of these restrictions particularly burdensome; she stowed the document in a bag tied round her waist, donned her 'travelling costume' of 'dust-coloured striped tweed, a bowl-shaped hat of plaited bamboo, laced boots of unblacked leather', gave instructions to her interpreter-guide, Ito, a furtive-looking youth of eighteen, and was ready to start.

The start was conventional – to the gorgeous grandeur of the shrines at Nikko, which had been a travellers' mecca since they were built in the seventeenth century. Pebbled courtyards paved a gracious way to some of the nation's greatest artistic masterpieces: bronze temple bells; treasure-houses sculpted with red-throated dragons, lilies, spike-toothed demons, topaz-eyed tigers; shrines whose roofs of weathered copper curved voluptuously skyward and whose interiors were hung about with brass incense-burners, and draperies of scarlet and pearl-white silk. On a fine day, light rebounded from the surfaces of polished lacquer, golden urns and porticoes vibrant with fabulous beasts and bursting blossoms. Yet, for Isabella, the shrines were at their loveliest when it rained and the sightseers stayed away. Then the purple curls of the thunder-god glowed deep and damp in his guardian niche, the cryptomerias behind the shrines dripped dark green, the little gold windbells rustled rainily from every eave, cascades of holy water plashed down into a stone cistern and the only other sound was that of straw-shoed acolytes scuffing to their rituals over the wet paving-stones.

The beauty of the shrines so made her prisoner that Isabella stayed on for a time in Nikko, where she acquired her very first taste of oriental village life, of which she was to have so much harsh, uncomfortable, fascinating experience during the next twenty years. It was a deceptively idyllic introduction to what lay ahead. Each village day was a rhythmical, placid imitation of the one before. At seven a.m. a drum-beat summoned the children to school where, with earnest docility, they studied their own tongue, Chinese, arithmetic, history and geography in a classroom which, with its blackboard, maps, desks, Isabella thought 'too Europeanised'. During the morning the cobbles were a clatter of wooden clogs as housewives hurried to buy cubes of jellied beancurd, strands of seaweed, pickled roots for lunch. Below Isabella's room, Kanaya (her host) pottered about among his azaleas, his floppy hat straw-gold in the sun, and the birds swooped for gnats over his dainty pond. Later, released, the children gathered along the streams which tumbled in stone channels down the middle of every street. Their ingenious toys – water-wheels, red windmills, cockleshell boats – bounced and spun in the current and when there was a disaster, a shipwreck or a broken wheel, the children at last forgot their staid sobriety and roared with glee or dismay. At sunset, the younger ones, warm-pink from the evening's hot bath, rode their father's shoulders about the streets or watched while he had his regular shave and haircut on the raised open front of the barber's shop. This operation, said Isabella, was one of Nikko's most entertaining sights: 'Soap is not used and the process is a painful one. The victims let their garments fall to their waists and each holds in his left hand a lacquered tray to receive the croppings. The ugly Japanese face at this time wears a most grotesque expression of stolid resignation as it is held and pulled about by the operator, who turns it in all directions that he may judge of the effect he is producing. The shaving of the face till it is smooth and shiny, and the waxing and tying of the queue with twine made of paper' completed the performance. This formal method of hairdressing was already old-fashioned; urban, modernised Japanese men, including the Emperor Meiji himself, had gone in for western hair-styles, cropped, tousled and chopped to various lengths above the collar. But the provinces were slow to respond to this, as to many of the drastic directives and fashions that emanated from the capital, and most of the Nikko men preferred to keep their hair long, waxed and bunched in a neat tail across the crown.

After the evening visit to the barber, as the light faded and street-channels ran darkly, the family gathered indoors and the *andon* was lit. This 'wretched apparatus' was a lamp with panes of white paper and inside them a dish of oil on which a pith of lighted rush floated. By its unpredictable flare, Kanaya's older children recited their morrow's lessons in a high monotonous twang that plucked at Isabella's nerves, adults played *go*, told stories, strummed an eerie *samisen* and passed the warmed *saké* cup. *Saké*, she noted, 'mounts readily to the head', and soon the singing began, a moaning two-note chant, that whined 'like the very essence of heathenness', while a half-witted manservant was excited into 'some very foolish performances' at which everyone cackled immoderately, except Isabella who felt ill at ease. At about ten, the *andon* being left to burn rancidly through the night, the wooden shutters were bolted tight, wadded quilts and wooden head-rests were produced, trays of sweetmeats were placed about in case anyone wanted a midnight snack, and then the family rolled themselves into their respective multi-coloured cocoons and slept.

Upstairs, alone, Isabella looked round her moonlit room, the one spray of azalea in a slender white vase, the filigree tracery of a cabinet, the hint of a misty landscape sketched on an ochre-gold screen – a room so exquisite that she went in constant dread of 'spilling the ink, indenting the mats, or tearing the paper windows'. And, remembering the vulgarity of the manservant's antics, the weird chill of the chant, she was uneasily aware that beneath the restrained and ordered beauty of her surroundings, and the placid village routines, shuddered an element that was bizarre, raw, totally alien to her understanding. And this sense of the essential outlandishness of the country and its people grew upon her as she journeyed northward into regions that were a world away both from the conventional globe-trotters' pictures of willow-pattern-pretty Japan, and from new Japan with its telegraph offices and station-masters in white kid gloves. The Japan she saw and, in a way, loved, was late-medieval: uncouth, ungilded, often unclean – also original, homespun, untrammelled.

The differences were apparent as soon as she and Ito, on two sorry mares, left Nikko and plunged north into forests through which, everyone said, no proper routes existed. And certainly the 'roads' soon dwindled to bridle-trails that slithered over log-bridges zigzagged among boulders and heaps of landslipped rubble, dabbled into quagmires. Villages degenerated into haphazard clusters of tattered single-room thatch huts with a much-decayed, much-trodden manure heap for a front garden, and one fouled stream where people washed themselves and their clothes. The people too degenerated – in so far as they became increasingly covered with dirt and sores instead of clothes. 'The men may be said to wear nothing. Few of the women wear anything but a short petticoat wound tightly round them or blue cotton trousers very tight in the legs and baggy at the top.' The petticoat, Isabella thought, was 'barbarous-looking' and when a woman thus clad, with a nude, diseased baby on her back stood and stared vacantly at the foreigner, Isabella could hardly believe herself to be in 'civilised' Japan.

Nor did the typical rural inn offer much to support her belief. Its rooms were draughty, smoky, humming with fleas and mosquitoes, reeking of sour sewage, their rafters crusted with dank soot, their walls a rickety clutter of dilapidated paper screens. These latter were her greatest trial, for, once the news of her arrival spread, crowds gathered in rooms adjoining hers and numerous holes began to appear in the screen-paper, to each of which was applied one Japanese eye, anxious to see what a female foreigner really looked like. It was unnerving and embarrassing to prepare for a night's rest under this silent, dark, eager gaze and on one occasion, when she felt particularly ill, Isabella prevailed upon the landlord to gum over every hole with strips of tough binding! In addition to the wondrous spectacle of Miss Bird herself, the crowds were immensely inquisitive about her possessions – the india-rubber bath, air pillow and her white mosquito net. Ito assured her he could have made a *yen* a day exhibiting these items to the public view, and policemen, who often called ostensibly to copy the details of her passport, actually came just to look at her and her marvellous accoutrements.

Occasionally, among all this dreary squalor, beauty graced their journeying: a line of trees woven together by a web of fragrant honeysuckle, a steep-thatched farmhouse roof glowing warm russet in a shaft of evening light, a row of stubby stone Buddhas, noseless but erect, showing the way to a neglected temple. But for much of the time, things were trying. The vicious Japanese horses stumbled, kicked and rocked like camels and always had to be led by a groom, so there was no hope of galloping off into the wild blue yonder as she had in Hawaii or Colorado. There was, in any case, little blue to gallop into, for unfortunately, the region was experiencing its wettest summer for thirty years. Rain plunged down day after grey day. Village streams and ponds overflowed, carrying ancient deposits of slime and refuse into damp dwellings; mildew flourished everywhere – in the rice she was offered for lunch, on bedclothes and towels, between the pages of the Transactions of the Royal Asiatic Society that she carried with her. She lived in a state of perpetual wet chill, subsisted on a diet of rice-mush, old eggs, slushy sago and cucumbers and was afflicted with spinal pain and bites from numberless insects that multiplied amazingly in the moist air. At one point, her foot was so hugely swollen with horse-ant bites and her hand by stings of both hornet and gadfly that, in desperation, she summoned a native doctor to her inn.

Ito, 'who looks twice as big as usual when he has to do any "grand" interpreting, and always puts on a silk *hakama* [jacket] in honour of it,' ushered into her presence a middle-aged man who bowed three times, sat on his heels and looked first at her 'honourable hand' and then at her 'honourable foot'. Then he sucked in his breath many times, gazed at her eyes through a magnifying glass, took her pulse and told her the bites were much inflamed, which was not news to her. Then he clapped his hands and a coolie appeared carrying a black lacquer chest on his back, inside which another gilt chest contained various medicines. The doctor concocted a lotion, bandaged her arm and told her to pour the lotion over it, then he made her a medicine and suggested she refrain from *saké*-drinking for a few days! There was something diffident and warm about him and they got on well. He showed her a box of 'unicorn's horn' which, he said, was worth its weight in gold, and told her that he relied mainly on it, acupuncture, rhinoceros horn and vegetable brews for his cures. He asked about western surgical methods and if chloroform was used in childbirth mainly to keep the population down. He stayed to dinner and gulped and belched with such gentility that Isabella nearly laughed aloud. After the meal, he asked her to join him in a smoke and assumed her refusal was on account of some strange religious vow. Tobacco had been introduced into Japan by the

Portuguese in the sixteenth century and almost all men and women smoked pipes. Doctors, Isabella noted, usually recommended the practice and she reproduces an amusing translation of a treatise on the attributes of tobacco – the 'Fools' Herb 'or 'Poverty Weed' as smug non-smokers called it. Smokers, contrariwise, swore that it 'dispels the vapours and increases the energies . . . affords an excuse for resting now and then from work, as if in order to take breath . . . and is a storehouse of reflection, giving time for the fumes of wrath to disperse'.

Perhaps Isabella should have taken up smoking to relax the nerves, for the records of her journey through North Japan have a nagging undertone of sour peevishness, only sometimes relieved with a jab of wry, self-mocking humour: 'Again I write that Shinjo is a wretched place. It is a *daimyo*'s town and every *daimyo*'s town that I have seen has an air of decay, partly owing to the fact that the castle is either pulled down or has been allowed to fall into decay. Shinjo has a large trade in rice, silk and hemp, and ought not to be as poor as it looks. The mosquitoes were in thousands, and I had to go to bed, so as to be out of their reach, before I had finished my wretched meal of sago and condensed milk. There was a hot rain all night, my wretched room was dirty and stifling, and rats gnawed my boots and ran away with my cucumbers.' To keep down the rats, incidentally, most houses kept a 'rat-snake' who lived unmolested in the rafters and who, if over-gorged with his favourite fare, occasionally tumbled off them on to bed or table below.

Root cause of Isabella's depression was that her frail physique had not dramatically strengthened with the stimulus of travel as it had done on her previous journeys to the Sandwich Isles and the Rockies. Exhaustion added to her woes, for she seldom seemed to get a good night's rest. At one inn five tobacco merchants thrumming on 'that instrument of dismay, a *samisen*' kept her awake till dawn; at another, the darkness throbbed to the clatter of drums and gongs keeping summer festival; at another the locals quietly removed the screens that made her room, and she woke to find herself completely surrounded by puzzled, staring faces. In her state of weariness she even allowed herself to be wheeled along in a *jinrikisha*, if one was available. These little 'two-wheeled prams', though a picturesque and intrinsic part of the traditional Japanese image, had only been invented about eight years previously, and were not widely used in these remote regions. In urban areas they were everywhere, crazy, rapid little vehicles that looked irresistibly funny at first to the foreigner's eye, including Isabella's: 'The shafts rest on the ground at a steep incline as you get in – it must require much practice to enable one to mount with ease or dignity – the runner lifts them up, gets into them, gives the body a good tilt and goes off at a smart trot. They are drawn by one, two or three men, according to the speed desired by the occupants. When rain comes on, the man puts up the hood, and ties you and it closely up in a covering of oiled paper in which you are invisible. At night, whether running or standing still, they carry prettily painted circular paper lanterns 18 inches long. It is most comical to see stout, florid, solid-looking merchants, missionaries (male and female), fashionably dressed ladies, armed with card cases, Chinese compradores, and Japanese peasant men and women flying along Main Street . . . racing, chasing, crossing each other, their lean, polite pleasant runners in their great hats shaped like inverted bowls, their incomprehensible blue tights, and their short blue overshirts with badges or characters in white upon them, tearing along, their yellow faces streaming with perspiration, laughing, shouting and avoiding collisions by a mere shave.'

That, of course, was a treaty port scene where there were lots of tourists about and all the runners were 'decently clad' in their blue tights in accordance with a law imposed by a government anxious not to offend western susceptibilities by any indecent display of coolie nakedness. In the hinterlands, as Isabella discovered, observance of the law was not so punctilious. Bowling along in a *jinrikisha* on a narrow country road, she and her runner 'met a man leading a prisoner by a rope, followed by a policeman. As soon as my runner saw the latter, he fell down on his face so suddenly in the shafts as nearly to throw me out, at the same time trying to wriggle into a garment which he had carried on the crossbar, while the young men who were drawing the two *jinrikisha* behind, crouching behind my vehicle, tried to scuttle into their clothes. I never saw such a picture of abjectness as my man presented. He trembled from head to foot, and illustrated that queer phrase often heard in Scotch Presbyterian prayers, "lay our hands on our mouths and our mouths in the dust." He literally grovelled in the dust, and with every sentence that the policeman spoke, raised his head a little, to bow it yet more deeply than before. It was all because he had no clothes on. I interceded for him as the day was very hot, and the policeman said he could not arrest him, as he would otherwise have done, because of the inconvenience that it would cause to a foreigner. He was quite an elderly man and never recovered his spirits, but as soon as a turn of the road took us out of the policeman's sight, the two younger men threw their clothes into the air, and gambolled in the shafts, shrieking with laughter!'

This incident nicely illustrates the provincial attitude to the waves of brand-new edicts that flooded the country during the decade: those in authority enforced them sternly and without questioning their relevance to a particular circumstance; the people, for the most part, accepted them with docility and made a great show of absolute obedience – nevertheless, when official-dom's back was turned, many reverted happily to their own well-tried ways, keeping the new ones handy, as it were, to put on quickly when authority reappeared.

II

Near the end of July, after bouncing like a baby in a *jinrikisha*, balancing atop the high-peaked saddles of various ill-tempered pack-horses, ploughing on foot over steep mountain tracks, even, on one occasion, straddling the blessedly firm back of 'a comely pack-cow', Isabella reached Kubota (now called Akita), capital of the north-western Akita province. She liked the town immediately, because it was entirely and typically Japanese, self-contained, unpretentious and thriving after its traditional fashion. She drifted into it on a flat scow up a narrow green river lined with derelict boat-yards; a grand mulberry-coloured mountain dominated its grey-green roof-line; a clean fresh breeze whipped in from the nearby Sea of Japan; she actually had a good beefsteak with mustard for dinner that night and began to feel better.

In olden times, Kubota, like dejected Shinjo, had been a *daimyo*'s town, and his castle, ringed by three moats, still looked imposingly feudal from afar, but was actually in ramshackle ruins. Nowadays, manufacturers and merchants propsered there instead, making and selling the subtly-toned blue-and-black silk much favoured by ladies, a white silk crêpe with raised woof much prized by sophisticates in distant Tokyo and clogs and screens for everybody. Along the main streets, women pattered among the usual conglomeration of native shops: switches of lustrous black hair and ruby-red hairpins shone in the local 'beauty salon'; demon-faced kites, paper carp and butterflies were anchored to the ridge-poles of the toy-store; ranks of watery-blue jars and musty gilt boxes of dried herbs lined the druggist's shelves; coopers and weavers displayed a lovely umber-and-tawny jumble of straw and wooden things – wash-tubs beautifully turned with copper ribs, cages of meshed bamboo, looking fine and large enough to cloister an eagle but actually used to hold stones in place as breakwaters, and tiny reed grasshoppers that looked real enough to hop straight out of your hand.

Western influence had penetrated to Kubota nevertheless, and its principal manifestations were a new hospital and the Normal School, both of which Isabella visited. The hospital's chief physician had been trained in western medicine and it was cheering to compare his methods with those of the dear old country doctor with his box of 'unicorn's horn'. In the Kubota hospital, local resistance to chloroform was being overcome and there were sufficient sprays of carbolic acid 'to satisfy Mr Lister himself'. The school too had changed from the old days when classical Chinese, native literature and the martial arts were its main subjects; now chemistry, Ganot's physics and the economic theories of J. S. Mill were added to the syllabus, and Isabella, as a representative of exciting western ideas, was positively lionised. As she was leaving, she asked one of the lecturers about religious instruction and he laughed, 'with undisguised contempt. "We have no religion," he added, "and all your learned men know that religion is false." '

This attitude greatly dismayed Isabella, as it did many of her contemporaries. For them the very existence of the so-called enlightened western institutions was indissolubly linked to Christianity, and to take the first without the second was like having a shell with no yolk, a carriage with no horse. Japan,

Isabella wrote, angered by this incident, was 'an Empire with a splendid despotism for its apex and naked coolies for its base, a bald materialism its highest creed and material good its greatest goal, reforming, destroying, constructing, appropriating the fruits of Christian civilisation but rejecting the tree from which they sprung'.

Ito, her interpreter, was a case in point. He was a sharp-witted, vain, bandy-legged youth with a passion for sweetmeats and tea-house girls, but 'no moral sense according to our notions'. He was rampantly chauvinistic and secretly despised westerners, declaring that when Japan had learned all she could from them, 'she will outstrip them in the race, because she takes all that is worth having and rejects the incubus of Christianity'. Fortunately he was also reasonably honest, industrious and ambitiously bent upon learning 'proper' English. When Isabella patiently explained that the phrase 'a devilish fine day,' that he had picked up in Yokohama was 'common,' he instantly erased it from his vocabulary. 'What a beautiful day this is,' he used to exclaim politely thereafter, as they rode together along some empty shore where sea and sky were blue.

When, at last, another blue day arrived, they left Kubota and continued north towards Aomori, whence steamers crossed to the island of Hokkaido. It was a long journey of about a hundred miles, took them a fortnight, and started off with a bang when on the first day they came upon a *matsuri*, a summer fair, in progress. The town streets were strung with joggling lanterns and people, 'monkey theatres and dog theatres, two mangy sheep and a lean pig attracted wondering crowds, for neither of these animals is known in this region of Japan; a booth in which a woman was having her head cut off every half-hour for two *sen* a spectator; cars with roofs like temples, on which, with forty men at the ropes, dancing children of the highest class were being borne in procession; a theatre with an open front, on the boards of which two men in antique dresses, with sleeves touching the ground, were performing with tedious slowness a classic dance of tedious posturings, which consisted mainly in dexterous movements of the aforesaid sleeves, and occasional emphatic stampings and utterances of the word *No* in a hoarse howl. It is needless to say that a foreign lady was not the least of the attractions of the fair.'

They left the town, which was called Minato, along a lovely
'avenue of deep sand and ancient pines much contorted and
gnarled. Down the pine avenue hundreds of people on horseback
and on foot were trooping to Minato from all the farming villages,
glad in the glorious sunshine which succeeded four days of rain.
There were hundreds of horses, wonderful-looking animals in
bravery of scarlet cloth and lacquer and fringed nets of leather,
and many straw wisps and ropes, with Gothic roofs for saddles,
and dependent panniers on each side, carrying two grave and
stately-looking children in each, and sometimes a father or a
fifth child on the top of the pack-saddle.'

But the fair respite was brief, the foul weather returned. For
days Isabella shivered in wet clothes, slept on a soaking bed;
trees and bridges were uprooted around them, hillsides and banks
slithered into torrents; straw rain-cloaks hung dripping under
every cottage eave, wet flanks of horses steamed; the last of the
bouillon cubes mildewed and water even infiltrated the tins of condensed milk. Under these conditions, every village inn was
swamped with stormbound travellers, men mostly, whom the local
geisha entertained with pluckety *samisens* and reedy songs that
shrilled eerily towards the grey heavens. Long into the night the
music continued, threaded among the slurps of noodles and
saké, the shouts of ribaldry, the creak of a windlass, the sloshing
about in bath-tubs and, finally, the snoring. Nor were the sounds
always outside Isabella's room. 'I had not been long in bed on
Saturday night,' she relates, 'when I was awoke by Ito bringing in
an old hen which he said he could stew till it was tender, and I fell
asleep with its dying squeak in my ears, to be awoke a second
time by two policemen wanting for some occult reason to see my
passport, and a third time by two men with lanterns scrambling
and fumbling about the room, for the strings of a mosquito net
which they wanted for another traveller.'

That particular interlude occurred in Odate; it was repeated,
with local variations on the stringiness of hens, the persistence of
policemen, the intrusiveness of other travellers, in one village
after another; for there was, she noted, a remarkable homogeneity
about the land and its inhabitants. 'Everywhere the temples and
houses are constructed on identically the same plan, and though
some may be large and some small, and wooden walls and mud

walls, thatched roofs and roofs of bark or shingles, may alternate, the interior of the dwelling-house has always similar recognisable features. Crops vary with the soil and climate, but there is no change in the manner of cultivation; the manuring and other agricultural processes are always the same. And far beyond all this the etiquette which governs society in all its grades is practically the same. The Akita coolie, boor as he may be, is just as courteously ceremonious in his intercourse with others as the Tokyo coolie; the Shirasawa maidens are as self-possessed, dignified and courteous as those of Nikko; the children play at the same games with the same toys, and take the same formal steps in life at the same ages. All are bound alike by the same rigid fetters of social order, a traditional code which, if it works some evil, also works so much good that I should grieve to see it displaced by any perverted imitation of Western manners and customs.'

On each similar landscape, similar figures reappeared. Thus, each village had its headman to oversee the collection of taxes after each harvest, to report on the conditions of ferries and bridges, and to keep the civil register up to date. To facilitate this, each house was legally bound to keep a tally hanging on the doorpost outside with the names, number and sex of its inhabitants inscribed thereon (in one village Ito counted 307 people in twenty-four houses!). Each village also had its priest, to guard the chill grey shrine, to bear the *saké* cup at weddings and the lotus blossom at funerals, and each had its blind masseur with a shaven pate who shuffled down the street at dusk blowing a bamboo whistle and offering to knead care away from the weary.

The same people seemed always to be trotting from one village to the next along the same sort of miry bridle-path: the *mago* or female groom, 'with her toil-hardened thoroughly good-natured face rendered hideous by black teeth', in trousers, sandals, a towel round her head, trudging with a firm steady stride through streams, swamps and tangles of undergrowth; swarms of 'gentle, naked, old-fashioned' children, carrying bundles, chasing dragon-flies, herding cattle; and, on every pass, baggage-coolies, gasping violently with exhaustion. It was sickening to see their distress, Isabella said, describing five she saw one evening: 'Their eyes were starting out; all their muscles, rendered painfully visible by their leanness, were quivering; rills of blood from the bite of insects which they cannot drive away were literally running all over their naked bodies, washed away here and there by copious perspiration. Truly "in the sweat of their brows" they were eating bread and earning an honest living for their families!'

This sense of continuity, order, familiarity and stability was somewhat modified once they crossed the Tsugaru Straits to the northernmost island of Hokkaido. Here was a life that was free, wild and random compared with that on the main island, with few headmen to count heads or policemen to check passports and blessedly bereft, she told a friend, 'of the fatiguing and clattering society of the English'. It was a land rich in minerals, virgin soil, bountiful fish-grounds, it was half-tamed and half-explored, with plenty of elbow-room for man and beast. Isabella spent about three weeks there, galloping at last, over plains speckled with damask roses and plumed grasses, rambling along desolate shores scattered with tatty fishing-nets, the bleached ribs of captured whale and ship-wrecked junk. And while there she made the acquaintance of the Ainu, the original inhabitants of the Japanese archipelago.

The Ainu were sturdy, hairy people of a mild and indolent disposition who lived in dirty lonely settlements along the shores and among the forests. Though primitive and generally held in contempt by the Japanese to whom they bore little physical resemblance, they were courteous and hospitable to strangers, and Isabella was made welcome in their lowly thatched huts, and accepted almost without question as quite 'one of the family'. Of her first night among them she writes, 'At this moment a savage is taking a cup of *saké* by the fire in the centre of the floor. He salutes me by extending his hands and waving them towards his face, and then dips a rod in the *saké*, and makes six libations to the god – an upright piece of wood with a fringe of shavings planted in the floor of the room. Then he waves his cup several times towards himself, makes other libations to the fire and drinks. Ten other men and women are sitting along each side of the fire-hole, the chief's wife is cooking, the men are apathetically contemplating the preparation of their food; and the other women, who are never idle, are splitting the bark of which they make their clothes. I occupy the guest seat – a raised platform at one end of the fire, with the skin of a black bear thrown over it.'

116

The hunting of the bear, which provided covers for their guest-seats, hide for their boots, meat for their stews and fat for their lamps, was the thrill and focus of the Ainu male's rather dreary existence. Hunting began in early spring when the village men, armed with knives, spears, bows and arrows tipped with a dark red poisonous paste made from monkshood-root, trooped off into the forest. Keen-eyed, with endless time and knowing where to look, they were sure, eventually, to find a little discoloured patch in the snow under which snuggled a hibernating bear. Often, though harassed by dogs, spears and sticks, the bear refused to leave his cosy hole, and when that happened a brave Ainu, taking comfort from the belief that bears did not attack while inside their own dens, went in after the poor beast. Apparently, the bear's most common reaction to this intrusion was to seize the man and simply thrust him behind his back, whereupon the man, very cool, pricked the animal's behind with his knife and thus sent him lumbering forth at last. Upon emerging into the unwelcome light, the bear was shot with poisoned arrows, bitten by dogs, punctured with spears, knifed through the heart, its head and viscera given to its killer, its immense carcass dragged back in triumph to the village. Isabella did not see an actual hunt, but numerous fleshless bear-skulls stuck on poles round the chief's house were trophies and evidence enough of the hunters' past victories.

Isabella visited several Ainu settlements, carefully noted all she saw and, in the evenings, sat round the fire with the village elders and, through Ito, plied them with questions. She admired their vigorous, thick-set, strong bodies, their lithe, graceful movements, their luxuriant black hair and beards. Compared to the puny Japanese, they are 'the most ferocious-looking savages, with a physique vigorous enough for carrying out the most ferocious intentions, but as soon as they speak the countenance brightens into a smile as gentle as that of a woman, something which can never be forgotten'. And so they answered all her questions with a courteous, if puzzled, patience and she learned that the gods they worshipped dwelt in every tree, rock, river and mountain, that they had no written history or law, that they hated the Japanese, but with a resigned and apathetic hatred, for they had no ambition to become part of the infinitely strange New Japan.

117

All the Ainu wanted of the Japanese was *saké*, for which they had a pathetic and ruinous addiction. 'They spend all their gains upon it and drink it in enormous quantities,' Isabella said. 'It represents to them all the good of which they know, or can conceive. Beastly intoxication is the highest happiness to which these poor savages aspire, and the condition is sanctified to them under the fiction of "drinking to the gods".' They drank the liquor from shallow bowls and used slender pieces of carved wood to hold aside their facial hair so that it did not get wet. These ceremonial 'moustache-lifters' were among their few prized possessions and were vaguely holy, as was the *saké* itself.

Apart from this craving, the Ainu were more or less self-sufficient. They made their own clothes of split bark-cloth and animal furs; they ate dried fish, pumpkin, seaweed, venison, bear and beans; they built their own houses of straw and wood, with convenient ante-chambers for the storing of looms, bows and arrows, nets, mortars and pestles, cooking-pots and tubs. When Isabella asked them if they wanted education for their children or greater opportunities for themselves, they simply smiled with a sad and yet sweet sort of resignation, as if to imply that they were as happy now as they could expect to be.

Isabella would have liked to stay longer among the Ainu, for she found their placid simplicity restful after the pushy noisy curiosity of the Japanese. But she had discovered that Ito had a contract with another foreigner who lived in Hokkaido, and so she insisted that he remain there to honour it, while she determined to 'buy her own experience' alone in South Japan. She regretted the necessity, for he had been faithful, honest and diligent in his fashion. 'Are you sorry it is the last morning? I am' was his question on the day before she left the island. And she smiled at his arrogant, wistful, intelligent face and agreed that she was indeed sorry their travels together were over.

When she reached the south a few weeks later, there was an autumn snap in the air. The fishing boats on the Inland Sea were trailing iron cages over their sides to catch the squid that would be dried for winter; people were burrowing in the leafy earth of the forests for the succulent mushrooms that came with the first frosts; in the country inns, guests sat swaddled in padded robes on the verandahs, sipped warm *saké* and looked out upon the hills where maples fired crimson, bamboos danced feathery-yellow and the conifers, as always, paraded in files of purple-green and black.

Back on the conventional globe-trotters' route, she went to Kyoto, the old capital, that was gay with tea-houses, sombre with shrines, rich in artistic treasures. And while there, Isabella made a genuine and conscientious effort, for the only time in her life, to comprehend Buddhism, a faith about which she had increasingly harsh things to say in later years. When journeying in rural Japan, she had spent much time considering the puzzle of Christian salvation – those diligent, innocent-seeming, merry grooms who led her horses, for instance; surely the immortality of their humble souls could not entirely depend upon the insufficient and tardy efforts of the 'niggard and selfish' Christian Church? Surely God numbered 'the heathen among his inheritance'? Perhaps the portals of Heaven were immeasurably wider than she had been taught in her childhood?

And so, beset by 'these solemn queries', she arranged a meeting with one Akamatz, the head of the Monto sect, a man of intellect, culture and energy, with a good command of English and a bright, keen, humourous eye. He and Isabella had one thing in common: they both deplored the increase of 'godless materialism' in the land and feared that the indiscriminate and popularised teaching of western scientific philosophy would undermine the people's faith in all deities, Buddhist or Christian. For the rest their ways diverged, and Isabella was soon tangled in a metaphysical web, 'lost in a chaos where nothing had form, and birth and death succeeded each other through endless eternities'. It was not her sort of ground; she had no aptitude for esoteric spiritual specu-lation. If she was to attain salvation, she felt it must be through a life of good works and moral endeavour rather than through mystic communion with the godhead. And so when the priest told her that 'the end of righteousness is rest,' and added, 'To attain Nirvana is to be delivered from the merciless necessity of being born again, to reach a state "in which there are neither ideas, nor a consciousness of the absence of ideas," ' it filled her only with a profound melancholy.

Akamatz, a courteous host, showed her temples and enchanted gardens where he and his followers dwelt, and conducted her into the former Shogun's residence where 'tea and bonbons were served on a gold lacquer tray in antique Kaga cups by noiseless attendants, in the large room of the summer palace, with its dark posts and ceiling and dull gleams of dead gold, the little light there was falling on the figure of the priest in his vestments, as he still discoursed on his faith. The solemnity was nearly oppressive, and the deserted palace, the representative of a dead faith (for dead it surely is), the deepening gloom, the sighing of a doleful wind among the upper branches, the rattling of the *shoji* [screens], the low boom of a temple drum in the distance, and the occasional sound of litanies wafted on the wailing breeze, wrought on me so like a spell, that I felt as if I were far from the haunts of living men.'

Depressed by this encounter, only confirmed in her view that Buddhism was a shell of a faith, beautiful, but empty of meaning and purpose, Isabella was relieved to return to the haunts of the living. There, in the streets near the temples, silk-robed salesmen, squatting on the matted floors of their open shops, gently offered tea and suggested she might like to look at their wares – those exquisite wares produced over centuries by this essentially materialistic 'nation of artists'. Brocades of stiff silver and gold that might soon emblazon the back of a shuffling old priest were unleashed before her, and mossy silks shadowed with a suggestion of bamboo; next door they offered creamy crackle-glaze vases, bulbous weedy-green teapots and angular bronze cranes with haughty glares. 'I long to buy things for all my friends,' she exclaimed, 'but either they would despise them or huddle them together with other things on some vile piece of upholstery!' It needed, she knew, a visit to Japan before most westerners of her acquaintance could begin to understand the meaning of artistic space, the harmonious wisdom of asymmetry. Nevertheless, she bore away the requisite globe-trotter's burdens of silks, screens and bronzes – and a mysterious object she called a *daimyo*'s bath – when she left Japan that winter. 'I am not fascinated with Japan,' she concluded, when writing to her publisher about the journey. 'It is deeply *interesting* and tempts one to make it a serious study,' but it had not taken her by storm. She retained that interest and revisited Japan – and her old friends there – several times during her second period of eastern travel in the

1890s; she grew more fond of it – as an orderly and delightful haven of rest from the wear and tear of dirtier, cruder lands.

But the most exciting and joyous experiences of this journey still lay ahead, south of Japan, south of China, where the hot gold Malay Peninsula thrust towards the Equator, full of apes, elephants and weird jungly things that screeched in the night.

CHAPTER IV

Malaya

'I HAVE no genius for titles,' Isabella once explained to her publisher John Murray. She hadn't; the only one of her books with a really good title is *The Golden Chersonese and the Way Thither* – and that was her sister's idea. It was rather over-ambitious though, for the name 'Chersonese', taken from Ptolemy via Milton, denotes the whole of the Malay Peninsula, and Isabella only visited its western coastal areas for six weeks on her way home from Japan via Singapore. But the title is felicitous because it conjures the book's flavour – the tale of a sunny, leisurely, exotic journey in an ancient eastern realm. Like several of her more successful journeys, the one to Malaya was quite fortuitous and grew out of a suggestion by the Colonial Secretary of Singapore that she might like to have a look at the nearby Native States. In the grand, but simple, manner of the age, he wrote a few letters of introduction to government officials on the route, arranged free transport for her and told her that a convenient steamer was about to leave. Was she ready to go? 'I was only allowed five minutes for a decision, but I have no difficulty in making up my mind when an escape from civilisation is possible,' Isabella commented, and the next day boarded the Chinese-owned steamer *Rainbow*, bound for Malacca.

The Golden Chersonese which resulted from this casual arrangement is one of the most delightful and accessible of all Isabella's books for the modern reader. It bubbles with exuberant anecdotes of funny people and funnier animals, it is colourful but not overwhelmingly lush, sharp with acute observation but not over-freighted with unadorned fact. Isabella herself never thought much of it, probably because it was eventually published in sad personal circumstances and contains such a large assortment of 'those small details and frequent magnification of trifles' which,

122

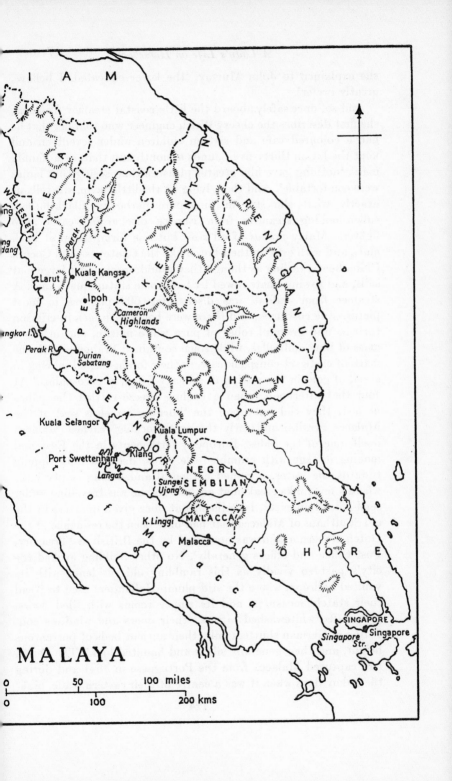

S I A M

KEDAH

WELLESLEY

P E R A K

K E L A N T A N

T R E N G G A N U

Perak River

Larut

Kuala Kangsa

Ipoh

Cameron
Highlands

angkor I.

Perak R.

Durian
Sabatang

S E L A N G O R

P A H A N G

Kuala Selangor

Kuala Lumpur

Port Swettenham

Klang

Langat

N E G R I

S E M B I L A N

Sungei
Ujong

K. Linggi

MA'LACCA

Malacca

J O H O R E

SINGAPORE

Singapore
Str.

Singapore

MALAYA

0   50   100 miles

0   100   200 kms

she explained to John Murray, 'the lesser educated, I believe, greatly prefer'.

And so, once safely aboard the little coastal steamer *Rainbow*, she first describes the cheery Welsh engineer who told her that he had a coloured wife and sixteen children under seventeen and kept the lot on thirty-five pounds a month and that, as a 'family man', 'nothing gave him greater pleasure than seeing that ladies were comfortable'. And then, lying on the little poop, she tells us exactly what she saw in Singapore harbour: 'Black-hulled, sullen-looking steamers from Europe discharging cargo into lighters, Malay *prahus* of all sizes but one form, sharp at both ends, and with eyes on their bows, like the Cantonese and Cochin China boats, reeling as though they would upset under large mat sails, and rowing-boats rowed by handsome statuesque Klings. A steamer from Jeddah was discharging 600 pilgrims in most picturesque costumes; and there were boats with men in crimson turbans and graceful robes of pure white muslin, and others a mass of blue umbrellas, while some contained Brahmins with the mark of caste set conspicuously on their foreheads, all moving in a veil of gold in the setting of a heavy fringe of coco-palms.' At four that afternoon, when a cooling breeze rattled the palms at last, they slid out upon the 'burning waveless sea' of the Malacca Straits; and early the next morning reached Malacca itself, one of the oldest European settlements in the East and looking its age with crumbled-tile roofs, decayed huts tipping towards the water, a ruined cathedral and a long empty jetty where a few junks creaked at anchor. As she was travelling under semi-official auspices, Isabella was at once given quarters in the old Stadthaus of Malacca that had once been the residence of the Dutch Governor and was now used by the British as 'Treasury, Post Office and offices generally'. No other building evoked the city's past so vividly as this rambling old residence with its vaulted ballroom where the stiff plump Hollanders used to tread their stately measures, and its empty rooms with tiled floors, blue walls, whitewashed rafters, 'their doors and windows consisting of German shutters only, their ancient beds of portentous height, and their generally silent and haunted look'. The Dutch had captured Malacca from the Portuguese in 1641 and during the palmy days when it was a centre of their eastern trade, pink-cheeked Dutch soldiers paraded in the square below the Stadthaus windows, Dutch bells called the merchants and their families to worship in the nearby church, sturdy ships of the Dutch East India Company, freighted with the products of the peninsula – peppers and gold, tapioca and cloves – left the harbour for Macao, Bombay or Amsterdam. But, partly owing to the Company's policy of monopolisation and an increase of trade at rival Penang, the importance of Malacca declined; the Company wound up its affairs there in 1799, and twenty-five years later the British took the port over. 'Portuguese and Dutch rule have passed away,' Isabella noted, 'leaving as their chief monuments – the first, a ruined cathedral and a race of half-breeds; and the last, the Stadthaus and a flat-faced meeting house.'

British occupation brought few monuments and little prosperity to Malacca, however, because, six years before it began, Stamford Raffles had landed on a swampy almost uninhabited island in the south called Singapore, and his coming soon resulted in the eclipse of the old port as a crossroads for the Far East trade. By 1879 few westerners lived there, no regular European steamers called, travellers seldom disturbed its somnolent beauty. The occasional visitor, like Isabella, quartered in the Stadthaus, was awakened each morning by a Mohammedan servant in white muslin bringing tea and bananas; before the sun grew molten, Mr Biggs, the colonial chaplain, student of hymnology, emerged from his bungalow and preserved his health and sanity with systematic constitutionals along the dusty streets; clouds massed above distant Mount Ophir and produced a shower every afternoon while the Portuguese half-castes took 'endless siesta behind their closely covered windows'; after the shower, 'The Governor's carriage, with servants in scarlet liveries, rolls slowly out of Malacca, and through the sago-palms and back again'; the Malays spent the time 'basking in the sun, or crawling at the heads of crawling oxen very like hairless buffaloes, or leaning over the bridge looking at nothing . . . their very movements making the lack of movement more perceptible'; at the end of the dreamy steamy day, alone in her room, Isabella breathed the languorous perfume of tuberose, bougainvillea, alamanda that twisted about the verandahs, listened to the aggressive whine of mosquitoes and the steps of two Malay guards thudding in the tepid dark below.

Most of the business that did function was in the hands of the Chinese, who, as Isabella was to discover, wielded considerable economic power throughout the Peninsula. Chinese junks still rolled into harbour during every north-east monsoon stuffed with hopeful coolies from Canton or Fuchow seeking work – thirty years before, a skilled carpenter or tailor could be bought outright for about twelve dollars, a strong coolie for about eight, a sick one for three or less. Descendants of such men who had been especially industrious or fortunate now rode through Malacca's streets in carriages as grand as the Governor's, lived in bungalows on their own sugar or pineapple plantations, and loaded their women and children with coronals of diamonds, necklaces of filigree gold and emeralds.

Lieutenant-Governor of this languid sinecure for many years was one Captain Shaw, a merry Irishman who arranged for Isabella to visit the nearby state of Sungei Ujong and asked her if she would take his two daughters with her to see the sights. Isabella was not at all keen on fledgling females as a rule, and though she agreed, it must have been reluctantly, for she was quite rude about them, even in print. The little party, 'under the efficient protection of Mr Hayward' the Police Superintendent, left by steam-launch a few days later, bound for the Sungei Ujong Residency, where the British Resident, Captain P. J. Murray, dwelt in unencumbered solitude.

One of the questions that greatly exercised the minds of administrators in the Colonial Office and the Straits Settlements Government at the time, and has continued to interest historians of Malayan affairs since, concerned the proper function and status of these Residents. It seems to be generally agreed that, by the late 1860s, most of the native states were reduced to a condition of near anarchy by constant warring of rival claimants to the various Sultanates, by violent piracy and bloody feuds between strong-arm Chinese secret societies. It seems agreed too that the British maintained a deliberate policy of non-involvement during the 60s and that their main concern was to secure peaceful conditions for the consolidation of trade in the area rather than any outright extension of British sovereignty.

By the early 1870s however, commercial pressures were so great and the States in such chaos, that the Colonial Office became convinced that, if it did not take an initiative, other European powers would intervene. Acting, therefore, on the time-honoured big-power strategy of staking the first claim, the new Governor of the Straits Settlements, Sir Andrew Clarke, came to office in 1873 with instructions to broach 'limited interference in the affairs of the Malay States for the preservation of peace and security, the suppression of piracy and for the development of roads, schools and police, through the appointment of a Political Agent or Resident for each State'. By the terms of the Pangkor Agreement which Sir Andrew ratified with certain Malay chiefs and Chinese headmen early in 1874, it was agreed that 'the collection and control of all revenues and the general administration of the Country be regulated under the advice of these Residents'. Or, as Sir Frank Swettenham, later a Resident himself, put it, their function was 'to advise the native Rulers and organise a system of government which would secure justice, freedom and safety for all with the benefits of what is known as civilisation'.

This was quite a tall order, considering that, in the Malay States at the time, there was no centralised system of government and no concept of any form of public institution. Justice depended mainly on the caprice of the Sultan or village headman; freedom was only for those not enmeshed in the widespread and pernicious system of slavery; safety was largely a matter of being able to draw a quicker *kris* (dagger) than one's enemy. The Residents were not invested with actual power to enforce the adoption of the counsel they offered, and there was constant disagreement between the Straits Settlement Government and the Colonial Office over how much initiative and authority they should be allowed. In these ambiguous circumstances, they had the choice, in the view of one modern historian, either of doing nothing much, or of giving 'advice' and then acting upon it themselves. Consequently it was already notorious that Residents and their Assistants, who were usually men of determination and energy, frequently exceeded their roles as mere counsellors and, to all intents and purposes, organised the affairs of the State to which they were assigned.

Isabella, as she admits, knew scarcely anything of all this before she went to Malaya, but she happened upon the scene at a time when there was such a dramatic difference in the methods adopted by the three Residents then in office and such exciting potential for experiment, improvement – and error – that she became quite fascinated by the situation. In her view, the position in Sungei Ujong was that the reigning Datu Bandar (ruler), troubled by internal rivalries and external threats, 'conceived the bright idea of supporting his somewhat shaky throne by British protection'. This roused some hostility from neighbouring chiefs at first, but after a small English force was sent in to kill off a few rebels, the situation stabilised, and by 1879 Resident Murray was 'practically the ruler' of the State. She concludes, 'It is scarcely likely however that Sungei Ujong and the other feeble protected States which have felt the might of British arms and are paying dearly through long years for their feeble efforts at independence, will ever seek to shake off the present system which, on the whole, gives them security and justice'. For Isabella, as for most of the colonial administrators she met, British was Best; she did not question the ethics of prescribing western codes of political and moral order for the ills of an alien eastern people (even though she had just observed, with less than bounding enthusiasm, the process of headlong westernisation in Japan). However, her imperial bias did not preclude her from being sharply critical of some of the colonial administrators' methods, and it was in this frame of mind – interested, observant, committed but not blindly prejudiced – that she, with the Misses Shaw and stalwart Mr Hayward, went to Sungei Ujong to meet its Resident.

There were, first of all, difficulties of locomotion. Their steam-launch – 'unseaworthy, untrustworthy, unrigged' – chuffed irregularly up the peninsular coast and then inland along the Linggi River. Like most Malayan waterways, this was a turgid, greenish-grey stream eddying between the slimy, dank roots of the mangrove swamp. Lithe vipers slithered; turtles, alligators and allied saurians snoozed on the steamy mudbanks, and birds came in pop-art colours – lime, lemon and post-office-red parrots; jazzy-blue kingfishers; starling-size rainbirds with feathers of rich claret and black, white stripes, cobalt and orange beaks and shining emerald eyes. But, as the noonday sun stabbed white hot, the animal kingdom retired to its holes and shades, the natives slept, only the mad British were about, and even among them conversation flagged. The copper sheath of the launch's gunwale blistered the touch, the Misses Shaw reclined, limp, pale, gasping under their parasols, the only sounds were the phut-phut of the dubious engine, the shrill of one wideawake insect, the leisurely plop of a submerging alligator.

At the village of Permatang Pasir it turned out that the messenger who had been sent ahead to make arrangements for the onward journey had 'served no other purpose than to assemble the whole male population . . . on the shore'. There they lounged, a sombre, aloof crowd, turbaned 'Mussalmen' in short jackets, full white trousers and red sarongs, and pot-bellied boys in 'silver fig leaves and silver bangles only'. Upon landing, the foreigners were told that it was impossible to proceed far that evening, and they were offered a rest in the local police station while the matter was debated. It was a nice station in its way, perched high on stilts, its verandah shaded with palms, containing two low beds ornamented with red silk and gold embroidery for the constables and displaying on its wooden walls a 'medley of rifles, *krises*, handcuffs, a "Sam Slick" clock, an engraving from the *Graphic*, and some curious Turkish pictures of Stamboul'. One policeman pulled a *punkah* outside for them, one brought coconut milk, and two mounted guard. Isabella would have enjoyed the experience but for the presence of the Misses Shaw, the younger of whom lay prostrate and shivering, stricken with a violent sick headache from the heat and declaring that she would not and could not move another inch.

A small police station in the Malay jungle was not suitable for the young lady if she were truly ill with bilious fever, and Mr Hayward and Miss Bird 'consulted assiduously' over what should be done. Mr Hayward who 'positively quailed at having the charge of these two fragile girls', sat in a chair, mopped his brow, and kept saying, ' "Oh . . . if anything were to happen to the Misses Shaw I should never get over it, and they don't know what roughing it is; they should never have been allowed to come." So I thought too as I looked at one of them lying limp and helpless on a Malay bed; but my share of the responsibility for them was comparatively limited. Doubtless his thoughts strayed, as mine did, to the days of travelling "without encumbrance". There was another encumbrance of a literal kind. They had a trunk! This indispensable impediment had been left at Malacca in the morning, and arrived in a four-paddled canoe just as we were about to start.' For start they did, after the sun went down, and they had dosed the patient with whisky to keep her upright. Worried Mr Hayward led the way, 'carrying a torch made of strips of palm branches bound tightly together and dipped in gum dammar, a most inflammable resin; then a policeman; the sick girl, moaning and stumbling, leaning heavily on her sister and me; Babu [the servant] who had grown very plucky; a train of policemen carrying our baggage; and lastly, several torch-bearers, the torches dripping fire as we slowly and speechlessly passed along. It looked like a funeral or something uncanny.'

After this dismal traipse, they boarded a long-boat with a low circular roof of *attap* (palm-leaf thatch), a craft most suitable for wriggling up the 'muddy hurry' of the shallow, corkscrew-twisted Linggi. The foreigners shared a blanket under the roof, the servants sat immobile in the prow, the voyage lasted for eighteen hours and was about as many miles long. Trees thrust out of the forest gloom, 'trees to right of us, trees to left of us, trees before us, trees behind us, trees above us, and, I may write, trees under us, so innumerable were the snags and tree trunks in the river. The night was very still – not a leaf moved, and at times the silence was solemn. I expected indeed an unbroken silence, but there were noises that I shall never forget. Several times there was a long shrill cry, much like the Australian "Coo-ee", answered from distance in a tone almost human. This was the note of the grand night bird, the Argus pheasant, and is said to resemble the cry of the "orang-utan", the Jakkuns, or the wild men of the interior. A sound like the constant blowing of a steam-whistle in the distance was said to be produced by a large monkey. . . . Then there were cries as of fierce gambols, or of pursuit and capture, of hunter and victim; and, at times, in the midst of profound still-ness, came huge plungings which I thought were made by alli-gators, but which Captain Murray thinks were more likely the riot of elephants disturbed while drinking.'

Intermittent streaks of blue lightning revealed opulent orange liana blossoms overhead, tendrils of blood-crimson climbers, the impassive white of a servant's turban. 'Pale green lamps of luminous fungus' glowed occasionally, and often the roof just above their heads was raked by black jungles of foliage that lunged at them from the dark. 'The Misses Shaw,' Isabella relates wearily, 'passed an uneasy night. The whisky had cured the younger one of her severe sick headache, and she was the prey of many terrors. They thought that the boat would be ripped up; that the roof would be taken off; that a tree would fall and crush us; that the boatmen, when they fell overboard, as they often did, would be eaten by alligators; that they would see glaring eyeballs whenever the cry "Rimou" – a tiger! – was raised from the bow; and they continually awoke me with news of something that was happening or about to happen, and were drolly indignant because they could not sleep; while I, a blasé old campaigner, slept whenever they would let me.'

At longed-for dawn, a cloying mist hung among the swamps and then, 'as the great sun wheeled rapidly above the horizon and blazed upon us with merciless fierceness, all at once the jungle became vociferous. Loudly clattered the busy cicada, its simultaneous din, like a concentration of the noise of all the looms in the world, suddenly breaking off into a simultaneous silence; the noisy insect world chirped, cheeped, buzzed, whistled; birds hallooed, hooted, whooped, screeched; apes in a loud and not inharmonious chorus greeted the sun; and monkeys chattered, yelled, hooted, quarrelled, and spluttered. The noise was tremendous. But the forest was absolutely still, except when some heavy fruit, over-ripe, fell into the river with a splash. The trees above us were literally alive with monkeys and the curiosity of some of them about us was so great that they came down on "monkey ropes" and branches for the fun of touching the roof of the boat with their hands while they hung by their tails.'

Later that eventful day, Mr Hayward, Isabella and the wilted Misses Shaw, their limp skirts trailing, were safely deposited as the Sungei Ujong Residency, where Captain Murray made them welcome. He was, she told Hennie, 'a most eccentric little man, never still for two minutes'; his manner was jovial, if jumpy, he hummed to himself, slapped people on the shoulder, laughed in the wrong places. He was kind-hearted and honest, in Isabella's view, 'thoroughly well disposed to the Chinese and Malays, but very impatient of their courtesies, thoroughly well meaning, thoroughly a gentleman, but about the last person that I should have expected to see in a position which is said to require much tact, if not finesse'.

Still, watching the Resident in action the next day at the local court-house, where he sat in judgement upon a Chinese accused of stealing a pig, she felt that his charity quite made up for any lack of ceremony. He had little of the magisterial manner, she told Hennie; 'He was hammering with a knife, whittling the desk, humming snatches of airs, making desultory remarks to me, exclaiming "Bother these fellows," or "What a pack of awful lies," or "Do get on and don't keep everyone broiling" ' – tactics which scandalised cautious Mr Hayward who interjected criticisms in a manner reminiscent of the White Rabbit. After listening to all the evidence, Captain Murray and Isabella decided that no judicial decision could be reached and the case was dismissed – 'He did steal that pig though!' she exclaimed. Her conclusion generally was that, while she could not say, 'the dignity of justice is sustained in this court, there is not a doubt that the intentions of the judge are excellent and if some of the guilty escape, it is not likely that any of the innocent suffer'.

The delinquent Chinaman, like most of his fellows in Sungei Ujong, was a tin-miner. The Chinese had pioneered tin-mining in the Malay States some forty years before and still arrived in their thousands, bringing with them their customary virtues – industriousness, inventiveness, enterprise – and their habitual vices – opium-smoking, gambling and internecine feuding. So industrious were they that they commonly worked twelve hours a day, panning for tin rather as the Californian forty-niners had panned for gold, and, unlike the forty-niners, most of them lived frugally. They ate and slept on a single mat in a communal shed, their sole possessions were a mosquito net, an opium pipe, a palm-leaf raincloak and a teapot swaddled in a basket. Time was measured in joss-sticks; money by the amount they could send to the folks back home. So inventive were they, that they had adapted the ingenious irrigation methods of their homeland to operate the mining sluices and irrigate their plantations; so enterprising were they, that many had given up mining for more congenial pursuits and their talents were diversified throughout the Peninsula. Chinamen flourished as sellers of pork, fire-crackers, sweetmeats, oil; as makers of bricks, lanterns, coffins, buggies; as boilers of soap and sugar; as smiths of tin, guns, locks; as burners of charcoal and lime; as carriers of water, cotton-bales and anything else portable; as pea-grinders, ivory-carvers, clerks – and as racketeers and pirates, which brings to mind their vices.

Of these, the treacherous feuds between the secret societies that honeycombed every Chinese community were the most socially disruptive. Each society imposed various mumbo-jumbo rituals upon its initiates, in a manner reminiscent of western Masonry, and demanded total and unquestioning allegiance from them. This was sometimes dangerous, for, while many associations had benevolent, mutually-protective aims, some were of criminal intent and their members committed blackmail, pillage and murder. Acknowledged leaders of the societies were known as 'Capitans China' – polite, wealthy, enigmatic men in black satin skull-caps who generally co-operated with the British, but who wielded no one quite knew how much power behind the scenes. It was this permeation of Chinese power and influence that so surprised Isabella at first. 'I have written a great deal about the Chinese and very little about the Malays, the nominal possessors of the country,' she admits after her descriptions of Sungei Ujong; but her impression was that the Chinese had practically over-run the region with their unfailing energies, their clandestine disciplines, their sobriety, thrift and unquestioning obedience.

Isabella also however, describes a visit she made with Captain Murray to the typically Malay home of the Datu Bandar, the second Rajah of the State. 'I thoroughly liked his house. It is both fitting and tasteful,' she decided. They were ushered into a small room through a doorway 'with a gold-embroidered silk valance. . . . There was a rich, dim light in the room, which was cool and wainscoted entirely with dark red wood, and there was only one long, low window, with turned bars of the same wood. . . . The furniture consisted of a divan, several ebony chairs, a round table covered with a cool yellow cloth, and a table against the wall draped with crimson silk flowered with gold. The floor was covered with fine matting, over which were Oudh rugs in those mixtures of toned down rich colours which are so very beautiful. Richness and harmony characterised the room, and it was distinctively Malay; one could not say that it reminded one of anything except of the flecked and coloured light which streams through dark, old, stained glass.'

Amid such elegance, where they were most courteously entertained by two of the Rajah's relatives – superb-looking men in red dresses and turbans – the 'sailor-like heartiness' of the Resident seemed particularly inappropriate. He slapped his hosts on the back, roared with hasty laughter, his thick-set, determined little body incongruous on the silken divan. Nevertheless, Isabella was sure his heart was in the right place and that he was 'much respected and loved . . . in spite of a manner utterly opposed to all Oriental notions of dignity, Malay or Chinese'.

The next day, they left the eccentric Captain Murray to his lonely problems as Judge, 'Superintendent of Police, Chancellor of the Exchequer, and Surveyor of Taxes' and returned uneventfully to Malacca, where Mr Hayward positively gulped with relief as he restored the two limp but essentially undamaged Misses Shaw to the arms of their fond papa. For them it was the end of the adventure; for Isabella much still lay ahead.

II

On 1 February she again boarded the quaint little steamer *Rainbow* which, at anchor in the Malacca Roads, was tipping and rolling as new 'cargoes of Chinese, Malays, fowls, pineapples and sugar cane' were shoved aboard to join the considerable numbers of Chinese, Malays, Javanese, goats, buffaloes and ducks already squashed on the decks. At last, with the sea running in at the scuppers and five little junks hooked on for a free ride behind and Chinamen still clambering in over the bulwarks and Isabella perched upon a hen-coop on the bridge, they all chugged away 'over the gaudy water into the gaudy sunset'. And the next part of her long 'Malay letter' was headed, 'British Residency, Klang, Selangor' – a name to conjure with, Isabella explained, that Hennie would probably be unable to find on any atlas.

Selangor was the middle State on the Malayan west coast, jammed between smaller Sungei Ujong to the south and larger Perak to the north. In its jungles some 15,000 Chinese worked, many of them in tin-mines; some 4,000 Malays lived, mostly in riverine villages and worked no more than they had to; a dozen or so Europeans were there, surveying for minerals, botanising, or organising institutions for the promotion of justice, freedom and

safety. Those engaged in the latter pursuit were British and lived
in or near Klang, the official capital, 'a mis-thriven, decayed,
defected, miserable-looking' cluster of dwellings on the banks of
the Klang River. Its houses, that crumbled along slushy alleys,
were surrounded by weed-choked fields and inhabited mostly by
pompous little armed policemen; its most prominent buildings
were the gaol, a large fort on a grassy mound prickling with
mounted guns, and above that a wooden bungalow before which
the British flag hung limply in the heat. At the Residency,
captain of all he surveyed, lived Mr Bloomfield Douglas, Resident;
'a tall, vigorous, elderly man with white hair, a florid complexion
and a strong voice heard everywhere in authoritative tones', was
Miss Bird's first impression of him. He met her at the jetty and
escorted her to his house which looked, she thought, like 'an
armed post amidst a hostile population'. A six-pounder graced
the front lawn; behind was a guard-room stacked with rifles,
bayonets, piles of shot; a bodyguard of twelve fully-armed men
was on permanent alert and 'a hundred more could be summoned instantly at the bang of a gong in the porch'. Douglas
spent most of his time inspecting his spruce soldiers (called
'policemen'), strutting about in a lavishly-gilded uniform,
barking orders and shooting snipe. He even concocted a little
'alarm' one evening, specially for Isabella; but 'I knew instinctively that it was humbug,' she explained, 'arranged to show the
celerity with which the little army could be turned out.' With all
these precautions for the safety of himself and his family, Douglas
must have been secretly terrified of the Malays, who undoubtedly
dubbed him a 'duck without spurs' – that is, a coward.

Isabella was appalled at the folly and boorishness of Douglas's
martial effervescence, at his evident ignorance of the people's
true needs, his disorderly administration and his contemptuous
bullying of the Sultan of Selangor himself. She visited the latter
in the Resident's company and watched while Douglas read out
the proceedings of a recent 'Council-meeting' and asked the Sultan
to confirm them, which he docilely did. 'The nominal approval of
measures initiated by the Resident and agreed to in council, and
the signing of death-warrants are among the few prerogatives
which "his Highness" retains,' she commented acidly, meaning
her readers to observe what slight resemblance this dictatorial

conduct of the State's affairs bore to the statutory roles of 'adviser' and 'advised'.

The pervasive feeling of being in hostile territory, engendered by Douglas's behaviour, was maintained during a short trip Isabella made in the official yacht, *Abdulsamaat,* together with the Resident, his son-in-law and a newly-appointed revenue collector. Thirty policemen escorted them and the trim vessel bristled with guns, bayonets and cutlasses. Their destination was Langat, where the Police Magistrate of the District, Mr Ferney, lived in a small bungalow on a hill. Isabella thought that Langat was a charming place – a typical Malay village, the houses tilting on stilts near the river, a few fishermen picturesquely floating about in canoes, grubby youngsters staring at her with their liquid brown eyes. It probably did not occur to her to wonder what it would be like to stay there for long – for a month perhaps, or a year.

In fact, one Englishwoman who had recently left after a year's detention there thought it was very like hell. She gives her reasons in a peevish, trivial, quaint little book entitled *The Golden Chersonese with the Gilding Off,* published a year after Isabella's book, and a direct riposte to it. Its author was Emily Innes who, as the wife of James Innes, the District Magistrate before Ferney, had been dumped on the banks of the river one hot day and rather left to sink or swim. Their 'residence' at first was 'an ordinary Malay wigwam of palm leaves and boards on piles,' Mrs Innes complained, and there was 'no garden, trees, flowers or society'. This was a truly extraordinary statement for her to make about her jungle surroundings, but she was clearly a patriot for whom a real tree was an oak or elm, a real flower a rose or hollyhock, and real people were all English.

Behind the Innes's 'wigwam', one slippery path bisected a paddy-field and petered out in an insect-ridden swamp, and, in the absence of a garden, 'we walked on the mud path every day in the year when the weather permitted it and when Mr Innes was away I walked on the mud path alone'. She recognised every worm as she trailed dismally along that path, her skirts draggling in the slush, her hat always protected by a parasol to preserve it from either the burning sun or the clinging rain. In the absence of 'society', Emily had to make do with the mild, inert Malay women who smelt of rancid coconut oil and plunked themselves down on her 'parlour' floor and stared at her for hours on end until she shooed them away. According to Mrs Innes, they asked but two questions: 'How much did her dress cost?' and 'How was Queen Victoria these days?' Their most disquieting feature was the horrid crimson trickle that flowed from the corner of their lips as they talked and made them look as if their mouths were full of blood. This was due to the habit of chewing betel-nut which was to the Malay, as opium to the Chinese or whisky to the Scotsman, a stimulant, luxury, necessity. Betel turned the chewers' teeth black, it wasn't particularly healthy and foreigners all thought it looked revolting, but it was the Malay 'thing'.

Mrs Innes's 'solitary comfort and pick-me-up' was her afternoon cup of tea, which she drank on the verandah, staring the while at the wide, fetid, sluggish river and the wide, fetid mudflat between her and it. The slime bubbled, spawned and stank. In its warm dank entrails, land-crabs scrabbled filthy holes, leeches sucked, rats slithered, eels wriggled, nameless reptiles with flabby bags below their mouths crawled, scavenger fowls clawed for worms, children dabbled their feet; shells of eggs and coconuts, skins of bananas and mangoes, faeces of people and buffaloes sank to rest there and so, on occasions, did all the magisterial papers of Mr James Innes, blown thither by a sudden gust of hot wind from the open-fronted court-room.

It was indeed a dolorous place for poor Emily, who was not one to make the best of a bad job, and her complaints, as she tears the gilt off the Golden Chersonese, are legion. Centipedes whose stings were deep and painful wriggled up at her out of the bath plughole, the tinned meat from Singapore was covered with mildew, flying blind beetles tangled in her hair, the servants would *not* learn how to whiten Mr Innes's topee properly; boiled scavenger fowls tasted like white wood and the river fish like mud; soursops were bland as cotton-wool steeped in sugar-water, jackfruit had the flavour of tinned railway butter; she discovered lizards on the table-cloth, an ants' nest in her jewel case, carpenter beetles in the soup and a scorpion in her hat-box; fowls laid their eggs in the pigeon-holes of Mr Innes's judicial desk and sometimes, from the hot dense night, the roar of the man-eating tiger rumbled so close that she thought she could see his fiery eyeballs burning.

And Emily Innes, standing on her lonely verandah, may have seen just that, for the Langat area was tiger-infested. During the short time that Isabella was there a beautiful dead tigress was dragged triumphantly back from the forest. 'All the neighbourhood, Chinese and Malay turned out,' Isabella says. 'Some danced; and the Sultan beat gongs. Everybody seized upon a bit of the beast. The Sultan claimed the liver, which, when dried and powdered, is worth twice its weight in gold as a medicine. The blood was taken, and I saw the Chinamen drying it in the sun on small slabs: it is an invaluable tonic! The eyes, which were of immense size, were eagerly scrambled for, that the hard parts in the centre, which are valuable charms, might be set in gold as rings. It was sad to see the terrible "glaring eyeballs" of the jungle so dim and stiff. The bones were taken to be boiled down to a jelly which, when some mysterious drug has been added, is a grand tonic. The gall is most precious, and the flesh was all taken for what purpose I don't know. A steak of it was stewed and I tasted it and found it in flavour much like the meat of an ancient and over-worked draught ox, but Mr Ferney thought it like good veal...'

But though the ways of the tiger were terrible and its howl chilled the blood, there was for Emily Innes when *she* lived at Langat a yet more dreadful sound – the shout from the river and the whistle of the *Abdulsamaat* that announced the arrival of her husband's boss Mr Bloomfield Douglas. His mien was overweening and his voice, Emily confirms, 'was pitched in tones that would have done admirably well for giving orders during a storm at sea'. He was always hungry and usually brought hungry companions, but was often without the precious provisions and mails from Singapore to cheer the marooned and boat-less Inneses. Upon his arrival therefore, the servants, the local policeman and a helpful Chinese shopkeeper ran about the mud-flats grabbing all the fowls they could lay hands on, which were hastily boiled in a curry stew for the 'guests'. The last tins of condensed milk were opened, the last claret uncorked and then, after the Resident and his friends continued on their merry way – taking with them all the snipe they had shot – Mrs Innes was left to pick up the pieces and make monetary recompense to indignant villagers for lawless seizure and premature decapitation of their poultry.

But Isabella Bird, as a member of the Resident's party, comfortably ensconced in a rattan chair on the deck of his yacht and later chewing her way through the tiger-steak at Ferney's new bungalow, knew nothing of all this. As Emily Innes bitterly explains, 'Miss Bird was a celebrated person and wherever she went she was well-introduced to the highest officials in the land. Government vessels were at her disposal and government officers did their best to make themselves agreeable, knowing that she wielded in her right hand a little instrument that might chastise or reward them as they deserved of her.' This contains more than a taste of sour grapes, and a somewhat exalted notion of Isabella's powers, but there is some truth in it, and probably Bloomfield Douglas *was* so attentive to Isabella mainly in the 'hope of an eulogy'. In that case, he was to be grievously disappointed, for the 'little instrument' in Miss Bird's hand is seldom more barbed than when it is describing the conduct of the bully Resident of Selangor.

She attended a sitting of the local court, as she had in Sungei Ujong, and decided that 'a most queerly muddled system of law prevails under our flag, Mohammedan law, modified by degenerate and evil custom, and to some extent by the discretion of the residents, existing alongside of fragments of English criminal law, or perhaps more correctly of "justice's justice", the Resident's notions of "equity" over-riding all else'. She visited the gaol, where the prisoners were marshalled for her inspection – half of them in irons, and Douglas roaring at the Superintendent, 'Flog 'em if they're lazy!' Standing on the *Abdulsamaat*'s deck, she watched Douglas strutting past the 'usual pomp' of his bodyguard and bellowing imprecations – *Chilaka* (worthless wretch) and *Bodo* (fool) – to everyone in sight. Describing this disgraceful scene, she adds a warning: 'The Malays are a revengeful people. If any official in British service were to knock them about and insult them one can only say what has been said to me since I came to the native States: "Well some day – all I can say is, God help him." But then if an official were to be *krissed*, no matter how deservedly in Malay estimation, a gunboat would be sent up the river to "punish", and would kill, burn and destroy;

there would be a "little war" and a heavy war indemnity and the true bearing of the case would be lost for ever.'

In this case, fortunately, the very evident risk of such an incident was averted, for some disquieting memoranda about Selangor affairs were already accumulating in the files of the Straits Settlement government. Frank Swettenham, for instance, then Assistant Colonial Secretary, visited the State around this time and the reports he submitted to headquarters were most unsatisfactory. Most of the revenue collected from fishing stakes on the Klang River was being spent on arms for the 'police', uniforms for the bodyguard and refurbishing of the *Abdulsamaat*, Swettenham discovered. In the District Land Office, records 'were conspicuous by their absence . . . There was no cash book, no register of permits and no rent roll.' When, in the following year, the Residency was moved to the fast-growing up-river settlement of Kuala Lumpur, other administrative irregularities and inefficiencies came to light. These were investigated by Swettenham and by James Innes, who had resigned from the service in bitter disillusion. The upshot was that in 1882 Douglas was offered the choice of facing an enquiry or resigning. He chose the latter and thus escaped with his skin intact, which in Isabella's view was almost more than he deserved. 'I think,' she wrote in a confidential letter to John Murray, 'that Mr Douglas is the most *fiendish* human being that I have ever seen. After close study I failed to find a redeeming point in his character. The mis-government of the State was gross and brutal. I saw scenes in which the Resident was the chief actor of the most brutal description and heard more than I saw. It was a rule of fraud, hypocrisy and violence.'

Considering all this, Isabella was extremely relieved to get away from the Selangor Residency, from the tense glitter of bayonets, the glare of sullen eyes under turban or highly-polished helmet, and above all from that awful bombastic florid man with his trumpeting voice and crawling inner terrors.

III

Isabella travelled to Penang aboard the *Abdulsamaat*, and her arrival was duly recorded by a reporter of the local *Gazette*: 'It may interest our Readers to learn that the distinguished *litterateur* (authoress) Miss I. Bird is on a visitation to these settlements and the Native States for the purpose of collecting facts and figures with a view to publication . . .' Endowed with this formidable, dreary-sounding reputation, Isabella was invited to a breakfast in honour of the departing Governor of the Straits Settlements, Sir William Robinson. Colonial officials from all the native States were present for the send-off and much jockeying for position was going on. 'There are people pushing rival claims, some wanting promotion, others leave, some frank and above-board in their ways, others descending to mean acts to gain favour, or undermining the good reputation of their neighbours; everybody wanting something, and usually, it seems at the expense of somebody else!' Watching the men's anxious, wary eyes, the veiled in-fighting, the assertive, deadly thrusts, Isabella felt a wash of relief that none of this concerned her personally. How interesting it all was from her neutral and privileged viewpoint at the Governor's right hand; how dreadful to be sentenced, at that starchy breakfast-table, to a further indefinite period in an *attap* hut on the edge of a swamp without hope of leave or recognition of services so conscientiously rendered, or to hear that the other fellow had just been offered the post you'd been sweating your guts out for during the past twelvemonth!

Among the officials present was William Maxwell, Assistant Resident of Perak, and Isabella's companion for the next stage of her journey. He was pleasant, clever, combative, dogmatic, energetic and 'thoroughly a gentleman', she decided – also bumptious, without tenderness or self-indulgence and over-hasty with the Chinese, she added for Hennie's benefit. But he was fond of the Malays and they, who had nicknames for all the British officials, called him the 'Cat-Eyed One'. Maxwell's (Assistant) Residency was in Larut, a swampy coastal province in the State of Perak, and she journeyed thither in the steam-launch *Kinta*, an unpretentious, peaceable craft unlike the *Abdulsamaat* and having, 'to use an expressive Japanese phrase, "very sick boilers"'. Also aboard was none other than Mr James Innes who, with his wife, had now been moved from Langat, Selangor to Durian Sabatang, Perak. The change, as Emily explains later in her woeful tale, was scarcely for the better – a plague of rats in the roof of her bungalow merely added to her trials. Perhaps Innes had been one of those who had unsuccessfully sought preferment at the Governor's breakfast-table, certainly he could have had no good news to cheer his melancholy spouse, for his manner, Isabella told Hennie, was 'feeble and despairing', his eyes 'dull and unfocussed'.

They left for Perak late at night: shadows of palm curved along the water's edge, and blanched casuarinas drooped graciously; 'the sea was like oil, the oars dripped flame, and seen from the water, the long line of surf broke on the shore not in snow, but in a long drift of greenish fire'. They sat on deck, lifting their faces towards the blissful hint of a breeze; Innes moped; one Captain Walker, just posted to Chief of Police in Perak, gushed over Isabella in 'an A.D.C. manner'; Maxwell expounded in some detail upon recently turbulent events in Perak.

Like its neighbours, Perak had been in a condition of near-chaos for most of the 1860s; it had been the first State to request and receive a British Resident – Mr J. W. Birch, appointed, with an Assistant, in 1874. The situation at that juncture, according to Frank Swettenham, was as follows: given: 'a beautiful fertile State, rich in minerals, splendidly watered, almost within shout of the Equator; imagine it sparsely populated by a peculiar, sensitive, courageous, superstitious, passionate and conservative people; suppose that not six white men had penetrated into this country within memory; that there were only twelve miles of cart road in the State and those only in one Province where Chinese outnumbered the natives of the land by ten to one; add that these Chinese had for over a year been in open warfare with each other, ignoring every authority, that they had burnt down every house; that all mining had ceased, that the only positions occupied were forts full of armed men, and coast villages the headquarters of pirates'; – to prove: 'that two Englishmen guarded by a handful of Sikhs could change all this and bring prosperity, law and justice to the land'.

As matters turned out it could be done more or less, but not by Mr Birch, who was a courageous, obstinate hothead, 'an idealist in a hurry', one modern historian suggests. After a month or so in office, Birch informed his superiors in Singapore that everything in Perak was 'of such an irregular character as to require immediate alteration', so he went bustling about telling the Malay headmen (through an interpreter) how they should levy taxes,

keep records and spend the money thus obtained. Early one
morning in November 1875 he visited an up-river village to post a
proclamation announcing an increase of British control over local
economic affairs; that afternoon he was stabbed to death in a
bathhouse by a band of Malays. At that point all nuances were
overlooked – as they would have been in Selangor had Douglas
been assassinated. A British officer had been murdered while in
pursuit of his legitimate duty; revenge must be exacted.

Details of the 'Perak War' that followed are tragical-farcical.
Frantic alarmist telegrams shot off in all directions from the
Straits Settlements Government (one read: 'Send ships and
reinforcements; the whole Malay peninsula is rising'), and soon
there arrived in disordered defenceless Perak a number of Sappers
and Miners from Madras, with a hundred miles of field telegraph;
a contingent of 5th Royal Artillery Battalion with four mounted
seven-pounders, two 5½ in. mortars, a hundred rounds of ammuni-
tion and two hundred rockets; officers and men of Her Majesty's
80th Regiment from Hong Kong; a contingent from Her Majesty's
"Buffs" and some Gurkhas from Calcutta. Perak's quiet green
coastline prickled with ships – H.M.S. *Modeste, Thistle, Philomel,
Ringdove* and *Fly*. Between them the troops managed to flush a
few fleeing Malays out of the jungle and burn down a few villages,
and then most of them withdrew. Later the complicity of some
Malay chiefs in Birch's murder was proved to British satisfaction,
one or two were executed, others banished to the Seychelles. A
Regent, Raja Yusuf, was inducted as puppet-ruler of Perak, and
in 1877 new British officials were given the ticklish posts of
Resident and Assistant Resident. They were Mr (later Sir) Hugh
Low and Mr (later Sir) William Maxwell, with whom Isabella
chatted that night aboard the steam-launch *Kinta*.

The following morning, Maxwell and Isabella were still swish-
ing along the Larut River. Blue-tailed bee-eaters with pale
chestnut throats and stomachs full of beetles, flies and (presumably) bees, flashed overhead, and golden-husked palm nuts
drifted downstream – but you didn't reach for them as you might
get your fingers snapped off by a passing alligator. On landing at
the filthy little pier of Teluk Kartang, the men went off to inspect
the Customs Post, and Isabella waited in an office 'where there
was a chair, a table dark with years of ink splotches, a mouldy

inkstand, a piece of an old almanac and an empty gin bottle. Outside, cockle-shells were piled against the wall; then there were ditches or streamlets cutting through profuse and almost loathsome vegetation, and shining slime, fat and iridescent, swarming with loathsome forms of insect and reptile life, all rioting under the fierce sun and among them, almost odious by proximity to such vileness, were small crabs with shells of heavenly blue. The strong vegetable stench was nearly overpowering, but I wrote to you and worked at your embroidery a little and so got through this detention pleasantly as through many a longer, though never a hotter one.'

When the men returned, Isabella and sombre Innes were fitted into a 'Larut gharrie' and went bouncing away over the buffalo tracks. These double-wheeled, low-roofed carts, just big enough for two, were usually owned and driven by Kling Indians, lithe harmless fellows who wore Turkey-red turbans, white loin-cloths and heavy jewelled rings in their noses. As a gharrie-passenger, 'you put up your feet on the board in front, and the little rats of fiery Sumatran ponies, which will run till they drop, jolt you along at great speed'. And in this fashion she came to the Assistant Residency – a substantial hill-top building with high-ceilinged rooms and an immense verandah 'like the fore-cabin of a great Clyde steamer'.

For the verandah and its marvellous view, the present incumbents could thank Maxwell's predecessor at the post, one Captain Tristram Speedy, as flamboyant a character as his name suggests, with a flowing blonde beard and a swashbuckling air that did not endear him to his superiors. The then Governor of the Settlements wrote in a dispatch to the Colonial Office: 'Captain Speedy is an altogether inferior order of being. He has apparently a delight in dressing himself in a gorgeous leopard skin with a grand turban on his head and still further exciting the curiosity of the natives by playing the bagpipes, an instrument on which he performs with much facility. If you have seen his elephantine frame, you will be able to judge what figure he would present under such circumstances.' Perhaps the natives enjoyed a bit of a show, certainly Speedy managed to impose some kind of order on the turbulent Larut region, centre for tin-mining, by establishing a magistrate's court and the nucleus of a police force. But he was accused of being inefficient and reckless with public funds – hence the size of his Residency and the lack of roads leading to it – and in 1877 he was more or less obliged to resign.

From Speedy's verandah, Isabella looked down upon the villages where Chinese miners lived, pits of stagnant water where some mines had been abandoned, a sparse yellow-leaved coffee plantation that wasn't doing very well and, at all the distances, 'miles of treetops as level as the ocean over which the cloud shadows sail in purple all day long'. She could see too the thin red lines of Sikh and Pathan soldiers parade every morning in the barrack square, 'classic', 'colossal' 'splendid-looking' men they were in scarlet coats, white trousers and blue turbans under which they tucked the ends of their long black plaited whiskers.

This colourful contingent was under the command of another colourful character, Major Paul Swinburne, of whom Isabella had already heard. His reputation as 'a brilliant, fascinating and altogether misplaced person' resounded 'in Japan, China, Singapore and all along here,' she told Hennie; when she left Malacca, Captain Shaw had said, ' "When you see Paul Swinburne you'll see a man you'll not see twice in a life-time". So yesterday' Isabella continued, 'when a tall slender aristocratic-looking man, who scarcely looks severable from the door-step of a Pall Mall Club, strode down the room and addressed me abruptly with the words, "The sooner you go away again, the better; there's nothing to do and nothing to learn," I was naturally much interested.' Refusing to be either overawed or offended by this opening gambit, Isabella soon found that Swinburne was indeed 'good company', 'a brilliant talker, dashing over art, literature, politics, society', though totally regardless of 'the equities of conversation'. He was a cousin of Algernon Charles Swinburne and took a somewhat uncharitable pleasure in describing his talented relation as 'a gifted wastrel, rich with all that life can offer within his grasp, but living for spirit-drinking and opium, in which, doubtless, some of his poems have found their inspiration'.

He and Maxwell were firm, fierce friends who spiked the lassitude of the tropical environment with inventive, vehement rows. Swinburne's habit was to begin 'in an aggravating tone . . . upon some peculiarity or foible, real or supposed, of his friend,

with a deluge of sarcasm, mimicry, ridicule and invective, torments him mercilessly, and without giving him time to reply, disappears, saying Parthian-like, "Now, my dear fellow, it's no use resenting it, you haven't a friend such as me in the world – you know if it were not for me you'd be absolutely intolerable!" '
The noise on these occasions was apparently appalling, fists thumped down, plates rattled, but afterwards they all felt better. So piquant and amusing was the company, so restful the hours Isabella spent alone in the large drawing-room where there were 'no women to twitter' as she 'read up the Native States in Blue Books, etc.' that she hated to leave. But she need not have minded, for the most joyous, exciting, extraordinary experiences of her entire journey in the Golden Chersonese still lay ahead – and began as soon as she left Larut for the main Perak Residency at Kuala Kangsa.

Maxwell escorted her for the first tramp through the jungle. Gaudy butterflies and monkeys cavorted among the trees, amber-and-turquoise bundles of humming-bird vibrated, and under the great glass-green leaves leeches listened for the rustling movements of an intruder so that they could stretch to their full extent and latch themselves firmly upon any passing flesh. Delicate coral-flecked spikes of orchid thrust at her, egg-yellow trumpets of blossom scrambled overhead among steely blue aspleniums and an unknown creeper of salmon-orange scalloped around velvet-black. Burnished gingerworts shone, red lilies flared, creamy oval fruits dangled, ferns, with serrated fronds six feet long, bowed, and she found three varieties of nepenthes, the blotched purple 'monkey-cups'. The lid of this pitcher-shaped flower was gilded with a nectar that attracted insects which flew into the cup, slipped on the smooth-as-satin interior walls and drowned in the quantity of water held in the base. Each grisly pitcher was packed 'with skeletons of betrayed guests' from which the insectivorous plant had extracted its food.

When they stopped for refreshment, Maxwell left Isabella, with the assurance that it was quite safe for her to continue her journey alone. And this she fully believed, 'any doubts as to my safety,' she explained, 'being closely connected with my future steed'. In due course the 'steed' arrived, as had been arranged, and Isabella takes up the story: 'Before I came I dreamt of howdahs and cloth of gold trappings, but my elephant had neither. In fact there was nothing grand about him but his ugliness. His back was covered with a piece of raw hide, over which were several mats, and on either side of the ridgy backbone a shallow basket, filled with fresh leaves and twigs, and held in place by ropes of rattan. I dropped into one of these baskets from the porch, a young Malay lad into the other, and my bag was tied on behind with rattan. A noose of the same with a stirrup served for the driver to mount. He was a Malay, wearing only a handkerchief and *sarong*, a gossiping careless fellow, who jumped off whenever he had a chance of a talk, and left us to ourselves. He drove with a stick with a curved spike at the end of it, which, when the elephant was bad, was hooked into the membraneous "flapper" always evoking the uprearing and brandishing of the proboscis, and a sound of ungentle expostulation, which could be heard a mile off. He sat on the head of the beast, sometimes cross-legged and sometimes with his legs behind the huge flapping ear-covers. . . . This mode of riding is not comfortable. One sits facing forwards with the feet dangling over the edge of the basket. This edge soon produces a sharp ache or cramp, and when one tries to get relief by leaning back on anything, the awkward, rolling motion is so painful, that one reverts to the former position till it again becomes intolerable. Then the elephant had not been loaded "with brains" and his pack was as troublesome as the straw shoes of the Japanese horses. It was always slipping forwards or backwards, and as I was heavier than the Malay lad, I was always slipping down and trying to wriggle myself up on the great ridge which was the creature's backbone, and always failing, and the *mahout* [driver] was always stopping and pulling the rattan ropes which bound the whole arrangement together, but never succeeding in improving it.

'Before we had travelled two hours, the great bulk of the elephant without any warning gently subsided behind, and then as gently in front, the huge, ugly legs being extended in front of him, and the man signed to me to get off, which I did by getting on his head and letting myself down by a rattan rope upon the driver, who made a step of his back, for even when "kneeling" as this queer attitude is called, a good ladder is needed for comfortable getting off and on.'

147

While the travelling-baskets were being 're-rigged', Isabella clambered up a ladder into a villager's house, a dwelling typical of its kind and perfectly attuned to its surroundings. It was raised on posts, with a steep palm-thatch roof, sides of split reed, bamboo rafters, the whole lashed together with the inevitable rattan. Inside it was as shady as grass under a tree, and filtered shadows fluttered across its simple furnishings – reed mats, circular bolsters, a spear, a few iron pots, fishing-rods. Black mynah birds, green pigeons, blue love-birds chattered inside cages swinging from the rafters. The natives snared them with horsehair nooses, tamed them fondly and taught them to 'speak'; a principal occupation of the household's round brown youngsters tumbling on the floor was the catching of grasshoppers to feed to them. The villagers seemed mild, lackadaisical, hospitable; one man sent an ape up a palm to fetch Isabella a coconut, others offered her bananas and buffalo milk.

At noon, when the sun's rays were streaming down from a too-blue sky, Isabella remounted her elephant by being hauled up over its head and 'the fearful joy' of the ride continued. Quite soon however, 'the driver jumped off for a gossip and a smoke, leaving the elephant to "gang his ain gates" for a mile or more, and he turned into the jungle, where he began to rend and tear the trees, and then going to a mud-hole he drew all the water out of it, squirted it with a loud noise over himself and his riders, soaking my clothes with it, and when he turned back to the road again, he several times stopped and seemed to stand on his head by stiffening his proboscis and leaning upon it, and when I hit him with my umbrella he uttered the loudest roar I ever heard. My Malay fellow-rider jumped off and ran back for the driver, on which the panniers came altogether down on my side, and I hung on with difficulty, wondering what other possible contingencies could occur, always expecting that the beast, which was flourishing his proboscis, would lift me off with it and deposit me in a mud-hole.

'On the driver's return I had to dismount again and this time the elephant was allowed to go and take a proper bath in a river. He threw quantities of water over himself, and took up plenty more with which to cool his sides as he went along. Thick as the wrinkled hide of an elephant looks, a very small insect can draw

148

blood from it, and when left to himself he sagaciously plasters himself with mud to protect himself, like the water buffalo. Mounting again, I rode for two hours, but he crawled about a mile an hour and seemed to have a steady purpose to lie down. He roared whenever he was asked to go faster, sometimes with a roar of rage, sometimes in angry and sometimes in plaintive remonstrance. The driver got off and walked behind him, and then he stopped altogether. Then the man tried to pull him along by putting a hooked stick in his huge "flapper" but this produced no other effect than a series of howls; then he got on his head again, after which the brute made a succession of huge stumbles, each one of which threatened to be a fall, and then the driver with a look of despair got off again. Then I made signs that I would get off, but the elephant refused to lie down, and I let myself down his unshapely shoulders by a rattan rope till I could use the *mahout*'s shoulders as steps. The baskets were taken off and left at a house, the elephant was turned loose in the jungle; I walked the remaining miles to Kuala Kangsa, and the driver carried my portmanteau!'

That ride, which Isabella quoted ever afterwards as being one of the most ludicrous of her entire life, was surely enough for one day. But not in Perak, where, as she said, circumstances had become quite singular and where it was immediately followed by the most astounding and hilarious repast she ever enjoyed. Mr Hugh Low, the Resident, was, as Isabella knew, away from Kuala Kangsa for a few days, and in his absence she was received at the Residency by a 'magnificent Oriental butler named Assam'. He showed her to her room, arranged for her bath and then informed her that dinner (or 'breakfast' as he chose to call it) was served.

'The word "served" was strictly applicable, for linen, china, crystal, flowers, cooking were all alike exquisite. Assam, the Madrassee, is handsomer and statelier than Babu at Malacca; a smart Malay lad helps him, and a Chinaman sits on the steps and pulls the punkah. All things were harmonious, the glorious coco-palms, the bright green slopes, the sunset gold on the lake-like river, the ranges of forest-covered mountains etherealising in the purple light, the swarthy faces and scarlet uniforms of the Sikh guard, and rich and luscious odours, floated in on balmy airs, glories of the burning tropics, untellable and incommunicable'...

'My valise had not arrived, and I had been obliged to re-dress myself in my mud-splashed tweed dress, therefore I was much annoyed to find the table set for three, and I hung about unwillingly in the verandah fully expecting two Government clerks in faultless evening dress to appear, and I was vexed to think that my dream of solitude was not to be realised, when Assam more emphatically assured me that the meal was "served", and I sat down, much mystified, at the well-appointed table, when he led in a large ape, and the Malay lad brought in a small one, and a Sikh brought in a large retriever and tied him to my chair! This was all done with the most profound solemnity. The circle being then complete, dinner proceeded with great stateliness. The apes had their curry, chutney, pineapple, eggs and bananas on porcelain plates, and so had I. The chief difference was that, whereas I waited to be helped, the big ape was impolite enough occasionally to snatch something from a dish as the butler passed round the table, and that the small one before very long migrated from his chair to the table, and, sitting by my plate, helped himself daintily from it. What a grotesque dinner party! What a delightful one! My "next of kin" were so reasonably silent; they required no conversational efforts; they were most interesting companions. "Silence is golden," I felt; shall I ever enjoy a dinner party so much again?'

Isabella's dining companions were Eblis (the devil) and Mahmoud. The former was about twenty-one inches high with a winsome, ancient face and baby-like hands and was much bullied by Mahmoud, who was about four feet high, very strong and lively and with a solemn hairy visage that distinctly reminded Isabella of a leading church dignitary in distant Edinburgh. On her very first day she saw Eblis being beaten with a stout Malacca cane by the vengeful Mahmoud and rescued the victim just in time. From then on, Eblis clung to her as to a saviour. Sometimes he took her pen daintily from her hand and tried to write with it, or he lay on her lap, murmuring 'ouf ouf' in loving tones, or, in a mood of self-advancement, he took from their envelopes all the Resident's official letters, held them up as if reading them, folded them and put them back.

It was like living in a zany zoo. She found two lizards nestling in her black silk dress and a snake under the counterpane; in

addition to Eblis and Mahmoud, the placid retriever loped around
the verandah, four elephants in red and gold regalia plodded about
in front of the bungalow, tigers snarled from the jungle at night
and an untamed gibbon that lived on the roof would suddenly
come plunging down into the drawing-room for a game. Describing
a typical morning scene, Isabella says that Eblis was crouching on
the table 'reading' one of her letters, the gibbon 'has jumped like
a demon on the retriever's back and, riding astride, is beating
him with a ruler; and jolly, wicked Mahmoud, having taken the
cushions out of the chairs, has laid them in a row, has pulled a
tablecover off the table, and having rolled it up for a pillow, is now
lying down in an easy, careless attitude, occasionally helping himself to a piece of pineapple.'

One of the elephants-in-attendance was Perak's Royal Elephant, colossal even by elephant standards, docile and noble, and
Isabella was offered a ride on him to atone for earlier mishaps. The
Royal Elephant was trained to grasp and peel a banana as skil-
fully as a monkey, to carefully clear the path of fallen tree-trunks,
to carry his passengers sedately over both land and water. And
so, at one stage of the ride, when they came to the broad river
Perak, Isabella and the elephant went down a steep bank and
'putting out from the shore, went into the middle, and shortly the
elephant gently dropped down and was entirely submerged,
moving majestically along, with not a bit of his huge bulk visible,
the end of his proboscis far ahead, writhing and coiling like a water
snake every now and then, the nostrils always in sight, but having
no apparent connection with the creature to which they belonged.
Of course we were sitting in the water, but it was nearly as warm
as the air, and so we went for some distance up the clear, shining
river, with the tropic sun blazing down upon it, with everything
that could rejoice the eye upon its shores, with little beaches of
golden sand, and above the forest the mountains with varying
shades of indigo colouring.'

Then she continues, 'There would have been nothing left to
wish for if you had been there to see, though you would have tried
to look as if you saw an elephant moving submerged along a
tropical river every day, with people of three races on his back!'
Suddenly, even there, came the desire for pale quiet Hennie, so
out of context among all that riotous life, extravagant colour,

151

gay freedom. She wanted to startle, to make Hennie see her for a moment at her very best, doing the sort of thing she was really good at. And yet, with the same thought, she knew the desire was hollow. For if Hennie, on some wing of enchantment, had been wafted to watch her elder sister floating down the River Perak on an elephant's back, she would have evinced no undue surprise, no unladylike agitation, she would, in fact, have cut the daring adventurer down to size with one unruffled glance. Hennie was so sane; she did not need to travel – and *should* not travel, for if she had, Isabella could not have written such vivid letters home.

Isabella's delightful interlude as Assistant Keeper of the Kuala Kangsa menagerie ended the next morning when a solitary bugle-blast from the jungle announced the return of the Resident – at which momentous note the bewitching Eblis flew from her shoulder to that of its true master. The man, Hugh Low, who stepped upon the verandah a minute later and disentangled himself from the hairy arms of his welcoming pets just sufficiently to shake hands, was in his fifties when Isabella met him, dark-bearded and with patient, slightly distant eyes. He had trained as a botanist, and plants were his first love, animals his second, people, on the whole, a rather poor third. He had been the Perak Resident for about two years and was well qualified for the post, having fluent Malay and a sympathetic understanding of the customs of the country. Before that, he had languished for nearly thirty years on the island of Labuan off the north-west coast of Borneo. In that dismal, flaccid backwater he had been jack of all trades that were thankless and routine – Treasurer, Police Magistrate, three times Acting Governor – and had been unfortunate enough to incur the enmity of the ebullient, brilliant James Pope-Hennessy, who, when Governor of Labuan, had married and carried away Low's only daughter, Kitty (his wife had died there years before). One way and another, Low's career had been hampered by the family bitterness which this union aroused, and by his withdrawn, rather gruff manner that did not facilitate his acquaintance with the right people back home. The appointment to Perak had been overdue recognition of Low's undoubted potential, and he was now getting into his stride, determined to show the Colonia Office what he could do when, at last, he was given the chance.

'He is working fourteen hours out of the twenty-four,' Isabella records. 'I think that work is his passion, and a change of work his sole recreation. He devotes himself to the promotion of the interests of the State and his evident desire is to train the native rajahs to rule equitably.' And so, nearly every day while Isabella was there, and before she had come and after she left, Hugh Low sat at a table on the verandah in the solitary bungalow with Eblis at his side 'like a familiar spirit', and the devoted dog at his feet; 'tiffin and dinner are silently served at long intervals; the sentries at the door are so silently changed that one fancies that the motionless blue turbans and scarlet coats contain always the same man; in the foreground the river flows silently, and the soft airs which alternate are too feeble to stir the over-shadowing palm-fronds or rustle the *attap* of the roof. It is hot, silent, tropical.' And from that calm, modest centre radiated a disciplined alien energy that changed the face of the land.

Low introduced stability where there had been continuous dissolution, a system of public revenue where there had been only extortion and piracy; eventually he brought freedom where there had been slavery. Industrious though he was, documents accumulated in his pigeon-holes: a letter from the Chinese fishermen at Tanjong Piandang asking to be relieved a tenth of the duty on their fish catches; a report from the Chief of Police on an outbreak of dysentery in the local gaol; explanatory diagrams for a new type of centrifugal pump that might be used to work the tin-mine sluices; a request from the overseer of the Kuala Kangsa road-gang for an extra horse; a petition from three slave-women seeking release from their debt-bondage. People came in person, not trusting the written word. 'Capitans China' called to tell him about increasing outbreaks of beri-beri among the miners, to settle a dispute over water-rights, to complain that a business-man who held the monopoly for selling opium in the area was making extortionate profits, to tender quantities of broken stones from the mines for the building of roads. (These had a high priority on Low's list, for the present 'roads' were mostly elephant tracks, and, as it was the immutable custom of elephants to plonk their massive feet in the holes gouged by their predecessors, the 'roads' were, as Isabella noted, 'a series of deep pits filled with mud and water'.) Malay chiefs came to Low, sprawled for hours on the mats and were offered tea and sweetmeats. They told him that a tiger had just killed every duck in the village, they asked him to settle a boundary dispute over their farming land, they offered buffaloes for sale to pull the carts loaded with road-building materials, they complained that two bond-slaves had escaped and the District Magistrate wasn't exerting himself to recapture them.

Occasionally, a solitary white man in a topee and duck suit found his way to Low's verandah – an aspiring planter from Ceylon perhaps, come to estimate the chances of growing coffee in Perak; a tough optimistic prospector from Australia seeking a mining concession, hoping to break the Chinese monopoly and make a Patino-size fortune; an agricultural surveyor from Singapore sent to assess land-values in the vicinity so that a fair system of land-renting could be established; or a wandering naturalist, a man after Low's own heart, with wine-red and silver-speckled butterflies eternally impaled, jars containing blotchy-yellow snakes curled in formalin, specimens of the rare scarlet-eared Barbet, an iridescent-emerald Javanese peafowl, a dusky pied hornbill tame in a cage and living on cake-crumbs and plantains.

One of the most frequent visitors to Low's verandah was the Regent of Perak, Raja Yusuf, a cruel and unscrupulous man by most accounts, though no one doubted his loyalty to the British, who supported him. When Isabella met him, she disliked his look of coarse and sensuous brutality, and the way he accepted a fan from her without a glance of acknowledgement, as if she were a slave. Apropos of which, she relates one of the current anecdotes illustrating his character: that he once punished a recaptured female slave for absconding by pouring boiling water down her back and then setting a red ants' nest upon it. Hugh Low, nevertheless, had managed to gain this man's confidence and respect, partly by his creation of a State Council made up of Yusuf, himself, Maxwell and leading members of the Malay and Chinese communities. The Council was concerned with law enforcement and administration; local headmen were encouraged to 'join the establishment' as it were by being appointed as policemen and revenue-collectors; courts of justice functioned along more coherent lines than those in neighbouring States; and, by curtailing the depredations of pirates and carefully husbanding revenue obtained from new methods of tax-collection and custom

duties, Low was in the process of making Perak economically
viable.

The thorniest of Low's problems was the Malay custom of debt
bondage, whereby ordinary people who had incurred any kind of
debt (or, sometimes, simply been accused of debt) were taken as
slaves by their village chiefs or the rajas. As all available monies
and resources were in the hands of their masters, it was well-nigh
impossible for slaves to free themselves once in bondage, and,
worse yet, their families and descendants were permanently
enslaved also. In consequence, there were a lot of bondspeople
in the Malay States and some were ill-treated and abused.
Naturally, every British Resident, fired with something of the
zeal and example of Wilberforce, abhorred the vicious system and
worked to abolish it; Birch, for instance, when he was Resident
used to harbour runaway slaves, which was said to be a major
reason for his murder. Low proceeded with more caution, understanding that, though the slave tradition was deplorable from a
western viewpoint, it had been firmly rooted in the native *mores*
for centuries and that, in the master's eyes, their slaves belonged
to them as rightfully and absolutely as did their houses, wives and
elephants. Cajoling, advising, offering restitution, Low finally
won, and slavery was officially abolished in Perak in 1884 – a
quiet achievement that at the time did not receive very much
attention from the outside world.

But Hugh Low didn't count on popular esteem; like Isabella, he
was an original – solitary, slightly eccentric, sensitive and unassuming. He and she were bound to like each other and they did.
He appreciated her independent unfussiness and her genuine,
intelligent interest in his work; she admired his honest diligence,
his tactful kindliness, above all the total absence of that blustering
arrogance which had been such an ignoble characteristic of the
Resident of Selangor. In the evenings, when the palms stood quiet
and black against a cool-lemon twilight and the green-gold lamps
of the fireflies jogged among the poinsettias, Low at last relaxed,
lit his pipe and talked with his guest. They talked, of course,
about personalities – about the unfortunate Birch, a high-handed
and officious fellow, in Low's view, who drank too much and more
or less deserved his fate. Probably they talked about Mr Pope-
Hennessy, Governor of Hong Kong, whom Isabella had recently

met and whose brand of pushy brilliance and rash idealism was anathema to both of them. Certainly they talked about the tyrannous reign of Bloomfield Douglas, and Low assured her that some two thousand Malays had actually fled to Perak to escape it.

They paused, perhaps, to watch a lizard zoom along the walls after flies, pausing that split-second before he actually swallowed his terror-struck victim; 'even a lizard gives the fly time to pray', Low quoted the Malay proverb. Then he went on to tell his guest about his experimental garden where he was trying to raise a number of small rubber-plants. They were, he said, two different sorts of South American indiarubber and had been sent from the Botanical Gardens in Singapore. These plants, though he did not yet know it, were to be historic. They grew into healthy trees eventually; in 1884 they shed their first seeds and Low invited planters to come to Perak and invest their capital in rubber instead of coffee – which was proving a risky venture. No one took him up at the time, and it was not until the turn of the century, years after Low had left Perak, that the rubber industry began to flourish there. But he could perhaps take comfort in his old age from the fact that part of the first consignment of rubber sent to London from Malaya in 1899 was produced from the seeds of those plants in his Kuala Kangsa garden.

That garden and its attendant livestock were Low's sole indulgence. He grew American corn and tobacco and tried to grow coffee, he bred turkeys and Nellore cows imported from India, and kept goats, sheep, ducks and widgeon for the table. Every guest commented how good the food was, and with it, on special occasions, the Resident served iced champagne – which could have unforeseen results. On February 18, Isabella notes in her journal, 'Major Swinburne and Captain Walker arrived in the morning and we had a grand tiffin at twelve, and Mahmoud was allowed to sit on the table, and he ate sausages, pommeloe, bananas, pineapple, chicken and curry and then seizing a long glass of champagne, drank a good deal before it was taken from him. If drunkenness were not a loathsome human vice, it would have been most amusing to see it burlesqued by this ape. He tried to seem sober and to sit up, but could not, then staggered to a chair, trying hard to walk steadily, and nodding his head with a would-be witty but really obfuscated look, then finding that he could not sit up, he reached a cushion and lay down very neatly, resting his head on his elbow and trying to look quite reasonable, but not succeeding, and then he fell asleep.'

Mahmoud woke bright-eyed and bustling as ever, but poor Eblis with the wistful face who cooed 'ouf ouf' when he was happy and screamed 'wah wah' when he was frustrated, completely lost his appetite and began to sicken. Hugh Low coaxed him with morsels of banana and poured drops of milk down his throat every half-hour. It was an affecting sight: 'The poor bewitching thing, which is much emaciated, clings to his master now the whole time, unlike other animals, which hide themselves when they are ill, puts out its feeble little arms to him with a look of unspeakable affection on its poor pinched face, and murmurs in a feeble voice "ouf ouf!" ' Poor Low was so miserable about Eblis that he nearly cried over him, Isabella tells Hennie, and he wrote to his daughter (now the Governor's Lady in Hong Kong) that 'he had never cared for anything in the world as for Eblis, except for her'.

Perhaps because he was feeling especially lonely just then, Low asked Isabella if she would like to stay for another month at Kuala Kangsa, and reinforced his invitation with a rare compliment: 'You've the pluck of six ordinary men,' he told her, 'and you glide about the house and never speak at the wrong time – if men are visiting me they never know when to be quiet but bother me in the middle of business.' And then the lively, odd little 'Perak crowd' positively deluged her with compliments. Maxwell, who had come over to see his chief, agreed that she was easier company than most men, and the dashing Swinburne, quite converted, said 'I admire you more than any woman I know – you know you are a splendid traveller – you know exactly what you can do and can't do.' Maxwell concurred in that too, saying he had suspected she was a 'real traveller' the moment he saw her land in Penang with 'only a bag and a roll'. And Isabella, not really accustomed to so much masculine acclaim, laughed and said well, yes, it *was* the one talent about which she was often complimented. Then added, 'without thinking', she explains to Hennie, ' "But I am always despised at first." At which they never ceased to laugh, but it is quite true, for my bodily presence is weak and my speech contemptible. And just because I "make no fuss" I generally lose a day or two at first by people thinking that I can't do the thing I have come to do.'

She didn't pursue the matter further, but it is interesting to note that Isabella saw herself as others sometimes saw her. Her manner was 'that of a gentlewoman' people recorded, perfectly self-possessed, but lacking flair or dash. Her voice, if not 'contemptible' was apparently slow, earnest, rather monotone, so that, initially, people tended to talk over her head – taking advantage of her diminutive stature. That was what Isabella meant, and it was an honest assessment, though, in later years, she fully compensated for her 'weak bodily presence' by an increasingly substantial reputation. But when she was in Malaya she still felt a little insecure at first encounters and so cherished these compliments from the men and carefully recorded each one for Hennie's benefit in a burst of naïve pride. And really it *was* quite an achievement for an unescorted middle-aged spinster to find her feet so capably and be so thoroughly well-liked in the uncompromisingly bachelor ambience of the Perak crowd. But then, an absence of womankind was, in Isabella's view, frequently a blessing. 'I think that Perak is fortunate in not having English ladies. You have no idea of the total want of occupation for any but the best kind of women,' she told Hennie, 'and they tattle and make mischief and create jealousies and undermine civil servants with a view of pushing forward their husbands and keep the little communities in constant hot water. There is not a European woman within a twelve-hour journey of Kuala Kangsa, and it is a happy thing.' One of the nearest was poor Emily Innes of whom Isabella had undoubtedly heard, and she was a case in point.

Yet, in spite of the cordiality and the lack of female tittle-tattle, the delights of ape and elephant, and the beautiful wild peace of her surroundings – of the fact, in short, that she liked 'Kuala Kangsa better than any place I have been in Asia', she refused Low's invitation to stay. She was 'disgusted with herself' for doing so, but confessed to Hennie, 'I cannot live longer without your letters and they, alas, are at Colombo' (whither she had originally been bound). So she left, pulled homeward, as many another traveller, by the invisible, infrangible thread of anxious love. She departed the Residency on a pony while the Royal

Elephant carried her baggage, and it was absurd to see the grand beast 'lie down merely to receive my little valise and canvas roll, with a small accumulation of Malacca canes, mats, *krises*, tigers' teeth and claws . . .' The sun had barely risen, globules of dew rolled along the pineapple leaves and tigers had only just retreated to their lairs, but Low was at his desk already, writing and nursing the sick Eblis at the same time, while the wild siamang peered down cheerily from the roof-beam.

As she rode through the jungle tracks, the early mists floated away in rose and gold, apes hooted their morning hymns to the sun, birds screeched, butterflies and orchids flopped in the hot light, dragonflies and honeysuckers shimmered. Isabella's eyes shone with the joy of it all, a joy that verged on sadness as her thoughts veered towards that 'dim pale island' to which she was returning.

Just before her final departure, Isabella received a telegram from Low: 'Eblis is a little better this morning. He has eaten two grasshoppers and has taken his milk without trouble, but he is very weak.' It was the only crumb of good news that mitigated her passionate regret at leaving, which suffuses the last paragraph of her book: 'We sailed from Penang in glorious sunshine at an early hour this afternoon and have exchanged the sparkling calms of the Malacca Straits for the indolent roll of the Bay of Bengal. The steamer's head points north-west. In the far distance the hills of the Peninsula lie like mists upon a reddening sky. My tropic dream is fading, and the "Golden Chersonese" is already a memory. . . .'

Part Two

A LADY'S LIFE

CHAPTER V

The Clergyman's Daughter

'How singular people all seem to me now who live on our dim, pale island and wear our hideous clothes,' Isabella remarked in a letter written one bright and carefree day under a tropical sun. And yet, when she returned from her travels in 1874 (with her collections of Hawaiian fern-prints and the kitten beaver fur presented by her favourite trapper), and again in 1879 (with her *daimyo*'s bath and the claws of a Perak tiger) she quietly merged into the sober landscape of home. She reverted, as a friend put it, to 'the timorous, delicate, gentle-voiced woman that we associate with Miss Bird of Edinburgh'. This second Miss Bird, who waited in the wings with a discretion proper to her sex and class, took competent command once Isabella had left the challenge and stimulation of foreign parts. It was she who set most of the scenes for the first forty years of their common life, she who was best known and best beloved by family and friends, she whom one would expect to emerge from her particular clerical nest. It is she who now deserves some attention.

Isabella Lucy Bird, born 15 October 1831, 'came of good stock', as the Victorians put it. The most dynamic and intellectual strain came through the family of her father, Edward Bird, which was quite closely related to the Wilberforces, and numbered among its members an impressive selection of eminent bishops, missionaries, clergymen and clerical wives. Running true to form, Edward, after first going to Calcutta as a barrister where his wife and infant son died of cholera, returned to England, became a clergyman and married Dora Lawson, a clergyman's daughter. The Lawsons, like the Birds, were responsible, solid members of the upper middle classes, and their family home was Boroughbridge Hall in Yorkshire, where Isabella was born.

The world into which she came was secure, earnest, dutiful,

kindly, devout. Among many of her relatives there was a strong, even passionate, urge towards practical Christian philanthropy. Aunt Mary was a missionary in India; her own mother used her pocket-money to hire a room for the holding of Sunday school classes; one of her cousins, another Mary Bird, later became a well-known missionary in Persia; and outstanding in the family annals was the name of William Wilberforce. He died when Isabella was only two years old, but his example as liberator, humanitarian and Christian gentleman was honoured by them all, most especially, says Anna Stoddart, by 'the lingering maiden ladies' of the clan, 'who treasured as mementoes of their great kinsman, lines inscribed by him on the blank leaves of their Bibles'.

Isabella's father did not make his total commitment to Christianity until he took orders at the age of thirty-eight, and for the next decade he worked at it with the obstinate zeal and dedication of the latecomer. He must have been an impulsive, passionate, uncompromising man, his rather frail physique stretched to breaking-point by the demands of his highly-strung temperament, and his elder daughter, who was like him in many ways, loved him fiercely. They moved to Tattenhall in Cheshire when Isabella was still an infant, and there a second girl was born and named Henrietta – after one Aunt Henrietta who, according to Anna Stoddart, 'had strong views on infant baptism and renounced on their behalf her clerical lover, at the sacrifice of her life'. Little Hennie's role too was to be partly one of renunciation in the cause of the stronger elder sister who dominated her life. Henrietta, we are told, was a faithful, unobtrusive, studious, gentle, dreamy child and she kept those qualities throughout her days – and chief of them was constancy.

Few 'cute' anecdotes of Isabella's childhood survive, but this one, from a friend, illustrates much: Isabella at the age of six sat listening to a gentleman 'who was canvassing Tattenhall in his own interest and who excited her distrust by his too obviously expressed admiration of lovely little Henrietta. She marched up to him and asked, in her incisive tones, "Sir Malpas de Grey Tatton Egerton, did you tell my father my sister was so pretty because you wanted his vote?" ' It showed a considerable grasp of language for a six-year-old to get such a very gentlemanly name correct! More significantly, the incident suggests two important facets of Isabella's character: a possessive, obsessive, rather masculine devotion to Henrietta (her protective stance before Sir Malpas is typical elder-brotherly); and secondly, a determined desire to free the truth, even if unpalatable, from the shackles of social hypocrisy. Throughout her life Isabella detested pretension and sycophancy, and in later years, when her pen had a certain power, she could not abide those who flattered her because, as it were, they wanted her vote.

Edward and Dora Bird were cultured, observant people; they soon realised that their elder daughter was endowed with exceptional intelligence and keen perspicacity, and they fed her eager mind with robust fare. She read no children's books, heard no baby talk, they found her lying in the stables quite absorbed in Alison's *French Revolution* when she was but seven. She had no formal schooling, but studied literature, history, drawing, French and the Scriptures at her mother's knee, learned Latin and botany from her father and later pursued her own studies into chemistry, metaphysical poetry and biology. As she had but one quiet sister, her days were not filled with childish romps, but each year the family went to Grandfather Bird's house at Taplow Hall where, in middle-class Victorian fashion, all the relatives gathered for the summer holidays, and all the children played together.

The Hall was spacious, with stables, paddocks, shrubberies and fields of clover where the 'Taplow grandchildren' could run reasonably wild. The days there began solemnly, Anna Stoddart says, with the family and all the servants 'outdoor as well as indoor . . . summoned to hear the Squire read the lessons and a prayer for the day out of "Thornton's Prayers"'. On the lawn was an aged mulberry tree, and the adults gathered beneath its shade in basket-chairs, sipping wholesome beverages, chatting, reading and writing letters, while their children raced and tumbled about the bordering banks of thyme, yarrow and bedstraw. The drawing-room was dignified with satin-wood tables, pot-plants and a piano around which the family again assembled in the evenings to sing appropriate airs, such as *The Captive Knight* and *The Curfew Bell*.

'The Taplow grandchildren,' says Miss Stoddart, 'breathed an atmosphere of "causes".' Letters from clerical relatives in India, 'framed with decorum for general reading', contained pathetic stories of poverty, moral degradation, spiritual barrenness, and urged the need for greater missionary endeavour; a guest, on leave, say, from some mission hospital in China or West Africa, told his tales of heathen suffering; the short-sighted maiden aunts, whose spectacles 'gave them an expression of sternness quite foreign to their natures', were stern nevertheless about their daily drinking of sugarless tea in the cause of West Indian slavery, long after the slaves had, in fact, been emancipated. The fervour of Protestant guilt ran high: it was early made clear to Isabella how lucky was her lot compared with that of the uneducated grass-hut native, the unwanted baby in the Calcutta streets. The relatively few abandonments to utter joy she ever knew were bound with that guilt, that deep sense of moral obligation towards the less fortunate.

But Isabella's fortune was by no means flawless; it was blemished from an early age by that ill-health which beset her whole life. Those maiden aunts were also stern in their insistence that all the grandchildren should stand throughout the endless Sunday services, for instance, and this, a weariness to the healthy, was a torture to Isabella with her incipient spinal disease. As Miss Stoddart suggests, 'Had her courage not ridden above it, she might have delivered herself over to confirmed ill-health and adorned a sofa all her days. But even as a child, her brave spirit scorned prolonged concession to this delicacy', and she rode, ran, climbed with the rest of the children, refusing to be outdone by any and more daring than the most reckless boy because she, in compensation for her physical weakness, had the strength of utter fearlessness.

When Isabella was eleven her grandfather died, a death that presaged the end of the halcyon gatherings at Taplow. That same year, seeking more testing mettle for his zealous spirit, Edward Bird moved with his family from Cheshire to a parish in Birmingham. Bird was an extreme and vociferous opponent of Sunday labour and, as such, had alienated many of the Tattenhall farmers whose cows were in the habit of producing as much milk on Sundays as on other days and who therefore continued to make their famous cheese on Sundays also. The Tattenhall church had apparently 'become discouragingly empty' by the time Bird left;

nevertheless, he at once raised the same battle-cry in Birmingham, where he found that 'his parish was given over to Sunday trading and the fight he had to wage on the Lord's side was with a very Apollyon'. It must have been a depressing change for Isabella, with her abiding dislike of the urban scene, to leave the fields and farms of Cheshire for the airless, overcrowded, sullen city. She gamely taught Sunday school classes of girls of her own age, trained a choir and continued her studies – which must have included a Tory-biased investigation into current politics, for her first published work, printed privately a year or so later, was a quaint and intemperate diatribe against the free-trade theories of Cobden and Bright. Meanwhile, Edward Bird struggled for the souls of his parishioners, many of which he found to be inert, oppressed and bitter. Though the congregations responded to the first flush of his febrile idealism, numbers of his flock soon fell by the wayside and some openly derided him over the vexed question of Sunday observance.

In 1848, Bird's physical health and the mainspring of his proselytising zeal broke down; Birmingham was left behind, and for the last ten years of his life Isabella's father was resigned to the little parish of Wyton, Huntingdonshire, which had a population of some three hundred souls who had never felt impelled to do a great deal of work on the Sabbath. The change benefited Isabella in some ways, though it meant that the family had in effect withdrawn in defeat from the harsh realities of the godless city. In Wyton, she could indulge her deep delight in nature, as she drifted along the flat reedy Ouse and rode over its misty water-meadows, and her social confidence increased as she made congenial friends among the local gentry and stayed at the cultured homes of her ecclesiastical relatives, the Bishops of Chester and Winchester.

When she was eighteen, Isabella underwent a partially successful operation for removal of a spinal tumour, but her health remained poor. It improved greatly in the Scottish highlands, where the family spent part of each summer; for Scotland appealed to them, on account of both its wild natural beauty and its stricter conformity to Mr Bird's belief on the sanctity of the Sabbath. But, returned to the flat Wyton, where the rooks cawed in the elms and the ivy hung damp on the garden walls, she dwindled, half-recumbent on the drawing-room sofa, listlessly pursuing her literary studies and needlework.

Clearly, as Isabella herself recognised, the trouble was partly psychological. Years later, a skilled Scottish physician diagnosed that she was 'one of those subjects who are dependent to the last degree upon their environment to bring out their possibilities. It is not a question of dual personality, it is the varied response of a single personality under varied condition . . .' Today, with a little more knowledge at their disposal, doctors would probably diagnose that the root cause of the ailments she suffered when 'in civilised society' was reactive depression, resulting from a temperament so at odds with its environment. Certainly her recurrent attacks of vague aches and pains, insomnia, mental lethargy, backache, and feelings of guilty insufficiency would suggest this; certainly too, the social environment in which she grew up must have been intensely frustrating, for it did nothing to 'bring out' her very special possibilities. Isabella's doctor at Wyton partly understood her predicament and prescribed a long sea voyage – classic remedy for single, highly-strung, rather too intelligent young women of the period. And so, in 1854, Isabella embarked on her first long journey abroad.

She was then twenty-three years old, she had startled none with her wit or beauty, never run away from home or questioned her parents' judgement, nor, as far as we know, had she ever fallen in love with any romantically suitable young man. She was not a literary prodigy and kept no intimate journal of her youthful joys and woes. Consequently, until the publication of her first book, she can only be seen from the outside, mainly through the eyes of her adoring hagiographer, Anna Stoddart. And the outside image is not very inspiring: Miss Bird, elder daughter of a country parson, devout, earnest, plain, charitable, high-minded, priggish, intelligent, delicate and, it must be said, a little dull. That was by no means all of Isabella, she was one of the most mettlesome daughters who ever flew from a rectory nest, but evidence of this from her early years is sorely lacking.

Miss Bird went to Canada and North America armed with a hundred pounds from her father and permission to stay away as long as it lasted. It lasted a long time, and she did a great deal with it. The book she wrote about that first journey is fairly informal, personal, discursive and gives considerable indication of her writing talent. It bustles with people who are keenly and sympathetically observed: the frontier town 'colonial ladies' who plied her with questions about Queen Victoria and the latest Paris fashions (which they naïvely imagined she was wearing); the Boston sea-captain who prided himself on being a 'thorough-going-down-easter' and poured scorn on the lazy 'Blue Noses' of Halifax; the kindly railroad conductor who wrapped her in a buffalo robe, gave her tea, explained the differences between English and American braking-systems; sturdy Kentuckians who slapped each other on the back and asked, by way of greeting, 'Well, old alligator, what's the time o' day?'; and the supercilious Englishman in the Canadian backwoods who sought to impress her with his tales of the dukes and duchesses he'd left behind. Later, and even more precisely to Isabella's taste, there were the thrilling wild men who boarded the trains as they went West: 'Californians dressed for diggings with leather pouches for the gold-dust, Mexicans with dark soft eyes singing plaintive Spanish airs, and real prairie rangers, handsome, broad-chested and athletic, with aquiline noses, piercing grey eyes and brown curling hair and beards. They wore leather jackets slashed and embroidered, large boots with embroidered tops, silver spurs and caps of scarlet cloth worked in somewhat tarnished gold thread, doubtless the gifts of some fair ones enamoured of the handsome physiognomies and reckless bearing of the hunters.' Clearly, Isabella had an early penchant for the Rocky Mountain Jim type.

The infinitely rich variety and quantity of the transatlantic scene, as she travelled a thousand miles west from Halifax and back again, amazed her, and she didn't miss a thing. Almost as soon as she landed, apparently, her pain and lassitude fell away, and she became immensely resourceful and energetic. In Nova Scotia she thumped in ancient coaches over corduroy roads made of pine-trunks, and, sitting outside on the box, regaled the coachman after dark with tales of ghosts and hobgoblins. She felt her success, she says, when he suddenly jumped with fright at the gleam of a nearby silver birch. In Saint John she loved the wharf-side bustle: 'a thousand boatmen, raftmen and millmen, some warping dingy scows, others loading huge square-sided ships; busy gangs of men in fustian jackets engaged in running off the newly-sawed timber . . .' And she relished the dramatic switch from one world to another, to, for instance, the 'parlour' in a Boston hotel: 'The carpet of the room was of richly flowered Victorian pile, rendering the heaviest footstep noiseless; the tables were marble on gilded pedestals, the couches covered with gold brocade. At a piano of rich workmanship an elegantly dressed lady was seated, singing "And will you love me always?" – a question apparently satis-factorily answered by the speaking eyes of a bearded Southerner, who was turning over the pages for her. A fountain of antique workmanship threw up a *jet d'eau* of iced water scented with *eau de Cologne*; and the whole was lighted by four splendid chandeliers interminably reflected, for the walls were mirrors divided by marble pillars. The room seemed appropriate to the purposes to which it was devoted – music, needlework, conversation, flirting.'

In Cincinnati, 'Palmetto hats, light blouses and white trousers were all the rage, while Germans smoke chibouks and luxuriate in their shirt sleeves' and 'dark-browed Mexicans in sombreros and high-slashed boots dash about on small active horses with Mamelouk bits'. Somewhere isolated and uncouth along the Mississippi, the breakfast served was 'johnny cake, squirrels, buffalo-hump, dampers and buckwheat, tea and corn spirit'; later at Chicago the only available fare was 'pork with onion fixings'. No cutlery was provided, so each diner hacked at the pork with his bowie-knife; 'Neither were there salt-spoons, so everybody dipped his greasy knife into the pewter pot containing salt' (which shocked Isabella).

The next day she crossed Lake Ontario in a gale, during which, she says, she was swept out of the steamer's saloon on one wave and back on its deck with the next. At Toronto they were cele-brating the Fall of Sebastopol, bonfires of tar-barrels were roaring under the sicklied gas-lamps, the crowd was shouting 'Down with the Rooshians, Hurrah for Old England', and Isabella was most gratified by their loyal sentiments. Back in New York, there were traffic jams: 'There are streams of scarlet and yellow omnibuses racing in the more open parts, and locking each other's wheels in the narrower – there are helpless females deposited in the middle of a sea of slippery mud, condemned to run a gauntlet between cart-wheels and horses' hoofs – there are loaded stages hastening to and from the huge hotels – carts and waggons laden with merchandise – and "Young Americans" driving fast-trotting horses, edging in and out among the crowd – wheels are locked, horses tumble down, and persons pressed for time are distracted. Occasionally the whole traffic of the street comes to a dead-lock, in consequence of some obstruction or crowd, there being no policemen at hand with his incessant command "Move on!"'

There is a surprising familiarity about several of her comments as a European seeing the American continent for the first time. Jewellery in the Broadway stores was preposterously expensive; men were uncomplainingly chivalrous; hotel rooms were unbearably over-heated; ice-water was happily ubiquitous; casually-met strangers were intimately loquacious – and yet chill; urban women were enviably slim and elegant; masculine yarns were extraordinarily chauvinistic; and everywhere there was the overwhelming sense of heterogeneity, change and impermanence, a fascination with the wealth and promise of the future. 'An entire revolution had been effected in my way of looking at things since I landed on the shore of the New World,' she declared with the earnest primness which characterises this early work. 'I had ceased to look for vestiges of the past or for relics of ancient magnificence and in place of these I now contemplated vast resources in a state of progressive and almost feverish development, and having become accustomed to the general absence of the picturesque, had learned to look at the practical and the utilitarian with a high degree of pleasure and interest.'

In fact the revolution in Isabella's thinking was by no means 'entire'; 'All my prejudices melted away as a result of these American experiences,' she states rather grandly in her preface. But she retained a fair number intact, though she did not then recognise them as such, rather as immutable laws ordained by God and proven on history's pulses. She deplored the lack of Sunday observance wherever she found it; truth, she felt, 'was at a fearful discount in America' compared with its rating at home; and, in comparison with the glorious constitutional monarchy of imperial Britain, Republicanism was a wayward, crude and feeble creature indeed and 'its present state gives rise to serious doubts . . . whether it can long continue in its present form'. Republicanism also resulted in a very peculiar 'mingling of ranks' (she once heard one chambermaid call another 'a young *lady*') but on the whole this was far from disagreeable, and its greater freedoms meant that she, an 'unattended young lady' could travel alone by train in a way that would have been quite inappropriate in dear England.

And so, much too soon, it was time to return to the proprieties, refinements, dutiful repose of her homeland, for which the orderly routines aboard Cunard's *America* bound for Liverpool somewhat prepared her. There were regular strolls on deck, too many large meals, interminable chess and card games, violins with afternoon tea, and to these she resigned herself with detached amusement. But she came alive when a gale suddenly blew up and the ship displayed 'its special capabilities for rolling'. 'The view from the wheel-house was magnificent. The towering waves which came up behind us heaped together by mighty winds, looked like hills of green glass, and the phosphorescent light like fiery lamps within – the moonlight glittered upon our broad foaming wake – our masts and spars and rigging stood out in sharp relief against the sky, while for once our canvas looked white. Far in the distance the sharp bow would plunge down into the foam, and then our good ship, rising, would shake her shiny side, as if in joy at her own buoyancy. The busy hum of men marred not the solitary sacredness of midnight on the Atlantic. The moon "walked in brightness", auroras flashed, and meteors flamed, and a sensible presence of Deity seemed to pervade the transparent atmosphere in which we were viewing "the works of the Lord, and his wonders in the deep." '

There was no surer proof of God's omnipotence than a display of the beauty he made, no more heady draught than one of nature's dramas spiced with danger, no more exhilarating stimulant than the novelty of constant change and movement. But once safely returned to port, slowed down and pampered with 'civilisation', her very sap drained away, leaving her distressed in mind and body; 'I always feel dil [dull and inactive] when I am stationary,' she wrote years later from the Sandwich Isles. 'The loneliness is dreadful often. When I am travelling I don't feel it, but that is why I can never stay anywhere.'

Stayed, perforce, at Wyton after her American adventure, she shelved the dilemma as she always did, by reliving her travels in writing. Her manuscript was shown to John Murray, who at once recognised its merits, and thus began the cordial friendship between Isabella and her publisher which lasted for the rest of her life. This first book, under the decorous guise of anonymity and the title *An Englishwoman in America*, appeared in 1856 and was accorded a fair success. But the following year her health again deteriorated in the spiritless environment of the Rectory; again she tried the cure of transatlantic travel (of which little record survives); and, very soon after this second journey, her father died. He had been 'the mainspring and object' of her life, she cried, in the fervour of that passionate grief which utterly swamped her on each occasion that she lost a member of her close family. And certainly his influence upon her was strong, his moral creed governed much of her thinking, and she modelled her obstinate integrity on his.

II

The father's death naturally meant that the Rectory had to be vacated, and early in 1860 the Birds moved to Castle Terrace, Edinburgh. It was one of those prim, trim, grim residences admirably suited to the housing of a reasonably well-off clergyman's widow and her two delicate spinster daughters. Isabella was then twenty-nine years old, and to her future biographer, Anna Stoddart, who first met her at this time, we owe one of the few descriptions of her youthful appearance. 'The memory of a small, slight figure dressed in mourning is still vivid – of her white face shining between the black meshes of a knitted Shetland veil; of her great observant eyes, flashing and smiling, but melancholy when she was silent; of her gentleness and the exquisite modesty of her manner; and above all, of her soft and perfectly modulated voice, never betrayed into harshness or loudness, or even excitement, but so magnetic that all in the room were soon absorbed in listening to her.' It is really not unkind to focus this slightly misty-eyed portrait by adding that Isabella had very prominent front teeth (a defect remedied by later dental treatment after a riding accident); that, 'Her quiet, slow, deliberate manner of speech might have been a little tedious in one less gifted', as a friend gently put it; that when she drew herself up to her full height it was, on her own admission, four feet, eleven and a half inches.

Isabella started her new life in the Scottish capital as a semi-invalid unable to rise before midday. During her bedridden forenoons, she wrote articles for worthy family periodicals such as *Good Words, The Leisure Hour, The Family Treasury*. Hymnology and metaphysical poetry were favourite themes, and her approach to them is lucid and erudite, her style muted, polished, conventional, devout, like a piece of best-quality grey silk. Rising in the afternoon, she busied herself with a number of local good works, attended committee meetings, often dined out.

The first 'cause' that aroused her charitable sympathy was that of the Hebridean crofters, whose plight she saw for herself during a tour of the Outer Hebrides in 1861. The 'Pen and Pencil Sketches' of that journey, which were later published, afford ample evidence of how vividly and directly she could write when stirred to compassion by first-hand experience of human misery. Entering a hovel on the Isle of Uist, she records, for instance, that 'The oppressive smell of dirt overpowered that of the peat smoke which was so thick that we could hardly discern anything and acrid enough to bring tears to the eyes; and tears were not inappropriate. The earthen floor was all holes, some dry, some wet. In one of the wettest, a crippled infant was dabbling its long lean fingers. There was no light but that which came through a smoke-hole and this also seemed to admit great gusts of the wind which blew the smoke down and left it to densify inside. Peat reek dripped from the roof, and the five human inhabitants looked as if peat smoke had so penetrated their tissues as to become part of their being. Over the peat fire which smouldered drearily, sat an ancient crone who had been dried in smoke till her skin was hard and withered like a mummy's and the puny infant on her knee looked up with old pinched features like her own. A sickly woman scantily clad sat on a heap of ashes rocking to and fro, the sick child lay on a dirty blanket on the floor with smoke and embers driving into its bleary eyes. There was no partition in the den, but two cows and some poultry seemed to understand that it was proper to keep at the other end of the room, at least while visitors were present.'

Something had to be done, and to Isabella and others of active conscience, the best solution seemed to be that of emigration to North America and Canada. In retrospect, this answer may not seem quite so satisfactory, but to those then concerned the issue was clear: here were crofters living in wretched conditions such as Isabella described; there were the empty, fertile, spacious lands across the Atlantic that she had also seen; and from them came the supporting testimony of many emigrants who had gone before and who reported back, 'We have plenty of food and grog'; 'We shall never want for timber and water'; and the famous, 'In America we have pies and puddings.' These were sound enough reasons for Isabella, who was always roused more by immediate social problems than by long-term historical perspectives.

She had a flair for organisation and personally supervised many of the practical arrangements. Wrote Mr Dunlop, a shipowner whom she approached in this connection, 'The impression left by our interview is of my great desire to serve the singularly gifted young lady well. She astonished me by her energy and her capacity in making arrangements . . . When all was settled and her people were about to embark, she was amongst them, seeing to their every want. The embarkation took place the day before their departure. Miss Bird remained with them all night, and when the official visit prior to their departure took place she had them marshalled in order, tidy and cheerful. The sadness at leaving their native shores had given place to cheerfulness – due to Miss Bird's presence among them.' The marshalling in good order of the 'tidy and cheerful' dispossessed has a distinctively bossy and patronising ring about it. Yet, Mr Dunlop adds, 'There was something about Miss Bird that filled every one with whom she came in contact with a desire to serve her. She never complained of inattention to her people, nor asked for special consideration for them or for herself. She was personally self-denying, her only wish being to make them happy. There was a fascination in all her ways. She was small of stature, simple and neat in her attire, and was full of a refined humour that brightened her conversation. There was always a grace in what she said, and an ever-present evidence of latent intellectual power; and presiding over all there was a dignity that forbade the slightest approach to familiarity.' Those qualities, so clearly discerned in her years before she began to travel seriously, were most important to her future success.

For it really seemed to be the case that coolies, interpreters, guides, muleteers were positively inspired to serve her with uncommon devotion, and that, though she moved so frequently in masculine domains, there was a presiding dignity about her which forbade undue 'familiarity'.

Isabella Bird's participation in local good works, allied to her social standing and that personal magnetism to which many who knew her refer, ensured that she soon had plenty of Edinburgh friends, most of whom were well known in the intellectual and philanthropic circles of the day. Anna Stoddart remembers 'Many a bright gathering at No. 3 Castle Terrace when artists, professors, poets and publishers were present. One occasion is specially vivid when Dr John Brown came, after taking precautions against "being mixed up with strong-minded women" and bandied genial quips with Professor Blackie, Dr Hanna, Mr Constable, Sir Noel Paton . . .' Among these, Isabella's closest friends were Professor John Blackie and his wife Ella. Blackie, Professor of Greek at the University, was a character in the city, an eccentric, rumbustious, clever, restless, huge man in a broad-brimmed hat, a student's cloak, with a long flowing beard and a kilt. His wife Ella was Isabella's closest friend for many years, but the configuration of her personality has been almost totally obscured by the shadow of her towering dynamic husband, in whose wake she lived. She was a highly-strung, deeply introverted woman with a beautiful melancholy intelligent face that suggests withdrawal and repression. She was thrifty, childless, and could make any place a charming home for her restless spouse when he cared to stay with her, which was seldom. She was, says Miss Stoddart, 'blighted with self-distrust', and in later years was a frequent victim of 'nervous depression', that disease so significantly prevalent among Victorian women and against which Isabella herself fought a lifelong battle. Isabella was a frequent visitor to Ella's drawing-room, a somewhat classical bower apparently, with walls panelled in ivory and gold, carved cornices and couches of crimson plush. To it, during the winter evenings of the 1860s, flitted a number of bonneted and cloaked young ladies of studious temperament, including members of the Stoddart and Cumming families, and the Bird sisters. Their conversation was impassioned upon such subjects as the schisms in the Scottish church, the rights of women, the merits of George Eliot's novels, and later, Anna says, when the kettle boiled, Blackie himself came stomping in 'with a crackling discharge of quips and compliments for the tea-drinkers'.

Isabella's letters to Ella (in which Blackie is referred to with affectionate forbearance as 'The Pro') are loving, intimate, frank, the chief surviving charts of her emotional life at this time. From them it seems that she was keenly interested in current influential philosophical and religious ideas, but that her intellectual enjoyment was marred, as so much of the enjoyment in her life, by a sense of guilt. 'I am in great danger of becoming perfectly encrusted with selfishness,' she told Ella, 'and this summer I have made very painful discoveries on this subject, and long for a cheerful intellect and self-denying spirit which "seeketh not its own and pleaseth not itself".' Yet the painful truth was that Isabella did not possess these gifts; she was a strong-minded, fairly self-centred person with a deep secret lust for simple selfish happiness that no amount of high-thinking and self-denial could totally assuage. But, because of her upbringing, she enormously admired and envied those to whom a selfless devotion to moral duty came easily – as it did, apparently, to her mother and sister.

In 1866, to the great sorrow of both sisters, Mrs Bird died, and from then on all Isabella's love was centred upon Hennie. Hennie was a less complex and passionate person than her elder sister. The prevalent clerical strain in the family had run true to form in her, and produced a shy, staid, gentle, studious, warm-hearted, good young woman, pure in mind and spirit and with a simple certainty of Christian faith that never faltered. She possessed a quality that Anna Stoddart terms 'unruffled peace' and allied to it was a timid grace, a responsive interest in the concerns of others that charmed Isabella's friends so that they became her friends too. She seldom sought friends of her own or ventured outside the tranquil warmth of the family circle; she shared little of her sister's intellectual breadth, few of her spiritual and emotional uncertainties, none of her drive. The initiatives that Hennie took were few: she sketched and painted in water-colours; she came third in Professor Blackie's Greek class for ladies; she leased the cottage in Tobermory on Mull which, after her mother's death, became her favourite refuge and where, Isabella says, she was always 'so happy and delightful'. Like Isabella, she took a deep pleasure in the apprehension of natural beauty, though her tastes were less dramatic, and she preferred the glow of burnet roses along the island shore, the tumble of a mossy burn to the cataracts and chasms that fed Isabella's imagination. In Tobermory where, according to Anna Stoddart, the villagers called her 'The Blessed One', she spread her wings with a barely perceptible rustle and arranged a number of tea-parties for friends. 'Henrietta's friends,' says Anna, 'were made for reasons very unusual; for the sake of their poverty and need of her, of their loneliness and dependence on her affection, of their sensitive youth and instinctive turn to her for understanding and guidance, of their sickness and sorrow and bereavement, and their faith in her sympathy and help.' It implies no denigration of these motives to add that Hennie, unlike her sister, had a strong and frustrated maternal instinct and that she half-adopted and paid for the education of a young girl in the village.

The Blackies, who had a house at Oban, occasionally visited the cottage on Mull, and one of these visits inspired the 'Pro' to a ballad about Hennie in her favourite setting. It is really quite a gem of its kind, apparently typical of the compositions that Blackie dedicated to various spinsters who adorned the fringes of his busy days, all of the verses, Anna explains, 'too rollicking to be dangerous'. It is called *A Ballad of Mull*:

> In a tiny bay,
> Where ships lie sure and steady,
> In a quiet way
> Lives a tiny lady;
> In a tiny house
> Dwells my little fairy,
> Gentle as a mouse,
> Blithe as a canary. . . .
>
> But above all fare,
> Of which my song is telling,
> Sits my lady there,
> The mistress of the dwelling.

Dressed in serge light blue,
With trimming white and snowy,
All so nice and new,
With nothing false and showy . . .

It goes on; incredibly, it gets worse.

Hennie, the reserved sister, composed all of a piece, would gladly have stayed the whole year in her tiny Tobermory dwelling; Isabella, a network of contradiction, needed the stimulation and challenge of urban life even while she hated its tiresome conventions and obligations. So they wintered in Edinburgh, and Isabella took up her second 'cause' – that of the city's slums. Again her pen was her most potent weapon, and her *Notes on Old Edinburgh*, published in 1869, are a furious and spirited indictment of the appalling conditions that existed less than a mile away from those trim terraces where she and her friends circulated. She describes the ragged, sore-blotched kids sitting stupefied in verminous gutters, the 'haggard, wrinkled vicious faces' peering from dirty windows, women shuffling along with buckets and waiting up to three hours to draw water from the one communal well, gratings 'choked up with fish-heads and offal', ashes and excrement. Inside it was worse: dark labyrinths of filthy rooms, in one a pregnant woman on a straw bed with her idiot child crawling in the grate; in another a dying man, covered with bed-sores, moaning for water; nearby, three half-clad prostitutes with their babies lying on the slimy floor, and brawling men plunging roughly down the stairs crying for a 'wee drap'. So, says Isabella, 'would the President of the Temperance Legion himself if he was hidden away in such a hole'. She pours vials of wrath on the landlords who charged extortionate rents for these wretched cells, with their walls swarming with lice, their floors with vermin, their foundations literally rotting with accumulated garbage of every odious sort. 'These miserable thousands are surely entitled to at least as much light, space and air as we give our beasts!' she exclaimed. Her report aroused some response, but, as Anna Stoddart says, 'philanthropy was only rubbing its eyes awake from slumber' in those days, and this was too vast a problem to be even partially remedied by the publication of one pamphlet, however powerful and inflammatory. Undoubtedly Isabella realised that, if she were truly determined to alleviate the slum conditions in the city, it would have taken some twenty years of wholehearted effort – a course that would have given her great moral satisfaction, but little health or true happiness.

Soon after these endeavours, her health deteriorated further. In June 1869 her doctor ordered that she must 'go to the sea, sleep on the ground floor and be out in a boat most of the day', says Anna Stoddart, who conscientiously documents the great variety of medical advice Isabella received over the years. The next month, Isabella, taking up the sad tale, admits that she has been 'as ill as could be with choking, aching, leeches, poultices, doctors twice a day, etc'. A year later she was still 'frail and in pain', Anna says, and her doctor 'suggested a steel net to support her head at the back when she required to sit up, her suffering being caused by the weight of her head on a diseased spine'.

In these distressing circumstances it was little wonder that deeper sloughs of depression and insomnia engulfed her. On medical advice, she took a chartered voyage to New York and back via the Mediterranean, but was too ill to leave the ship, and returned in worse health, and even more beset by a frustration that was physical, mental and spiritual. Yet still the doctors could only come up with the same suggestion – travel. And so in the summer of 1872 when she was forty years old and in a mood of kill-or-cure desperation, Isabella resolved to go to the very Antipodes in search of whatever it was her body and spirit craved. At last, in the enchanted Sandwich Isles and the rugged Rockies, she found her own very individual way to happy and creative fulfilment. And the puzzle of it all was that the frail lady who could not lift her head from the pillow without support in the summer of 1870 climbed Mauna Loa, the 'Matterhorn of the Pacific', three years later, and then went on to round up wild cattle in the Rockies.

CHAPTER VI

The Doctor's Wife

HENRIETTA BIRD, writing to Ella Blackie from Mull in the summer of 1873, reported that she had recently received 'three delightful cheerful letters from Isa. . . . They have not contained a single word which has left other than a pleasant impression. Is not this delightful?' The cheer and delight continued during the years spent abroad, as we know, and these and other brimful letters positively bounded into the sedate Tobermory cottage, sparkling with details of Isa's marvellous adventures on the other side of the world. And Hennie – 'My Dearest Pet', 'My Ownest', as her sister called her – sipping a cup of tea by the fire or ensconced in the window-seat overlooking the bay, read and re-read the letters with pleasure and shared their contents with her intimate friends.

First came the stories of the dangerous climb to the top of the volcano on Hawaii, with Isa actually sleeping in a tent on the crater's very edge, and that was followed by Isa's reckless winter ride in the Rockies, and her friendship (if not more than friendship) with poor Mr Nugent, who sounded such an extraordinary man. Then after Isa had been at home again, which, alas, didn't seem to suit her at all, came the letters from North Japan, describing those terrible flea-ridden inns in which she had stayed during the wet summer of 1878. So much of that Japanese journey had sounded very dismal and bad for Isa's health – but then the 'Great Perak Letter' had arrived, a hundred and sixteen pages of it and each one a burst of colour and vitality. And soon after, in the early spring of 1879, the still waiting, faithful, patient Hennie heard that darling Isa was truly coming home again at last. She was stouter, she said in her last letter from Malaya, and even her face was fatter, and the tropic sun had browned her so much that she 'could be taken for a Portuguese'! And everyone everywhere –

in Hawaii, Colorado, Japan, Perak – had liked Isa; and so they should because she was extremely intelligent and most interesting to listen to, and so loving, sympathetic and really most amazingly courageous and enterprising. It would be very delightful to see Isa again.

II

On her way home from the Golden Chersonese, Isabella stopped at Cairo where she contracted a fever; while still weak, she went off to camp on the slopes of Mount Sinai for four nights alone; she developed pleurodynia (rheumatism of the chest muscles). So, when she finally reached the shelter of the Tobermory cottage in May 1879, she was not as robust and brown as a Portuguese after all, but something of a physical wreck. To Ella she wrote, 'My body is very weak and I can only walk about three hundred yards with a stick, but my head is all right, and I am working five hours a day in this delicious quiet. Hennie has improved wonderfully since I came and we are very happy together. I feel that "goodness and mercy have followed me" and the joy of returning to Hennie's unselfish love and the precious affection of many dear friends is new every morning.' Hennie's love was large enough to bask in, it was pure, total, undemanding and threatened no unforeseen invasions of body or mind. It was enough for Isa; there was, she concluded that peaceful summer, 'no room for a third'.

The third, aspiring intruder, the man who worshipped Isabella with a devotion and constancy akin to Hennie's love, was Dr John Bishop, an Edinburgh physician. Bishop, ten years Isabella's junior, a native of Sheffield, had settled in Edinburgh some years before. He had been resident surgeon at the Royal Infirmary, a private assistant to Sir Joseph Lister and had then set up in private practice. He was a favourite of his patients, many of whom, Anna Stoddart says, 'belonged to the more intellectual class of that generation'. Among them, not surprisingly, were Hennie and Isa, both of whom were in distressingly frequent need of medical attention.

Friendship blossomed between John Bishop and the sisters during the mid-seventies when, after her Sandwich Isles journey, Isabella pursued the study of histological botany, in which

Bishop was something of an expert. The general scientific field then called simply 'microscopy' so fascinated Isabella for a while that she contemplated giving up her literary work for it and, though dissuaded from this, she and Bishop spent much time together, enthusiastically 'busy with the marvels of the Atlantic ooze', as Anna Stoddart puts it. Bishop was immensely attracted by Isabella's intelligent grasp of the subject and by much else besides – her charm, her charitable concern for others' welfare, her breadth of interest. He had first proposed to her in 1877 and Isabella's reply must have been of the 'shilly-shally' kind that she usually deplored. In a letter to her publisher at that time she reported her 'conditional engagement' and hoped that Murray still had 'romance enough to sympathise with a "love match" '. Anna Stoddart however says that, even then, Isabella persuaded Bishop 'to let their friendship abide undisturbed by considerations which she was unwilling to face', and that he resignedly acquiesced in this. Nevertheless, the doctor continued to dance a variety of attendances, and Isabella told Ella a month later that he was staying at Tobermory 'healing the sick' – the quotation marks are hers.

It was partly to escape from this new emotional pressure and its attendant threat of 'becoming an invalid wife' as she put it, that Isabella had gone to Japan and Malaya; now she was back and patient John still waited. This time she definitely refused him, explaining gently that she was 'scarcely a marrying woman'. He forbore to press her further and, she wrote, 'He has acted nobly and sweetly to me, never saying one word about his own suffering.' 'Noble' and 'sweet' are words that Isabella and Anna continually use about both John Bishop and Henrietta, who thus emerge as holier-than-life figures bathed in a saintly glow. Like Hennie apparently, Bishop was quite unselfish, kind-hearted, immensely loyal; like Hennie too, his nature was retiring, conscientious, quite unassuming and with that same quality which Anna calls 'a rare simplicity and purity', a certain spiritual grace. In appearance, as Isabella describes him to a friend, he was 'a little under middle height, very plain, wearing spectacles and is very grey', with a 'high broad intellectual brow' that confirmed his cultured and 'very artistic tastes'. He must have had a quiet sense of the droll too: 'Isabella has the appetite of a tiger and the digestion of an ostrich' was how he diagnosed the amazing capacity of one so frail to travel so far. A man so similar in temperament to Hennie, sharing her talent for patient and undemanding devotion, could not but be a little *de trop* in 1879 when the two sisters were so happily and satisfyingly reunited. His role in Isabella's life lay in the near future.

In the meantime, that October, *A Lady's Life in the Rocky Mountains,* the somewhat reticent story of Isabella's Colorado adventures, finally appeared in book form and was greeted with rave notices. Her 'spontaneous and unadorned narrative', applauded the *Spectator,* was 'of more interest than most of the novels which it has been our lot to encounter, and in fact comprises character, situation and dramatic effect enough to make ninety-nine novels out of a hundred look pallid and flat in comparison'. Others concurred in their praise of her unforced, vivid style, her skilful combination of the dramatic and the natural, and not one, to Isabella's relief, 'scented out any imagined impropriety' – at least, not as far as Jim Nugent was concerned. The reviewer of *The Times* while acclaiming it as a bright and lively book, commented in passing that Miss Bird 'donned masculine habiliments for her greater convenience and backed such half-broken horses as she happened to hire'.

Masculine habiliments indeed! This evoked in Isabella an unusual burst of really vindictive fury. She wrote to Murray straight away, making it quite, quite clear that 'the Hawaiian riding dress', as she described it, was 'a dress worn by *ladies* at Mountain Resorts in America and by English and American *ladies* on Hawaii. The full-frilled trousers being invaluable in mountaineering or riding'. She continues, 'My indignation and disgust have not cooled down yet. I can imagine a lady who "dons masculine habiliments" quite capable of thrashing an editor on less provocation', and she apparently suggested that, as she was a properly-attired lady, Mr Murray might like to undertake the thrashing on her behalf? This he declined, and offered instead the soothing suggestion that a short prefatory note and a sketch to suggest the very feminine nature of the author's riding costume would be more appropriate. These duly appeared in most subsequent editions (of which there were seven) and they somewhat mollified Isabella. The sketch, though, was 'rather Amazonian and the horse unlike my little pet "Birdie" ', she complained, but at least, 'the costume is *not* "masculine habiliments"'. At any rate, Dean Stanley told Mr Murray that everybody was asking, 'Have you read *The Rocky Mountains*?' – it was that successful.

As for Isabella's response to *The Times* review, it is surely justifiable to suppose that her quite immoderate rage was closely related to her emotional state at that period. She had, after all, just refused the hand of a man in order to continue living in devoted harmony with her sister for whom she cherished an abnormally intense love. It was a most inappropriate moment to so much as hint that Isabella was in any way 'masculine', wanting perhaps in the conventional responses to the opposite sex, and flaunting her difference by the wearing of trousers. In fact, there is really little question but that she was normally sexed, though most of her passion was diverted into channels other than sexual. She probably feared the physical intrusion of sex and, even more, the curtailment it would have imposed upon her freedom of action, especially while she was of child-bearing age. Clearly, she had no maternal instinct whatsoever, preferring, in the legendary British fashion, the company of horses. And so really Isabella's reason for wearing trousers was simple, as the reviewer had in fact said: they facilitated the riding of horses astride. That travellers were 'privileged to do the most improper things with perfect propriety' was, after all, her lifelong principle, in time people accepted it from her, allowing her, by the rigid standards of the day, both to have her cake and eat it.

The row simmered down and the sisters left Mull for the winter. Describing that summer they had spent together in the Tobermory cottage, Isabella wrote, 'I think perhaps that I shall never again have such a serenely happy four months. I shall always in the future as in the past have to contest constitutional depression by earnest work, and by trying to lose myself in the interests of others; and full and interesting as my life is, I sometimes dread a battle of years.' The most pressing 'earnest work' was the writing of her book about Japan, which, she feared, would be 'dull and flat' after the Rockies. And it would have been more so perhaps if John Murray had carried his point, for he urged her to 'tone down' somewhat her brutally frank descriptions of Japanese peasant life. This she refused to do, saying that she 'wanted to speak the truth' – to chip a little of the sugar off the cherry-blossom image that was already forming around Japan.

When the manuscript was completed, Isabella went on one of her visiting treadmills among friends and relatives, while Hennie returned to Tobermory. Late in April, Isabella had a telegram to say that her sister was seriously ill, and, rushing to the cottage, found her prostrate with typhoid. Dr Bishop was at once sent for, and as, by almost providential chance, he had recently broken a leg, he gave up his normal practice and devoted himself entirely to Hennie. 'There is such a strength in having so good a man and so skilful a doctor, who knows her constitution thoroughly, in the house', Isabella wrote. The trial was a long one; hope ebbed and revived; the islanders brought masses of spring flowers, stood outside the gate to hear of her progress. In early June Hennie died.

Isabella was broken. As some mothers for their children, some spouses for their mates, some children for their parents, so Isabella was cast into a pit of total desolation by the death of her sister. 'The anguish is awful . . . She was *my world*, present or absent, seldom absent from my thoughts . . . She is not – and the light, life and inspiration of my life have died with her', she wrote to Ella Blackie, who later recalled Isabella's 'white face, the rigidity of a grief that chilled and devitalised her, the awful loneliness that wrapped her round'. 'I knew it would be terrible, but never knew half *how* terrible. I feel as if most of myself had gone,' Isabella continued in despair. And indeed, whether consciously or not, Isabella had for years envisaged herself and Hennie as being, to an extent, one entity. The letters Isabella wrote home from abroad contain many passionately affectionate passages in which Hennie is referred to as 'it'. For instance, 'I delight in my darling and the only pleasure I have is knowing it has something it can like'; and 'Each letter that I get gives me such a wild despairing wish to get back and see its well-beloved face, for it is my own and only pet'. Occasionally, Isabella refers to herself as 'it' also; she signed some of her letters 'Its being'; a term of mutual endearment was 'Its own pet'. The implication is that the sisters formed a mutually absorbed and absorbing 'it', a being that was indivisible, interdependent, complementary. Anna Stoddart quotes a friend of their early years who saw this clearly: 'The two sisters were widely different in girlhood, their temperaments and characteristics as well as their intellectual tastes and acquirements varying greatly, but both were charming companions and able to converse well on many subjects. What one lacked, the other possessed and thus together they formed a perfect combination.'

Within this 'combination' their later roles were clearly defined along lines similar to those of the male and female in primitive societies: Isa was the dominant leader, the wanderer, thinker, 'man of action'; Hennie was the admiring comforter, home-maker, still centre to whom Ulysses returns. But this is something of a simplification, because, as clearly emerged from the row over the riding-dress, for example, Isabella never consciously aspired to masculinity, rather, she needed Hennie's warm and simple femininity to complete her as a woman. Again, like many a wanderer's, her response to the home-maker's devoted love was ambiguous. Undoubtedly it was true, as Anna Stoddart said, that one very important element in Isabella's life was 'her deep home affection' – for father, mother and then all concentrated on her sister. Nevertheless, Isabella found most of her happiness and fulfilment in far-flung places, and when Hennie made a nest for them in Tobermory, Isabella was never there for more than a few months at a time, because, she asserted, the Mull climate greatly disagreed with her! (And so, perhaps, did living in the one ambience that Hennie had made her own.) When not abroad, therefore, it had long been Isabella's habit to go away for months on a series of visits to numerous friends and relatives, as she had been doing when Henrietta was taken ill.

In consequence, added to Isabella's sense of loss of half of her being was a racking guilt because she had so often neglected her sister's warm and loving presence in the past. Now she had lost it, and she passed into those involutions of grief through which, as through the circles of birth and love, there is no short cut. She yearned to die herself – 'I seem hardly to care what happens to me', she wrote; drearily she reiterated the sad litany of her loss – Hennie was 'the inspiration of all my literary work, my best public, my home and fireside, my most intimate and congenial friend', she told John Murray. She went to Tobermory, sorted through the beloved's possessions, tried to take up her sister's local charity work; 'The things I am interested in are *her* interests and for *her* sake I have become attached to Tobermory', she declared.

The copies of the just-published *Unbeaten Tracks in Japan* arrived, and she put them aside unopened. Murray, with kind intent to ease her sorrow, told her of its reception: 'How can I convey to you the tidings of your own praises which are resounding everywhere and with a unanimity of which I have had no previous experience in my long career as a publisher?' Isabella quotes this in a letter to Ella, and adds, 'But all this avails me nothing'. There was no joy in it for her, though she admitted 'a lurking satisfaction in having vindicated a woman's right to do what she can do well'.

And it was the book about Japan that firmly established her in the public mind as no mere 'lady adventuress' but as a perspicacious and very intelligent observer of the social and political scene in the Far East. 'I am specially pleased', she told Murray who had sent her a batch of favourable reviews, 'that the reviewers have not made any puerile remarks on the feminine authorship of the book or awarded praise or blame on that score.'

Her eventual interest in the book's reception indicated the first spark of returning life. The following January, six months after Hennie's death, John Murray may have been a little surprised to read the following from his favourite lady traveller: 'Perhaps you may remember that before I went to Japan I told you of the possibility that on my return I should accept a very faithful love that had long been mine. However, bad health and the filling up of my life by the affection and companionship of my sister, made me regretfully decide against marrying. It is all changed now, and Dr Bishop's devotion to her in the last six weeks of her life and her great wish that I should accept the care and devotion of one whose character and worth she had thorough trust in, have largely helped to make me feel that were I now to decide against him I should be casting away a very precious treasure. We shall be married in the spring . . .'

It would be crude to suggest that John Bishop was a mere 'substitute' for her dead sister, yet there was some small comfort in the similarity of their temperaments. Now, in addition, John offered his long-tested devotion, a 'home and fireside' from her deep sense of loneliness, a sympathetic community of interests and enthusiasms, and a fatherly bulwark against total despair – 'I now realise', she wrote later, 'that his devoted love has stood between me and the worst desolation ever since he led me from the death-chamber in Tobermory.' The engagement was entirely on Isabella's terms. 'It is understood that if I again need change, I am to be free for further outlandish travel,' she told Murray, and Bishop, accepting the condition, used to say quizzically, 'I have only one formidable rival in Isabella's heart, and that is the high tableland of Central Asia.' Isabella also insisted, with painful single-mindedness, on the paramount claims of her grief for Hennie. 'It touches me much that he recognised the truth that I should mourn all my days and instead of aspiring to fill the place which will always be vacant, he only asks to be allowed to take care of me and soothe my sorrow', she wrote to a friend.

Isabella was to be married from the home of her Warwickshire relatives, and John Bishop joined her there a day or so before the ceremony. 'The dear soul arrived early on Saturday', she told Ella, 'radiant, gentle, unselfish and well-dressed. I never saw him appear to so much advantage and my critical family are all quite delighted with him.' Impeccable though the bridegroom's behaviour was, Isabella, the fifty-year old bride, deliberately blighted the ceremony by her dramatic and ruthless insistence that it should resemble a second funeral. Just beforehand, she was 'half-blinded with tears, shrinking from all congratulations', she told Ella. For the actual wedding, which took place on 8 March 1881, she wore deep mourning of braided black serge and a black hat; there were no wedding guests; the church, she told her friend, was old and beautiful, and on its stained-glass windows 'the gridiron of St Lawrence is conspicuous'. Presumably, no one even suggested anything so joyously intimate as a honeymoon.

Back in Edinburgh, Isabella's behaviour would have strained to breaking-point the adoration of a lesser man, and she herself wondered 'If even his devoted love will grow weary of my abiding grief.' She returned to Tobermory, still 'drunk with loss', fearing now that she had 'ventured all that I had to give upon her life and exhausted my power of absorbing love upon her'. And if she had no use for Bishop's devotion, then their marriage would be barren indeed. Perhaps for his sake she concealed this turn of the screw at least, for he seemed 'very happy . . . his refined and reverential tenderness is truly beautiful'. It could not but also be just a little dull; it did nothing to satisfy Isabella's secret craving for drama and romance; Bishop did not have in his whole body one single spark of that brilliant reckless dazzle that had fired the fascinating Jim Nugent. 'I wish it had seemed more of a *step*', she confessed soon after the marriage, 'more novel and exciting, but I was so used to him before and the great intimacy of the terrible time at Tobermory makes meals and going about together seem merely a continuation of that'. And that others both recognised her plight and regarded it with some malicious amusement is suggested in a story current at the time: that, before her marriage, Isabella had intended to travel in New Guinea, but had given up the idea because it was not the sort of place you could take a man to!

And so, defiantly, and probably in the face of a good deal of unexpressed scepticism, Isabella tried to come to terms with what she called 'the everyday drudgery of life' that constantly defeated her. She moved into the marital home in Walker Street, Edinburgh; she gave the drawing-room 'an Oriental character, sustained by Eastern cabinets and palms which stood in the *daimyo*'s bath', Anna Stoddart says; she filled the rooms too, 'with picture of my darlings' – her family. 'We are just renewing the lease on the Cottage', she tells a friend. 'It is a shrine, but a pivot also . . . My husband is considerate, devoted and unselfish beyond anything . . . for him I truly regret the incurable nature of my grief.' And that apparent incurability induced self-pity. Soon she was complaining to Ella that she had hardly seen John for days, that he was always out while she was cooped up alone with her back trouble. This was wilful; she was seldom alone except by choice. The Bishops entertained and dined out, and Isabella habitually left her husband 'alone' for weeks on end, when she was fit enough, to go and stay with friends in London.

During one of these visits, her publishers held a party in her honour, at which Marianne North, a somewhat less adventurous 'adventuress', was introduced to Isabella. According to Miss North, Isabella was attired with considerable bravura for the occasion: 'She was seated in the back drawing-room in a big armchair, with gold-embroidered slippers and a footstool to show them on, a petticoat all over gold and silver embroidered wheels, and a ribbon and order across her shoulders, given her by the King of the Sandwich Islands'. She was, Miss North concluded, 'a very solid and substantial little person, short but broad, very decided and measured in her way of talking, rather as if she were reciting from one of her books'. This was not very flattering, but Isabella's earnest, unruffled demeanour did not rouse everyone's enthusiasm, and in any case she was seldom at her best during this period of her life. Even Anna Stoddart intrudes an unusual note of censure with her comment that, in the months following her marriage, Isabella 'had allowed herself to be captured by a morbid obsession' over Hennie's death and that 'this morbid strain exaggerated her personal moods'.

In November, when Isabella was at Tobermory and Bishop was 'alone' in Edinburgh, he was struck down with the painful skin disease erysipelas after performing an operation on a sailor with it. From this infection, apparently much more serious in those days, he never fully recovered, and its effects, allied to Isabella's troubles, blighted the remainder of their married life. She was ill next, with 'carbuncles on the spine' and 'nervous prostration' as the limitations of a conventional home and marriage began to chafe. When she was able, she took 'elderly rides' on a side-saddle in her husband's company and felt a 'crippled fool' the while. But though she may have burned in secret fury at the convention imposed upon her sex, she never once defied it by putting on her 'Hawaiian riding dress' and revelling in the therapy of a 'good gallop'. Instead she decided to satisfy her yearning for speed with a tricycle and corresponded with her publisher as to whether she should buy a 'National' or a 'Salvo' – eventually concluding that the latter was too slow for her 'somewhat fast notions of locomotion'. Whether she actually possessed a tricycle when in Edinburgh is not on record – it is, in any case, the sort of eccentric detail that Anna Stoddart would have refrained from mentioning. Years later, however, when Isabella was back in London, John Murray apparently presented her with one, and the story goes that she learned to ride it in Albemarle Street.

During her second year of married life Isabella, who was still restless and melancholy, continued work on her book about Malaya, but she wrote listlessly, for now that the inspiration of her sister had gone, she cared 'nothing for fame or money'. By this time in her life, she probably had no need to worry about the latter. She had undoubtedly inherited money as sole survivor of her close family, her husband earned quite enough to support her, and in addition her books were beginning to make a considerable profit. Her book about the Sandwich Isles, of which only a thousand copies were printed, had done little more than cover costs, but there was a continuing steady demand for her book of Rocky Mountain adventures. In fact, its sales, combined with those of *Unbeaten Tracks in Japan*, which was also very popular, brought her a cheque for £1,447 from John Murray. 'I, at all events, have no cause to complain of my publishers', she told him warmly. However, this represented something of a high point in the profits she made from her writing; from her next book, *The Golden Chersonese*, for instance, published in 1883 and dedicated to Henrietta, she reaped an eventual reward of only £370. Critically the latter book was well received, though one or two reviewers did comment on a certain waspishness of tone, a lack of sympathy for those less tough than she – such as the limp young Misses Shaw.

But there was no sinew of toughness now, as poor Isabella and John simply staggered from one illness to the next. They went south in search of health, where Bishop completely collapsed and pernicious anæmia, probably linked to the erysipelas infection, was diagnosed by London specialists. 'He has become a skeleton with transparent white hands and his face is nothing but a beard and beautiful eyes', Isabella wrote. 'He is always happy, everything, however distressing, is "all right". He says that these weeks have been the happiest time of his life. His mind is very clear and bright; he is full of fun, interest and thought for others.' That was written in September 1884, and for the next eighteen months Isabella devoted herself unstintingly to the welfare of this saintly, luckless, brave man she had married. There were dreary rounds of medical consultations; dismal and unsuccessful convalescences during which Dr Bishop was wheeled in a bath-chair along various sea-fronts to get the benefit of the fresh sea air; there was a brief hopeful return to Tobermory where John managed to stroll to the village with the aid of a stick, and then the desperate flight to the Riviera away from the brutal Scottish winter.

Henrietta Amelia Bird

John Bishop

John Murray, Isabella's publisher and friend, a portrait by Sir George Reid, R.A.

Wyton Rectory, near Huntingdon, where Isabella lived as a young woman

Tobermory in 1904. 'The Cottage' can be seen half way up the hill at the extreme right of the photograph and the Henrietta Bird memorial clock tower stands on the quayside to the right of the church

Leh, 'a flat-roofed, squat, vermilion-and-brown town'

ft: *A lama, photographed for William Carey's book, described as 'standing in that wild theatre, with his trumpet of human thigh-bone'*

ght: *Usman Shah, Isabella's Afghan guide, whose colourful costumes azed and delighted her. She was unable to finish this sketch to her liking he Afghan was arrested for murder while actually posing*

A gopher – the native coracle-like craft of the Euphrates and Tigris. Isabella spent some time in one with, among others, Mr Curzon, but unfortunately there is no record of their conversation

George Curzon, who at the time of Isabella's visit was gathering material for his authoritative book on Persia

A dervish

A Persian woman 'bedizened creatures confin... in their languid over-perfumed rooms'

Isabella (right) and tent on the fringes of the Bakhtiari country. In the centre is Miss Bruce, daughter of Dr Bruce, the nineteenth-century crusader

Isabella on horseback at Erzerum, on her return journey

Isabella's 'travelling party' in Korea

Isabella took this photograph of an unidentified missionary family in the Far East

The King of Korea

*'The Reverend Heywood
Horsburgh in native dress'*

*Isabella the photographer 'a snapshot taken of Mrs Bishop at
Swatow by Mr Mackenzie'*

'*The author's trackers at dinner*'. *The specks on this photograph are particles of Yangtze mud which adhered to the plate during the developing process (see p. 312)*

(see p. 312)

One of Isabella's own photographs of three members of the China Inland Mission dressed in native clothes

All this time, Anna says, Isabella 'never recorded a word about herself or her ailments . . . Her diary is filled with entries concerning him – his doctors, nurses, movements, daily condition.' For the poignant truth was that now, during John's last lingering illness, she found herself truly and dependently in love with him – a love awakened by the noble qualities she admired and his courageous battle against affliction. Following medical advice, they went to Cannes, Geneva, Glion (whence Isabella had to return to London briefly for an operation on her back!), to St Vissoie, St Luc, to Cannes again . . . a painful procession of cheerless spa hotels, foreign nurses and menservants, friends coming and going, sleepless nights and lack-lustre days of sickroom waiting. At Cannes, Sir Joseph Lister, under whom Bishop had once worked, came over to carry out a transfusion of blood, taken from 'a sturdy young Italian peasant who was willing to risk it for a large sum of money'. This, not surprisingly, was of no avail, and Bishop wasted slowly day by day. 'Oh my idol, my treasure, my noble and spotless love', Isabella wrote to Ella in anguish. 'His dark eyes look out strangely from the small face which, for the last week, has worn the serene contented look of one who has entered into rest. When those eyes see me they brighten and the whole face lightens into rapture, and the weak voice utters words of wildest love and worship!' A few days later, on 6 March 1886, two days before their fifth wedding anniversary, Bishop died. 'So happy my own bride', were his last direct words to her, Isabella recorded. At first she was stunned: 'His extraordinary patience, self-control and cheerfulness and intellectual activity blinded all who were about him for the last sixteen months to the extent of his deprivations and sufferings. He was always so happy, so interested in every one and everything, so enthusiastic, so grateful and loving that it did not seem as if he *could* die.'

When the impact of her new loss struck her, it was 'simply awful . . . John's long and weary illness had made him the object of all my thoughts, plans, hopes, fears, interests. . . . Was it not strange', she asked Ella, 'that so late in life and so unwillingly on my part the unequalled unselfish devotion and increasing beauty of his character should win my *whole* heart and that then he should leave me?' Her morbid obsession with Hennie's death had blighted the first year of their marriage; it had been mitigated only by the onset of her husband's fatal illness; during his endurance of that illness, he had truly won her heart; now she had lost him – and that loss too was tinged with guilt because she had not responded earlier to his love, had never rested long in its shelter. It is a touching, melancholy story of patience, ill-starred devotion, suffering and sheer misfortune.

III

Back in Tobermory, Isabella wore the sad garb of mourning again, again tended 'Henrietta's poor', again sorted through heart-rending memorabilia of the beloved beset by 'rushes of desolation', and then, painfully, turned her thoughts forward. She had, she told John Murray, 'ample' financial means and was 'absolutely without any ties so that I can, if any measure of strength returns, shape the remainder of my life as I please'. (And she, who so dearly loved freedom, must have felt some small stir of pleasure in her newly unencumbered state.) 'But I am no longer young and shall never be as strong as I was and shall never have the same spirit. As to travelling, that is a subject which I hope to consult you about. . . . After a time it may seem desirable, but I should not be inclined, as my last great journey before settling quietly in my own country, to do anything that is not very well worth doing, and which would not enable me to bring back a rich cargo of knowledge. When I have thought of travelling and when my husband and I talked it over, it has always been of Asia that I have thought and of that country which lies between China and N. India.' Later she again pursues the theme, proposing a tour of medical missions, 'with the object of taking and sending home private notes of the working of each with the variation in the mode of working . . . The scheme commends itself to me from my beloved husband's and my own very deep interest in medical missions, and from my desire to erect a memorial to him in the shape of a medical hospital.'

And so she began to erect the elaborate façade of reasonable and virtuous motives for the wild escape she planned: she was going for a *last* journey, she would secure 'a cargo of knowledge', she was going to inspect missions, to build memorials. She was going because it was her only chance of health and happiness, but that she did not dare admit, because it was such an ignobly selfish reason, compared with the consistently selfless deeds of the beloved dead. In practical preparation, she took a three-month course of nursing training at St Mary's Hospital, Paddington, and she reactivated her journalistic talents with some on-the-spot reports for *Murray's Magazine* on the latest bout of Irish troubles. On her return, she confessed to Mr Murray, 'my health improved very much in Ireland. I became more vigorous and enterprising daily . . . It is rather a sad fact – but rough knocking about, open-air life in combination with sufficient interest is the one in which my health and spirits are best.'

Even so, her long siege of grief and anxiety had left her bruised, cantankerous, uncertain of her physical and mental capabilities, and she procrastinated, fearing the outcome. Acting on impulse, she bought a house in Maida Vale, London, which she purposed to use partly 'as an invalid home'. A Derbyshire farmer was her 'first patient'; a 'person from the East End' her second. Isabella was a poor judge of her own psychology; she never accepted that she was truly not cut out to be an angel of mercy, or that, though she could cope admirably in a log-cabin with a couple of buckets, a pinewood fire and a hunk of venison, she was quite incapable of establishing smooth and viable domestic arrangements for herself in such a place as Maida Vale. The house brought only disappointment, melancholy, 'carking cares', and she sold it within a year. 'I surrounded myself with my relics, thinking that I might find a sort of ghostly companionship in them and that I might make my house useful in entertaining guests who could not "recompense" me', she explained. 'Both these plans have failed – the relics mock me and the guests are too great a fatigue . . . The cottage at Tobermory will then be home, if any place can be home to one so frightfully bereft.'

For a few months she again teetered on the verge of total emotional collapse. 'In truth unrest had seized her', Anna Stoddart surmised, 'and she mistook its fever for the misery of solitude.' In this precarious state, Isabella even quarrelled with the abiding shelter of the established Church, deploring its 'reactionary tendency . . . The church of my fathers has cast me out by means of inanities, puerilities, music and squabbles', she whined petulantly. So she turned to the nonconformists and underwent what Miss Stoddart terms 'the ceremony of immersion without joining the Baptist body'. It was a special arrangement apparently, and Isabella makes no further mention of any particular attachment to the sect. Added to her spiritual turmoil was the continued plague of ill-health. Doctors diagnosed rheumatic gout, 'threatened rheumatic fever', said her heart 'was much affected' and that she would never regain much strength. Nevertheless, she told Murray in the summer of 1888, 'I hope in a few months I shall gain enough to embolden me to carry out a scheme of travel which has been simmering in my mind ever since I was left alone.'

Back again at Tobermory, where the salt winds tossed the rows of sweet peas and pinks in Hennie's gentle bower, she was sewing a 'complete outfit' of Jaeger flannel, reading books about the 'country which lies between China and N. India' – and giving lectures to the local young women on 'Dress', 'Thrift' and 'Courtesy'. When, late that autumn, she bolted the door and shuttered the windows of the cottage shrine, she resolutely pushed grief away from her at last. 'When I leave the dear ones here I shall feel as if the bitterness of death was past', she wrote in January 1889, just before she sailed. 'The voyage will be a strange time, a silent interval between the familiar life which lies behind . . . and the strange unknown life which lies before. I wish you could see my outfit, packed in four small boxes, 20″ long, 12″ high, 12″ wide, and a brown waterproof bag containing a canvas stretcher bed, a cork mattress, blankets, woollen sheets and a *saddle*!'

Part Three

❧ ❧ ❧ ❧ ❧ ❧

A LADY'S LIFE
ON THE BACK OF YAK,
PONY, MULE AND STALLION;
ON JUNK, WUPAN, STEAMER,
SAMPAN;
IN TENT, STABLE,
HUT, CARAVANSERAI;
ACROSS THE DESERTS,
AND OVER THE PLAINS
AND UP THE MOUNTAINS

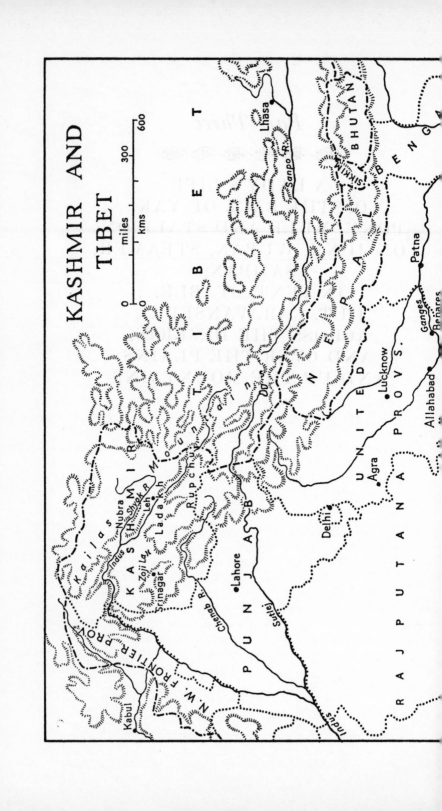

CHAPTER VII

Kashmir and Tibet

MRS ISABELLA BISHOP, in bleak and empty mood, was bound for one of the bleakest, emptiest lands in the world – Tibet. She had no one especially to preserve herself for any longer; she was footloose to a new, alarming, depressing degree. Now Hennie was dead, there was no one with whom her travels could be truly shared. 'I feel most keenly the difference between this and former journey', she told her publisher in a letter from Tibet. 'My sister seems to die afresh with everything I see and the enjoyment, though not the *interest* of travel has died out.' She was prone to emotional over-dramatisation, and in fact quite a few rays of pure, forgetful, exultant pleasure still shine from her books, but there was a significant change of emphasis. Her later letters are not so spontaneous, uninhibited or personal as those written to Hennie; never again had she to concentrate every faculty in the effort of conveying each immediate nuance of her experience in order to send it home to her sister fresh, intact, with the bloom still on it. She was keeping a sort of diary for six friends, she told Murray, but no friends, however dear, could command such emotional allegiance; they were not 'with her in spirit' as she went. And, for her last two major works, she reluctantly relinquished the 'letter' form altogether.

So, from now on, it was principally *interest* that sustained her, a highly developed and trained interest that continued to broaden and invigorate her intellect as she grew older; but which did not quite compensate for the loss of that outgoing and candid joy. Compared with her earlier writings, the three full-length books that Isabella wrote after her sister's death are heavier to pick up and harder to appreciate. They are increasingly authoritative and contain considerable insight into the moral, political and social structures that frame people's lives, but there is less detail about her relationships with individual personalities. They are not however dull, for Isabella's interest illuminates them, that lucid, careful, responsive attention to every detail of the immediate environment which never failed her and made her one of the great travel-writers of her day.

During the spring of 1889 which she spent in Kashmir, Mrs Bishop's interest was focused on the founding of a mission hospital at Srinagar. It was to be called the John Bishop Memorial Hospital – a fitting tribute to the man. During her later years, and partly from the proceeds of her books, she financed the establishment of several other hospitals and orphanages in various parts of the East, most of them staffed by qualified medical missionaries and under the trusteeship of the Church Missionary Society. Her personal tastes were simple, and these institutions were her single extravagance – if the term is appropriate to describe these acts of generous and disinterested private benevolence. Present day opinion looks askance at the evangelical stratagem of the medical mission, where, it has been said, 'the heathen sick were bribed with the promise of Christian health'. But it should be remembered that during the nineteenth century there were certainly few other places where the poor of the East could hope to receive skilled, sophisticated medical attention. Mission staff were invariably tireless workers, they soothed diseased eyes, prodded tumours out of diseased flesh, strengthened rickety limbs, cleansed festered sores. Even if the patients were surrounded by texts from the New Testament and did have to recite a short prayer before receiving their medicine, it was a small price to pay – and usually the only one, for benefactors such as Isabella footed the bills.

Once the construction of the hospital was under way, there was little to detain Isabella in Srinagar and much to send her away. By mid-June Kashmir was 'in season': 'There is an English hubbub most monstrous and the wretched coolies are beaten and cheated and lawn tennis, polo and horse racing, which have been played out below, invade the most secluded valleys, and the country is over-run by tourists and sportsmen from the plains', she complained bitterly – and if there was one thing Isabella never could stand it was the bray of the upper-middle-class English on selfish pleasure bent. So she planned escape. She hired a Punjabi interpreter, a willing Kashmiri lad called Mando, and three mules and drivers for a shilling a day each, to carry camping equipment, folding chair and bedding. She was provided, perforce, with an 'escort' made up of one Afghan soldier from the local Maharajah's troop of irregular mercenaries. 'This man, Usman Shah, was a stage ruffian in appearance. He wore a turban of prodigious height ornamented with poppies or birds' feathers, loved fantastic colours and ceaseless change of raiment, walked in front of me carrying a big sword over his shoulder, plundered and beat the people, terrified the women and was eventually recognised at Leh as a murderer and as great a ruffian in reality as he was in appearance.' She concluded drily, 'An attendant of this kind is a mistake.'

Remedy and crown among her new acquisitions was Gyalpo, a buoyant, silver-grey Arab steed 'as light as a greyhound and as strong as a cart-horse. He was higher in the scale of intellect than any horse of my acquaintance. His cleverness at times suggested reasoning power, and his mischievousness a sense of humour. He walked five miles an hour, jumped like a deer, climbed like a yak, was strong and steady in perilous fords, tireless, hardy, hungry, frolicked along ledges of precipices and over crevassed glaciers, was absolutely fearless , and his slender legs and the use he made of them were the marvel of all. He was quite untameable, rejected all dainties with indignation, swung his heels into people's faces when they went near him, ran at them with his teeth, seized unwary passers-by by their *kamar bands* and shook them as a dog shakes a rat, would let no one go near him but Mando, for whom he formed at first sight a most singular attachment, but kicked and struck with his forefeet, his eyes all the time dancing with fun, so that one could never decide whether his ceaseless pranks were play or vice . . . I was never weary of watching him, the curves of his form were so exquisite, his movements so lithe and rapid, his small head and restless little ears so full of life and expression, the variations in his manner so frequent, one moment savagely attacking some unwary stranger with a scream of rage, the next laying his lovely head against Mando's cheek with a soft cooing sound and a childlike gentleness . . . His wild eyes were like those of a seagull. He had no kinship with humanity.' 'He was not exactly an old woman's horse', she added in a letter, 'but I contrive to get on with him.'

Mrs Bishop and her colourful company left Srinagar at the end of June, and she quickly imposed a strict daily marching routine upon them all. This she did during all her later journeys by allotting fixed hours for travelling, eating, pitching tents and so on. It makes her sound something of a martinet, but it was an effective way of enforcing her authority as a lone woman over assorted coolies, guides, muleteers. Thus, as they followed bridle-tracks that spiralled 13,000 feet high over the Kashmiri mountains, the order of the day was: 'In bed before nine; tea and toast at six; dress, pack, start with the Afghan and *seis* (groom) at seven – having sent on a coolie eight miles with the servants' square tent, the luncheon basket with rice, hard-boiled eggs, cold tea, and cherries, and my cork mattress. Halt at ten; pitch the tent, lie down for two and a half hours (such a luxury but for the proximity of things that creep), and go on again for another hour . . .' And on and on, among spruce forests and valleys starred with white jasmine, until they reached a treeless region spiked with 'mountains of bare gravel and red rock, grey crags, stretches of green turf, sunlit peaks with their snows . . . eastwards and beyond a long valley filled with a snowfield fringed with pink primulas; and that was CENTRAL ASIA'. She writes it like that, in defiant, triumphant capitals, to remind herself of John Bishop's wry comment that it was 'the only formidable rival' to him in Isabella's heart. She had lost him; but Central Asia at least she would have.

The part of the promised land she chose to explore first was Ladakh, a part of western Tibet that since 1841 had been a dependency of Kashmir. The province was governed, with varying degrees of inefficiency, by Kashmiri officials; Her Britannic Majesty's Commissioner resided in Leh, its capital, for four months a year only; its boundaries, in defiance of the British urge for definition, were still ambiguous. For most of the nineteenth century the Tibetan government, under Chinese suzerainty, had adamantly refused to allow foreigners access to 'Tibet proper', and thus the country had become to the West a symbol of the ultimately remote and mysterious in the generally remote and mysterious East. Not that all foreigners obeyed the prohibition, for, as the historian Sir Thomas Holdich says, 'The chronicles of Tibetan exploration are full of the records of vain attempts to unveil the mysteries surrounding that holy of Buddhist holies –

the city of Lhasa.' A few intrepid European explorers, missionaries and spies of the Indian government had penetrated the forbidden barriers; all suffered great hardship and some did not return. Isabella, however, seems not to have succumbed to this 'Lhasa or bust' fever, and perhaps she was wise, for, again according to Holdich, when the 'veil was torn aside' by the members of the Younghusband Expedition in 1904, mysterious Lhasa proved to be but 'a scattered unkempt and ill-regulated town full of impurities, infested with savage dogs, obscene pigs and night prowlers revelling in many most unholy institutions'.

Anyway, when Isabella was in the area, the veil was still untorn, and the outlying provinces of Ladakh and Baltistan were under the 'protection' of the Indian government in order to keep that section of the precious Himalayan frontier cushioned off from unpredictable, Chinese-infiltrated Tibet. Not that the Ladakhis knew or cared much about such great-power manoeuvres. They continued to trade extensively with China and Russia, and to a smaller extent with India; their country was geographically and climatically part of Tibet; they owed all their cultural, moral and religious allegiance to the Dalai Lama in Lhasa. So, though most of Isabella's explorations were confined to Ladakh and neighbouring provinces, she was justified in calling her writings on the subject *Among the Tibetans*.

She met her first Tibetans at the village of Shergol, near the Kashmiri border, and at that point 'the intensely human interest of the journey began'. In place of the handsome, cringing, sullen Kashmiris she was greeted by the 'ugly, short, squat, yellow-skinned, flat-nosed, oblique-eyed, uncouth-looking' Shergolians, to whom she at once took. The headman courteously showed her the local sights: 'a *gonpo* or monastery built into the rock with a brightly coloured front, and three *chörten* or relic-holders painted blue, red and yellow and daubed with coarse arabesques and representations of deities, one having a striking resemblance to Mr Gladstone'. The 'sights' were religious; in Tibet they always were.

Each dim and smelly home into which Isabella was invited had its shelf of wooden gods, each village its *chörtens*, its statues of Buddha, its prayer-wheels – revolving wooden cylinders filled with rolls of paper inscribed with prayers. The cylinders were frequently

turned by the villagers, who muttered, as they did so, the universal prayer, *Om mani padme hum* (O jewel in the lotus O). This oddly
appealing mystic formula was the legend, anthem, ave maria,
slogan, charm of the people, its continual repetition was a means
of acquiring merit, its delineation on wood, stone or paper a
philanthropic act. It was inscribed everywhere: on cotton banners
in the market-place, on cliff-sides, on personal seals, on large
slabs of tinted butter, on monastery bells, bridges, pebbles. In
some villages there were a hundred or more prayer-wheels in a
row, each emblazoned with '*om mani*' and with more '*om manis*'
churning out of them, some so large that water power was used
to revolve them. Said a British missionary who had lived there, 'If
you were to introduce steam-power into Tibet tomorrow, probably
the first use made of it would be to turn a prayer-wheel.'

The continual hum of devotion that vibrated through the bleak
land twanged into a positive cacophony inside the *gonpos*, whence
blasted a daily oratorio of religious music. Each *gonpo* sheltered
some three hundred lamas, and Isabella estimates that the total
lama population in Ladakh alone was at least 11,000. They were
everywhere. Some were solitary, unaffiliated wanderers, 'travelling
without any end in view', said one historian, 'so that the places
they reach are always those they sought'; others, who dwelt in the
monasteries, went jovially in companies – 'Passing along faces of
precipices and over waterless plateaux of blazing red gravel . . .
the journey was cheered by the meeting of red and yellow lamas
. . . each lama twirling his prayer-cylinder, abbots and *skushoks*
(the latter believed to be incarnations of Buddha) with many
retainers or gay groups of priestly students, intoning in harsh and
high-pitched monotones, *Om mani padme hum*.' 'The lama', wrote
William Carey, a well-known traveller in Tibet, 'holds the people
in the hollow of his hand and many forces meet in that magnetic
and masterful grip.' The forces were Buddhism, Hinduism and
demon-worship; they spawned in the mind of the average lama
a nightmarish chaos of gods, devils, hobgoblins and saints.
Dressed in filthy petticoat-like robes of yellow or red (according
to sect) and pointed hat tricked out with coloured feathers,
tassels and trailing flaps, carrying holy water in a leathern bottle,
pen, purse, and *dorje* (dumb-bell-shaped badge of office symbolising
a thunderbolt) the lama, ignorant, idle and unscrupulous as he

204

sometimes was, embodied the learning, culture and wealth of the
land.

Lamas were the only Tibetans permitted to read the nation's
sacred literature, which was contained in volumes of exquisite
parchment, that, according to Isabella, 'when divested of their
silken and brocade wrappings' often contained 'nothing better
than fairy tales and stories of doubtful morality'. Lamas produced
most of the country's music, or what she terms 'the wild dissonance' that resulted from the warble of silver horns, the thunder
of yak-skin drums, the whistle of conch-shells, the boom of a
golden gong. Lamas alone could divine the future, by interpreting
the 'meaning' of the cracks that appeared in the shoulder-blade
of a sheep after it had been charred. Thus they were indispensable
for every enterprise – the trading of China tea for Kashmiri silks,
the sowing of barley-seed, the celebration of birth, marriage,
death, all would surely fail unless they had the lama's blessing.
William Carey conjures up the eerie appearance of the Tibetan
holy man when he writes, 'In any other environment the lama
would be merely a dirty and revolting pretender. But strutting in
that wild theatre with his trumpet of human thigh-bone at his
lips and a skull in his hand, he is the very embodiment of the
spirit that haunts the mountains and broods over the wide
inhospitable deserts and makes a sport of men. It is the spirit of
awe and mystery that smites the heart with panic and congeals
the blood. And this is the enchantment with which the land is
enchanted.'

Such a country, subjugated and dedicated to this consuming
religious spirit, would seem stony ground indeed for the Christian
missionary, but there were the resolute few, as Isabella found when
she eventually reached Leh. On the way to the capital, her expedition crossed arid mountain ridges where the lowest valleys were
more than 11,000 feet high. By day the sun banged down un-
hindered through the rarefied air, shuddered above the rocks and
cooked up a temperature between 120° and 130°; at night the
mercury slithered below zero. 'I did not suffer from the climate,'
Isabella explained, 'but in the case of most Europeans, the air
passages become irritated, the skin cracks, and after a time the
action of the heart is affected. The hair when released stands out
from the head, leather shrivels and splits, horn combs break to

pieces, food dries up, rapid evaporation renders water-colour sketching nearly impossible and tea made with water from 15 to 20 degrees below the boiling-point is flavourless and flat.'

After a 160-mile 'delightful journey' in these conditions, she saw Leh in the distance, a flat-roofed, squat, vermilion and brown town huddled below a range of 18,000-foot-high mountains and encircled by a plain of blazing-hot gravel. She was expected, for the Tibetans had their own bush telegraph to report the movements of such a rare bird as a female foreigner, and so she was met at the city gates by 'the wazir's *jemadar* or head of police, in artistic attire with attendants in apricot turbans, violet *chogas* and green leggings, who cleared the way with spears, Gyalpo, frolicking as merrily and as ready to bite, and the Afghan [Usman Shah] striding in front as firmly as though they had not marched for twenty-five days through the rugged passes of the Himalayas'. Though Isabella, in her dusty tweed suit, could not compete with the gay motley of the police escort, Usman Shah did his best on her behalf. As she had noted earlier, the little swashbuckler had exploded into rainbows of colour as the journey progressed. At first he wore, 'black or white leggings wound round from ankle to knee with broad bands of orange or scarlet serge, white cambric knicker-bockers, a white cambric shirt with a short white muslin frock with hanging sleeves and a leather girdle over it, a red-peaked cap with a dark blue *pagri* wound round it, with one end hanging over his back, earrings, necklace, bracelets and a profusion of rings'. Later, 'he blossomed into blue and white muslin with a scarlet sash, wore a gold embroidered peak and a huge white muslin turban, with much change of ornaments, and appeared frequently with a great bunch of poppies or a cluster of crimson roses surmounting all'.

Thus flamboyantly preceded, Isabella rode to the bungalow of the British Joint Commission in Leh. The Commissioner was absent, but she was soon called upon by one of the city's very few permanent white residents, Mr Redslob of the Moravian Mission. Redslob, a large, cheery German, and linguist, artist, botanist, scholar of all things Tibetan, had spent twenty-five years in the country, during which he and his colleagues had been beating their evangelical heads almost entirely in vain against the unyielding walls of lamaism. Among his successes in Leh were a school, a hospital and a printing press for Tibetan translations of the Gospels. During his visit, jolly Mr Redslob told Isabella some of this, and also asked if she would like to accompany him on a journey to the northern province of Nubra. This meant leaving the capital she had just reached almost immediately, but she did not hesitate, for she was still as ready to go further from 'civilisation' as she had been when offered the chance to visit the Malay States from Singapore ten years before. And anyway, her impromptu expeditions often turned out best.

II

Isabella had intended to take Usman Shah on her new adventure, but unfortunately Leh was the end of the road for that colourful buccaneer. While she was sketching his fantastic rig-out that same afternoon, he was recognised by the chief of police as one of a gang of mercenaries who had plundered the town and mortally stabbed an officer but a few months before. So tiny unrepentant Usman, still swaggering, was marched out of town, and Isabella was a little sorry, for he had been completely faithful to her in his fashion and was such fun to look at – though she shuddered to recall how often she had been completely at the mercy of that bright jewelled scimitar he always carried over his shoulder.

The next day, she, Redslob and a scholarly monk called Gergan began their ascent of the Kailas mountain range that lay between the capital and Nubra province. Before nightfall, they reached an altitude of 18,000 feet, men and beasts (but not woman) suffering dreadfully from mountain sickness and wild Gyalpo 'stopping every few yards, gasping with blood trickling from his nostrils and turning his head to look at me, with the question in his eyes, "What does this mean?" ' The following dawn a series of 'gruntings and low resonant bellowings' outside the tent announced the arrival of a new animal in Isabella's life – the yak. He was a beast of uncertain temper, sturdy, hairy, his ferocious eyes glinting from under a tangle of black curls, given to barging at a prospective rider with his thick curved horns, and to 'executing fantastic movements on the ledges of precipices', when the rider was actually astride. He disdained the plough, but condescended to carry burdens when led by a rope through the nostrils, and,

usefully, he thrived at altitudes above 11,000 feet. The yak was to
the Tibetan what the bear was to the Ainu, the buffalo to the
Indian – provider of all good things. The people put yak fat in
their cakes, yak meat in their stews, yak butter in their tea and
yak dung on their fires; yak skins made carpets and tents; long
yak hair was dyed red and exported to China where it was used to
decorate the hats of a certain class of mandarin; bushy yak tails
were set in silver-tipped antelope horn and exported to India
where princes in their carriages used them to fan away the flies.

Isabella's first yak was deceptively quiet and looked almost
elegant with her well-worn Mexican saddle and striped blanket
thrown among rather than upon his shaggy locks. 'His back
seemed as broad as that of an elephant, and with his slow, sure,
resolute step, he was like a mountain in motion.' Mounted thus,
she crossed the precipitous Digar Pass in a snowstorm and
descended into the valley below. It was strange terrain: wolves
lurked among the tamarisk thickets, yellow gorges cut deep into
the yellow gravel of the rock, patches of loose-grained barley and
lucerne sprouted about the villages, and trading cravans, following the route to Yarkand, slithered down from the glaciers to
ford the ice-grey Shyok River that roared in full summer spate.
On the outward journey, the party were poled across the Shyok
in a leaky scow, but on their return, after a week of wandering
among the mountain villages, they learned that the scow had been
totally wrecked in the rapids two days before, and they would just
have to wade. That night, round a camp fire, a noisy group of
'water guides' and local headmen cheerfully informed them that
the waters were rising steadily as the glaciers above melted, and
the consensus seemed to be that the fragile little foreign lady on
her 'spider-legged' horse would never reach the far bank alive.

However, unless Isabella wished to spend the next few months
in the valley, there was no choice; and the next morning, under a
magnesium-white sun that was unhelpfully dissolving the snow-
fields at an ever-increasing rate, they prepared for the crossing.
A friendly headman pressed upon Isabella the loan of a huge
Yurkand horse, 'which nearly proved fatal'; the Tibetan servants
knelt on the banks and prayed for safety; Mando and the interpreter, white-lipped with terror, wore dark goggles so they might
not see the booming surge; everyone dashed quantities of the

ice-cold water over their faces 'to prevent giddiness'; girths were tightened, loads hoisted higher, and with shouts of encouragement the whole caravan plunged in. Isabella's horse was led by one of the 'water guides' – near-naked brown creatures who 'with elf-locks and pigtails streaming from their heads and their uncouth yells and wild gesticulations looked like true river-demons'. 'Louder grew the yells as the torrent raged more hoarsely, the chorus of the water guides grew frantic, the water was up to the man's armpits and the seat of my saddle, my horse tottered and swerved many times, the nearing shore presented an abrupt bank underscooped by the stream. There was a deeper plunge, an encouraging shout, and Mr Redslob's strong horse leapt the bank. The men encouraged mine; he made a desperate effort, but fell short and rolled over backwards, into the Shyok with his rider under him. A struggle, a moment of suffocation, and I was extricated by strong arms, to be knocked down again by the rush of the water, to be again dragged up and hauled and hoisted up the crumbling bank. I escaped with a broken rib and some severe bruises, but the horse was drowned.' Mr Redslob and the guides were so upset by the accident that she felt bound to make light of it, saying that it was the sort of thing for which one must be prepared when wandering about in Central Asia.

And certainly the fording of Tibetan rivers was a notoriously hazardous business, and western travellers have told several chilling tales on the theme. The chilliest comes from the 1840s and is told by the lively Jesuit missionary Abbé Huc, who, with one companion, made the extremely arduous and perilous journey across Mongolia and eastern Tibet to Lhasa. At one stage, the missionaries' caravan had to ford twelve wide branches of a half-frozen river during the night. 'Ice cracked in all directions', Huc explained, 'animals stumbled and splashed up the water and men shouted and vociferated . . . When day broke, the Holy Embassy was still dabbling in the water, and when re-formed at last on the opposite bank, it presented a truly ludicrous appearance. Men and animals were all covered with icicles. The horses walked on very dolefully, evidently much incommoded by their tails, which hung down, all in a mass, stiff and motionless as though they had been made of lead instead of hair. The long hair on the legs of the camels had become magnificent icicles which knocked one against the other as the animals advanced, with harmonious discord . . . As to the long-haired oxen [yaks] they were regular caricatures; nothing can be conceived more ludicrous than their appearance as they slowly advanced with legs separated to the utmost possible width in order to admit of an enormous system of stalactites which hung from their bellies to the ground. The poor brutes had been rendered so perfectly shapeless by the agglomeration of icicles with which they were covered, that they looked as though they were preserved in sugar candy.'

Compared to this, Isabella's crossing, though painful, was comparatively easy, and after it they all camped in some apricot orchards to recuperate. 'There I put into practice what I had learned about broken ribs in St Mary's Hospital', she told John Murray, and it must have been most effective, for she makes no further mention of her injury. In the orchards, bundles of gold fruit swung above their heads and they were welcome to eat as much as they wanted, provided they returned the vital stones to the proprietor. From the stones' kernels women were extracting drops of clear fragrant precious oil that was used to illuminate the shrine-lamps which burned before all those dusty-gilt Buddhas. Babies were given balls of apricot oil and barley mush to suck and their mothers oiled their grubby little bodies with it instead of washing them. The dirtiness of the Tibetan was as legendary as the perils of his rivers. His was not the fecund, loose, shifting dirt of the tropics, but the barren, hard-glazed, ancient filth of a life-time that no apricot oil could hope to dislodge. An eighteenth-century English traveller, George Bogle, recorded that he once prevailed upon a Tibetan woman to wash her child's face so that he could see the true colour of its skin. The infant, he says, nearly died of convulsions. 'As for the garments of the Tibetan', remarked William Carey, 'they are a zoological perserve.' But this, the people thought, was as it should be, for didn't the old proverb tell them that lice and riches went together and he who divested himself of the former was doomed to lose the latter also?

In these circumstances, wise Isabella always slept in her own tent, except at the village of Hundar, home of Gergan the monk, which they reached the next day. Redslob had been there before and the whole population turned out to greet them. At Gergan's house, 'Everything was prepared for us. The mud floors were swept, cotton quilts were laid down on the balconies, blue corn-flowers and marigolds were in all the rooms and the women were loaded with coarse jewellery' – turquoise amulets, silver and brass bangles. It was a typical land-owner's dwelling, built of stone and sun-dried brick, its ceilings of peeled poplar rods, its living-room floor of split white pebbles set in clay, in the centre of which stood a clay fireplace with brass cooking-pots, bars for roasting barley and a large wooden churn. This was in constant use for the making of that abominable Tibetan tea which only a few stalwart foreigners learned to love. Isabella gives the recipe: 'For six persons. Boil a teacupful of tea in three pints of water for ten minutes with a heaped dessert-spoonful of soda. Put the infusion into the churn with one pound of butter and a small tablespoonful of salt. Churn until as thick as cream', – and then slurp from bowl. Often, a mush of parched barley was added to the brew to form a sodden brown tea-ball which was then eaten rather than drunk. To the westerner's palate, the butter was rank with the flavour of the ancient goatskins in which it had been too long kept.

The skins and other stores were kept in the small dark rooms that opened off the main living-room, above which, Isabella continues, 'were the balconies and reception rooms. Wooden posts supported the roofs, and these were wreathed with lucerne, the first fruits of the field. Narrow steep staircases in all Tibetan houses lead to the family rooms. In winter the people live below, alongside of the animals and fodder. In summer they sleep in loosely built booths of poplar branches on the roof. Gergan's roof was covered, like others at the time, to the depth of two feet with hay, i.e. grass and lucerne, which are wound into long ropes, experience having taught the Tibetans that their scarce fodder is best preserved thus from breakage and waste. I bought hay by the yard for Gyalpo.

'Our food in this hospitable house was simple: apricots, fresh or dried and stewed with honey; *zho*'s milk, curds and cheese, sour cream, peas, beans, balls of barley dough, barley porridge, and "broth of abominable things".' The people pressed this fare upon her and were jolly, friendly and most anxious to amuse her. She liked their broad placid faces and easy ways, though she could not but deplore their polyandrous marital arrangements. (In other parts of Tibet, according to other authorities, polygamy was the rule instead, but allied to a system of 'temporary marriage' – a state of affairs which an American traveller uncompromisingly described as little removed from promiscuity, which is, after all, but "indefinite polyandry joined with indefinite polygamy" '). Anyway in Hundar, according to Isabella, who checked her facts with Redslob, only the eldest son might marry and the bride 'accepts all his brothers as inferior or subordinate husbands . . . all children being regarded as legally the property of the eldest son, who is addressed by them as "Big Father", his brothers receiving the title of "Little Father" '. The system might logically lead to a superfluity of women, but Isabella does not mention this – perhaps the Tibetan spinster moved to a polygamous district, or found some consolation in Leh, where there was a large colony of Moslem merchants. The married women at any rate were convinced adherents of the system and sympathised greatly with Isabella in her dismally manless state. Monogamy, they explained, must be a very tedious affair and might result in one's becoming a 'widow' – a term of abuse and reproach hurled only at men and animals!

Perhaps in these circumstances of domestic rivalry between the various sizes of brother, a husband had to woo his shared bride constantly, which may account for the exceptional charm of some Tibetan love-songs. This excerpt, translated by a colleague of Redslob's, suggests the prevailing tone which, with its hyperbolic promises of eternal devotion, is oddly reminiscent of a musical-comedy lyric:

> If she, taking the shape of a turquoise dove,
> Should go to soar in the highest skies,
> I, taking the shape of a white falcon,
> Will go to take her home again . . .
> If she, taking the shape of the fish gold-eye
> Should go to float in the deepest ocean,
> I, taking the shape of a white-breasted otter,
> Will go to take her home again . . .

Polyandry also brought different divisions of labour between the sexes. Men wove all the family clothes from the hair of sheep, goat and yak; men also ploughed, and the women followed breaking up the clods. Women cooked the everyday 'coolie soup' of dried apricots and spread dung on their house-roofs to dry for fuel. Junior husbands served as yak-drivers, goatherds and churners of the abominable butter. And, in times of discord, men and women beat each other.

The life was pretty rough, but Isabella saw no dire poverty, and the villagers pressed gifts upon her because she was in Redslob's company. 'He drew the best out of them', she declared. 'Their superstitions and beliefs were not to him "rubbish" but subjects for minute investigation and study.' Consequently he had made many friends, though few converts, and even had *entrée* to the nearby monastery of Deskyid, and arranged for Isabella to accompany him thither, – a rare privilege for a female foreigner.

Deskyid, at an altitude of 11,000 feet, was jumbled on top of a perpendicular spur, a 'vast irregular pile of red, white and yellow temple towers, storehouses, cloisters, galleries and balconies rising for three hundred feet one above another, hanging over chasms, built out on wooden buttresses, and surmounted with flags, tridents and yaks' tails'. The main temple, dedicated to 'Wrath and Justice', suggested to her a hideous inferno: 'Demon masks of ancient lacquer hung from the pillars, naked swords gleamed in motionless hands, and in a deep recess, whose "darkness was rendered visible" by one lamp, was that indescribable horror the executioner of the Lord of Hell, his many brandished arms holding the intruments of torture, and before him the bell, the thunderbolt and sceptre, the holy water and baptismal flagon. Our joss-sticks fumed on the still air, monks waved censers, and blasts of dissonant music woke the semi-subterranean echoes.' In the incense-sodden chapel of meditation some lamas were mumbling over their rosaries in a way that the Tibetans themselves likened to the purr of an elderly cat. Their rosary beads came in several exotic varieties: yellow ones from the seeds of a rare Chinese tree, bony ones made from snake spines or discs cut from human skulls, red sandalwood ones, nut-brown beany ones or specially efficacious little nodules dug out of an elephant's brain. The object of the prolonged rosary-telling was to plunge the devotee into a state of ecstatic contemplation, and though a few seemed very pious, Isabella suspected that the majority were 'idle and unholy'.

Unholiness commonly took the form of extortion, for which a

lama had ample opportunity. For instance, when attending a funeral his task was to read aloud from a sacred book during the mourning feast – and this he would gabble at the highest possible speed because he was paid by the page. Another of his functions was to exorcise evil spirits from the sick. Again he was paid according to the amount of effort involved. This often resulted in a poor man having but one easily-ousted demon in residence, while a rich man was likely to have been invaded by two or three most tenacious major devils and a whole legion of little servitor hobgoblins who took a very long time to dislodge.

After seeing the temples, Redslob entered into a good-natured disputation on religious matters with the monastery's abbot. The monks in attendance laughed 'sneeringly' at the foreigner's efforts – perhaps at his sheer effrontery. But Redslob persevered as he always had, and pressed a copy of the Gospel according to St John upon the abbot, who observed that St Matthew, which Redslob had left on a previous visit, had 'made very laughable reading'. Perhaps, for the abbot, gospel wit lay partly in its stunning brevity: the equivalent Tibetan sacred work ran to a hundred and eight volumes of 1083 pages each and twelve yaks were needed to carry it.

III

A few days after their expedition to Deskyid, Redslob and Isabella returned to Leh through snowstorms that made it seem as if the very mountains were falling apart. The cold was of the searing kind in which metal would stick to the fingers and the skin be torn off in its removal. The scenery was awe-inspiring: scintillating spires and plains of snow stabbed with dramatic flares of colour – blotches of rose-red primulas, sheets of edelweiss, a chasm of ice-green water, a golden eagle feeding on the carcass of a black horse. They ascended a 17,500-foot-high glacier by means of narrow slippery ledges cut into the ice by their guides, and, as even Gyalpo's clever steely legs were unequal to the challenge, she again rode yak-back.

The descent was a miserable stumble down miles of crumbling zigzags, and it was a pity that they couldn't have tried instead the 'glissade' method much appreciated by Abbé Huc in similar circumstances. First, he tells us, one of his 'yaks advanced to the edge of the ice and blowing through his large nostrils some thick clouds of vapour, he manfully put his two front feet on the glacier and whizzed off as if he had been discharged from a cannon. He went down the glacier with his legs extended but as stiff and motionless as if they had been made of marble. Arrived at the bottom he turned over and then ran on bounding and bellowing over the snow'. Then it was the good fathers' turn: 'We seated ourselves carefully on the edge of the glacier, we stuck our heels close together on the ice as firmly as possible then, using the handles of our whips by way of helm, we sailed over those frozen waters with the velocity of a locomotive. A sailor would have pronounced us to be going at least twelve knots an hour. In our many travels we had never before experienced a mode of conveyance at once so commodious, so expeditious and above all so refreshing!' It sounds a pretty tall travellers' tale too – but how funny it must have looked, and how Isabella would have enjoyed a similar slide.

However, she returned conventionally to the capital astride Gyalpo and pitched her tent for a fortnight close to the British Postal Agency. In her absence, tribes of merchants from far-flung parts had arrived and 'the din and stir of trade and amusements ceased not by day or night'. In Leh's huge bazaar 'mules, asses, horses and yaks kicked, squealed and bellowed; the dissonance of bargaining tongues rose high; there were mendicant monks, Indian fakirs, Moslem dervishes, Mecca pilgrims, itinerant musicians and Buddhist ballad-howlers; bold-faced women with creels of lucerne on their backs and the wazir's *jemadar* and gay attendants moved among the throngs'. And for a while Isabella was there too, breathing its smells of dry fodder, mules' dung, musty saffron and sour curds, absorbing its colours of apricot and brassy gold, rusty red of dried peppers and lamas' robe, slithering emerald of brocade, and feeling the push and jostle of a thousand alien shoulders, the alien stare of a thousand slanting eyes. Under tattered awnings, squat men from veiled Lhasa exchanged incense sticks and sacred medallions (guaranteed to contain the ashes of a genuine holy man) for Kashmiri silks, indigo and wheat; merchants from northern Yarkand, padded in sheepskin and astride stout Turkestan horses, offered hemp and received in return borax, turquoise and deer-musk; thickset traders from Afghanistan, their broad faces creased by the wind, spilled out for sale bales of broadcloth and brassware, and bought, in exchange, the thin bright Tibetan gold.

Gold, Holdich mentions, has been associated with Tibet since the days of Herodotus, who refers, in some wonder, to a well-known travellers' tale about a race of huge black ants that dwelt to the north-west of India and clawed gold-dust out of the mountains. Traders, mounted on swift camels, who occasionally tried to plunder the precious heaps accumulated by the ants were driven away by ferocious animals. The legend, repeated and embroidered by several chroniclers, lingered for centuries; about the middle of the nineteenth century, Indian survey-spies reached the gold-mining districts of western Tibet. There they found miners grovelling in the ground muffled from head to foot in thick black blankets to protect them from the elements; they were scratching dust from the soil with a very primitive tool – a two-pronged antelope horn, which looked very like antennae; around their bleak huts, fierce Tibetan mastiffs kept constant guard. A grain of truth, like a grain of gold, had survived for a long time.

Around the end of August the traders roped up their bales again, counted their gains or losses, beat their steeds into action and went stringing away over the desert or the mountains to points north, south, east and west. And Isabella went too, sad to leave Leh, but fortunate to have seen it in 1889 before its 'civilised amenities' burgeoned. Soon, British interest in Tibet and its neighbours increased, owing to those ineradicable Foreign Office fears about Russian expansionism in Asia, about which Isabella was to hear much. And so, particularly after Lord Curzon became Viceroy of India in 1898, Britain tightened its hold on Ladakh. The bridle-track that Isabella had followed from Kashmir to Leh was widened to cart-width in case of military need, a British Commissioner went to live year-round in the capital, and gatherings for Tea (unbuttered) and Badminton were held in the Residency bungalow. The Commissioner's Visitor's Book became full of names of travelling missionaries, army surveyors, ladies who rode side-saddle from Srinagar, cavalry officers on leave from the Indian hill-stations come up for the huntin'. The British sportsmen shot deer, antelope, wild asses and the elusive ibex when they could sight him, and they invariably brought a fox-terrier with them for company. To accompany the terrier was a coolie whose function was the bearing of a basket in which the animal could rest if it became footsore or started to spin round with mountain-sickness.

From all this clack of too-comprehensible tongues Isabella would have fled as she had fled from the Kashmir season, and perhaps would have been driven on towards the fastnesses of the Tibetan interior. But as it was, she felt she had escaped far enough. On leaving Leh, still astride her wild Gyalpo, she made a detour to the south-eastern Rupchu region, a high-lying gale-torn gravel desert inhabited by nomad Chong pas, wild horses, goats and sheep, then crossed three airless mountain passes and came down to the province of Lahaul or 'British Tibet' as it was often called. There, she was approached by 'a creature in a nondescript dress speaking Hindustani volubly. On a band across his breast were the British crown and a plate with the words, "Commissioner's *chaprassie*, Kulu District". I never felt so extinguished. Liberty seemed lost, and the romance of the desert to have died out in one moment!'

And so she left that harsh and eerie land. Its most characteristic sounds were the spooky shrieks and thumps of monastic music echoing round the rocks, the bray and bellow of wild ass and yak, the thrashing howl of a wind that chilled the marrow and left the scant grass in the valleys brittle as bone, hard as wire; its most characteristic sights were greasy placid peasants chewing sodden barley balls and mumbling incantations before the dim and dirty godshelf, and the pantomime-antics of frenzied lamas twirling prayer-wheels, exorcising demons; looming over all was what William Carey describes as 'that unspeakably solemn horizon of snowy peaks over which a dazed eagle may flutter in convulsive flight or the thin black line of trade slowly crawls, dropping its frozen dead as it goes'.

Carey's writing, like that of several other western travellers, captures this sense of Tibet – its ghostly enchantment, its cruel unresponsiveness, its isolated majesty, its inert, spirit-ridden outlandishness. But Isabella somehow fails to capture the character of the country. She writes about the customs of the people, the work of the few devoted missionaries, the bustle of trade, but it is all a bit too cosy, clean, prosaic. Perhaps she could not bear to plunge so deep at that vulnerable point in her life; perhaps she did not travel far enough. She must have been dissatisfied with her own records of the journey, for the book she had tentatively planned and which, she tells Murray, would have been called *A Lady's Ride through the Western Himalayas* was never written. In 1894 the Religious Tract Society brought out a short unrevised, mapless account of her journey under the title *Among the Tibetans*. It was the only one of her books not published by John Murray (apart from a volume of her Chinese photographs, *Chinese Pictures*, published by Cassell's in 1900) and the one which received, and deserved, the least critical attention.

CHAPTER VIII

Persia and Kurdistan

F ROM Lahaul, Mrs Bishop trotted in leisurely fashion down through the Punjab and reached Simla in mid-October. The height of the summer season was over and the hill-town was cool, mellow, sedate as Cheltenham. It was not at all in Isabella's line and she began to contemplate reluctantly a return to empty England. One day, however, during a lunch at the Residency, she met Major Herbert Sawyer of the International Branch of the Quartermaster's Department of the Indian Army, and he changed all her plans.

Major Sawyer, whom Isabella got to know quite well during the next few months, was an irascible, intelligent, energetic, obstinate, brave man of thirty-eight years. His tall, strikingly handsome, military figure had, Isabella remarks, 'a look of distinction and command, so that people would always say, "Who is that?"' Ordinarily his manner was pleasant, if chill – he seldom took the trouble to know anyone well, a friend of his told her; when roused, he was peppery and outspoken – 'He has a crotchetiness which, of all mental peculiarities, bothers me most', she told a friend, 'and is restless and fitful besides being sarcastic.' She continues, 'He was distracted for the loss of his wife who died in April, but I cannot spend much sympathy on him because the more distracted men are [in contrast to faithful womankind is the implication] the sooner they re-marry!' Sawyer was about to leave India for a geographical-military reconnaissance to parts of western Persia, an area that much interested Isabella, but which she had been dissuaded from visiting by tales of its rigours and perils. It was partly the hope that she might help to ease his 'distraction' with her kindly but unprovocative companionship that persuaded Sawyer to offer her an escort – at least as far as Tehran. And he might also have decided that the company of a patently non-combatant middle-aged lady was an effective 'blind' for certain of his reconnoitring activities which he did not particularly want the Persian government to know about.

Whatever the basic reason, everyone thought that Sawyer's offer was 'the acme of good fortune as a traveller', Isabella wrote in wry amusement. And probably there *were* several bored pretty ladies of Simla who would have adored the chance to risk their all and go galloping away into the wild deserts with dashing, eligible Major Sawyer for company. 'But *I* quite feel that it involves a certain abridgement of my liberty', Isabella points out. 'I should much prefer to travel alone.' And she stipulated that time and tribulation should decide whether or not she accompanied him beyond Tehran into the 'unknown hinterlands'. For she had her reservations about him: she liked his sense of fun, his straight-forward briskness, his manliness; but she knew he would bully anyone if given the chance and 'I am trying feebly to assert myself from the first as my age entitles me to do!' she declared, conjuring a picture of frail and helpless widowhood that could scarcely deceive those who knew her well. It might, at first, have deceived Sawyer; if so, time would undeceive him.

Sawyer's mission to Persia was a minor strategic move in what might be called the Great Game. The Game had been going on for most of the century; its contestants were the Empires of Britain and Russia; its ultimate stakes were the military and economic domination of Central Asia; its biggest single prize, possessed by defensive Britain, threatened, it was thought, by aggressive Russia, was India. 'Without India', wrote George Nathaniel Curzon, 'the British Empire could not exist. The possession of India is the inalienable badge of sovereignty in the eastern hemisphere.' In Curzon's view, almost that entire hemisphere was a sort of great chessboard, a tantalising, unpredictable, tense arena where the wrong move might be disastrous, the right strategy result in greater power, security and prosperity for the British. As early as 1889 Curzon was convinced that the Russian policy was one of hostility and almost limitless expansionism, and that the British, to maintain their supremacy, must meet aggression with aggression.

It was a current nightmare of Curzon's (whose nightmares were undoubtedly political) that on one dreadful day those tough

Black
Sea

Trebizond
(Dec. 12th)

Erzerum

RUSSIA

Caspian
Sea

TURKEY

Bitlis

Van (Oct. 31st)

Urmi
(Oct. 7th-14th)

Kurdistan

R. Euphrates

R. Tigris

Kermanshah

Khannikin

Baghdad
(Jan. 10th)

Hamadan
(Aug. 26th-Sept. 15th)

Kum (Qum)

Tehran
(Feb. 26th-c.March 18th)

Borujird
(Aug. 9th)

Isfahan
(c. April 1st-
April 30th)

Julfa

Ardal

PERSIA

Luristan

Karun R.

Basra

PERSIA
KURDISTAN
AND TURKEY

miles   300

kms   500

patrols that prowled about the bleak and lonely frontiers of the Indian north-west would suddenly spot a row of Cossack fur hats popping up over the nearby mountains – the vanguard of a Russian military avalanche that could roll across Central Asia and penetrate the British defences at one of their weakest points. In 1888 Curzon toured the area and declared that Russian Central Asia was 'a vast armed camp'. His dry, sonorous tones crackled out to the Foreign Office, the India Office, and the readers of *The Times* an abrasive, verbose beadroll of dire omens: Russian railways reached to the shores of the Caspian and Russian ships dominated its waters; Russia had already annexed Transcaspia, Bokhara, Samarkand, to mention but an exotic few, and, most alarmingly of all, the next place on the Czar's list was Persia. The military position of Russia along the entire northern frontier of Persia was already one of unassailable military superiority. 'Whenever Russia desires to enforce with peculiar emphasis some diplomatic demand at Tehran, a mere enumeration of the Russian garrisons within a few hundred miles of the Persian capital is enough to set the Council of Ministers quaking and to make the Sovereign think twice', Curzon wrote in his ponderous, brilliant book, *Persia and the Persian Question*.

He was collecting material for this opus in 1890, which was why, early that January, he was chugging up the Tigris towards Baghdad in the steamer *Mejidieh* and met, on board, a certain Dr Bruce of the Church Missionary Society Mission in Julfa, Major Herbert Sawyer of the Indian Army and his rather unlikely travelling companion, Mrs Isabella Bishop. 'I do not think that any of my fellow-travellers can be guaranteed as non-explosive', Isabella told her friends in the first of her 'Persian letters'. And indeed as the group of foreigners glided past that timeless Middle-Eastern landscape – sandy plains with drab-brown sheep and drab-brown camels, the flat oblong mud hovels, the shrouded faceless women, the wiry armed men, the occasional date-palm and sprig of wormwood – they found much to disagree about. Curzon undoubtedly monopolised the conversation. He had just spent Christmas prowling around the River Karun which had been opened to all foreign commerce for just over a year. As a trade route for British goods it was unsatisfactory at present, he told his companions, for it lacked wharves and warehouses, was impeded by rapids and passed through insecure territory. In passing, Curzon tipped a vial of vitriolic scorn (of which he possessed a limitless supply) on all those who had prematurely heralded its opening 'on so loud and foolish a trumpet' as a great diplomatic victory. Two years later there appeared in Curzon's book a sixty-page chapter on the River Karun which said everything one could possibly want to know about that particular waterway – its history from the time of Alexander, the naming of its parts by Arab geographers, the geological and botanical features of its neighbouring region, the character of nearby towns and their inhabitants, a summary of his own experiences and those of other Europeans who had travelled thereon, bloody tales of rebellions that had occurred in the vicinity within the last hundred years or so, the hydraulic ingenuity of the canals leading from the river to the town of Shuster, the opportunities for hunting lynx or lion, sticking pigs, shooting teal and francolin, and detailed references to all those who, in a multitude of tongues, had ever written, thought, talked about the River Karun, from the Arab historian Abulfeda to the lady traveller Mrs Bishop. That was Curzon's method; it was bombastic, prolix, exhausting, sublime; how could one hope to get in a word edgeways in such a man's company?

One of Curzon's talents however was to pick the brains of lesser mortals when it suited his purpose, and so he probably *did* give Isabella a chance to say a few words, for she had just left Tibet, a country which Curzon saw as another vital piece (a castle perhaps) on his chessboard. In retrospect, it is more with Tibet than with Persia that his name is linked. For, within a decade, Curzon's meteoric rise to power would culminate in the office of Viceroy of India, and his cold bland face, set with disdainful confidence above the gold foliage of his viceregal costume, would turn in meditation towards that mysterious land beyond the Himalayas. As a result of his meditations, the British bayonets would go pricking off to Lhasa in 1904 in that same obsessive cause – the defence of India.

But when Curzon was going up the River Tigris in 1890, the problems of the Middle East seemed much more crucial to British security, and so, after learning that Isabella had, after all, only pottered about the Tibetan fringe, he probably lost interest and launched on another of his favourite themes: the strengthening of Persia. The theme was a popular one among eastern experts in the Foreign Office, the India Office and the War Office. In their eyes, the Shah's large, under-populated, under-developed kingdom had for long been a mushy mollusc, a decayed, squashed fruit; it needed some backbone injected into it, some manly gumption, guts, get-up-and-go. 'Our policy should be, as far as we can, to make Persia *something*', wrote one British diplomat that year; Lord Salisbury had several remedies under consideration 'for the stiffening of Persia'; 'Is it *possible* to make Persia strong and have her for an active ally?' asked General Sir Garnet Wolseley, in near despair. But, declared a *Times* leader of the previous year, 'The day of doing nothing and letting the over-ripe Persian pear fall in Russia's mouth seems to have passed away', and the stiffening process was just beginning. In order to engineer such a stiffening it was vital to improve and create lines of communication – roads, railways, navigable rivers – which, stretching like ramrods over its spineless southern and western parts, would both encourage the growth of trade and provide transport for the military if necessary.

That was why Curzon, the political chess-player, and Sawyer, the military surveyor, were abroad the steamer *Mejidieh*, quarrelling with each other, Isabella says, because they were almost equally self-opinionated and, for light relief, both rounding upon the milder-mannered missionary Dr Bruce. The doctor told Isabella in confidence that Curzon was one of the most offensive people he'd ever met; Curzon returned the antipathy with interest and disseminated it in his inimitable, merciless, piquant style: 'Dr Bruce,' he wrote in his tome, 'is as good a type as can anywhere be seen of the nineteenth century Crusader. In an earlier age, the red cross would have been upon his shoulder and he would have been hewing infidels in conflict for the Holy Sepulchre instead of translating the Bible and teaching schools in Julfa.' The fractious little group separated as soon as they reached Baghdad. Bruce set off for Julfa to continue his *ersatz* Crusade; Curzon headed for the Persian south-west provinces to inspect the tribal loyalties of the Lurs, the beliefs of the Sabians, the prodigious mounds of Susa, the Tomb of Daniel, the water-mills of Dizful, the crops of the Ka'ab Arabs and so on; Mrs Bishop and Major Sawyer were left to make final preparations for the five-hundred-mile ride to Tehran. Before boarding the *Mejidieh*, Isabella had hired a man-of-all-work whom she simply calls 'Hadji'. He was a large, tough Gulf Arab, with knives and rosaries in his belt, his head swathed in a red and yellow turban with tassels hanging down his back, his hide boots turned jauntily up at the toes. He proved to be a big mistake. At that point, indeed, Isabella wrote home, she feared that the whole adventure was a mistake. Sawyer's behaviour so far had dismayed her. He went through the local bazaars 'holding a handkerchief to his nose and looking utterly *blasé* and disgusted at everything'; he bullied his subordinates so much that she felt she would be safer without him, and he insisted that she carry a revolver, which she secretly filled with blank cartridges. Her riding dresses, for some unaccountable reason, were suddenly too short and she hurriedly 'had to lengthen one with the other'; she was nervous about riding a mule on an untried saddle and her knees were so rheumaticky that she feared she would be unable to mount the beast anyway.

But it was too late for retreat and she left Baghdad on a bright cold morning in mid-January safely perched on the mule, in full marching equipment 'of two large holsters, with a revolver and tea-making apparatus in one, and a bottle of milk and dates in the other. An Afghan sheepskin coat is strapped to the front of the saddle, and a blanket and stout mackintosh behind. I wear a cork sun-helmet, a gray mask instead of a veil, an American mountain dress with a warm jacket over it, and tan boots, scarcely the worse for a year of Himalayan travel. Hadji is dressed like an Ishmae-lite.' Gaily she trotted out through the northern gate, the clatter of the bazaars fell away and there was the desert – limitless, naked, lonely, silent, free. 'I felt better at once in the pure exhilarating desert air and nervousness about the journey was left behind. I even indulged in a gallop, and, except for her impetuosity, which carried me into the middle of a caravan, and turning round a few times, the mule behaved so irreproachably that I forgot the potential possibilities of evil.' And thus happily began the toughest single journey of her life.

It was mid-winter. Snow-thick winds screamed across the plains from the gaunt snow mountains, rain stiffened to hail, ragged webs of mist drifted about the hills, occasionally cold white sunlight trickled over the leagues of sodden ice and was swamped by purple sloughs of cloud that threatened worse weather for each morrow. Sunsets were beautiful and melancholy: 'Mountain ranges were painted in amethyst on an orange sky. Horsemen in companies galloped towards tents which were not in sight, strings of camels cast their long shadows on the purple sand, and flocks of big brown sheep, led by armed shepherds, converged on the reedy pools in long brown lines.' The very featurelessness of these wastes and the monotonous drudging lives of their inhabitants engrossed her interest at once. Weather-bound for several days at the Governor's house in the cheerful-sounding town of Khannikin near the Persian frontier, Isabella recorded with scrupulous and loving attention the very cheerless world next door. 'My neighbour's premises consist of a very small and mean yard, now a foot deep in black mire, a cow-shed and a room without door or windows, with a black uneven floor, and black slimy rafters – neither worse nor better than many hovels in the Western Isles of Scotland. A man in middle life, a woman of dubious age, two girls from eight to ten years old, and a boy a little older are the occupants. The furniture consists of some wadded quilts, a copper pot, an iron girdle, a clay ewer or two, a long knife, a wooden spoon, a clay receptacle for grain, two or three earthenware basins, glazed green, and a wicker tray. The cow-shed contains – besides the cow, which is fed on dried thistle – a spade, an open basket and a baggage pad. A few fowls live in the house and are disconcerted to find that they cannot get out of it without swimming.

'The weather is cold and raw, fuel is enormously dear, work is at a standstill, and cold and *ennui* keep my neighbours in bed till the day is well advanced. The woman gets up first, lights a fire of tamarisk twigs and thistles in a hole in the middle of the floor, makes porridge of some coarse brownish flour and water, and sets it on to warm – to *boil* it, with the means at her disposal, is impossible. She wades across the yard, gives the cow a bunch of thistles, milks it into a basin, adds a little leaven to the milk, which she shakes in a goat skin till it is thick, carries the skin and basket to the house, feeds the fowls from the basket and then rouses her lord. He rises, stretches himself, yawns, and places himself cross-legged by the fire, after putting on his *pagri*. The room is dense with pungent wood smoke, which escapes through the doorway, and only a few embers remain. The wife hands him an earthen bowl, pours some porridge into it, adds some "thick milk" from the goat skin, and stands before him with her arms crossed while he eats, then receives the bowl from his hands and kisses it, as is usual with the slaves in a household.

'Then she lights his pipe, and while he enjoys it she serves her boy with breakfast in the same fashion, omitting the concluding ceremony, after which she and the girls retire to a respectful distance with the big pot and finish its contents simultaneously. The pipe over, she pours water on her lord's hands, letting it run on the already damp floor, and wipes them with her *chadar*. No other ablution is customary in the house.

'The woman, the busy bee of the family, contrives to patter about nearly all day in wet clothing, carrying out rubbish in single handfuls, breaking twigs, cleaning the pot and feeding the cow. The roof, which in fine weather is the scene of most domestic occupations, is reached by a steep ladder and she climbs this seven times in succession, each time carrying up a fowl, to pick for imaginary worms in the slimy mud. Dyed yarn is also carried up to steep in the rain, and in an interval of dryness some wool was taken up and carded. An hour before sunset she lights the fire, puts on the porridge, and again performs seven journeys with seven fowls, feeds them in the house, attends respectfully to her lord, feeds her family, including the cow, paddles through the mire to draw water from the river, and unrolls and spreads the wadded quilts. By the time it is dark they are once more in bed, where I trust this harmless, industrious woman enjoys a well-earned sleep.'

And that is Isabella 'doing what she can do well'. If anyone then, now, in the future, is curious about peasant family life in a desert town in the winter – there it is, every thistle and puddle of it. The weather did not improve, she and Sawyer simply decided to plough through it, and their first night on Persian mud was, in its unmitigated comfortlessness, as typical of the country as its peasant home-life. The village caravanserai was abominably dirty and too ruinous to afford shelter from the driving sleet, so they passed into 'the great lofty mule stable, on both sides of which are recesses or mangers about ten feet by seven and about eight feet high. . . . There were at least four hundred mules in this place, jangling their great bells, and crowds of muleteers and gendarmes, all wet and splashed over their heads with mud, some unloading, others making fires and feeding their mules, all shouting when they had anything to say, the Babel aggravated by the clatter of the rattles of a hundred curry-combs and the squeals of fighting horses. The floor was deep with the manure of ages and piled with bales and boxes. In the side recesses, which are about the height of a mule's back, the muleteers camped with their fires and their goods and laid the provender for their beasts in the front . . . The odour was overpowering and the noise stunning, and when our wet mud-covered baggage animals came in, adding to the din, there was hardly room to move, far less for the roll in which all mules indulge when the loads are taken off; and the crush resulted in a fight and one mule got his fore-feet upon my "manger" and threatened to share it with me. It was an awful place to come to after a six hours' march in rain and snow, but I slid off my mule into the recess, had it carpeted, put down my chair, hung a blanket up in front and prepared to brave it, when the inhabitants of this room, the one place which has any pretensions to being a room in the village, were bribed by an offer of six krans (about four shillings) to vacate it for me. Its "pretensions" consist in being over a gateway, and in having a door and a square hole looking out on the street; a crumbling stair slippery with mud leads up to it. The roof leaks in every direction, and the slimy floor is full of pools, but it is luxury after the caravanserai stable, and with one waterproof sheet over my bed and another over myself I have fared well, though the door cannot be shut. . . . In front of this room is a broken ditch full of slimy greenish water, which Hadji took for my tea! We have now reached a considerable altitude and may expect anything. Hadji has just climbed the stair with groans of "*Ya Allah*" and has wailed out, "Colonel says we go – God help us." '

The name of Hadji's god was on his lips at every catastrophe – when the girths broke and the mules' loads fell in the slush, when he was reprimanded for offering food on a filthy plate, when water froze in the tea-urn, when he was cheated over the price of a hen. The name of Isabella's god was often in her mind, for this was biblical country. That first gruesome mule stable reminded her of the inn at Bethlehem and she imagined the humiliation and mess of a birth in 'the crowd and horrors of such a stable'; the Persian *mise en scène* was peopled with Old-Testament figures – an aged Kurdish patriarch with turban and long grey beard crouched over a fire, dirty shepherds sleeping in slumped heaps on the stable straw, morose, black-robed women ladling grain from clay-fired jars. Chaldeans, Israelites, Nestorians, Zoroastrians had all passed that way, and some of the villagers round about were Davidites, who venerated the nearby tomb of King David and believed in a thousand and one reincarnations of the Godhead, from Moses through to Imam Ali, cousin of Mohammed. The ancient bleak setting stirred Isabella's imagination and nourished her faith; the bigotry of Islam and its oppressive hold on the people, especially the women, sickened her, and these influences, acting upon her throughout her travels in the Middle East, undoubtedly contributed to her adoption of an increasingly convinced and militant pro-Christian attitude.

For the time being, she needed all her spiritual and physical resources simply to survive. After bitter nights under the leaking roofs of various filthy caravanserais, they were up at icy dawn to tramp across uplifted snow-plains marked only by the hieroglyphs of birds' feet and the trailing dents of a caravan gone before. The track was a corrugated, one-mule-wide trench running between drifts and fell into the latter of the two categories of Persian 'road' that Curzon defined as those 'upon which some, however slight, labour has at one time been spent, and those to which no labour had ever been devoted at all'. When two caravans met Isabella tells us, 'the question arises who is to give way?' The question arose one afternoon when they saw bearing down upon them a string of sixty mules loaded with huge packing-cases. Mule-like 'they could not and would not give way, and the two caravans came into collision. There were mules struggling and falling, loads overturned, muleteers yelling and roaring, Hadji groaning "God help us!", my mule, a new one, a big strong animal, unused to a bit, plunging and kicking, in the middle of a "free fight". I was struck hard on my ankle by a packing-case and nearly knocked off. Still down they came, in apparently endless hordes; my mule plunged her bridle off, and kicked most violently; there were yells all round. My snow spectacles were knocked off and lost, then came another smash, in which I thought a bone was broken. Fearing that I should be laid up with a broken limb for weeks in some horrible caravanserai, and really desperate with the danger and confusion, I called over and over again to Hadji to get off and pull my mule into the snow or I should be killed! He did not stir, but sat dazed on his pack moaning "God help us" till he, the mule and the load were rolled over in the drift. The orderly contrived to get the bridle on my mule, and to back his own in front of me, and as each irrepressible animal rolled down the bank he gave its load a push, which, nicely balanced as these loads are, made it swerve and saved me from further damage. Hadji had rolled off four times previously and the last I saw of him at that time and of the caravan was a man, five mules and their loads buried in the snow. The personal results to me of what is euphemistically called a "difficulty" are my blue glasses gone, a number of bruises, a badly-torn riding skirt, and a bad cut, which bled profusely and then the blood froze.'

They floundered on at about fourteen miles a day. They spent one night in a frigid hovel where even the floor was a glacial sheet, even the plaster on the walls was fringed with icicles; they blundered through a blizzard at three degrees below zero and, on arriving at the inn, Isabella was literally frozen to the saddle and had to be prised off and carried inside. Nearly three weeks out from Baghdad they reached Kermanshah, where, at the home of the British Agent, she and Sawyer, their limbs tingling at the promise of warmth, were conducted 'into a handsomely-carpeted room with divans beside a blazing fire, a table in the centre covered with apples, oranges and sweetmeats, and the large Jubilee photograph of Queen Victoria hanging over the fireplace'.

The Agent's sitting room was one of the few comfortable places in Kermanshah, a town with a sorry past of 'plague, pestilence and famine', its present population shrunken and oppressed, its dwellings, alleys and warehouses crumbling, its pervading atmosphere, like that of most other provincial centres, one of forlorn and listless decay. Appropriately, as it was the first sizeable Persian town Isabella had seen, Kermanshah was famous for its carpets. This was a lucrative trade (though seldom so for the weavers themselves), because Persian carpets were much in vogue. As Curzon puts it, 'The upper-class householder in England or America is rare who does not think the acquisition of such an article, whether genuine or spurious, an indispensable testimony both to culture and civilisation.'

Isabella tried to see the carpets in the bazaar, but was rudely hooted and jostled by the Moslem males, even though she had veiled her face in deference to custom. She visited the shops where the weaving was carried on – a beautifully simple process in which the wool was stretched on a primitive loom and pure vegetable dyes were used of deep madder red, pale indigo and soft turquoise on a white ground that would mellow to primrose in a decade. The weavers were women, and, as men were present, they had to hold their thick veils across their faces, which greatly impeded their movements. She watched the scene with pitying dismay, seeing, as foreigners usually did in Persia, the drama of its contrasts: the grace and beauty of traditional, creative work; the ugly, barbaric restrictions imposed upon the workers.

A prime reason for the generally dismal state of affairs in Kermanshah, as in other towns, was the nature of local maladministration, of which Isabella had a glimpse during her visit to the District Governor. This functionary, a grotesque, squat figure in long full skirts, a brocade coat and black Astrakhan hat, had a face like an ape, she decided, and a loud fatuous giggle to match. He curtly asked Isabella if the rumour was true that she was going to Tehran to take up the post of doctor in the Shah's harem, and then offered Russian tea and *gez*, 'a mawkish white exudation from a desert plant akin to manna', another English traveller explains. 'When mixed with pistachio nuts and sugar it is cloyingly sweet, clamps itself firmly around the inner jaws and renders conversation impossible for a considerable period.' If Isabella could not talk, she could observe, and she liked little of what she saw – ragamuffin armed soldiers propped against the doorways of the Governor's citadel, 'obsequious crowds of native and negro servants' lounging about the reception-room that was 'a dismal combination of Persian and European taste' with its tea-tables covered in tawdry cretonne, its simple lofty walls bedizened with hanging wax grapes *à la française*.

Justice was dispensed with unwonted zeal by the Governor and his subordinates from this turgid centre, for, as Curzon explains, 'nothing is so welcome to the Persian Governor as a street row, a blood feud, a murder or a quarrel within his jurisdiction. Down come his officers on the delinquents and from their pockets out come the fines. If litigation ensues, so much the better for the provincial exchequer, since every wheel of the judicial machine will require constant greasing.' By this system most wealthy offenders escaped unscathed, though poorer, but for the truly impoverished a gruesome assortment of humiliations and tortures was supplied. A woman caught in adultery might have her head shaved and be led through the jeering town tied on an ass: for a man, the commonest punishment was the bastinado, whereby he was slung head downwards from a bar and the soles of his feet were beaten raw with pomegranate-wood switches kept damp and flexible for the purpose. (Those with a little cash might bribe the beaters to whip with less ferocity.) There were one or two other oriental specialities such as, for stealing telegraph posts – fasten delinquent by one ear to a post in the middle of the desert; for the murder of an official – brick murderer up to his neck in a wall, enclosing the head in mortar and leave to set hard . . .

After the Kermanshah sights, the little group trotted on, faces muffled now in lined face-masks, feet in sheepskin bags. Isabella, Hadji, the cook and two baggage mules formed what Sawyer was pleased to call 'the light division' and rode ahead each day into the venomous hiss of a continual gale. It was a demon wind, 'a steady blighting, searching, merciless blast, no rise or fall, no lull, no hope. Steadily and strongly it swept, at a temperature of 9° across the glittering ascent – swept mountain-sides bare; enveloped us at times in glittering swirls of powdery snow which after biting and stinging careered over the slopes in twisted columns; screeched down gorges and whistled like the demon it was, as it drifted the light frozen snow in layers, in ripples, in waves, a cruel, benumbing, blinding, withering invisibility! The six woollen layers of my mask, my three pairs of gloves, my sheepskin coat, fur cloak, and mackintosh piled on over a swaddling mass of woollen clothing, were as nothing before that awful blast. It was not a question of comfort or discomfort, but of life or death.' She was not exaggerating, either; the following day they passed the corpses of five muleteers shrivelled by the gale's fury.

Isabella had never experienced such suffering on a journey. They crossed a 7,000-foot mountain pass, scintillating in frigid sunlight that mocked their distress and froze their masks to cheek and lip; many many times the baggage straps broke and the ill-balanced loads, with servants atop, rolled away into the drifts, and Hadji, calling upon his god, lay spread-eagled and motionless waiting to be picked up, just like, said Isabella, 'a shot soldier in a war picture'. The cook 'was all to pieces'; the muleteers suffered fevers and snow-blindness; when she dismounted cramps tortured her every joint, and both she and Sawyer endured agues and frostbite. Isabella survived this on a diet of sour wafers, dried soup, dates and goat's milk. Every sunset, huddled in a smoke-stifled hovel, she was besieged by peasants begging for medical aid to cure their scrofula, tumours, ophthalmia, smallpox and other divers maladies interpreted to her by Hadji 'with brutal frankness'; at night, she shared sleeping-space with sundry animals and her blankets froze to her head; each new dawn Hadji cried to Allah and swore he would be dead before dark. Her response to all this was astonishing: 'I have chills but in spite of them and the fatigue am really much better than when I left Baghdad, so that though I exercise the privilege of grumbling at the hardships, I ought not to complain of them, though they are enough to break down the strongest men. I really like the journey, except when I am completely knocked up, or the smoke is exceptionally blinding.'

In fact, she seems to have been the fittest of the lot, for even Sawyer's 'herculean strength is not what it was'. A few days later only one of the seven servants was still on his feet and affairs seemed to have touched rock-bottom. 'Mustard plasters, Dover's powders, salicylate of soda, emetics, poultices, clinical thermometers, chlorodyne and beef tea have been in requisition all day. The cook, the Afghan orderly and Hadji seem really ill. At eight this morning groans at my door took me out, and one of the muleteers was lying there in severe pain, with the hard fine snow beating on him. Later I heard fresh moaning on my threshold and found Hadji fallen there with my breakfast. I got him in and he fell again, upsetting the tea, and while I attended to him the big dogs ate up the *chapatties*! He had a good deal of fever and severe rheumatism and on looking at his eyes I saw that he was nearly blind . . . He thinks he will not survive the night and has just given me his dying directions!'

Hadji did rise again the next day when the caravan staggered on, but feigned deafness as well as blindness so that he would not have the bother of any more interpreting. When they reached Kum a few days later Isabella decided she had had more than her fill of this whining, incompetent, malingering Arab; she dosed him with brandy and milk, gave him more than his wages, some warm clothing and told him to be off. The result was miraculous: he lost his deafness, blindness, fever and 'palsied gait' within the hour, and the last she saw of him was an erect and active man swaggering away beside his mule 'with at least forty years thrown off'.

The worst of their hardships ended at Kum, from which one of Persia's main roads stretched across the bleak plains to the capital. The caravanserais along it were like Grand Hotels compared to those in which they had been staying – stained gilt mirrors glared from the mud walls of Isabella's tawdry 'suite' and there was stabling for 1,500 mules. Forty-six days after the departure from Baghdad (during which period, Isabella told a friend, she had lost twenty-two pounds in weight!) she and Sawyer left the rest of the caravan and galloped ahead for Tehran. In the early evening, when they were still floundering through the muddy dark, they heard an incongruous familiar whistle, a roar and a rattle of lights as a train lurched by on Persia's only five-mile-long railway, 'taking away with its harsh western noises that glorious freedom of the desert which outweighs all the hardships even of a winter journey'. By this time, Isabella was faint with hunger and exhaustion and her spine was in agony; for the last few miles even the horses tottered with fatigue and she could scarcely hold on to the saddle. ' "Are you surviving?" ' Sawyer kept inquiring out of the darkness, and her answer was increasingly dubious.

At long last they lurched through a gateway, and there was the British Legation, large, dignified, unruffled before them. 'Every window was lighted, light streamed from the central door, splashed carriages were dashing up and setting down people in evening dress, there were crowds of servants about, and it flashed on my dazed senses that it must be after eight and that there was a dinner party! Arriving from the mud of the Kavir and the slush of the streets, after riding ten hours in ceaseless rain on a worn-out horse; caked with mud from head to foot, dripping, exhausted, nearly blind from fatigue, fresh from mud hovels and the congenial barbarism of the desert, and with the rags and travel stains of a winter journey of forty-six days upon me, light and festivity were overwhelming.

'Alighting at a side door, scarcely able to stand, I sat down in a long corridor, and heard from an English steward that "dinner is waiting". His voice sounded very far off, and the once familiar announcement came like a memory out of the remote past. Presently a gentleman appeared in evening dress, wearing a star, which conveyed to my fast-failing senses that it was Sir H. Drummond Wolff. It was true that there was a large dinner-party and among the guests the Minister with thoughtful kindness had invited all to whom I had letters of introduction. But it was no longer possible to make any effort, and I was taken up to a room in which the comforts of English civilisation at first made no impression upon me, and removing only the mackintosh cloak, weighted with mud, which had served me so well, I lay down on the hearthrug before a great coal fire till four o'clock the next morning. And "so the tale ended", and the winter journey with its tremendous hardships and unbounded mercies was safely accomplished.'

II

Tehran, capital of Persia since about 1785, was a half-westernised, half-oriental city dumped on a stony plain that burned in summer and froze in winter. Spring, which arrived two days after Isabella, conjured violets, willows and irises for its irrigated gardens and, for its people, the first little cucumbers sent up from the south wrapped in rose-leaves. Its walls, eleven miles in circuit, marked spring's boundaries, for the desert that lapped against them was practically changeless. Its gates, Curzon said, consist 'of lofty archways adorned with pinnacles and towers and present from a distance a showy appearance which has caused to some incoming travellers paroxysms of delight' but which, on closer inspection, proved to be 'gaudy and tasteless erections of crumbling glazed tile'.

Inside the city walls, its bazaars were crammed with foreign goods – cottons from Berlin, Austrian chandeliers, China tea, Dutch candles, brass bowls from Lucknow and, from the two imperial rivals, Russia and Britain, bevies of rose-rimmed teapots and ornate picture-frames, mounds of brash magenta cloth and cheap tin trays, galaxies of glass trinkets, tasselled oil-lamps and flashy beads. 'A stroll through Tehran's bazaars shows the observer something of the extent and rapidity with which Europe is ruining the artistic taste of Asia', Isabella remarked. The city's womenfolk, creeping in nearby alleys, were shapeless blue-black bundles, on the way, perhaps, to the public baths, where they could cast aside their shrouds and gossip with friends as they languidly awaited the weekly beauty treatment: a stain of henna to keep the soles of the feet, the fingernails and palms a nice reddish-brown, and a paste of indigo leaves to keep the hair blue-black. The men of the city by contrast, bustled and flaunted, drank lots of thick coffee in cafés and arak (surreptitiously), smoked their gurgling water-pipes with ceremonious gusto (often smoked opium also), called each other son-of-a-burnt-father and/ or of-a-dog with exceeding frequency, bullied, cheated, laughed a lot, and for recreation hunted beyond the walls in the sudden spring, with falcons to catch pheasants and with greyhounds to catch gazelles.

One of the capital's keenest sportsmen was The Asylum of the Universe, the King of Kings, the Shah-in-Shah Nasr-ed-Din himself, who, Curzon tells us, 'may frequently be encountered riding out of the city to one of his numerous shooting boxes in the mountains, attended by a large camp-following and solaced by a selection from his extensive seraglio'. Nasr-ed-Din, he continued, possessed other qualities which, like his love of the hunt, were characteristic of his lineage: 'a genius for paternity, a fair intelligence, handsome features and remorseless economy'. The Shah's economy was practised mainly on his subjects, for his Palace, which Isabella visited in company with Sir Henry Drummond Wolff, was a dream of oriental splendour. Sweeping staircases of creamy alabaster curved into halls of blue and white marbled stucco that were furnished with tables of beaten gold, and numbered among these magnificent anterooms was one of the greatest multi-millionaire shows on earth: rows of glass cases 'full of pearls, rubies, diamonds, sapphires, emeralds, flashing forth their many-coloured light – treasures not arranged, but piled like tea or rice'.

The immense Pleasure Gardens outside enshrined the familiar

masculine Paradise – sparkling fountains, nightingales, roses, with women's apartments (*anderun*) adjoining. The latter sported, according to Curzon, 'a subterranean bathroom in the centre which has a circular pool lined with blue tiles, whilst at the extremity of the chamber is an inclined plane of polished marble, down which, it is understood, that the shiftless naiads used to slide into the arms of their royal adorer and were by him pitched into the pool – a feat of no common exertion, considering that is at some distance'. Probably Sir Henry did not show Isabella this slippery slope, but he did present her to the Shah, the royal pitcher, who appeared informally while they were there. The King of Kings pushed up his big horn spectacles and focused upon her eyes 'about which there is something very peculiar'; he asked a few brusque questions and walked away – a rather 'rough-looking man', she decided, 'with neither eastern nor western polish' about him and having in his broad hands enough wealth to alleviate much of the misery and poverty she had seen in his domains, had he felt so inclined. Such a royal inclination was improbable. 'The Shah', pronounced Curzon, 'is about as likely to undertake a genuinely great public work as he is to turn Protestant.'

In extenuation however, Curzon adds that the Shah often intended to remedy certain abuses, but his good intentions were frustrated and defeated by a traditional system of venal corruption allied to 'a great dearth of administrative energy'. In Curzon's view, 'Half the money voted with his consent never reaches its destination, but sticks to every intervening pocket with which professional ingenuity can bring it into even transient contact; half the schemes authorised by him are never brought any nearer to realisation, the minister or functionary in charge trusting to the oblivious caprices of the sovereign to overlook his dereliction of duty.' Other western observers, including Isabella, bear out these strictures. The 'oriental squeeze' operated with rare finesse in Persia, where it was called *modakel*. *Modakel* worked at all levels, but increased in geometrical progression according to the status of the parties concerned. Thus a muleteer might pay nine *krans* for a load of hay, and charge his master ten *krans* for it; but a chief of police might buy his appointment for a thousand *krans* and extort from the local citizenry twice as much within six months. The marketing of official positions in this fashion did nothing to encourage a sense of security, because, once in office, a man spent much of his time and money protecting it from other aspirants – as the Persian proverb put it, 'While the jay eats the grasshopper, the hawk waits for the jay.' In these precarious circumstances it was an official's usual policy to collect as many 'grasshoppers' as possible before the hawk swooped, that is, to 'squeeze' everything procurable by means of bribery, crippling taxation and general skulduggery from his every subordinate down to the lowliest peasant, who, Isabella says, 'is the ultimate sponge, to be sucked dry by all above him'.

With all this going on there was indeed, as Curzon remarked, a dearth of enthusiasm and resourcefulness for the furthering of new, expensive schemes of westernisation, but in 1890 fresh efforts were begin made in this direction by the clever, optimistic British Minister, Sir Henry Drummond Wolff. Sir Henry believed that the best way to strengthen 'sick man' Persia was to encourage the British to invest in the building of its roads and railways. The Russians, however, had similar ideas, and the whole question of when Persia should get its modern communications depended more on international economic and military strategy than on the needs or wishes of the people themselves. Even the Shah had no final say, for he was pulled in different directions by the vociferous claims of the two big powers as they busily staked out their 'spheres of influence' – Russians in the north, British in the south. And, during her three-week stay at the Legation, Isabella noted that within the foreign community 'the relations of England and Russia with each other and with the Shah afford a topic of ceaseless interest'. Her interest in such topics was waning, however, and she soon planned escape.

Isabella does not refer to Major Sawyer at this point, but during the journey from Baghdad she learned to suffer his 'crotchetiness' and found him to be resourceful, game and reliable under stress. Sawyer, for his part, must have had secret misgivings about the wisdom of encumbering himself with a small, delicate-looking widow nearing sixty, but her performance had been a remarkable one and she presumably passed his every test. They agreed to meet later in Isfahan, a long way south, and from there to explore together the savage and empty country of the Bakhtiari tribes that was the object of Sawyer's survey mission.

For the new stage of her journey, Isabella hired as interpreter and attendant a cheerful young Brahmin called Mirza Yusuf. Tehran milled with these *mirzas* – secretary-scribes – and many of them danced perpetual if unproductive attendance on the various Ministers of State, playing rhubarb-and-custard bit parts in the Alice-in-Wonderland world of Persia's mobile administration. Curzon describes the rituals with some amazement: 'A Ministry in Persia consists of the minister and some scribes (*mirzas*) without any determinate place of office or any of the apparatus that appears indispensable to Europeans. A bureau is set up at whatever spot the minister happens to be, whether in his house, or in an ante-room or a court of the Royal Palace or perchance in . . . a coffee house. His swarm of scribes buzzes after the chief on all his marches, each bearing with him in his pocket the necessary writing apparatus and documents. Accordingly an office can be rigged up any or everywhere in a trice. In the pockets of such a *mirza* are often to be found the documents of a series of years past consisting of little scraps of paper which he has come to regard as private, and in no sense official property.' Perhaps Mirza Yusuf's pockets were full; anyway, he was, Isabella says, 'willing to do anything to get to England'.

So a few days later she, Mirza Yusuf and a Persian cook with a 'grotesquely hang-dog look' started on the breezy easy journey to Isfahan. The plains were 'reddish, yellowish, barren, gravelly or splotched with salt', their flatness occasionally broken by grisly hunks of decay – choked irrigation tunnels, a ruined, untenanted hovel, the corpse of a camel festooned with replete vultures. Rutted tracks ground into the gritty land by the beasts of a million ambling caravans marked this ancient way; but the sky above was newly streaked with the wires of the Indo-European Telegraph Company that hummed importantly with up to a thousand messages a day – coded lengthy dispatches from the India Office in Whitehall to the Viceroy in India and equally lengthy summaries of Indian news from Calcutta for the columns of tomorrow's *Times*. The new verbose pompous mumbo-jumbo of the British Empire vibrated meaninglessly above; below, the ancient, equally verbose, pompous and meaningless mumbo-jumbo of the dervishes still held sway; the contrast was absolute.

There were always dervishes shuffling along between Tehran

and Isfahan, telling fortunes and stories, stealing, praying, cursing, selling talismans (dried sheep's eyes to ward off snake-bite, lucky blue beads to sew on horses' tails), sleeping against the telegraph poles in the desert. These were the wandering lamas of Persia, less consequential in the main than their Tibetan confrères, but equally idle, dirty and given to weird musical and terpsichorean exhibitions designed to demonstrate their familiarity with the prevailing godhead. Like the lamas, some were truly devout; many, according to one long-term western resident, 'had no religion save that of doing no work'. So they scrounged, demanding shelter and alms by fixing their victims with a glittering eye, brandishing a bowl and hiccuping out with alarming ferocity the sound '*Huk – yac, huk*'. One of the dervishes on the Isfahan road must have intimidated Isabella a little for she reluctantly allowed him a night's lodging, though he was not a congenial guest: 'He carries a large carved almsholder; and the panther skin on his shoulders, the knotted club and his lean, hungry, fanatical face give him a dangerous look. All I have seen on this march have worn long matted bushy hair, often covering their shoulders, an axe in the girdle, and peculiar turbans decorated with phrases from the Koran.' She was fortunate to shake him off the next day, for dervishes frequently moved in upon the wealthy for weeks, even months on end. If their demands for alms were ignored, they simply squatted in the courtyards, yelled '*huk, huk*' for hours, blew their wailing buffalo-horns all night, poured a stream of imprecations on their 'hosts' and even planted seeds of barley in the garden, thereby signifying their intention of staying until the crop ripened, or they were bought off. They were seldom forcibly ejected, for a vague odour of sanctity clung to them along with less fragrant smells, and most people were a little afraid of their licentious, bizarre theatricality.

The day after her encounter with the dervish, Isabella reached Isfahan, the former capital of Persia that until the mid eighteenth century had been a magnificent eastern city, and since, according to Curzon, had bewailed its lost splendours 'in perpetual sack-cloth and ashes'. Such sorrow and deprivation begat envy and malice; the Isfahanis were notorious for their niggardliness, their conceit and their religious intolerance. Neither Jews, Armenians nor other Christians dared to live in the city itself for fear of persecution, and as Isabella passed through its streets she she was jeered and spat upon by howling men. It was a relief to cross the River Zainderud into the suburb of Julfa where all the religious minorities lived in uneasy proximity and thus where Dr Bruce, Curzon's Crusader, had established a large Church Missionary Society mission, in which she stayed. Naturally, she regarded Bruce's endeavours much more warmly than did Curzon, and praised its 'solid and suitable' teaching of Armenian girls, its orphanage and medical centre.

Isabella did however express reservations about the wisdom of sending untried young Englishwomen to such a post, and cited the case of 'Miss V . . .' who had recently arrived at the Julfa mission and died there within a few months, 'her life sacrificed to over-study of a difficult language and neglect of fresh air and exercise'. Cut off from all family ties, the idealistic newcomer, 'dreaming of a circle in all respects consecrated, finds herself among frictions, strong difference as to methods of working, not always gently expressed . . . Is it wonderful', Isabella asks, 'that supposed slights, tiffs, criticisms which would be utterly brushed away if a good walk in the open air or a good gallop were possible, should be brooded over till they attain a magnitude which embitters and depresses life?' She constantly advocated the therapeutic value of a 'good gallop' and felt that, though the actual dangers of missionary life were often exaggerated, the insidious long-term effects of isolation, confinement and sickness due to unfamiliar food, climate or conformity to native custom were not sufficiently taken into account by mission boards. Delicate, sheltered, dedicated, unskilled, sometimes faint-hearted and highly-strung young women were given a great send-off into the heathen wilderness where, quite often, feeling neglected and futile, they simply wilted and died.

Mrs Bishop's enlargement on this particular theme at this point in her journey was not fortuitous; she undoubtedly had in mind her own cousin, 'Mary Bird of Persia' as she was later called, who arrived to work at the Julfa mission about a year after Isabella was there. Mary was then thirty-two, and had led 'a sheltered home-life' up to that time, according to a memoir about her; she was delicate in health, small in stature and had no professional training. But she must have possessed some of Isabella's fearlessness, pertinacity and practical zeal, for she did not succumb in the least. She taught herself how to extract teeth, sew up ears torn in harem fights, cauterise boils, and she insisted on ministering to the poor in Isfahan itself, in defiance of the bigoted hostility that assailed her. To some missionaries these were courageous acts, performed in defiance of the sort of overwhelming odds against which crusading Christians are intended to wrestle; but the lay view was different. 'Miss Bird's recklessness is a constant source of anxiety to the English officials who are naturally desirous that, as a British subject, no harm should befall her,' wrote a member of the Julfa telegraph staff. 'It is a question calling for serious consideration whether proselytising missionaries in such a country as Persia do not defeat rather than promote the cause of Christianity by exciting or intensifying antipathy to European ideas. They certainly tend to endanger the safety of all European residents there.' Many of the secular foreigners subscribed to this opinion, and the mission was equally unpopular 'with the Armenian hierarchy who look upon its agents as poachers on their own preserves', Curzon comments. The hierarchs had a point in so far as the only converts made by the mission in its twenty years of operation were Armenians who had discarded their own brand of Christianity for the Anglican variety. Moslem children were forbidden to attend its school and the legal penalty for Moslem apostasy was still death.

Dr C. J. Wills of the Persian telegraph service, like his colleagues, has some harsh things to say about this religious imbroglio. In his view, 'The Isfahani looks upon the Julfa Armenian as a race apart and merely a panderer to his vices and a maker of intoxicant liquors; and the hangdog Armenian with his sham Turk or European dress and the bottle of arak in his pocket staggers in secure insolence, confident in the moral protection given him by the presence of the English whom he robs, respecting neither his priest whom he despises, nor the missionaries whom he dislikes at heart (though they educate his children gratuitously) and whom his priest openly reviles.' Wills spoke from first-hand experience for he once lived in the Armenian quarter along the street of the liquor-makers and Persians often knocked on his door by mistake calling for crude arak – 'fixed bayonets' as it was known.

As a secular male doctor, Wills was one of the few foreigners who could move freely about Isfahan, which Isabella hardly saw. Crossing the Julfa bridge early in the summer mornings, he would pause to watch the calico rinsers at work. They were up to their knees in the shallow river, thwacking the long strips of calico against mill-stones, and from the half-dyed fabric clouds of multi-coloured spray sprang up against the sunshine. After rinsing, the strips were stretched on the gravel banks – rich purple and coppery brown they were, turkey-red, saffron and larkspur blue. Each rinser had his own mill-stone, his brushwood hovel on the shore, his donkey, guard-dog and a boy to keep the material damp by dashing sheets of water over it. The rinsers roared a tuneless song, the boys shouted, the donkeys brayed, the dogs barked, the water splashed and the coloured calico slapped rhythmically against the stones. It was one of those bright timeless scenes that had gone on for centuries along the banks of the Zainderud and warmed the spirits of all who saw it.

Later, after dealing with his patients, Wills used to wander round the bazaars, selecting and eating his lunch as he went – crackle-crisp kebobs garnished with sorrel and ground figs, hot flapjacks, a succulent slab of mutton from the sheep-on-a-spit, a bowl of cucumbers or wild asparagus, and to top it off a bowl of sherbet flavoured with tamarind juice or a bunch of long white juicy grapes called 'old man's beard'. Then he'd stroll along to watch the printers stamping the traditional designs of peacocks, lion-hunts, elephants, soldiers and beardless disdainful noblemen on the famous Isfahan curtains, or he'd visit the artists in the Gulshan caravanserai to admire the decoration of an exquisite pill-box, and he'd usually end up at the Maidan (the place) where the haughty, gracious, fiery, superb Persian horses were put through their paces. Wills bought as many of these as he could afford and mentions that in his stable, as in all others, the grooms kept one wild pig because its breath was supposed to be good for the other inmates. These piggy mascots were always called *Marjan* (Coral); they devotedly trotted behind the horses like pet dogs and the horses often repaid their affection by refusing to gallop too fast, so that little Coral could keep up!

'The fury of Islam', as Isabella called it, effectively prevented her from enjoying the pleasures and beauties of Isfahan, and she went to the city but once, under escort, to meet some Persian women in their *anderun*. Life in an *anderun* was petty, stilted, prurient, catty, cushioned, hopeless and unhealthy. In obedience to the Moslem concept of 'not opening the eyes of the women too wide', females received scant education of any kind. Their apartments were silken, gilt, tasselled, thickly carpeted, decorated with alabaster vases, glass lustres, lamp-shades, candelabra; for the Persians adored glassware and, Curzon supposed, 'would have no hesitation in pronouncing the Crystal Palace to be the *maximum opus* of the world's architecture'. Inside these padded cells, the women passed the time in banging tambourines, making bonbons and cucumber jams, gossiping, occasionally tearing each other's hair out, chalk-whitening their necks, clown-reddening their cheeks, smearing eyes and lashes with black *kohl*, concocting love-potions to excite the enthusiasm of their lords and watching performances of bawdy plays, on which, Isabella felt, 'unaccustomed English eyes could not look'. Lacking exercise, eating too many bonbons, the women were invariably puffy-fat and pallid, they tottered rather than walked and wore the most extraordinary indoor costume, which she thought 'as lacking in delicacy as it is in comfort'. It consisted of a 'chemise' of tinselled silk gauze 'so transparent as to leave nothing to the imagination', a short velvet wide-open bolero covering the arms, but not the breasts or upper abdomen, and an enormous stiff bouffant mini-skirt with white knee-length socks to match. To the eyes of the nineteenth century westerner this bizarre rig-out, topped by the painted docile face and dyed, plastered hair was hideously ludicrous rather than provocative, though, as Dr Wills says, 'the effect of a lady sitting down astonishes the beholder and would scandalise the Lord Chamberlain'.

How lucky and untrammelled Isabella suddenly felt in comparison with these bedizened creatures confined for most of the time in their languid, over-perfumed, stuffy rooms; how glad she was to get back to Julfa and concentrate on preparations for the forthcoming adventure – such as 'refitting my dear old tent with new ropes'. Herbert Sawyer arrived in April and, she told her friends, he made 'an immense sensation in this minute community which vegetates in superlative stagnation. His splendid appearance, force of character, wit, brutal frankness, ability and kind-heartedness made a "great breeze" and I hear that his sayings and doings are the one topic.' Quite probably there were one or two missionary maidens in Julfa who, like the Simla ladies, would have gladly taken Isabella's place and faced the perils of the Bakhtiari country in such manly company, but the dashing eligible widower and the tough ageing widow were, she says, 'good comrades' and had reached their compromises. They agreed that Isabella's caravan was to be almost independent, it would simply camp at night within the ring of Sawyer's sentries, and that 'I am to keep my rough ways in dress, etc'. Her four mules carried bedding, stores for forty days (including a quantity of much-vaunted "Edwards' Desiccated Soup"), 'presents for the savages' (it is her joke) and three skin tents. One of these was a small 'bathroom tent' which it was difficult to use during daylight because the space between it and the ground was usually knobbed with open-eyed, open-mouthed faces of local urchins. The modern reader may wonder how Isabella with her scrupulous regard for the feminine proprieties, dealt with matters of evacuation and personal hygiene during this and most of the other journeys when men were in constant and close proximity. Surely the question must have occurred to many of her friends and readers; but it is doubtful if any summoned the courage to ask her, and certainly, she never mentioned the subject herself. Anyway, on this excursion she at least had a bathroom tent, and also, most precious and important of all, a portable medicine-chest given her by Messrs Burroughs & Wellcome, containing fifty bottles their special 'tabloids', quinine, ointments and some surgical instruments.

III

Mrs Bishop and Major Sawyer left Julfa on 30 April, the best time of the year. Willows, hazy-green with spring, lined the river banks, apricot and walnut orchards were in bloom, fields of opium-poppy glowed white and clouds of blue-grey pigeons drifted about the nearby pigeon-towers. These towers, some of them eighty feet high, decorated with arabesques of red and yellow ochre, were colourful, quaint features of a monotonous landscape. Their walls were honeycombed with pigeon cells and their object was to enable the easy collection of pigeon guano for the raising of early melons. In the past, the trade had flourished, but early-melon demand had slackened and most of the towers were in ruins, though the pigeons still liked them and used them as bases for extensive depredations of the surrounding crops.

Within a few days the caravan shook down nicely and the free ways of the wilds were hers. Each cool dawn began with the shout to 'Boot and Saddle' from Sawyer, whom she had dubbed 'The Sahib' in recognition of his typically Anglo-Indian mien. Then came the sunrise sounds of animals chewing fodder, the clack of cooking-pots, the shouts of muleteers; later the rhythmical thud of hoofs on gravel slopes, the smells of tamarisk and animal dung, the touch of a cool breeze swirling through the hair of horse and rider, the sudden surprise of beauty, such as rows of red-legged storks fishing along the blue-green of the Seligun Lake. 'This is a purely wandering life', Isabella wrote in her first letter from the Bakhtiari country. 'We never know in the morning where we shall be at night, but if a place looks nice and there is water we decide to camp there. I *like* it.'

Real travellers invariably liked it. Even the sophisticated George Curzon, a figure more fitted to the halls of public debate, liked it, for he found that Persia brought out the nomad in him. 'Perhaps it is that, in the wide landscape, in the plains stretching without break to mountains and mountains succeeded by plains, in the routes that are without roads, in the roads that are without banks or ditches, in the unhampered choice, both of means of progression and of pace, there is a joyous revulsion from the sterile conventionality of life and locomotion at home. Something, too, must be set down to the grateful spirit of self-dependence which legions of domestics have not availed to subdue, and to the love of adventure which not even the nineteenth century can extinguish. Or is it that in the East and amid scenes where life and its environment have not varied for thousands of years, where nomad Abrahams still wander with their flocks, there Rebecca still dips her skin in the well, where savage forays perpetuate the homeless miseries of Job, western man casts off the slough of artificial civilisation and feels he is breathing again with his ancestral stock, the atmosphere that nurtured his kind?'

If this were so (and Isabella would have concurred with all these reasons), then certainly the Bakhtiari among whom she now found herself offered ample inducement for the casting-off of civilisation's sloughs, for they were a people much given to Old Testament scenarios, savage forays and Job-like miseries. Most of them, to use the lifeless phraseology of the geography text-book, were 'pastoral nomads' who wintered along the warm plains of Khuzistan and summered among the high cool affluents of the Upper Karun. They usually dwelt in carpeted tents. The carpets 'served as chairs, tables and beds and the low wall of roughly-heaped stones at the back for trunks and wardrobe, for on it they keep their "things" in immense saddlebags made of handsome rugs. The visible furniture consists of a big copper bowl for food, a small one for milk, a huge copper pot for clarifying butter and a goat-skin suspended from three poles, which is jerked by two women seated on the ground, is used for making curds'. In addition to the curds, they ate the produce from a few scant crops and their herds of goats and sheep, supplemented by hares and ibex, acorn bread and the occasional bowl of bustard soup.

Bakhtiari ideas on boundaries were hazy, but they lived mostly to the west of Isfahan, an area of precipitous mountains and plateaux, foaming gulleys, empty alpine valleys. They retained a sort of quasi-independence under the Shah and owed monetary tribute to Isfahan. But such payment was seldom obtained for, as Curzon suggests, 'the intrusion of a civil revenue officer among them would be a perilous exercise'. In any case, the Bakhtiari did not really feel part of Persia, for though they spoke a Persian dialect their origins were as vague as their boundaries. 'They appear never to have developed a folk-lore or produced a book or harboured a historian,' Curzon comments, and their few traditions 'are swift to lose themselves in the fabulous'. Those traditions they did possess were vainglorious embroideries of their more violent forays, bitter inter-tribal feuds that had crackled on for centuries and had earned the Bakhtiari a formidable reputation for cruel ferocity; it was proverbial, for instance, that they had been obliged to forego the reading of the *Fahtihah* or prayer for the dead, because otherwise they would not have had time for any other occupations. Isabella, in quoting this legend, felt it was too harsh, for in her experience the people were so sorely afflicted with all the miseries of Job that they had little stomach for fighting.

Owing to the possession of the Burroughs & Wellcome medicine-chest, she was assumed to be a *hakkim* (doctor) and word of her approach spread like blossom on the breeze. Men, women and children crowded round her tent at every halt, bringing their cataracts and glaucoma, their scabies, epilepsies and snake-bites, their dyspepsia and rheumatism ('wind-in-the-bones', they called it) for her attention. Dismayed and harassed, seeing up to two hundred patients a day, Isabella found she needed every ounce of that medical training she had received at St Mary's Hospital three years before. It must have been quite an ordeal – the rows of silent, miserable, accusing people huddled outside her tent, pathetic old women praising Allah as they bore away their doses of medicine in broken egg-shells, flies feeding on the open sores of wailing children, the smell of sick, unwashed bodies, above all their unquestioning faith that she could perform medical miracles. The stone-blind stumbled from afar pleading for eye-lotions, the stone-deaf thrust their ears at her to cure, the harem women with wild handsome nut-brown faces pleaded for love-potions or for malignant draughts to disfigure the favourite wife.

Except in the latter case, Isabella did all she could without flinching, conscious that she was setting a Christian example. From Julfa a few weeks before she had written to a friend, 'I have just read "The Greatest Thing in the World" and wish to act out the courtesy and kindness which it enjoins, among the savages, muleteers . . . I am always seeing more strongly that *doing* is Christianity and possibly many of us have paid a disproportionate attention to what we believe. It is a striking remark that at the judgement a verdict is given only on what has been done or not done'. Her efforts were, then, a working out of this practical Christian philosophy; they were tokens of gratitude for her intensified, vitalised faith; they were also, undoubtedly, gestures of affection and respect for that kind John Bishop, who would have so heartily approved. Certainly it was in the spirit of true Christian charity that Isabella laboured to help these people, for they constantly repaid her kindnesses by robbing her and the rest of the caravan of everything they could lay dirty hands on – except the medicine-chest, which was never touched!

Some time in May (they had by now lost track of the exact date) she and Sawyer reached Ardal, the 'capital', where the Ilkhani, the Bakhtiari chief, was temporarily housed in a forlorn and crumbling fort. While Sawyer argued with him over the hire of an armed escort for the wilder regions beyond, the thankless task of 'harem-visiting' fell to Isabella's lot. Bakhtiari women were more rowdy, robust and importunate than the pallid Persians, and, crowding round her in dozens, they besieged Mirza Yusuf with questions: 'How old was this foreign woman?', 'Why didn't she dye her hair?', 'Did she whiten her teeth?', 'Why didn't her eyebrows meet in the middle?', 'Did she know a cure for wrinkles/jealousy/simple ugliness?', 'How many wives had Sawyer at home?', 'Did he want a Bakhtiari girl?' 'Did foreigners get indigestion because they ate too much celery in sour milk?' 'Would the lovely foreign lady give them some of her pretty buttons, or scarves, or bangles?' It always ended the same way – the women offered a few gluey sweetmeats, then gradually relapsed into sullen envious silence, broken by wails of self-pity at the dull inactive degradation of their lives.

As soon as she decently could, Isabella literally tore herself away, feeling sad, helpless, angry at their plight. As she left the native settlements the noises of the makeshift, nomadic life brayed after her – whine of women, squawk of babies and fowls, snort, bleat, bawl of tethered animals, yelp of dogs and boys, bang of tambourine, screech of pipe, clatter of guns and basins, bellows of men demanding food and quarrelling. 'Savage life does not bear a near view,' she decided after two months among the people. 'Its total lack of privacy, its rough brutality, its dirt, its undisguised greed, its unconcealed jealousies and hatred, its falsehood and its pure selfishness and treachery are all painful on a close inspection.'

Nevertheless, it was clear to her that such people must be treated with that extra kindness and forbearance due to those who were innocently ignorant of the Christian virtues. By the time they reached Ardal, it was equally clear that Major Sawyer did not share these views. This tension is only suggested in the book, but in two letters that survive it seems that the relationship between the two became very fractious over the question of 'dealing with the natives'. Sawyer's approach was blatantly and unashamedly imperialistic. 'Tell him if he doesn't bring wood I'll go with my men and tear down every roof and door-post in the place,' was the message that poor Mirza Yusuf was told to convey to a headman who had refused them fuel. 'And then tell him to go the devil,' Sawyer added for good measure. When they reached Ardal, Sawyer's choler effortlessly expanded to include the Ilkhani, his sons and all the minor *khans* within shouting range. 'Imagine the toil I have here,' Isabella suggests to her friends – who, worthy maiden ladies in distant Edinburgh, probably couldn't begin to imagine any such thing – 'when the Sahib ought to be most friendly and polite to the great feudal chief whose guest he is, and yet is most desperately insolent in manner. As yesterday, when the two sons of the Ilkhani called at the *durbar* tent, and he coolly went out at once, saying to me, "Now do the best you can with them!" After which he stood outside the tent within earshot, cleaning his sextant and making a snort of ridicule and saying sarcastic things in a whisper about my feeble efforts, which Mirza heard and kept giggling in his interpretation. . . . His behaviour is a frightful political mistake and a mistake in every way,' she concludes. Plainly, Sawyer had cast her in the thankless role of mediator between himself and the unruly tribal chiefs, relying on her popularity as a *hakkim* and her conciliatory, friendly behaviour to gain the sympathy and co-operation that he couldn't be bothered to win on his own behalf. She did it, but it was impudence on his part to expect it. After all, it was his mission, and *his* was all the credit when they returned home, the mission safely accomplished.

Nor was this the only role that Isabella had thrust upon her. Unfortunately, Sawyer's only reliable surveyor caught an eye-infection that incapacitated him for weeks – and she was the only possible substitute. 'The Sahib has just told me that I am to help him with the observations and in a few minutes I shall have to take the chronograph record of the sun crossing the meridian, twenty-four observations for the latitude and *then* there will be the stars for the longitude. Alas, alas!' wailed Isabella, but secretly revelling in this exercise, for she always enjoyed the collection of records and measurements that, she hoped, might contribute a mite to the sum of human knowledge. 'And now,' she continues breathlessly, a page or so later, 'the Sahib has just told me that he'll want me from 9.30 till eleven tonight to work on the stars. It is terribly hard work, my hands gets shaky and icy cold and I get some very sharp words. A single mistake of sight and the base from which the survey starts would be vitiated and all the elaborate astronomical calculations will be upset.' One night apparently the words 'You'd turn a saint into a devil' were thundered at her, 'amidst much else – and all because I asked for the repetition of three figures to make sure that I had heard them rightly.' It is one of the most amusing and engaging pictures of Isabella's later years to imagine her standing late at night on the great gritty empty plains of Persia, very small, tired, cold, and trying, with desperate and child-like conscientiousness to hold the sextant, chronograph or whatever *quite* steady while Sawyer barked at her out of the darkness about her really rather minor inadequacies!

At such times, the Major was at his worst; at other times they rubbed along well together, she, at least, relaxed by the freedoms and 'utter sartorial licence of camp life'. 'I am so much better as usual since I came into camp and have not to do "company"', she explains. In the absence of company, clothes were simply 'a sort of loose grey ulster' and Bakhtiari rag shoes; food was gobbled greedily off a tray; light was a candle on a saucer; sleep was a soft oblivion as she rolled in a sheepskin among the saddlery in a dim corner of the tent. During the midday halts, which grew longer as the heat increased, Sawyer, in old flannel shirt and breeches, would come to lie outside her tent with his handsome head in its shadow and she would read *Ben Hur* aloud for their mutual entertainment, and sermons on Sundays for their mutual enlightenment.

After leaving Ardal they climbed to the steep watery uplands north of the Upper Karun, along with straggling processions seeking summer pastures. 'Loaded cows and bullocks, innumer-able sheep, goats, lambs and kids,' trailed past, 'big dogs, weakly sheep tied on donkeys' backs and weakly lambs carried in shepherds' bosoms; handsome mares each with her foal running loose or ridden by women with babies seated on the tops of loaded saddle-bags made of gay rugs; tribesmen with foot-long guns slung behind their shoulders and big two-edged knives in their girdles'. In these wild regions every man was a walking arsenal, the authority of the Ilkhani was uncertain, and at every halt the camp boiled with rumours – that the Ilkhani was going to murder his nephew and there would be tribal war, that some of the *khans* were going to murder the Ilkhani, with similar consequences, that the Ilkhani and/or his nephew was going to cut the throats of the rich, intrusive foreigners. One day, a group of tribesmen armed with clubbed sticks surrounded Sawyer, who coolly fired his revolver in the air and passed the incident off as a joke; on another occasion Mirza actually overheard some of the men making plans to kill them all. No wonder that Sawyer was secretly concerned when Isabella trotted away alone to collect alpine plants or view a particularly dramatic mountain pass. 'I was undressing that night,' she tells her friends, after one such expedition, 'when some beast kept poking round my tent, now here, now there – violently. I whistled and called Mirza, upon which it seemed to raise itself up as if it would break down the curtains of the tent. I was really frightened and with my alpine stock struck the creature a violent blow, as I thought on its nose, thinking it was a bear, when a human yell answered, followed by "You hit awfully hard!" – It was the Sahib who I hadn't seen since the day before, come to see if I had got back safely.'

Because of the disturbed state of the country, muleteers absconded, armed escorts from the chiefs did not arrive, the survey schedule fell further behind and Sawyer got 'furiouser and furiouser'. 'I don't believe there would be one difficulty here but for his awful temper and complete contempt of thought and manner for coloured people,' Isabella wrote. After venting his spleen on all the coloureds within sight, he turned on her 'with such a causeless ebullition of rage that I decided we must part company and that I must tell him so'. Such was the force of the Major's personality, however, that it took her three tries before she eventually screwed up courage to do this. Sawyer 'took her head off' at first, and launched into a catalogue of her shortcomings, among which that of her voice figured prominently. 'It had begun to irritate him the day we left Karachi, he told me, and at times nearly maddens him!' But in fact she was well-nigh invaluable to him just then, in spite of her voice, and she was enjoying herself after her original fashion. So he promised to curb his temper and be less rude to the natives, and she agreed to stay.

But those joys she did experience during the last six weeks of their journey together seldom leap from the pages of her published narrative. As they scrambled west across the mountain ranges, she provides a quantity of geographical information, her interest in the subject sharpened by her enforced participation in the survey-work, and this is occasionally brightened by vivid descriptions of the scant human activity around. Clearly, it was a hot, tedious journey undertaken at considerable risk, for the threat of violence – reckless, causeless, almost innocently savage – throbbed ceaselessly in the rarefied air. On two occasions their caravan was fired upon by tribesmen outlined in traditional fashion on the hill-crests; and once they found themselves in the middle of a tribal fracas. 'Bang, bang. The firing is now close and frequent,' Isabella records, 'and the dropping shots are varied by straggling volleys.' As she trained her field-glasses on the combatants, who were scuffing up and down the hillsides shooting and yelling, she thought what stupid dreary warfare this was. For such a torn and untamed land, the only real remedy would be her favourite one – the benevolent overlordship of British rule. 'Why don't the English come and give us peace?' the Bakhtiari apparently asked her on many occasions. But she realised that had the British, the Persians or anyone else come to tame these predatory nomads, most of them would have fought to the joyous death to preserve their savage freedom and any alliance they made would founder on the treacherous sands of greed and deceit.

Though Isabella is at pains to point out the Bakhtiari virtues – their love of children, occasional merriment, familial loyalty – they sound the most dangerous and unpleasant people she ever travelled among, and she was most fortunate to emerge from their territory without being 'left to stand in her skin', their graphic way of describing the state of those they had plundered. But she did, and on 9 August reached Burujerd, where Sawyer's mission ended. Isabella's letters to her friends end earlier, so there is little hint of how the two seasoned travellers parted. Anna Stoddart, who always thought the conventional view was the nicest, says 'they bade each other goodbye as comrades who had gone through difficulty, danger and privation together'. Probably they did, but certainly Sawyer was glad to hear the last of that

over-careful ageing voice of Isabella's, and she expresses relief
'that no call to boot and saddle' would break the sleep of future
dawns.

IV

To substitute for the unpredictable stimulating companionship
of the handsome Major, Isabella bought 'Boy', a powerful
compact stallion, 'with a big ugly head and flopping ears' and a
proud, uncut tail 'carried in fiery fashion'. He was unsuspicious,
affectionate and engaging, but a real coward and would turn
tail and bolt at the whiff of a camel. Like all Persian horses, he
wore a surprising quantity of clothes, even in summer: 'a *parhan*
or shirt of fine wool crossed over the chest, then a similar garment
of thicker material and at night a *namad*, 'a piece of felt half an
inch thick, so long that it wraps the animal from head to tail
and so deep as to cover his body down to the knees'. During the
first day out on the journey west from Burujerd, Boy came walking
into her tent and 'made it very apparent that he wanted me to
divide a melon with him'. Grapes were his next penchant – he
would eat up to ten pounds a day 'for dessert' – then cucumbers,
pears and biscuits. When she sat outside, he was tied to her chair
and rubbed his nose against her face for the occasional pat;
when she walked, he followed like a dog and watched with
interest when she picked flowers, and when she rode him frolicked
happily, sure-footed and beautiful.

It was harvest-time, and at the oasis town of Sahmine, two
marches from Burujerd. 'All the open spaces were threshing-
floors'. Heaps of wheat were 'tossed into the air on a fork, the
straw is carried for a short distance and the grain, falling to the
ground, is removed and placed in great clay jars in the living-
rooms of the houses. All the villages are now surrounded with
mounds of *kah* (broken straw) which will be stored before snow
comes. The dustiness of the winnowing process is indescribable.
I was nearly smothered with it in Sahmine, and on windy days
each village is enveloped in a yellow dust storm.'

When there was no wind, however, the last fierce heats of
summer hung in thick, almost tangible wedges over the plains,
and Isabella who had born the sharp cold of the uplands with

equanimity came down with fever. On one such day, when the air stormed with sand-flies, and the steel-white sun almost scorched the hair from her head, she could no longer bear to ride, and lay down in a roadside ditch to rest. The following vignette amusingly suggests how she surmounted sudden difficulties – with resource, determination, asperity and not a little luck. She was aroused by 'Mirza's voice saying in cheerful tones, "Madam your horse is gone!" "Gone," I exclaimed, "I told you always to tether him." "I trusted him," he replied sententiously. "Never trust any one or any horse, and least of all yourself," I replied unadvisedly. I sent him back with his horse to look for Boy, telling him when he saw him to dismount and go towards him with the nose-bag, and that though he would approach it and throw up his heels and trot away at first, he would eventually come near enough to be caught. After half an hour he came back without him. . . . He said he saw Boy, rode near him twice, did not dismount, held out to him not the nose-bag with barley but my "courier bag", and that Boy then cantered out of sight! For the moment I shared Aziz Khan's contempt for the "desk-bred" man.

'Mirza is so good that one cannot be angry with him, but it was very annoying to hear him preach about "fate" and "destiny" while he was allowing his horse to grind my one pair of smoked spectacles into bits under his hoofs. I only told him that it would be time to fall back on *fate* and *destiny* when, under any given circumstances, such as these, he had exhausted all the resources of forethought and intelligence. My plight was a sore one, for by that time I was really ill, and had lost, as well as my horse and saddle, my food, quinine, writing materials and needlework. I got on the top of the baggage and rode for five hours, twice falling off from exhaustion.' At length they reached a village, where she went to bed in her tent, promising a large reward for anyone who found Boy. 'The next morning a gentle thump, a low snuffle and a theft of some grapes by my bedside announced that Boy was found.' And the contents of the holsters, which were missing, were later returned to her also.

Her fever continued, and when she reached the city of Hamadan she stayed three weeks to recuperate. At Hamadan, in her circumstances, anyone with less of an insatiable appetite for comfortless and perpetual motion would surely have called it a day, packed up and gone home the easy way by Baghdad and Cairo. The fever had left her debilitated, all her stores had again been stolen, another winter lurked behind the mountains. But such a temptation, if indeed it was one, gained no ground with her. When *she* looked at the map, the obvious way home seemed to be a north-westerly overland journey of a thousand miles through west Persia, parts of Kurdistan and Armenia to Trebizond on the Black Sea. It was not a route with much popular appeal and local muleteers offered various excuses for refusing to take it – it was too late in the season, they would all be robbed, they didn't know the way. But at last she made a contract for mules, men and supplies with 'a well-dressed Turk' who proved as untrustworthy as he looked, and left Hamadan in mid-September.

Her 'marches' averaged eighteen miles a day, and by the sixth of them there were so many Kurds about and so little Persian was spoken that, though officially still in Persia, she felt she had reached romantic Kurdistan. Kurdistan, 'a name in very common use upon the title-page of travellers' books,' wrote Lord Curzon, turning his mocking gaze in Mrs Bishop's direction, 'is no more than a convenient geographical expression for the entire country estimated at over 50,000 square miles that is inhabited by Kurds. This region has no natural or political boundaries; it includes both Turkish and Persian territory and it contains many other elements, Turkish, Persian, Chaldean and Armenian in the population as well'. The various elements squabbled among themselves as usual, and the Kurds, bigoted, fiery, ruthless people, had, Curzon adds, 'proved a thorn in the side of every ruling power' that had ever established sovereignty in western Asia. He utterly disapproved of their predatory activities and their 'sullen swagger' so 'usually associated with picturesque ruffianism'. But Isabella, who always had a sneaking admiration for the ruffian type, was prepared to like the Kurds very much, though she learned so many unpleasant things about them that she later had to revise her opinion.

The men were wild-looking, gay, festooned with swords, long knives, guns, with garlands of bullets round their waists, and quite free from the distasteful 'Persian cringe'. The women were

'unveiled, bold-faced and handsome in the Meg Merrilees style'
and it was refreshing to see 'their firm elastic walk after the
tottering gait of the shrouded formless bundles which pass for
Persian women'. They were hospitable and invited her into their
houses, gloomy labyrinths of clean low-roofed clay-floored rooms.
They enthroned her on piles of quilts, offered Russian tea,
warned her of the fearsome perils of the road ahead, chatted
about their crops and animals of which they seemed to have an
abundance. Other travellers comment on the pressures of Kurdish
hospitality, and one recalled that, as a gesture of friendship, a
chief would 'select a particularly greasy lump of lamb's fat from
the stew and stuff it well down into the guest's mouth with his
dirty fingers, on which one is supposed to choke out, "The Lord
be praised, it is excellent".' Isabella contrived to avoid this
amiable custom, but the men did thrust upon her the traditional,
hectic escort when she left each village – a 'throw on the road',
as it was called. They charged around her, wheeling their steeds
in ever-narrowing circles and 'sometimes tearing up and down
steep hills, firing over the left shoulders and right flanks of their
horses, lunging at each other with much-curved scimitars, and
singing inharmonious songs'.

This was all thrillingly interesting and Isabella felt happy
again. The air had a spirited edge that restored her health, the
nearest European was miles away, galloping on Boy was a daily
delight. On these western plains no rain had fallen for months
and the prevailing colours were cobalt, ochre and buff-brown.
The distant mountains provided the cobalt, dissolving into a
washy-blue horizon; ochre were the nearby houses and the stacks
of fodder on the roofs, and buff-brown the near foothills, the
dried straw-beds, the mud walls of ruinous forts, the hides of
ploughing oxen, the dusty fat-tailed sheep. She came upon a
Seyyid one day, a Moslem holy man with a commanding physique
and the frigid pride of the ascetic, who preached with such
fervour about the virtues of 'Houssein' that his hearers beat their
breasts and howled with conviction; she came upon strings of
carts with huge creaking wheels drawn by four buffalo and a
boy who sat on the back of one crooning a perpetual melody – if
he stopped, so did the beasts.

And then, really too soon, she came upon the plain of Urmi,

the 'Paradise of Persia' where the waters began and so the grass was green, the orchards fruit-laden, the fields golden. Looking down upon the region on a bright autumn day she watched the activity of this suddenly fertile land: 'Here the wine-press is at work, there girls are laying clusters of grapes on terraces prepared for the purpose, to dry for raisins; women are gathering cotton and castor-oil seeds, little boys are taking buffaloes to bathe, men are driving and loading buffalo-carts, herding mares, ploughing and trenching, and in the innumerable villages the storehouses are being filled; the herbs and chillies are hanging from the roofs to dry, the women are making large cakes of animal fuel . . . and are building it into great conical stacks, the crones are spinning in the sun, and the swaddled infants bound in their cradles are lying in the fields and vineyards while their mothers are at work'.

Rich, tranquil Urmi marked the end of the most interesting parts of this journey – or at least, the end of Isabella's most interesting accounts of it. From there, she ascended the lonely mountains of Kurdistan, where settlements of Syrian and Armenian Christians were being murdered, robbed and persecuted by bands of armed Kurdish brigands. She visited the Patriarch of the dispossessed Syrian church in his mountain retreat at Kochanes and journeyed towards the Black Sea via Van and Erzerum. She was horrified to discover that, throughout the whole area, the Syrian and Armenian peasants were cruelly impoverished and oppressed by both Kurds and local officials. She became furiously indignant at the situation, and it was an indignation that spurred her into action on behalf of these mild, defenceless people when she reached England.

On the last day of October, a day away from the relative security of Van, she wrote: 'As I have no lodging but a dark stable, I am utilising the late afternoon, sitting by the village threshing floor, on which a mixed rabble of animals is treading corn. Some buffaloes are lying in moist places looking amiable and foolish. Boy is tied to my chair. The village women knit and stare. Two of the men, armed with match-lock guns, keep a look-out for the Kurds. A crystal stream tumbles through the village, over ledges of white quartz. Below, the valley opens and discloses ranges bathed in ineffable blue. The mountain sides are aflame with autumn tints, and down their steep paths oxen are bringing the tawny gold of the late harvest on rude sledges . . .'

It is an attractive, typical last picture of Isabella's great middle-eastern safari, as she sat writing by the side of a threshing-floor, with peasants and animals about her, beloved Boy tethered to her chair, and the sounds and sights of wild nature brilliant and close. The best of it was over by then, although she took more than another month to reach Trebizond in easy stages. Communications were most effective in those days, once on the well-beaten tracks. She left Trebizond on 13 December by steamer, went to Constantinople, was in Paris on Christmas Day, in London at six a.m. on Boxing Day, where she breakfasted with her publishers, Mr and Mrs Murray, travelled to Edinburgh that night and there came to temporary rest at the home of Professor and Mrs Grainger Stewart in Charlotte Square.

CHAPTER IX
Korea

MRS ISABELLA BISHOP faced the New Year – her sixtieth. On New Year's Day she made a pilgrimage to Tobermory. It was an inappropriate time to choose, with the Hogmanay whisky flowing and the Hogmanay pipes skirling, and no one probably having much in mind, just then, pious little Miss Henrietta Bird who died there eleven years before. Isabella stayed just two days and returned miserably to Edinburgh. There were aching voids in familiar places where the well-beloved faces had been; it was much more painful than when she was abroad, distanced from these poignant emptinesses. She told Ella Blackie, 'It is *most desolate* to return after two years and have no home to go to and no familiar things about me.' Nevertheless, she was temperamentally incapable of making a home for herself, as she already knew, even though she went through the motions of inspecting various Edinburgh houses – only to reject them all. 'It is so so difficult to decide on anything like *settling*,' she concluded.

And she did not settle; instead she swamped any wish to do so in a positive mill-race of private visits and public professional obligations that lasted for the next three years, and from which she then again fled abroad. Several impulses prodded her into this compulsive activity: an increasing sense of social responsibility that made her attempt to alleviate a little of the suffering and hardship she had seen on her travels; a growing belief that Christianity was a force for good in the world and that its message could be most effectively spread through the work of medical missions; a personal conviction, verging on guilt, that she had not the moral strength, the charity of soul or the sweetness of temper that graced those whom she had so loved in the past. Compared with theirs, her life had been one of thoughtless

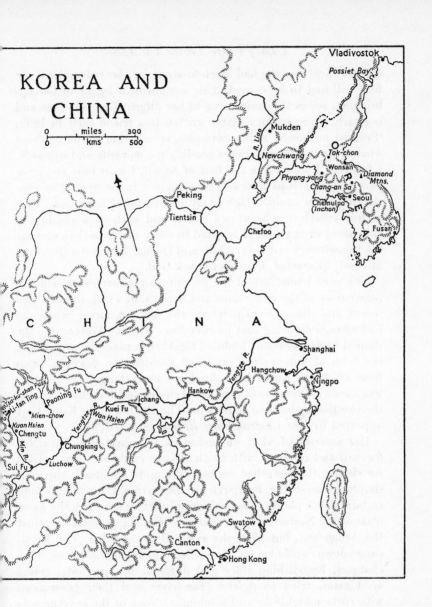

KOREA AND
CHINA

miles 0 300
kms 0 500

Vladivostok
Possiet Bay

Mukden
R. Liao
Newchwang
Tok-chon
Wonsan
Phyong-yang
Chang-an Sa
Diamond Mtns.
Chemulpo (Inchon)
Seoul
Peking
Tientsin
Chefoo
Fusan

C H I N A

Shanghai
Hangchow
Ningpo
Nisa-ku-shan pass
Li-fan ting
Paoning Fu
Ichang
Hankow
Yangtze R.
Mien-chow
Kuan Hsien
Chengtu
Kuei Fu
Wan Hsien
Min R.
Sui Fu
Luchow
Chungking

Swatow
Canton
Hong Kong

self-gratification; she had much to atone for; *her* redemption, she
felt, still had to be earned. This sentiment, a legacy of her upbringing, seems the mainspring of her diligence at this time and
is clearly expressed in a letter written to a friend early in 1892:
'Beloved memories, noble examples, stimulating words of those
whom I have lost are always goading me onwards and upwards.
I feel that I *must* make the best of myself, I *must* bear an active
part in life, I *must* follow their examples to be worthy of ever
meeting them again, which is my one personal hope. And thus
with a ceaseless ache at my heart, and without a shadow of
enjoyment in anything, I respond to every call to action, and my
life though very sad is very full, and though I cannot enjoy I am
intensely interested. For this I thank God.'

The most immediate of the pressures upon her concerned the
persecution of the Armenians and Syrians, of which she had had
recent and dramatic experience. She did not forget what she
had witnessed during that journey from Urmi to Trebizond – the
ill-used Syrian peasants huddled together in caves for protection,
the tales of kidnapping, rape and murder, the desolate farms
from which the Kurds had plundered everything. The question
was already a vexed one in political circles and Isabella increased
the vexation by her two articles on 'The Shadow of the Kurd' that
appeared in *The Contemporary Review* in mid-1891.

Her account of what was going on is unhysterical, straight-
forward and resonant with truth. As she explained, her motives
for visiting the disturbed regions were quite apolitical: she went
simply to meet the Patriarch of the Syrian Church and 'add
certain alpine plants to my collection'. Before she went she knew
little of the Nestorians and 'shared a common prejudice' against
the Armenians, but what she saw had enraged her. The Kurds
came down wolf-like on the village folds, mounted on fiery
chargers, brandishing rifles and daggers; the peasants, riding
aged asses, tried to defend themselves and their possessions
with rusty matchlocks and pitchforks. None of the governments
concerned made any effort to protect their Christian subjects:
the peasants, Isabella explained, 'know nothing of justice except
that it may be bought and they are too poor to buy it'. And
the condition of the Syrians, 'squeezed between the rapacity
and violence of the Kurds and the oppression of the Turkish

officials', must surely be 'one of the most pitiable on earth'. The voice of Mrs Bishop was now of some account in the land. Even before the articles appeared, Isabella was invited to dine at John Murray's to meet his friend, Mr Gladstone. 'The great statesman took her down to dinner,' Anna Stoddart says, 'and questioned her keenly about the Kurdish atrocities amongst Nestorians and Armenians.' Undoubtedly she answered him intelligently and meticulously in that slow gentle voice of hers. Then she said, ' "And now Mr Gladstone, you have asked me a great many questions and I have done my best to answer them; may I venture to ask you one?" "Certainly," he said. "Then what was the Nestorian heresy?" "Ah," said he, laying down his knife and fork and wheeling round in his chair, "that is a matter in which I am profoundly interested." And he entered on a long, learned and precise exposition of the heresy, quoting historians, Fathers of the Church, modern critics, without pause or failure of memory, and at the end of half an hour left her not only amazed at his vast and accurate knowledge, but conversant with the whole schism.' In retrospect, it sounds a somewhat sombre occasion, but it is the only one recorded of Mrs Bishop's dining with such a very eminent politician. And it is pleasant to imagine that Isabella later enlivened proceedings by telling Gladstone about the red and yellow deity on the relic-holder in Shergol that bore such 'a striking resemblance' to him.

Her political involvement was not over. After the publication of the articles, she was invited to speak in a Committee Room of the House of Commons about what was already being called 'The Armenian Question' and would of course, become much more tragic and inflamed in the future. She spoke well, apparently, though in a state of extreme and almost incapacitating nervousness. Isabella never learned to bloom and cavort in the limelight, and demanding public occasions brought her much panic and little pleasure. As she wrote to the secretary of the Royal Geographical Society on a later occasion when he asked her to speak, 'I cannot get over a diffidence which I feel about everything, and no amount of success relieves me from the fear of failure. I always do my best, but . . . am always thoroughly dissatisfied afterwards.'

Still, she continued to do her dutiful best and it kept her from moping. 'I am most thankful for all new interests out of myself, for I feel that without them my sorrowful solitude would be greater than I can bear', she told Mrs Grainger Stewart, with whom she had recently stayed. The next major interest was the writing of her book, *Journeys in Persia and Kurdistan,* in the preface of which she apologises for 'the lack of vivacity' due to 'the heavy and abiding shadow' cast by her sister's and husband's deaths. This lack, which is indisputable, made the task an irksome one. Many of her notes and letters had been stolen or lost in the Persian postal service and those that survived seemed without zest or even interest. 'Persia is dull and ugly and my journey seems very flat and the tribes and their *khans* are as monotonous as Layard's,' she tells Ella, and, in a later mood of impatient depression about the book, she snaps, 'I shall never publish my letters again, though some I believe prefer their petty details.' Nor did she publish in letter-form again, though fortunately not all the 'petty details' are expunged as a result. In accordance with an agreement made with Sawyer, her accounts of their journeys together had to be vetted by the International Department of the Indian War Office, 'a truly hampering arrangement' and one which now seemed a heavy price to pay for the irascible Major's company. She had several cordial meetings with him, though, and consulted him over the map of the Bakhtiari country, which gave no end of trouble. She had to ask the head of the Indian Government Survey about it and he told her the matter 'was a delicate one' – it might be strategically imprudent to indicate the route that Sawyer had surveyed for military intelligence. As she had already decided, when she and Sawyer sailed from Karachi under sealed orders, 'Mystery is the joy of the Indian Government.'

She escaped to Mull to finish the book and found that the island's postal service was little more reliable than the Persian. Her correspondence to Murray about the map was mislaid and she explains, 'The Post Office here is generally distrusted and the postmaster has been twice suspended. It is generally believed that a kettle is kept on the stove for the purpose of steaming open letters which may prove interesting! A common practice in West Highland offices.' This letter of Isabella's was sent from Mull, and it is surprising that it survived. Probably the postmaster's interest in the maps of the Bakhtiari country had rapidly waned.

In spite of the difficulties, the book was out before Christmas 1891, just about the time that Isabella gave a talk to the Tobermory Y.W.C.A. (which she had founded) on 'Persian Manners and Customs' illustrated by two members wearing costumes brought from Isfahan. And in spite of her fears the book was extolled by the critics, though with a hint of stay-at-home exasperation at the needless though shining endurance of those who went so far and did so much – particularly when they were ladies. But a lady, conceded *Blackwood*'s reviewer, apropos of Isabella's book, 'whose comfort is secured by a little hot water and a pinch of tea is really better off than him to whom stronger stimulants and more extensive meals are necessary'. In fact, in the field of travel-literature, 'it is the man who gets writer's cramp and breaks down in health . . . while the woman, his contemporary, goes on serenely with a smile piling up volume after volume with the measured and sedate force of a conscientious day-labourer'. This was rather grudging, and Isabella undoubtedly preferred the critic who wrote that she 'could not have served the cause of medical missions better than by her poignant descriptions of the crowds round her tent' begging for the *hakkim*'s ministrations.

While the critics pronounced judgement, Isabella stayed on Mull through the wild dark rages of the Highland winter, pottering about in the draughty cottage and existing on a diet of dry toast, mutton hotch-potch and a glass of port wine daily in a belated attempt to melt a few pounds of her 'too too solid flesh'. This unjust and apparently irreducible plumpness incidentally, allied to her short stature, offered little scope for the sartorial dramatics in which she might well have indulged had she been six inches taller and willowy. As it was, she confined herself to severe black silks for nearly all formal occasions, with an occasional blooming into oriental brocades, as at the party described by Marianne North; for the rest, she relaxed into a comfortable and unstudied eccentricity – a black ulster, warm serge petticoats and old jerseys. 'Her costume,' says Anna Stoddart, 'shocked some of the good Tobermory people, and indeed it was adapted rather for convenience than beauty. A servant lassie, listening to her praises from her mistress, who descanted on the courage with which she overcame the difficulties of travelling amongst half-savage peoples, said scornfully, "It's no wonder she gets through – no one would look at her. " '

The islanders were glad of her presence nevertheless when, as the weather worsened, everyone went down with influenza or pleurisy and Isabella helped the overworked doctor; her little leather medicine-box was gaining as much reputation as among the Bakhtiaris, she told Ella. Gales bellowed, bringing down telegraph-poles and delaying the mail-boats; wan mists and snow 'unsunned and sodden' clung along the burns; black rains soused the hairy moors. When the weather was at its foul worst, Isabella habitually donned her rubber boots, an officer's mackintosh and sou'wester and blundered out into it; 'The Stormy Petrel' people called her, knowing her preference for the drama of the wildest days. Gathered to a friend's fireside, she compared rheumatic symptoms with old Mrs MacLachlan of Badarroch or talked gardening with the Allans of Aros House; she plied 'Henrietta's poor' with beef jelly or chicken soup; she lectured to the Y.W.C.A. on such uplifting subjects as 'Tit for Tat', 'Getting On' and 'Thrift' – again thrift, it was a recurrent theme. The trouble with many of the islanders, in her view, was that they were notoriously unthrifty, and had little desire to 'get on'. They were 'charming', but she confided to her mainland friends that they nearly all 'suffered from brain-rust', while some of the lower orders, with 'their cunning, moral timidity and plausibility' reminded her of 'savages of rather a low type'. During the next winter, which she again spent on the island, she tried to organise cookery classes for the local women. 'It has been awful work because the people are so dilatory and shilly-shally,' she complained to Ella. It was the old story in fact – the poor and meek never quite managed to live up to the high standards she expected of them. In spite of all her endeavours, Isabella could not suffer fools gladly, as even her most devoted biographer admitted; she just had not the temperament to encourage every faltering step with sweet patience, win over every backslider with gentle persuasion and make charitable allowances for the unredeemably mediocre.

Her talents were broader, more forceful than these; as a writer, she could enlighten and interest the minds of many; as a speaker, her influence was now considerable. During these years she used her abilities to further the work of medical missions and encourage sympathy and understanding for the parts of the world she had explored. In these causes, the figure of Mrs Bishop, short, undeniably plump, sheathed in black silk, with her calm intelligent face and gentle voice, became a familiar and respected one throughout the country. She spoke to the Moravian Mission about Tibet, to Church Congresses in Wakefield, Southampton, Glasgow, York, to Syrian Christians in Leeds, to the British Association and the Royal Scottish Geographical Society about the Bakhtiari.

Isabella had been made a fellow of the Royal Scottish Geographical Society, and when the Royal Geographical Society in London agreed to admit members of other geographical socities it was faced with the proposition of admitting women members to its cloistered ranks. This caused a fine furore, as the Council of the R.G.S. first elected Isabella along with fourteen other 'well-qualified ladies' to be fellows and then faced a furious rearguard attack from its many misogynist members. The columns of *The Times* boiled with the debate and Admirals (who had spent years at sea escaping their wives) thumped the tables of the Council Chamber in protest against the flimsiest shadow of a petticoat rule. At a special General Meeting, the vote went against the admission of ladies, and an uneasy compromise was eventually reached whereby those female fellows already elected had special dispensation to remain, but no more of their weak sex were to be admitted. Isabella, who was in a strong position to enter the lists, remained publicly aloof from the controversy. The fact was that she did not have enough faith in or sympathy for the great majority of womankind to be any sort of suffragette. Though she must have realised that the educational, social and professional restrictions imposed upon her sex cramped and frustrated her own natural development, particularly during her earlier years, she seems always to have assumed that she was an inexplicable and not very laudable exception to the general rule, and that most women were neither deserving of nor particularly fitted for the greater freedoms allowed to men. So she confined her disgust to private correspondence. 'I don't care to take any steps in the matter as I never took any regarding admission. The fellowship as it stands at present is not worth making any trouble about. At the same time, the proposed act is a dastardly injustice to women.'

Probably the aspect of the affair that most offended her personally was the utterly irrational attitude of Curzon, with whom she had been on friendly terms, so she thought, since their meeting on the Tigris. He had given her practical advice with her book and an excellent review of it, but then, at the height of the silly controversy, he announced his violent opposition to the admission of women to the Royal Geographical Society on the somewhat irrelevant grounds that 'Their sex and training render them equally unfitted for exploration, and the genus of professional female globetrotters with which America has lately familiarised us is one of the horrors of the latter end of the nineteenth century.' Curzon's own book on Persia did not appear until several months after Isabella's, because of a certain amount of political hocus-pocus. Soon after his return, Curzon had been appointed by Lord Salisbury to the Under-Secretaryship for India, a post he much coveted. In his newly-elevated state, however, it was considered that the strictures he had made on the Shah's administration in the first draft of his book were too harsh. He and Salisbury corresponded on the matter, Curzon protesting that everything he had written was quite true, to which the Prime Minister replied, in a masterly example of political double-think, 'But your plea on behalf of your utterances that they are all *true* is quite inadmissible. That is precisely the circumstance that will make them intolerable to the Shah.' The book, with the offending passages duly toned down, eventually appeared and was hailed as a standard work in many quarters. But several thought it was extremely hard going – 'nearly seven pounds weight of solid print', moaned one critic; and another, irritated by Curzon's customary tone of effortless superiority, commented, 'Mr Curzon seems to be under the impression that he has discovered Persia and that having discovered it he now, in some mysterious way, owns it.' Comments like that perhaps gave Isabella some satisfaction, although she was not malicious and did not harbour grudges.

She hadn't time to, for one thing, as she rushed from one speaking engagement to another, her most noted achievement in this field being the address she gave to the Gleaners' Union in Exeter Hall, London in November 1893 on 'Heathen Claims and Christian Duty'. Quotations from the speech are interesting because they show Isabella's definite change in attitude towards evangelism. She described herself as 'A traveller who had been made a convert to missions not by missionary successes, but by seeing in four and a half years of Asiatic travel the desperate needs of the un-Christianised world. There was a time when I was altogether indifferent to missions, and would have avoided a mission-station rather than have visited it. But the awful pressing claim of the un-Christianised nations, which I have seen, had taught me that the work of their conversion to Christ is one to which one would gladly give influence and whatever else God has given to one.' The broad tolerance and uncritical detachment of the sound journalist unhappily fled when she addressed such assemblies: Buddhism and Mohammedanism were both 'corrupt'; the Asian continent 'is the scene of barbarities, tortures, brutal punishments, oppression, official corruption which is worst under Mohammedan rule'; the whole un-Christian world, devoid of the 'sanctities of home', of righteousness, temperance and knowledge of the judgement to come, rolled pitifully in the heathen dark.

Her plea was for dedication to the service of mankind, to those who were ill and suffering. 'Throughout the East,' she concluded, 'sickness is believed to be the work of demons. The sick person at once becomes an object of loathing and terror, is put out of the house, is taken to an outhouse, is poorly fed and rarely visited, or the astrologers or priests or medicine men and wizards assemble, beating big drums and gongs, blowing horns and making the most fearful noises. They light fires and dance around them with their unholy incantations. They beat the sick person with clubs to drive out the demon. They lay him before a roasting fire till his skin is blistered and then throw him into cold water. They stuff the nostrils of the dying with aromatic mixtures, or mud, and in some regions they carry the chronic sufferer to a mountain-top, placing barley-balls and water beside him and leave him to die alone. . . .' It was strong, persuasive stuff, much of it was true and it went down well.

In all these causes Isabella wore herself out, and yet it was to the 'corrupt and vicious' East she turned in search of solace, enthusiasm and delight. She told herself that one of the reasons for her journey was to report on the work of missions in Korea and China; in the preface of her book on Korea she says her journey was 'part of a plan of study of the leading characteristics of the Mongolian races'. She went, surely, because she was thoroughly weary of clerical drawing-rooms and church congresses, of petty wrangles over women's rights, of rather dull admiring friends and relatives, of drear rooms filled with mementoes of the beloved dead, of editors, critics and the fulsome compliments of presiding chairmen, of 'door-bells and please me'ms', of the tribulations of the Armenians and the insufficiencies of the western islanders. She yearned to straddle a steed and go galloping over some airy plain, she longed for another encounter with the bright eyes of danger and for the stimulation of fresh sights, strange sounds, the jostle of unknown bodies, and the warm, spicy, fetid, perfumed, musty, lush, stewed stinks of the East.

She was sixty-three and physically in poor shape. During her time at home doctors had told her that she was suffering from rheumatic gout, over-exhaustion, an infection of one lung and 'fatty and calcareous degeneration of the heart'. 'I have become very elderly – indeed I may say an old woman, and stout!' she warned one friend who had not seen her for a time. 'My hair will not turn grey, and thus I am deprived of the softening, and almost renovating influence which silver hair exercises on a plain face. I still wear deep mourning, but not a cap of any kind.' But, she added, 'Mentally I think and hope that I am more sympathetic, and that my interests outside of myself are larger and wider, but probably this does not appear, as my manner is quieter than ever. I have written this much to prepare you for a "little soul" in a big body!' That quietness of mien was perfectly self-assured, and by now it sheathed a well-furnished, keen, disciplined mind, an astonishing capacity for reckless courage and endurance, that same absorbing, unstinting God-given faculty of being interested which never failed.

Early in January 1894 Mrs Bishop boarded the steamer *Mongolia* bound for Yokohama. The more she travelled the lighter she went, but this time her luggage did include two cameras, for she had recently attended an advanced photography class at the Regent Street Polytechnic. Anna Stoddart saw her off at the docks and says, 'When bidding me farewell, she seemed to be wrapped up in the sombre expectation of death in the East.' Mingled perhaps with that gloomy expectation was an equally sombre realisation: that Mrs John Bishop, missionary advocate, authority on Kurds and Persians, celebrated writer, public speaker, helper of the needy, was essentially a lonely, not very happy person. It was Isabella Bird, traveller extraordinary, who had the gift of happiness, and she owed no deep allegiance now to anyone or to any place, so that, if she had died alone, in some far-flung corner of a foreign field, it would have been quite fitting.

II

During the next three years Isabella circulated between Tokyo, Seoul and Shanghai as other elderly widows of comfortable means might savour the delights of London, Paris and Carlsbad. She wrote little more about Japan, that had become, as it were, the London, familiar sanctuary of her wanderings. Her interest and enthusiasm centred on Korea and parts of China, and she wrote comprehensive accounts of each in *Korea and Her Neighbours* and *The Yangtze Valley and Beyond*. She went first to Korea and spent four months there, during which, she told John Murray, it 'took less hold of me than any country I ever travelled in. It is monotonous in every way, and the Koreans seem the dregs of a race – indolent, cunning, limp and unmanly.' But that was a premature judgement, for Korea, like, say, Bolivia or Finland, is an acquired taste on the traveller's palate, and Isabella was already unconsciously acquiring it.

In 1894 Korea was still known as 'The Hermit Nation' that turned an unsociable, unchanging, elderly face to the world. So unsociable was it, the story went, that its coastal areas had been deliberately deforested in order to present the bleakest, most inhospitable and discouraging aspect to the stranger. And the lack of change was such that its King belonged to a dynasty dating from 1392, which managed to survive until 1910. But the Korean image was disintegrating, had begun to do so in 1866 when citizens of several western nations landed 'to trade, rob, kill or, what was equally obnoxious to the regent and his court, to make treaties,' says William Griffis, the American historian, who concluded that 'the fires of civilisation were beginning to smoke out the hermit'. During the next decade or so 'obnoxious treaties' which opened some ports to foreign trade were forced upon the Korean authorities, who sent this plaintive note to the leader of one early American expedition: 'This people and Kingdom have lived in enjoyment of their own civilisation for four thousand years and want no other. We trouble no other nations. Why should they trouble us? Our country is in the furthest east, yours in the furthest west. For what purpose do you come so many thousands of miles across the sea?'

It was an exceedingly good question, but one unlikely to deter either the Americans or the other major powers that soon arrived upon the scene, and forced Korea into the thankless role of 'buffer', 'shuttlecock', 'pawn on the international chessboard', 'pigskin in the world's football game' and other sporting paraphernalia with which historians seek to enliven their pages. Korea, wrote one, was 'patronised, cajoled, bullied and caressed' by the powers that were, and by none more so than by the Japanese who, having themselves responded quite differently to the challenge of the West, delighted in the pleasurable exercise of forcing upon someone else a dose of the same medicine they had been given (to use one of those enlivening historian's metaphors). In 1876 the Japanese made a Treaty of Peace and Friendship with Korea and, then proceeded to secure a position of economic and commercial ascendancy in the country that threatened to out-rival the Chinese who, in the past, had maintained undisputed suzerainty over Korean affairs. So Japan and Korea became locked in a bitter and stormy relationship, and Isabella was on hand during the enactment of some of its cruellest, most dramatic collisions.

When she first arrived, in March 1894, Korea was still under its last three months of Chinese suzerainty, but precariously so, its weak government 'confronted with the ill-suppressed cupidity of Russia, the mysterious latent force of China, the jealous and vainglorious interest of Japan.' These were the words of George Curzon, who, on his Grand Tour of Asia, had preceded Isabella by a few years. Because, when he chose, he was eminently capable of packing a great deal of succinct, crackle-sharp commentary into the nutshell of a paragraph, let him describe this typical 'old-style Oriental state' as he saw it, and it still was in 1894: 'A royal figurehead enveloped in the mysteries of the palace and the harem, surrounded by concentric rings of eunuchs, ministers of state, officials and retainers and rendered almost intangible by a predominant atmosphere of intrigue; a hierarchy of office-holders and office-seekers, who were leeches in thinnest disguise, a feeble and insignificant army, impecunious exchequer, a debased currency and an impoverished people – they are the invariable symptoms of the fast vanishing regime of the older and unredeemed oriental type. Add to this the first swarm of the flock of foreign practitioners who scent the enfeebled constitution from afar and from the four winds of heaven come pressing the pharmacopoeia of loans, concessions, banks, mints, factories and all the recognised machinery for filling western purses at the expenses of eastern pockets . . .' and that was Korea, an ailing land, stumbling defenceless into the late nineteenth century, like a reluctant, grubby, rather dull-witted Rip Van Winkle.

And it had this air of shabby melancholy at first sight, as Isabella thought when she landed at the port of Chemulpo. The roadstead was a slimy mud-flat where turtles, crabs and octopuses wriggled and crept, a drizzly rain fell on the deliberately denuded hills. Chemulpo – the name meant 'various-articles-river-bank' – contained a few European merchant houses, an imposing Japanese consulate, tea-garden, Shinto shrine, a foreign club with a billiard-room, a noisy Chinese settlement and a 'comfortless and unworthy building' where dwelt the British Vice-Consul, who was later to cause Isabella considerable inconvenience. She stayed just long enough to observe the tight grip of Japan on the place – a Japanese bank and postal service, an influx of cotton-bearing steamers from Nagasaki and of Japanese agents buying up all the rice they could find to stockpile for the coming war, which, at that time, only they knew was imminent – and then she was carried the twenty-six miles to Seoul in a chair with six bearers.

The entrances to walled Seoul had resounding names: the Gates of Elevated Humanity, High Ceremony and Bright

273

Amiability, but the city inside them had little of the pomp of a capital. Viewed from a hill-top, in fact, Isabella thought it looked like 'an expanse of over-ripe mushrooms'. Yet the old place had a weird appeal that grew upon her. 'I knew Seoul by day and night, its palaces and its slums, its unspeakable mean-ness and faded splendours, its purposeless crowds, its medieval processions, which for barbaric splendour cannot be matched on earth, the filth of its crowded alleys, and its pitiful attempt to retain its manners, customs and identity as the capital of an ancient monarchy in face of the host of disintegrating influences which are at work, but it is not at first that one "takes it in". I had known it for a year before I appreciated it, or fully realised that it is entitled to be regarded as one of the great capitals of the world.'

The magic of the city, to judge from several visitors, including Isabella, lay in its national peculiarities of sound, sight, smell, apparel, custom and a general air of rigid conservatism which Isabella terms 'grooviness'. In no other capital did the chair-coolies sing so hauntingly, or the great bronze bells (hung in 1498) boom so thrillingly, or the magpies chatter so brashly – beloved birds these, because they ganged up to kill house-snakes. Certainly in no other capital was the clatter of laundry-sticks the one and only sound to be heard after nightfall. The women wielded these sticks over their menfolk's clothes which were always white and had to be washed every day and beaten, instead of ironed, to a dull satin polish every night. White was the traditional mourning colour and the custom of always wearing it was said to date from a time when three Korean kings (each deserving of a three-year national mourning) died in one disastrous decade. After that the men decided it was easier to keep in mourning; Curzon, the misogynist, wrote that the men adopted white beaten-smooth robes 'for the excellent purpose they serve in keeping the women busy'.

Peculiar then to Seoul were the streets, filled almost exclusively with men all wearing those same baggy white robes but topped with different hats. 'It is only in Korea,' remarked an American traveller, 'that one realises the infinite possibilities of the genus hat . . . hats for fair weather, hats for foul, indoor hats, outdoor hats, everyday hats, court hats, immense hats, almost no hats', mourners' hats like colossal soup-plates of plaited straw and hats sprouting wings like ping-pong bats. Occasionally, scuttling among this lordly hatted crowd 'which swayed and loafed and did nothing in particular' in Isabella's view, one would see a working woman in a green coat, clutching a bundle of yesterday's masculine laundry to be washed in the nearest fetid ditch. The ditches stank in a manner characteristic of an old-style oriental state, but there were other, distinctively Korean odours. The lacquer of the men's hats smelled sickly in the sun; *kimchi*, the national vegetable dish, a mixture of cabbage, garlic and turnip, imparted to every house and its inhabitants the smell of aged sauerkraut; towards sunset, piles of brushwood were lit for the cooking of the evening meal and every foul alley was sweetened with a haze of aromatic pine smoke. The brushwood was brought into the capital each day on the backs of bulls, and these too were a singular phenomenon – gentle, ruddy-coloured beasts whose loads filled an entire street-width, led by drivers who wore their particular variety of straw-hat – very broadly-brimmed, in order, said the foreigners, that they could jostle you rudely out of the way while pretending they hadn't seen you.

There were few 'sights' to break the monotonous filth of this depressed, eccentric city where 'the ordinary sightseer sees his vocation gone'. There were hardly any magnificent temples, because Buddhism, formerly the official religion, had been disestablished for some three hundred years. Ancestral and demon worship had taken its place and the lovely hillsides around the capital were monopolised by the dead, horizontal under grassy mounds, encircled by crescents of pines, stone lanterns statuary, and thus in a state of spacious dignity which they had seldom attained when vertical. Below one of the highest hills sprawled the Mulberry Gardens, surrounding an ancient royal Audience Hall. The Hall was haunted by demon hordes; cries of murdered kings and of those killed violently on the battlefield screeched across its gilded rafters at night; leopards were said to lurk in the stone drains under the mulberry-bushes; the only living voices heard were the dismal ones of two aged guardian eunuchs.

Clean, thrifty, matter-of-fact, separate on another hill, a colony of some five thousand Japanese throve; near them was the Palace of the Chinese Minister Resident, guarded by dragon-gods and 'a number of big supercilious men dressed in rich brocades and satin'. In enclaves too the westerners resided; most of them, predictably, were American, British or German, consular, missionary or mercantile, and little love was lost between the various factions. Isabella's main contacts were, as usual, with the diplomats and missionaries. Some of the American missionaries had already spent up to ten years in Korea and, as they had been white pioneers on the Korean scene, their view of the country, like that of the missionaries in the Sandwich Isles, was paternalistic and vaguely proprietorial. The missionaries were encouraged too by the heaven-sent void in Korean spiritual life caused by the absence of an official religion, and they were hastening to fill it with a cornucopia of various Christian endeavours. The Roman Catholics had a cathedral with a small spire, the Methodists a mission school, the Presbyterians a hospital, the Anglicans a mission press and English church of the Advent, the Sisters of St Peter a Community House. Isabella visited some of these as was her wont, and at the Boys' Boarding School met Mr F. S. Miller who eventually accompanied her on her journey up the north branch of the River Han to the Diamond Mountains.

It was not a particularly congenial arrangement, for Isabella would have preferred to go by herself, but even she couldn't tackle the Korean interior without an interpreter, and a native one had proved impossible to find. So Mr Miller with his 'imperfect knowledge' of the language was pressed into service, Bishop Corfe lent her his Chinese servant Wong, and she hired a twenty-eight-foot long sampan for the journey. Her preparations were thoroughly spartan and business-like by this time: 'I discarded all superfluities such as flasks, collapsing cups, hand-mirrors, teapots, sandwich tins, lamps and tinned soups, meats, bouillon and fruits', she explained for the benefit of the less initiated, and she took the barest of kitchen necessities, two changes of clothing, a folding chair, bedding, Korean string shoes and the two cameras. The chief burden was money, for the only acceptable coin outside Seoul was *cash*, a pitiful mite with a hole in the middle rated at 3,200 to the dollar. *Cash* was threaded in hundreds on straw strings and it took six men or one pony to carry the equivalent of £10. So the sampan had to be ballasted with *cash*, and was pretty crammed also with sacks of tea and flour, charcoal for the brazier, Isabella herself, Wong, Mr. Miller and his servant, the owner of the boat, (one indolent, ancient Kim), and his assistant who paddled it.

They started on 14 April, an auspiciously gay day: 'The environs of Seoul were seen through a mist of green, and plum and peach blossom was in the ascendant, and the heliotrope azalea was just beginning to tint the hillsides and the air was warm and muggy . . .' According to the Korean Almanac, a kind of Shepherd's Calendar issued every two years by the Korean Astronomical Board, it was the period of the fourth moon, when 'Behold the cry of the water chicken is heard in the land and the earthworm crawls out of his hole. Bitter weeds and barley start and last year's grass dies. Beetles crawl and it is a good time to plant beans.'

For the next five weeks, while the earthworms oozed into the spring sunshine and everyone dutifully planted beans, Isabella and her five male companions floated along the River Han in the sampan. Each dewy morning, lying in her trestle bed under the vessel's makeshift roof of dried pheasant-grass, she awoke to the sounds of 'the bellowing of cattle, shouts and laughter of boys and yelping of dogs as bulls young and old were driven to the river banks to be tethered in the flowery grass'. The river itself was 'cheery with mallard and mandarin duck, geese and common teal', and in the nearby paddies 'the imperial crane, the egret and the pink ibis with the deep flush of spring on his plumage' prodded for food. It was a 'sportsman's paradise' for the few male westerners who passed that way, but no paradise for boatmen. Sometimes the water of the Han dissolved to a pebbly trickle over which even the shallow sampan had to be dragged, sometimes it cascaded down rapids up which everything had to be hauled, and sometimes it flowed nicely wide and green, lapping amicably against the junks carrying salt, tin kettles, dried peppers and Japanese cottons to the interior.

Isabella was contented and busy with her numerous occupations: talking with the people through Mr Miller, 'taking geographical notes, temperatures, altitudes, barometric readings and measurements of the river (nearly all unfortunately lost in a rapid on the downward journey), collecting and drying plants, photographing and developing negatives under difficulties – all the blankets and waterproofs in the boat being requisitioned for the creation of a "dark room" '. At about five o'clock each evening Kim feigned exhaustion, 'a deception to which his lean form and thin face with its straight straggling white hair lent themselves effectively', and there was much bother about the night's anchorage and much haggling with the locals for a hen or its eggs, and much breaking of faggots, frying of rice fritters, gossiping, belching, pipe-tapping and finally snoring from the crew's foredeck. And Isabella too slept soundly, hunched in her trestle bed, looking forward to the simple sounds of animals and people that would wake her at daybreak.

The people of the Han valley were docile, indolent, friendly, robust and they lived in warm, mud-walled homes alongside large stinking pigsties. Each dwelling, however humble, had a best 'gentleman's only' room with matted floor, wooden pillows and large hat cases hanging from the rafters. Here the men were served huge meals on low wood tables and they ate voraciously. Eating was a principal hobby among Koreans, for 'from infancy onwards one object in life is to give the stomach as much capacity and elasticity as possible'. In order to reach the desired amplitude, 'A mother feeds her young child with rice and when it can eat no more in an upright position, lays it on its back on her lap and feeds it again, tapping its stomach from time to time with a flat spoon to ascertain if further cramming is possible.' In later life, therefore, everything was grist to the capacious and omnivorous Korean maw. 'Pork, beef, fish, raw dried and salted, the intestines of all animals, all birds and game, no part being rejected'; fermented beans, seaweed fried in fat, sweet potatoes, lily bulbs, chestnut cakes and baked dog were among other delicacies. Isabella watched people eating over three pounds of meat at a sitting, plus several bowls of rice, topped off perhaps by twenty-five peaches or melons. After the men showed that they 'had reached the desirable state of repletion by eructation, splutter-ings, slapping of the stomach,' they rolled out into the sun to sleep it off and the women came creeping into the room and 'gobbled up their lords' leavings'.

This was indicative of the Korean woman's domestic status.

She had no claims on her husband, only duties towards him.
At the age of puberty she was 'bundled up in a mass of wedding
clothes' and her eyelids were sealed together so that she did not
see the unknown male to whom she was then married. Hence-
forward, she was known only as 'the wife of so-and-so', or the
'mother of such-and-such a son'; her husband called her 'what's-
her-name' or '*ya-bu*' that meant roughly 'look here', and when
he tired of her he took a concubine or perhaps a second wife.
The women of the upper classes led empty, silent, secluded lives;
peasant women were, in a sense, more fortunate, for they could
forget their troubles in work. They fed the bristly black hogs,
cleaned rice with pestle and mortar, beat those lordly robes,
shredded cabbage and turnip for pickled *kimchi*, strung up orange
and ginger peel to dry in the sun. Probably, as Isabella says, it
had never occurred to any humble wife to turn suffragette and
so they, like their husbands, seemed reasonably contented with
their monotonous unadorned lives.

There were just two feared and hated disruptions to the peaceful patterns of Korean rural life, and the darker *bête noire* of
these was the tiger. As Isabella travelled further inland, she heard
ever more bloody tales of tiger depredations. Domestic beasts
and poultry were frequently attacked and so, apparently, were
vulnerable humans – children, isolated woodcutters, lone travellers at night. Isabella was sceptical at first, but the genuine and
voluble terror of the people convinced her that such tales were
true, and indeed they must have been, for deaths-by-tiger were
reported in the respectable missionary-sponsored periodical *The
Korean Repository* with the frequency and gruesome prosaicness
of traffic accidents. For example: 'A son of Mr Kang of Wonsan
aged 12 years was coming home from a neighbour's house some
yards distant when he was caught by a tiger and carried off.
His skull and feet were found next day on a hill, back of the
French missionary Père Boret's compound.' The very prevalence
of such disasters had its uses: a standard way of avoiding creditors
or escaping from the law was to leave bits of one's shredded
clothing in the lonely woods and abscond . . . 'taking a tiger' it
was perhaps called? 'The Korean hunts the tiger one half of the
year and the tiger hunts the Korean the other half' ran the
jeering Chinese proverb. The men who did the half-hearted

hunting were a very special brigade, tough, honoured and singled out for valour like commandos. They wore loose blue uniforms, seed necklaces and special conical hats and were armed with rusty matchlocks charged with three pea-sized balls of shot apiece. The hunt was a risky business, though the rewards were great – tiger insides were coveted by the Chinese for medicines (as in Malaya) ,tiger claws were much prized by wealthy ladies, and tiger skins graced the floors of wealthy homes.

The other curse of the countryside, as predatory, unpredictable and almost as savage as the tiger, was the *yang-ban*. *Yang-bans* were the 'licensed vampires of the nation' in Isabella's view, landed squires, pretentious parasites, high-ranking holders of official sinecures that entitled them to idle in luxury paid for by excessive taxes and forced 'loans' exacted from the humbler classes. Convention forbade a *yang-ban* to work, to bear any burden as heavy as a pipe or book – or even to support the full weight of his own body. Attendants carried his every requirement and supported him on each side as he strutted along at a slow, pompous pace. 'Unsupported,' Curzon suggests, 'he would I suppose fall to the ground from the sheer weight of his own importance.' *Yang-bans* simply lived off the land, entitled to free services, board and lodging wherever they went, and to requisition animals, women or junks as the fancy took them. Peasants hid their daughters, ponies and fattest hens if they knew one was coming, and were sometimes sullenly unhelpful to Isabella's servants, fearing they would browbeat them as did a *yang-ban*'s entourage.

After five weeks on the River Han, Isabella and Miller reached the northernmost navigable point and the journey culminated dramatically in 'a superb mountain view of saddle-back ridges and lofty grey peaks surrounding a dark expanse of water, with a margin of grey boulders and needles of grey rock draped with the *ampelopsis*, a yellow clematis, and a white honeysuckle'. She longed to go on, but the rapids ahead were so fierce that Kim went utterly on strike, so they turned downstream and, a few days later, she and her little party regretfully left the sampan and took to the roads.

For ferocity and pigheaded recalcitrance, the Korean pony was unequalled, even in Isabella's considerable equine experience. When saddled, the beast 'performed the singular feat of bending his back into such an inward curve that his small body came quite near the ground'; when faced with another pony, he went for it, hooves flying, teeth bared, squealing and trumpeting with fury; at night, his bony head was chained to the trough and his body partially slung to the roof-beam in order to prevent him from maiming his stable-mates. Each pony had its own *mapu* (groom) who fed it thrice a day on a brown slush of beans, millet-stalks, rice-husks and water. The animals liked the beans best, and another of Korea's characteristic sounds was the flappety-flop of a pony's long tongue delving to the bottom of the trough and slurping every accessible bean into its mouth. Well-fed though they were, the ponies took a malicious delight in keeping their riders in a state of alarmed suspense by suddenly lying down in the road, or collapsing on their forelegs with their skinny rumps in the air, or even starting off backwards at a brisk trot. Dearly as Isabella loved horses, she never made friends with one of these.

With Mr Miller the question was not so much one of friendship as of simple survival. He wrote a brief account of his journey with Isabella in *The Korean Repository* and made it sound extremely uncomfortable and joyless. While on the sampan he suffered an acute rash, caused, he eventually discovered, by the fleas and other vermin which, descending from the oarsmen's clothes stowed above his bed, took up residence in his underwear. When they changed to ponies, poor Mr Miller rapidly learned that 'I could not ride on a pack-horse as well as I thought I could.' He soon fell off, in fact, into a shallow muddy gulley and lay there 'holding my feet up to keep them dry and looking back to see if Mrs Bishop's horse would step on and soil my shirt bosom. I might have turned a somersault and lit on my feet,' he explains grandly, 'but I was particularly cautioned before leaving home to be sure under all circumstances to keep my feet dry.' How Isabella must have chuckled to herself when she came upon this troubled evangelist with his precious feet in the air! He must have been rather a wet young man however dry his feet, but she gave him some marks for effort, recording that 'though not an experienced traveller' he 'preserved the serenity of his temper under all circumstances'.

And circumstances seemed designed to test the serenity of the most unflinching, especially when they centred upon the Korean inn. They came in two (unstarred) varieties: irregular and regular. The former were untenanted hovels with a few troughs for the beasts. The latter consisted 'of a filthy courtyard full of holes and heaps, entered from the road by a tumble-down gateway. A gaunt black pig or two tethered by the ears, big yellow dogs routing in the garbage, and fowls, boys, bulls, ponies, *mapu*, hangers-on and travellers' loads make up a busy scene.

'On one or two sides are ramshackle sheds, with rude, hollowed trunks in front, out of which the ponies suck the hot brown slush which sustains their strength and pugnacity. On the other is the furnace-shed with the oats where the slush is cooked, the same fire usually heating the flues of the *kang* floor of the common room, while smaller fires in the same shed cook for the guests. Low lattice doors filled in with torn and dirty paper give access to a room the mud floor of which is concealed by reed mats, usually dilapidated, sprinkled with wooden blocks which serve as pillows. Farming gear and hat-boxes often find a place on the low heavy cross-beams. Into this room are crowded *mapu*, travellers, and servants, the low *residuum* of Korean travel, for officials and *yang-bans* receive the hospitalities of the nearest magistracy and peasants open their houses to anybody with whom they have a passing acquaintance. There is in all inns of pretensions, however, another room, known as the "clean room" 8 feet by 6, which, if it existed, I obtained. If not I had a room in the women's quarters at the back, remarkable only for its heat and vermin, and the amount of *ang-paks*, bundles of dirty clothes, beans rotting for soy and other plenishings which it contained, and which reduced its habitable portion to a minimum. At night a ragged lantern in the yard and a glim of oil in the room made groping for one's effects possible.

'The room was always overheated from the ponies' fire. From 80° to 85° was the usual temperature, but it was frequently over 92°, and I spent one terrible night sitting at my door because it was 105° within. In this furnace, which heats the floor and the spine comfortably, the Korean wayfarer revels.

'On arriving at an inn, the master or servant rushes at the mud, or sometimes matted, floor with a whisk, raising a great dust, which he sweeps into a corner. The disgusted traveller soon perceives that the heap is animate as well as inanimate, and the groans, sighs, scratchings, and restlessness from the public room show the extent of the insect pest. But I never suffered from vermin in a Korean inn, nor is it necessary. After the landlord had disturbed the dust, Wong put down either two heavy sheets of oiled paper or a large sheet of cotton dressed with linseed oil on the floor, and on these arranged my camp-bed, chair and baggage. This arrangement (and I write from twenty months' experience in Korea and China) is a perfect preventive.'

A few days later they began an ascent of 1,320 feet across the Pass on Tan-pa Ryong and into the Diamond Mountains, where hundreds of Buddhist monks, who had been banished from all the cities, dwelt in a state of unharassed disestablishment. It was an enchanted region, beautiful beyond her telling. The nearby hills were a tangle of maple, hazel, chestnut and pink azaleas; serrated grey peaks and billows of woodland bunched the distances; valleys were trim old-gold with buckwheat and maize; blue shadows lay along the pines. They spent the night at the monastery of Chang-an Sa, the 'Temple of Eternal Rest' and a model of medievalism with its dormitories, refectories, and infirmary for the halt and blind, cells for wayfarers and temples instead of high-arched churches. The monks, gentle and jolly-seeming fellows, wore hats with long fringes, cultivated persimmons, lived on pine-nuts, rice and honey, and rose at midnight and four a.m. to peal their devotional bells.

'A full night's sleep is not easy of attainment in a Korean monastery,' complained Curzon, who had also passed that way. In his opinion few of the bonzes were true believers, and the continuing yield of acolytes was due less to spiritual hunger than to the fact that monks were able to 'subsist in the main upon the charity of others – an occupation in which the Korean finds an enchantment that personal exertion can never supply'. Isabella agrees that the monks seemed rather lazy, were reputed to be profligate, and 'their religious performances are absolutely without meaning to them, and belief, except among a few, does not exist'. And yet – it was all so beautiful, courteous, orderly in a timeless oriental way that Isabella almost forgot the unkind things she had said about Buddhism to the tight white faces in Church Assembly Halls in Leeds, York, Coventry and points south. The monks were so hospitable, serene, benevolent, and 'I am compelled to admit that they exercise a certain fascination and that I prefer to remember their virtues rather than their faults,' she concludes. But that was not her final conclusion; returned, two years later, to the assertive pressures of Christian evangelism, she would respond as she always did to the occasion and denounce the degenerate evils of Buddhism in no uncertain terms.

By the time they reached the costal plains it was early June, the season when, according to the Korean Almanac, 'The tongue of the oriole turns over in its mouth, putting an end to its song, and the horns of the elk drop. Beetles and locusts arrive.' And so did the heat. Villagers were knee-deep in the steamy paddies puddling rice and the spindly pink legs of the ibis were also submerged as they speared frogs from the warm mud. Coolness was promised only by the cooing of wild doves on a lake-shore and the sight of a seaside village, which did not, however, live up to expectation. 'In the early twilight, when the fierce sun-blaze was over, in the smoky redness of a heated evening atmosphere, when every rock was giving forth the heat it had absorbed in the day, across the stream which is at once the outlet of the lake and the boundary between the provinces of Kang-won and Ham-gyong, appeared a large, straggling, grey-roofed village, above high-water mark, on a beach of white sand. Several fishing junks were lying in shelter at the mouth of the stream. Women were beating clothes and drawing water, and children and dogs were rolling over each other on the sand, all more or less idealised by being silhouetted in purple against the hot lurid sky.

'As the enchantment of distance faded and Ma-cha Tong revealed itself in plain prose, fading from purple into sober grey, the ideal of a romantic halt by the pure sea vanished. A long, crooked, tumble-down narrow street, with narrower offshoots, heaps of fish offal and rubbish, in which swine, mangy, blear-eyed dogs and children, much afflicted with skin-disease, were indiscriminately rooting and rolling, pools covered with a thick brown scum, a stream which had degenerated into an open sewer, down which thick green slime flowed tardily, a beach of white sand, the upper part of which was blackened with fish laid out to dry, frames for drying fish everywhere, men, women and children all as dirty in person and clothing as it was possible to be, thronging the roadways as we approached, air laden with insupportable odours, and the vilest accommodation I ever had in Korea have fixed that night in memory.'

The accommodation at Ma-cha Tong must have been execrable, a real hell-hole, for Isabella to single it out from her dire and drear litany of Korean inns. And one reviewer of her eventual record of the expedition, *Korea and Her Neighbours*, voices a complaint that many readers must have shared at about this stage: 'Not a single discomfort is omitted; we are not spared an ounce of dust nor a single predatory insect. Inn after inn is more detestable than the last . . . it is all a little hard on the meritorious and sympathetic public which was guiltless from the beginning of sending out the forlorn pilgrim. We take it for granted that pilgrims shoulder the wallet and strap on the sandal shoon for love of the pilgrimage. Then why dilate on mud and dirt and starvation and hungry myriads who inhabit darkness? They are themselves apt to beget weariness and make the impatient reader inquire with an objurgatory sniff, "Then why on earth did you go there?" ' The public was used to travel writers omitting most of the unsavoury details from their narratives. Nevertheless, the critic is right to suggest that Isabella did lay the filth on with a trowel during this particular journey, and it is quite a relief to learn that she and Miller eventually reached the main road to Wonsan, with telegraph poles sprouting incongruously on either side and the promise of a comfortable billet at its end.

The comfort of the billet, which was at the American Protestant Mission, was somewhat disturbed by the rumours that had been humming along the telegraph wires from Seoul to Wonsan during the last few weeks and which Isabella had not heard until then. The tales were all of war: of clashes between the Tong-haks (the rebel faction) and Royal troops in the capital, of bloodthirsty mobs gathering to march on the treaty ports, of invasion from Japan, from China, from Russia, perhaps from all three together. Isabella calmly discounted them all, brooking no such upstart interference with her plans, and on 19 June took a steamer round the coast to Chemulpo.

There she discovered that, for once, her unflappability had

not paid off: it *was* war and she had landed herself in the thick
of it. 'Japanese transports were landing troops, horses and war
material in steam launches, junks were discharging rice and
other stores for the commissariat department, coolies were
stacking it on the beach, and the movement by land and sea was
continuous. . . . On landing, I found the deadly dull port transformed: the streets resounded to the tread of Japanese troops
in heavy marching order, trains of forage carts blocked the road.
Every house in the main street of the Japanese settlement was
turned into a barrack and crowded with troops, rifles and
accoutrements gleamed in the balconies, crowds of Koreans,
limp and dazed, lounged in the streets or sat on the knolls,
gazing vacantly at the transformation of their port into a foreign
camp.'

III

The Sino-Japanese war, though not officially declared for several
weeks, was virtually under way. It eventually resulted in agonies
of loss and humiliation for the Chinese, new forms of national
chaos and frustration for the Koreans, and, for the victorious
Japanese, triumphs which soon lost their savour and turned to
gall. Ostensibly, Japan had sent the troops which Isabella saw
to help the Korean King quell the Tong-hak rebellion which
had indeed broken out, and to protect its own nationals. In
reality, their coming was the result of long-term military and
political strategy aimed at ousting China from its traditional
position as suzerain over Korea, and implementing instead a
Japanese policy of reform and indirect control. Already the
Chinese whom Isabella saw that eventful June day in Chemulpo
seemed to have foreseen the worst results of this exercise. They
had quite lost their heads, she says, and 'frenzied by race-hatred
and pecuniary loss' were transformed into madmen.

Another man in Chemulpo who lost his head that day was the
British Vice-Consul, who arrived in a very agitated state at
Isabella's inn to say that, in his view, the situation was perilously
explosive and that she, a defenceless elderly widow, should leave
the country immediately. Indeed he positively insisted, and she
reluctantly obeyed, though under protest, for she had left her

decent clothes, passport and money in Seoul whither she had
been bound. 'It is one of my travelling rules never to be a source
of embarrassment to British officials,' she explained, and so
boarding a little Japanese steamer, she went to Chefoo on the
China coast. She arrived wearing her dirty, travel-stained tweed
suit and with just four cents in her pocket, and hung shyly
around the British Consulate for some time, summoning courage
to approach its suddenly imposing portals. 'I experienced,' she
admits, 'something of the anxiety and timidity which are the
everyday lot of thousands, and I have felt a far tenderer sympathy
with the penniless, especially the educated penniless, ever since.'
She need not have worried; her name was passport enough. The
Consul welcomed her warmly and arranged for her bank credit,
his wife made up a bundle of summer clothes, she tiffined with
one Lady O'Connor and was very soon on her pilgrimage again.

At first, it was a series of minor disasters. She went from
Chefoo to Newchwang in Manchuria and from there up the
River Liao in a 'pea-boat' as she called it, towards Mukden.
She lay for several days in the pea-boat's cabin stricken with
severe fever while the worst tempests for years tore the countryside apart around her, and swamped the hold so that her bed and
belongings were sodden with filthy bilge-water. Still, in the
resultant floods, also the worst for years, the best place to be
was in a boat, for, during the rest of the lunatic journey, they
floated past children paddling about in wash-tubs and people
perched in tree-tops holding babies, pigs and hens in their arms.
For the last stage of the adventure she hired a wooden cart,
which overturned in a quagmire, rolled down a bank and deposited her on a house-roof, with a broken arm and many bruises.

Nevertheless, by 1 August, when the Sino-Japanese war was
officially declared, Isabella, battered but undefeated, was in
Mukden, describing and photographing the Chinese troops as
they went tramping through the old Tartar city on their way to
Korea. They looked the losers they would be, she thought. Their
clothes were stagy and unserviceable – loose-sleeved red jackets,
blue or apricot trousers, boots of thick black cotton cloth; their
weapons were of mainly historical value – muzzle-loading muskets,
spears and bayonets; and their general impedimenta were
medieval – paper fans and umbrellas, silk banners and singing

birds tethered to sticks. It was a sad, colourful pageant shambling loosely through the muddy streets; 'It was nothing but murder to send thousands of men so armed to meet the Japanese with their deadly Murata rifles'. And murder it was during the next few months as the Japanese relentlessly pushed the Chinese back out of Korea during a series of sharp, cruel encounters.

While these were in progress, Isabella 'was hunted from pillar to post by "scares" with which I had no sympathy,' she complains to John Murray, seeming to look upon the conflict as something of a personal affront, and eventually, in early November, she 'escaped from the grandmotherliness of consuls and the fortunes of war in a little German vessel trading to Vladivostock'. While in Russia she visited the Korean settlements in Siberia that were the main object of her journey. The settlers, living in neat, prosperous villages in the region of Possiet Bay, were proof, in her eyes, that the Korean could develop into an industrious, honest, orderly worker if conditions were favourable. Consequently, a principal thesis in her book on Korea is that the people were redeemable and had great potential; it was the corrupt and oppressive system of government that had so impoverished and devitalised the country.

In January 1895, Isabella was at last able to return to Korea, whose affairs had dominated her interest during the six months' absence. In Manchuria the war still raged and the Japanese were still winning it; in Korea, according to the Almanac, 'The wild goose stands with its face to the north and the magpie builds for itself a nest. The crow of the pheasant is heard on his hillside, hens feed on milk and the lake's stomach becomes solid.' But the lake was one of the few solid things left in the land during this period of flux and chaos. The Japanese, headed by astute Count Inouye, were in control and were trying to impose their policy of reform and modernisation on the stubborn, reactionary Koreans. Inouye, as 'adviser', attended every meeting of the Korean cabinet; the King 'had become little more than a "salaried automaton" '; the Six Boards by which the country had been misgoverned for so long – of Civil Affairs, Ceremonies, War, Revenue, Punishments and Works – had been swept away and replaced by Ministerial Departments with Japanese supervisors and go-ahead titles such as Education, Justice and Foreign

Affairs. The situation was politically complex and fascinating, and Isabella responded to it with the fervour of a keen foreign correspondent. In a letter to a friend, she explained, 'I am staying with Mr Hillier, the British Representative, and find the new regime wonderfully absorbingly interesting, and I have all facilities for studying it. The weather is superb; the severe cold suits me. I have freedom and you know how I love that! I have a Korean soldier of the Legation Guard to go out with me and carry my camera and a horse and a charming host. . . . I am utterly steeped in the East. I think, taken altogether, that this journey is wider and more absorbing in its interests than any I have ever had. I am so thankful for my capacity for being interested. What would my lonely life be without it?'

Thus engrossed in Korea, Isabella was very much pleased to be granted an audience with its King and Queen in the Kyeng-pok Palace. The Korean Queen was very much the power at the side of the throne, a ruthless, sharp-witted, conservative woman who favoured continued alliance with the Chinese instead of the Japanese – a predilection that would soon cost her her life. 'A nice-looking slender woman' she was, Isabella recorded, 'with glossy raven-black hair and a very pale skin, the pallor enhanced by pearl powder. The eyes were cold and keen, and the general expression of brilliant intelligence. As soon as she began to speak, and especially when she became interested in conversation, her face lighted up into something very like beauty'. Beside this brilliant personage, dressed in blue and crimson brocades, the King drooped, 'short and sallow, certainly a plain man wearing a thin moustache and a tuft on the chin', with nervous twitching hands and mild frightened eyes. This unhappy pair, surrounded as they were by secret enemies and court intrigue, were won over by Isabella's air of confident and sympathetic integrity. She was summoned to three further audiences, and during the last, held in strict privacy, the King entrusted her with a top-secret communication for the Foreign Office in London. Isabella was rather taken aback by this, and not knowing quite what to do with such a very august missive, eventually sent it to her resourceful publisher. John Murray, opening the latest news from his most astonishing lady traveller, must have been rather startled to read: 'Dear Mr Murray, The enclosed is a confidential message from the King of Korea to the British Foreign Secretary . . .'

The trouble was that practically all Koreans, from the royal family downwards, traditionally and thoroughly hated the Japanese, and the Japanese, pursuing their policy of modernisation with the hot-headed zeal of the newly converted, lacked tact and consistency of judgement. They poured a series of proclamations over the heads of the sullen people: 'One day a decree abolished the three-feet-long tobacco pipes which were the delight of the Koreans of the capital; another, there was an enlightened statute ordering the planting of pines to remedy the denudation of the hills around Seoul, the same *Gazette* directing that duly-appointed geomancers should find "an auspicious day" on which the King might worship at the ancestral tablets! One day barbarous and brutalising punishments were wisely abolished; another, there appeared a string of vexatious and petty regulations calculated to harass the Chinese out of the kingdom and appointing as a punishment for the breach of them a fine of 100 dollars or a 100 blows!'

One of the many consequences of these indiscriminate reforms was an epidemic of government resignations on the time-honoured oriental ground of 'official sickness'. To these, the King usually published, in that same *Official Gazette*, a standard reply: 'We have examined your resignation. These are times of re-organisation when the entire realm is affected and things profitable and harmful are to be determined. Why then do you plead sickness? Resign not, but take up your duties and attend immediately (or soon) at your Department.' Probably the official thus 'advised' did return to his department; equally probably he did nothing much when he got there. *Yang-bans* were past masters of the arts of inertia and passive non-cooperation, and the Japanese soon found that it was much easier to defeat the Chinese in battle than to reform the Koreans at home. In April 1895, the treaty of Shimonoseki brought the Sino-Japanese war to an end, and as the Japanese had been completely victorious they naturally expected to retain supremacy in Korea – but the opportunity was bungled.

Meanwhile, Isabella had left Korea for the summer, but had decided to stay in the East. 'I find it quite impossible to tear myself away,' she told Murray – her health was so much improved,

events were all so fascinating. So she went to China for a few
months, where she lectured to the Hong Kong Literary Society
on Korea and Lesser Tibet and then travelled by houseboat to
Swatow, Hangchow and Shao Hsing. At the latter place, she
stayed with the Rev. W. G. Walshe, and he put on record for
Anna Stoddart's biography one of the very few really lively,
revealing accounts of Isabella at this restless period in her life.
'Her visit to me was very interesting in every way. I introduced
to her notice some new features of interest daily, and her stock
of photographic plates soon came to an end in her endeavour to
secure lasting pictures of the ancient buildings and monuments
in which our city abounds. She usually rode in a sedan chair on
her expeditions, and, though generally very much exhausted
when the close of the day came, she appeared to be tireless so
long as anything of interest remained to claim her attention.
She was very easy to entertain, and my bachelor establishment
had no difficulty in supplying her wants, so long as she was
provided with indigestible things in the way of pastry. She
generally breakfasted in her room and rose late, retiring at night
about 11 p.m. apparently worn out; but she always had sufficient
reserve of strength to occupy an extra hour or two in the development of her photographs. . . . A special fancy of hers was the
study of our local flora and fauna, and new varieties of trees and
shrubs were her particular delight. Her absolute unconsciousness
of fear was a remarkable characteristic; and even in remote places,
where large crowds assembled to witness her photographic
performances, she never seemed in the least to realise the possibility of danger. Had she done so, she would have missed a great
deal of what she saw and learned. On more than one occasion I
was conscious of a feeling of nervousness, though I flattered
myself that I knew something of the character of the people
among whom I lived; but even in the face of the largest and
noisiest crowds, Mrs Bishop proceeded with her photography
and observations as calmly as if she were inspecting some of the
Chinese exhibitions in the British Museum.

'On her return to the coast, via Ningpo, I insisted on escorting
her by canal to the river, where a house-boat was to await her;
but she entirely declined to accept any further attention and I
reluctantly took leave of her there, with a journey of two days

before her to be accomplished without any companionship. I shall never forget the picture of the white-haired lady sitting alone in the front of the boat, as she waved her farewells – it was so characteristic of her to stand alone and independent of help, even when most cheerfully volunteered. She would not even accept a reasonable provision for the journey and contented herself with a few necessaries, including filtered water and some fresh eggs; and as it happened she was not destined to enjoy even these, for, owing to her ignorance of the language, she was not able to express her wishes to the boatmen, and as a result they boiled the eggs in the filtered water for the first meal, leaving her without any drinking water for the rest of the journey. Mrs Bishop was very anxious to conciliate the natives of whatever country she passed through, and when travelling in the interior of China, she generally adopted a costume which was designed to fulfil the Chinese canons of good taste. The principal feature of it was a large loose jacket, or mantle of "pongee" which effectively disguised the figure of the wearer, but which unlike Chinese garments generally was furnished with the most capacious pockets, in which she carried all sorts of travelling paraphernalia, including some articles of her own design. Amongst other things she used to produce from one of the pockets a portable oil lamp, ready for use at a moment's notice, and it seemed rather remarkable that the oil did not leak. . . . Mrs. Bishop impressed me as being a woman of unusual gifts, not only as a speaker and writer, but also as an observer and collector of information, possessing so much courage and force of character as to make her practically fearless, undismayed by obstacles, and undeterred by physical weakness; and yet there was nothing of that masculinity which is so common a feature of women who have made their mark in distinctively masculine fields of activity. Her nature was most sympathetic and wherever she went her first consideration was to study the social condition of the country, the position of women, the treatment of the sick, etc., and to devise means for the alleviation of pain and distress. My association with her, though covering but a short period, will ever be one of my happiest memories.' The Walshe vignette is interesting because it suggests, without maliciousness, her slight dottiness, and confirms that in her old age she was sustained by that same blend of fearlessness, resourcefulness and womanly sympathy which had so impressed people twenty-five years before.

After leaving China, Isabella went briefly to Japan: 'I am ill with rheumatism and sciatica, and am going next week to Tokyo for the best advice and afterwards to some baths', she explained to a friend. 'My plan is to get quietness and seclusion if possible, and to wear Chinese dress, in which it is possible to be easy and comfortable. I am in rags and most of my stockings have no feet. My boots were so absolutely done that I had to wear straw shoes over them, but I have now got Japanese shoes.' However long Isabella travelled she never learned to cope with shoes and stockings; they, together with servants and doorbells, were among the most infuriating of civilisation's 'everyday drudgeries'.

Her ailments and desire for quiet seemed to evaporate when, in early autumn, she heard rumours of fresh disasters in Korea and, like a good war reporter on the scent, took the next steamer back to Chemulpo. The rumours were true, Seoul was in uproar and things were as bad as they could be. The Korean Queen had been murdered, and the assassination, it turned out, had been perpetrated with the connivance of the new Japanese Resident, Viscount Miura, an unscrupulous man of military background who had replaced Count Inouye in office the month before. The killing itself, as Isabella reconstructs it from eyewitness accounts, was accomplished with brutal efficiency. 'Japanese troops entered the Palace, and formed in military order under the command of their officers round the small courtyard of the King's house and at its gate protecting the assassins (Korean troops, drilled by Japanese). As the Japanese entered the building, the unfortunate King hoping to divert their attention and give the Queen time to escape, came into a front room where he could be distinctly seen. Some of the Japanese assassins rushed in brandishing their swords, pulled His Majesty about and beat and dragged about some of the Palace ladies by the hair. . . . The Crown Prince, who was in an inner room, was seized, his hat torn off, and threatened with swords to make him show the way to the Queen. . . . The Crown Prince saw his mother rush down a passage followed by a Japanese with a sword, and there was a general rush of assassins for her sleeping apartment. . . . Kyong-jik, Minister of the Royal Household, seems to have given the alarm, for the Queen was dressed and was preparing to run and hide herself. When the murderers rushed in he stood with outstretched arms in front of Her Majesty, trying to protect her, furnishing them with the clue they wanted. They slashed off both his hands and inflicted other wounds, but he contrived to drag himself into the King's presence, where he bled to death. The Queen, flying from the assassins, was overtaken and stabbed, falling as if dead, but one account says, that recovering a little, she asked if the Crown Prince, her idol, was safe, on which a Japanese jumped on her breast and stabbed her through and through with his sword.'

After this tragedy, the King, utterly distraught, was imprisoned in his Palace. He feared greatly for his own life, and would eat only eggs boiled in their shells or food sent in locked boxes from the various legations, and begged the foreign missionaries to keep guard outside his chambers, for they were the only people he could trust. The missionaries were generally held in high esteem in the country, and Isabella formed a high opinion of their work in the fields of education and social reform. Yet, though one of her ostensible purposes was to report on their work, she only devotes to them about fifteen of some five hundred pages on Korea, and it is plain that her chief interest was in social and political change, the effects of the Japanese take-over on the country and the ordinary everyday life of its peasantry.

In pursuit of these concerns she again went exploring, this time up the north-west coast along the old main road to China. Travelling conditions were much as before: the roads as foul, the ponies as cantankerous, the inns as loathsome, and readers are still not spared 'an ounce of dust nor a single predatory insect'. It was a grand little trip nevertheless, Isabella thought, and some of her descriptions are novel and breezy. She visited the royal city of Song-do, famous for wooden shoes, pounded capsicums, coarse pottery, oiled paper and above all for the cultivation of that mysterious panacea, *ginseng*. *Panax ginseng*, to give it its botanical name, was a root plant considered tonic, febrifuge, stomachic, the very elixir of life by the Chinese and was therefore a major export of the Koreans, who scoured their mountains for the specially-precious wild variety as if searching for gold in the Klondike'.

The season was at its height in Song-do when Isabella was there and the people, seemingly untouched by the momentous upheavals going on in their capital, 'talked, thought and dreamed *ginseng*'. Its roots were planted and transplanted under reed roofs inside fenced areas which, at certain crucial times, had to be guarded by watchmen who howled and beat drums throughout the night in order to ward off thieves and evil spirits (surely one of the world's most extraordinary jobs – that of *ginseng* guard!) After seven long years of unstinting care the *ginseng* was dug up – a pallid tuber with 'beards and tails' that bore 'a grotesque resemblance to a headless man'. It is possible, Isabella adds, 'that the likeness is the source of some of the almost miraculous virtues which are attributed to it,' meaning, presumably, its reputation as a potent aphrodisiac. The root was then boiled and dried, its 'beards' and 'tail' cut off for humble home consumption, and its trunk, looking then 'like a piece of clouded amber', was packed 'waterproofed and matted and stamped and sealed by the Agricultural Department as ready for export'. One basket fetched up to 14,000 dollars, Isabella says, and one root of the extra-efficacious wild variety up to £40 – so no wonder there was so much fuss about it.

From Song-do, she continued north to Phyong-yang, which, the previous year, had been the site of one of the decisive battles of the Sino-Japanese war. For the Chinese the engagement had ended in massacre or ignominious flight, and desolate evidence of the conflict still littered the area. Houses were in ruins, shell-fragments were embedded in the gilt temple carvings, the pines were notched with bullets, human bones glared from amid the rows of cotton and beans, and in the ditches lay pathetic scraps of paper fans, umbrellas, silk banners like those Isabella had seen among the Chinese who had gone shuffling through Mukden the year before.

The further north she went the poorer the land became. At Tok-chon, the most distant town she reached, only officials could afford to eat rice; peasants scratched meagre crops of potatoes and millet from stony soil, ate also scraps of stiff ancient fish and seaweed, made nothing but skimpy gauze for cheap black hats. Pedlars, who staggered up from the south bearing silk girdle cords, Japanese lucifers, indigo dyes, sticks of candy stuffed with sesame seeds, green-glaze pickle jars and amber buttons, had to carry nearly everything away unsold, for money there was as scarce as 'frogs' teeth, crabs' tails or eunuchs' whiskers', to use a picturesque native phrase. Tok-chon was truly the end of the road: 'the ruin and decay of official buildings and the filth and squalor of the private dwellings could go no further', she concluded, adding, 'As I sat amidst the dirt, squalor, rubbish and odds-and-endism of the inn yard before starting [on her return journey] surrounded by an apathetic, dirty, vacant-looking open-mouthed crowd steeped in poverty, I felt Korea to be hopeless, helpless, pitiable, piteous, a mere shuttle-cock of certain great powers, and that there is no hope for her population of twelve to fourteen millions, unless it is taken in hand by Russia, under whose rule . . . I had seen Koreans transformed into energetic, thriving peasant farmers in Eastern Siberia.'

But no country, just then, seemed to take Korea in hand. The Japanese were proving incompetent at it, the newly-defeated Chinese were incapable of it, the Russians, on whom Isabella pinned rather excessive hopes, were biding their time. When Isabella got back to Seoul some weeks later, the King was still a prisoner, the government was still in chaos, the Japanese, though increasingly discredited and detested since the murder of the Queen, were still issuing their decrees for reformation. Then, at the very end of that disastrous year, the conquerors compounded their errors by the promulgation of a really terrible edict that plunged the nation into new depths of farcical-tragical confusion: the Royal Proclamation recommending the cutting off of the Korean top-knot. 'This set the country aflame,' Isabella wrote. 'The Koreans who had borne on the whole quietly the ascendancy of a hated power, the murder of their Queen and the practical imprisonment of their King, found the attack on their hair more than they could stand.'

As she went on to explain, the top-knot of the Korean was no inconsequential tuft but a symbol of manhood bestowed upon the male in a solemn investiture. At this ceremony, a boy's hair was scraped up into a bundle on the crown of the scalp and arranged with strings into a firm twist 'which stands up from the head slightly forward like a horn'. Over this a crownless skull-cap of horsehair gauze was bound so tightly across the brow that it gave its wearer a headache for a week and, in the opinion of one irreverent foreigner, 'acted as a successful barrier to the ingress of any new ideas for the rest of the man's life'. Over this cap a tall black gauze hat was fastened through which the top-knot could be clearly seen like a cocky little bird in a cage. This hat too, Isabella explained, 'is a source of ceaseless anxiety to the Korean. If it gets wet it is ruined, so that he seldom ventures to stir abroad without a waterproof cover for it in his capacious sleeve, and it is so easily broken and crushed, that when not in use it must be kept or carried in a wooden box, usually much decorated, as obnoxious in transit as a lady's band-box. . . . The Top-Knot is often decorated also, with a bead of jade, amber or turquoise, and some of the young swells wear expensive tortoise-shell combs as its ornaments. There is no other single article of male equipment that I am aware of which plays so important a part or is regarded with such reverence or is clung to so tenaciously, as the Korean Top-Knot.'

For the Japanese therefore to demand the severance of this venerated institution in the name of western-style progress was almost tantamount, in Korean eyes, to the urging of mass castration upon the nation's manhood – and they reacted accordingly. The King and the Crown Prince were the first victims of the dreaded Japanese shears and most of the Cabinet were similarly denuded. 'But the rural districts were convulsed. Officials even of the highest rank found themselves on the horns of a dilemma. If they cut their hair, they were driven from their lucrative posts by an infuriated populace, and in several instances lost their lives, while if they retained the Top-Knot they were dismissed by the Cabinet. . . . All through the land there were Top-Knot complexities. . . . Countrymen, merchants, Christian catechists, and others who had come to Seoul on business and had been shorn, dared not risk their lives by returning to their homes. Wood and country produce did not come in, and the price of necessaries of life rose seriously. Many men who prized the honour of entering the Palace gates at the New Year feigned illness, but were sent for and denuded of their hair. The click of the shears was heard at every gate in Seoul, at the Palace and at the official residences; even servants were not exempted, and some of the Foreign Representatives were unable to present themselves at the Palace on New Year's Day because their chairman were unwilling to meet the shears!'

The shorn King, tool of the Japanese, issued a soothing proclamation to the effect that 'The Top-Knot and hair band were regarded as novelties when first introduced and became fashionable only because people liked them. But that they stand in the way of activity and health goes without saying. Nor is it right in these days of communication by ships and vehicles that we should stick to the old customs of the exclusive past.' Perhaps not, but the people wanted none of this tousle-headed Japanese-western hybrid of modernity and nor, secretly, did the King. On 11 February 1896 Seoul was again convulsed with the news that His Highness had escaped from the Palace and sought asylum in the Russian Legation.

It was a momentous and terrible day in Korean history. Following the royal flight, the Prime Minister and other members of the Cabinet were beheaded by furious mobs, prisons were opened and their inmates released, innocent Japanese were lynched. Within a few hours of his escape, the King issued a quaintly woeful statement, which Isabella quotes. It began, 'Alas! Alas! on account of Our unworthiness and maladministration the wicked advanced and the wise retired. Of the last ten years, none has passed without trouble. . . . Our dynasty of five centuries has thereby often been endangered and millions of Our subjects have thereby been gradually impoverished. These facts make Us blush and sweat for shame.' After more in this breast-beating vein, the King continues: 'As to the cutting of the Top-Knots – what can We say? Is it such an urgent matter? The traitors by using force and coercion brought about the affair. That this measure was taken against Our will is, no doubt, well known by all. Nor is it Our wish that the conservative subjects throughout the country, moved to righteous indignation, should rise up, as they have, circulating false rumours, causing death and injury to one another. . . . As to the cutting of the Top-Knots, I say, no one shall be forced as to dress and hats. Do as you please . . .'

At this dispensation, the people breathed a sigh of relief and returned to their normally passive and disengaged state. From the security of the Russian Legation the King ruled or rather misruled the nation for a year, spurning the endeavours of the Japanese and almost ignored by the Chinese, while the Russians, in the view of many historians, were deliberately giving Korea enough rope to hang herself. The impetus towards reform faltered and fell away, in spite of a nascent progressive movement among a few Koreans in the capital. Some of the Japanese forces were withdrawn; Viscount Miura, though harshly censured in a Japanese court for his complicity in the Queen's murder, was acquitted on technical grounds; the bones of the Queen's little finger, all that was left of her, were immured in a colossal cata-falque in the grounds of the New Palace. The King reverted with cheerful incapacity to his groovy well-tried ways and one Lady Om, an Imperial Concubine of the First Class, gradually attained a position of ascendancy in the dead Queen's stead.

In the winter of 1896 Isabella returned briefly for the last time to the eccentric, secluded, dun-coloured Korean capital. A few changes had taken place, she noted: main streets had been widened and some slums cleansed; dirty, sturdy little boys were actually selling newspapers along these wider streets, and groups of Korean policemen, 'with shocks of hair behind their ears and swords in nickel-plated scabbards by their sides', slouched about them, their numbers and superfluous equipment suggestive of 'useless and extravagant expenditure'. But much of the irre-deemable Orient remained unscathed: bulls loaded with brush-wood plodded by, coolies still sang and the tattoo of the women's laundry-sticks still echoed in the twilight. 'Incipient Top-Knots were everywhere,' Isabella reported, and, on being granted an audience with the unrepentant King, she saw that the royal appendage also 'seemed to have resumed its former proportions'. The regeneration of Korea, such as it was, still lay in the future, and Isabella was to have no first-hand experience of it.

CHAPTER X
China

WHEN Isabella looked lovingly and knowledgeably, as she often did, at the map of the Far East, she saw a vast gap in her experience of it. Her first approach had been from the Pacific when she had explored its exotic Japanese fringe and had then touched upon its mainland at Hong Kong. Ducking out from behind the deck-house on a storm-ridden day in December 1878, she had seen 'the coast of Asia, the mysterious continent which has been my dream from childhood – bare, lofty, rocky, basaltic; islands of naked rock separated by narrow channels, majestic perpendicular cliffs, a desolate uninhabited region lashed by a heavy sea, with visions of swirling mists, shrieking sea-birds and Chinese high-sterned fishing-boats with treble-reefed, three-cornered brown sails appearing on the tops of the surges, at once to vanish'.

And on shore the cities of Hong Kong and Canton had been equally intoxicating, her first draught of 'true Orientalism'. And she, drinking everything in, wished every day 'that the sun would stand still in the cloudless sky, and let me dream of gorgeous sunlight, light without heat, of narrow lanes rich in colour, of the glints of sunlight on embroideries and cloth of gold, resplendent even in the darkness, of hurrying and coloured crowds in the shadow, with the blue sky in narrow strips high above, of gorgeous marriage processions and the "voice of the bridegroom and the voice of the bride", of glittering trains of mandarins, of funeral processions, with the wail of the hired mourners clad in sackcloth and ashes, of the Tartar city with its pagodas, of the hills of graves, great cities of the dead outside the walls, fiery-red under the tropic blue . . . of the wonderful river life and all the busy, crowded, costumed hurry of the streets . . .'

The oriental magic of that journey had culminated in the

Golden Chersonese; next, she had aspired to the Tibetan passes of the Himalayas and then turned back. Circling again, she had, in the mid-1890s, visited Eastern Siberia, revisited Japan, explored the Chinese coastal plains as far south as Swatow, been three times to Korea. And there, between her eastern and western approaches, between the ranges that dominated the familiar valleys of the River Shyok and the Yellow Sea which lapped the familiar shores of Chemulpo, was the gap. It was a very wide gap, but it was more or less bridged by the River Yangtze which flowed from the Tibetan highlands to China's east coast. And so, early in January 1896, when she was sixty-four years old, Isabella went purposefully to Shanghai, where the River Yangtze joined the sea.

Shanghai was by then one of the most cosmopolitan and sophisticated of all the treaty ports in the East, and for that very reason held no charms for Isabella. But for many of more extrovert and conventional temperament, Shanghai was a jolly place, a 'model settlement' with an elected Municipal Council to keep everything spick and span. Water-carts laid the dust, scavenger carts allayed the smells, a spruce force of Chinese, Sikh and European policemen waylaid undesirables, and, in short, all the strange magnificent squalor of China was kept at a safe and hygienic distance. In its place, Isabella saw, stretched 'ranges of great godowns, wharves, building yards, graving docks, "works" of all descriptions, filatures, cotton mills and all the symptoms, in smoky chimneys and a ceaseless clang, of the presence of capital and energy'.

Away from the commercial hubbub, macadamised roads were lined with 'private houses of the most approved and massive Anglo-Oriental architecture' and the wide, tree-lined Bund was dignified with the Grand Hotels of France, Britain, Germany. Newspapers and periodicals from every 'civilised' western nation lay on the green-baize tables in their public rooms; in their dining-rooms and verandahs guests sipped vermouth, ate chicken patties and caviare, talked about last night's performance of the visiting Italian operetta group. From the hotels' windows the scene was a lively one: 'Single and two-horse carriages and buggies, open and closed, with coachmen and grooms in gay and often fantastic cotton liveries, dash along the drive. Hackney victorias abound, and there are *jinrikishas* . . . in hundreds, with Chinese runners.'

Most of this traffic was made up of foreigners dashing madly from one entertainment to another, for, as Isabella says, 'The tremendous energy with which Shanghai amuses itself during seven months of the year is something phenomenal. It is a fatigue even to contemplate it.' There were clubs for drag-hounds and dramatics, bowling, lawn-tennis (Chinese lads in cotton uniforms made nippy little ball-boys) and cricket (the 'Feebles v. Duffers' match was an event of the season); there were societies for fireflies, astronomy, philharmonics, and looming largest of all was that for 'the racing fraternity'. 'The morning gallops extract people from their beds at unwonted hours, and in spring and autumn the prospects of the stables make great inroads on conversation', Mrs Bishop noted tartly. But it depended, of course, on how you looked at it. Oliver Ready, for example, author of *Life and Sport in China*, long-term Shanghai resident, thought that Race Days were the greatest fun: 'Everyone knows everyone else, the names of ponies entered have been household words for weeks [as Isabella said] while their supposed merits are open secrets. The jockeys are personal friends, the weather is bright and warm, the ladies wear their smartest dresses, the course is kept and order maintained with the aid of blue-jackets from the gunboat in port, while her drum and fife band or nigger troupe render selections of varied merits.' And then there was the delectable champagne lunch on the grandstand to look forward to, and even if your particular favourite hadn't been first past the post, all the exercise and excitement helped to 'shake up the old liver'. For that, as Ready explained, was the cure for all Shanghai ills, and the ardent pursuit of many 'manly sports' kept the livers of the young men so well shaken, that they were invariably fitter than either the ladies or the Chinese.

Another infallible liver-shaker was to do a bit of shooting in the autumn. It was grand sport too, if you owned a shooting-boat (staffed with half-a-dozen coolies, a cook and boy, loaded with food and claret) in which to go floating past the low-lying bean-fields around the Yangtze delta. Flocks of partridge, teal, snipe, flushed out by boys and dogs, sprayed up from the reedy islands, and the hunters' guns crackled. There was, however, one untoward hazard about shooting in the Shanghai area – that of 'Accidental Shooting', which is referred to in the local *Sportsmen's Diary*. This cautionary note is necessary, the writer explains, 'because the country people *will* lie *perdu* in the most unlikely spots, jumping up at the very moment the trigger is pulled'. It was an extremely irritating habit, for 'the results of wounding a native, male or female, may be so serious that the ever-present danger does not conduce to that steady nerve and calm demeanour proper to a sportsman. I believe,' the writer concludes, 'that nearly every man who has shot in China will agree with me that if this risk did not exist, or if it only existed to the extent that it does on an English estate, his shooting would be greatly improved.'

'But I will go no further,' as Isabella says, to curtail her caustic compilation of Shanghai pastimes; enough has been said to suggest, as she did, that the prevailing tone was one of frivolity, philistinism and an unblushing disregard of China and its people. 'May it be permitted to a traveller to remark.' Isabella concludes, 'that if men were to give to the learning of Chinese and of Chinese requirements and methods of business a little of the time which is lavished on sport and other amusements, there might possibly be less occasion for the complaint that large fortunes are no longer to be made in Chinese business.' Several times during her journey inland she returned to this theme, noticing that the British were allowing the China trade to fall into other hands. In Chinkiang and Hangchow the Germans had set up flourishing albumen factories and were monopolising the trade; Americans had taken the lead in the import of kerosene oil; Russia was out-pacing the British in the tea market and the Japanese were everywhere. They alone had trained Chinese-speaking agents 'to find out what the people want and supply it', and, at the up-country markets of the Yangtze basin, she repeatedly noted that, among the jumbles of bamboo hats and baskets, preserved eggs and beancurd patties, were just two imported items: American hardware and Japanese cottons. British cloth, she was told, came in the wrong width and bound in wrappers of unlucky colours. Following treaties forced upon the reluctant Chinese in 1860 and 1876, some of the ports along the River Yangtze had been opened to foreign trade, and an increasing number of foreigners – consular officials, missionaries, a few enterprising merchants – settled in the more accessible of them. After the humiliating defeat in the war against Japan, the central Chinese government was seriously weakened both economically and politically. Several major European powers seized this opportunity to lay claims to various parts of the Celestial Empire and a territorial scramble for 'spheres of influence' ensued – entered into, wrote one historian, 'with all the zest of a Cornish wrecking raid'.

This process was just getting under way in 1896 when Isabella was there; two years later, and before her book *The Yangtze Valley and Beyond* appeared, the British informed the world that the valley was now in their 'sphere of influence'. This was a most unfortunate term, Isabella suggested in a paper to the Royal Geographical Society, and it carried 'all sorts of evils in its train'. In her view the bullying western expansionism – for which the term was a euphemism – could only result in violence and disruption within the Chinese Empire while giving its statesmen 'a glorious opportunity . . . to play off one set of foreign interests against another', and she therefore advocated a policy of prudence and a patient reform of the existing regime, in default of a better. Her forecast of the violence that would result from the West's aggressive policy was amply borne out; her views on the possibility of improvement under the Manchus were, as a reviewer said, 'rather too roseate'; her general observations on the state of the land were sensible and well-founded, for she, unlike most of its foreign residents or visiting dignitaries, certainly saw the 'real' China, as it was in 1896 and, in some respects, probably still is.

The Yangtze is 3433 miles long; it is the largest river in Asia; 'more like a sea than a river,' thought Marco Polo; the Chinese call it the 'Great Long River,' the 'River of Golden Sands' in its upper reaches, or, succinctly, 'The River'; by any name it is a vast body of water forever surging towards 'its imperial audience with the ocean'. The river's lower reaches are usually opaque grey-yellow like muddied topaz; its rapid late-spring rises wash seeds from the nearby paddies and rats from their mud-holes; its equally sudden falls reveal dangerous sandbanks and stinking flotsam. In the course of its seaward journey, the Yangtze cleaves through gorges – those of the Rice Granary,

the Horse's Lung, the Tiger's Teeth, the Wind Box, for example;
it swirls past massive mid-stream rocks – the Heavenly Needle,
the First, Second and Third Pearls, the Goose Tail, the Little
Deer's Horn; it eddies among the Three Lotus Whirlpools and
the Saw-Teeth Shallows and pours down the cataracts of the
Three Yellow Cows, the Temple Stairs, the Get-Down-From-
Horse Rapids. When Isabella sailed that way, the main sources
of the Yangtze had not been fully explored, its upper reaches
were not navigable by steamer and its heaviest traffic was that of
salt junks, 'from seventy to one hundred tons burthen, with
their lofty, many-windowed sterns like the galleys of Henry IV,
their tall single masts and their big brown-amber sails of woven
cane or coarse canvas extended by an arrangement of bamboo,
looking heavy enough to capsize a liner, and with hulls stained
and oiled into the similitude of varnished pine'.

All her sympathies were with those huge ancient vessels, even
though she began her journey prosaically aboard the *Poyang*,
one of those modern river steamers that at once 'dissipate the
romance of travel by their white enamel, mirrors, gilding and
electric light'. It was early in the year and the weather was raw,
damp misted the offending mirrors, and she was the only foreign
passenger leaving the securities of Shanghai for the uncertainties
of the interior at such a bleak time. The *Poyang* called at each
treaty port, where there was a trim paved Bund along the water-
front, a clutch of factory chimneys and godowns, a rotting fringe
of 'semi-amphibious native life' with decayed and ragged crones
peering out from hovels of wet straw. None of these ports much
interested Isabella, who conscientiously noted the presence of
consulates, chambers of commerce, custom and mission houses,
tennis courts and clubs 'and other necessaries of the British
exile's life', and then hastened on her way.

Matters became more inspiriting at Ichang, about a thousand
miles upstream, an impressive city with towers, temples and
sturdy battlements. It looked prosperous, but in the recent past
had had some considerable trouble with its *feng-shui*. *Feng-shui*,
that is, geomancy, was a potent force in everyday Chinese life
and foreigners who belittled its influence did so at their peril.
No prudent Chinaman would build a house or bury his grandfather without first consulting the local geomancer to ensure

that the proposed site was propitious. Cities also had to be careful where they put themselves and, for many years, Ichang had suffered from being under the baneful influence of a great pyramid-like hill on the Yangtze's opposite bank. Because of this Ichang's citizens felt they had fallen on hard times and some of their most promising sons had failed in the triennial examinations. So, as the geomancers advised, a huge pavilion was erected on another hill to counteract this evil shadow, since when, naturally, the city's prosperity had increased and undoubtedly a respectable number of local candidates had passed their triennials. Another conceivable reason for Ichang's improved state was that, in 1887, it became the new upstream terminal point for the steamers and therefore a centre for the transhipment of goods from steamers to junks, and vice versa.

At Ichang, therefore, Isabella hired her first native boat. It was quite a luxurious vessel compared with the Korean sampan with its roof of pheasant-grass, for it had a projecting rudder, a tattered sail and a 'passenger cabin' opening on the bow-deck where sixteen oarsmen laboured to heave its twenty tons up the torrents. The ship's master, the *laopan*, was a shifty character 'with the leanest face I ever saw, just like very old, yellow, mildewed parchment strained over bones, sunken eyes, no teeth, and in the bitterly cold weather, clad only in an old blue cotton garment, always blowing aside to show his emaciated form'. Also aboard were the lean one's 'loud-mouthed virago' of a wife, her interpreter, Be-dien, two English missionaries, to whom she gave passage part-way, and the usual concomitants of babies, dogs and hens.

It was grand to be off at last, on the first day of February, when 'With a strong fair wind our sail was set; the creak and swish of the oars was exchanged for low music of the river as it parted under our prow; and the deep water . . . of a striking bottle-green colour, was unbroken by a swirl of ripple and slid past in grand, full volume. The stillness was profound, enlivened only as some big junk with lowered mast glided past us at great speed, the fifty or sixty men at the sweeps raising a wild chant in keeping with the scene.' For the landscape was wild enough. On either side of them towered the cliffs of the Ichang gorge, a bizarre conglomeration of pinnacles, grottoes and stalactites garlanded with mauve primulas, maidenhair fern and, wherever the rock sloped to anything less than the utterly perpendicular, with arable patches 'not larger than a bath-towel' to which the peasants lowered themselves on ropes. Limestone pillars, like 'gigantic old women gossiping together in big hats' abutted the cliffs, alongside boulders adorned with Chinese writing. The writing did not, as might similar manifestations in the West, proclaim the merits of 'spic-sparc soap powder or Bottomley's beans,' but reminded the passing voyager that 'The hills are bright and the waters dark' or 'The river and the sky are one colour.'

Before leaving Ichang, Isabella had asked one of its foreign residents how travellers were wont to pass the time on the long upstream voyage, to which he had replied, 'People have enough to do looking after their lives.' And this turned out to be no more than the truth, as Isabella discovered as soon as they approached the first of the notorious Yangtze rapids and saw the signs of disaster on every side. 'Above and below every rapid, junkmen were encamped on shore under the mats of their junks, and the shore was spread with cotton drying. There were masts above water, derelicts partially submerged in quiet reaches, or on some sandy beach being repaired, and gaunt skeletons lay here and there on the rocks which had proved fatal to them. The danger signal is to be seen above and below all the worst rapids in the shape of lifeboats, painted a brilliant red and inscribed with characters in white: showy things, as buoyant as corks, sitting on the raging water with the vexatious complacency of ducks, or darting into the turmoil of scud and foam where the confusion is at its worst, and there poising themselves with the calm fearlessness of a perfect knowledge of every rock and eddy.' Before tackling their first rapid, Isabella's crew slew a fowl as a hostage to fortune and smeared its blood on the bow-sweep; and she, watching the scene, commented that while 'the deterrent perils' arrayed before the eyes of aspiring travellers were often greatly exaggerated, those of the Yangtze rapids, 'fully warrant the worst descriptions which have been given of them'.

The method of ascent was painful, dangerous, gruelling, infinitely slow: 'trackers', attached to long tow-ropes, simply hauled the vessels up the thundering cataracts. 'The huge coil of plaited bamboo, frequently a quarter of a mile long, is landed after being passed over the mast-head, a man on board paying out or hauling in as is required. . . . The trackers uncoil the rope, each man attaching it to his breast strap by a hitch, which can be cast off and rehitched in a moment. The drum beats in the junk, and the long string of men starts, marking time with a loud yell – "*Chor-chor*", said to mean, "Put your shoulder to it". The trackers make a peculiar movement; their steps are very short, and with each they swing the arms and body forward, stooping so low to their work that their hands nearly touch the ground, and at a distance they look like quadrupeds.

'Away they go, climbing over the huge angular boulders of the river banks, sliding on their backs down spurs of smooth rock, climbing cliff walls on each other's shoulders or holding on with fingers and toes, sometimes on hands and knees, sometimes on shelving precipices where only their grass sandals save them from slipping into the foaming race below, now down close to the deep water, edging round a smooth cliff with hardly foothold for goats, then far above, dancing and shouting along the verge of a precipice, or on a narrow track cut in the rock 300 feet above the river, on which narrow and broken ledge a man unencumbered and with a strong head would need to do his best to keep his feet.' In short, these trackers, their sallow, scraggy bodies clad only in soiled cotton drawers, their skins scarred with cuts and sores, performed 'the hardiest and riskiest work I have seen done in any country, inhumanly hard, week after week, from dawn to sunset', was Isabella's conclusion. Yet they were astonishingly resilient, 'full of fun, antics and frolic; clever at taking off foreigners; loving a joke'.

If the spectacle of the ascent was sensational, as the great vessels trundled, tottered and reeled up the tumbling waters, threatening at every instant to break loose and go careering on to the rocks below, the method of descent was positively heart-stopping. The huge junks, masts lashed to their sides, came bounding broadside towards the slippery slope of water at the rapid's summit and 'make the leap bow on, fifty, eighty, even a hundred rowers at the oars, standing face forwards, and with shrieks and yells pulling for their lives. The plunge comes; the bow and fore part of the deck are lost in foam and spray, emerging but to be lost again as they flash by, then turning round and round, mere playthings of the cataract, but by skill and effort got bow on again in time to take the lesser rapid below. It is a sublime sight. *Wupans* and *sampans*, making the same plunge, were lost sight of altogether in clouds of foam and spray, but appeared again. Red lifeboats with their smart turbaned crews, dodged in the eddies trim and alert, crowds of half-naked trackers, struggling over the boulders with their 1200 feet of tow-rope, dragged, yelled, and chanted, and from each wild shore the mountains rose black and gaunt into a cold grey sky.'

At the highest cataracts, cool, invaluable pilots took command of each vessel and gave orders by drum-beat and gong to trackers and oarsmen. Each pilot, Isabella discovered, was accompanied by 'a curious functionary . . . a well-dressed man carrying a white flag, on which was written "Powers of the waters, give a lucky star for the journey." He stood well forward, waving this flag regularly during the ascent to propitiate the river deities, and the cook threw rice on the billows with the same object.'

In spite of the flag-bearer, the cook's rice and the pilot's skill, disasters were alarmingly frequent, and the whole procedure was accomplished in such a frighteningly makeshift and last minute sort of way, that foreign travellers usually anticipated even more than there were. A Mr Parker, who went *Up the Yangtze* some years before Isabella, nicely captures this sense of nonchalant brinkmanship: 'The trumpery old sail and the provoking old sweeps, the sockets which are perpetually slipping off their pins and require a man to wax them with the sole of a cast-off straw shoe, seem to work wonders at most distressing crises. Knots are carelessly tied; pipes are lit when hands should be otherwise employed; cooking utensils are always in the way; blocks wobble about and are so loosely fixed that the already frayed ropes are almost invited to tear themselves; and yet everything seems to blunder somehow round again to safety.' Nevertheless, the Ichang Consul reckoned that one junk in twenty was lost, and that each year one tenth of the shipments arrived damaged.

At the approach to each cataract, every boat had to join a queue for ascent, and sometimes this meant a whole night of waiting, moored at the base of the next morning's glittering challenge. 'Miserable nights they were. It was as bad as being in a rough sea, for we were in the swell of the cataract and within the sound of its swish and roar. The boat rolled and pitched; the great rudder creaked and banged; we thumped our neighbours and they thumped us; there were unholy sounds of tom-toms, the weather relapsed, the wind howled, and above all the angry yells of the boat baby were heard. The splash of a "sea" came in at my open window and deluged my camp bed and it was very cold.'

Sometimes, if the surrounding terrain was very precipitous, Isabella stayed aboard for the ascent and took her chance with the crew; sometimes she landed and spent hours standing about or climbing while her boat went up. At such times, curious, gossipy groups of villagers gathered around her who, she learned, were telling each other that her blue-grey eyes could see three inches into the earth and that, with the additional aid of her binoculars, she could see even deeper to where the treasures of the mountains – precious stones and golden cocks – lay hid. Moreover, a little black devil dwelt in her shrouded camera who came out at night and dug up the golden cocks that she had so shrewdly seen – which of course explained why her boat lay so low in the water: it was ballasted with 'these auriferous fowls'!

At length, another rapid conquered, the golden cocks unscathed, Isabella's boat went scudding into ever lovelier country. They passed 'spurs crowned with grand temples, below which picturesque villages cluster, and whitewashed, black-beamed, several-gabled, many-roofed, orange-embowered farmhouses; and every slope and level is cultivated to perfection, the bright yellow of the rape-seed blossom adding a charm to greenery which was never monotonous'. They passed coal workings high on the lateral cliffs that were mere holes shored up with timber, 'out of which . . . strings of women and children were creeping with baskets of black dust on their backs'. They passed through the "Witch's Mountain Great Gorge", an uncanny place of black swirling water and cold rock on a gloomy winter's day, and the reach above it, 'The Iron Coffin Gorge', was no cheerier.

At the port of Kuei Fu, about 1200 miles up-river, the Chinese New Year came upon them and everyone except Isabella determinedly downed tools for a few days. Tremendous, malodorous feasts of salt pork, dried fish and vegetables were cooked up, from a nearby festive 'sing-song boat' came the thrum and wail of dancing girls, and Isabella's lean *laopan* escaped into a two-day opium-inspired Elysium, 'his toothless, mummified face . . . expressive, usually, of nothing but fiendish greed, with its muscles relaxed and its deep hard lines smoothed out'. Most of the crew were opium smokers, and at night the stern of her boat 'was a downright opium den with fourteen ragged men curled up on their quilts with their opium pipes beside them, in the height of sensuous felicity'. In the western province of Szechuan, where the poppy was grown – its floppy white petals shining innocently in the sunlight – she found that 'opium houses are as common as gin shops in our London slums'. The prevalence of 'the foreign smoke', as the Chinese called it, was deplored by the authorities, and by foreigners who affirmed that it was a main cause for the country's economic decline. 'Edicts are still issued against the use of opium,' remarked Dr George Morrison, the famous *Times* correspondent who had travelled along a similar route across China some months earlier. 'They are drawn up by Chinese philanthropists over a quiet pipe of opium, signed by opium-smoking officials whose revenues are derived from the poppy and posted near fields of poppy by the opium-smoking magistrates who own them.' In these circumstances there was little hope of controlling the drug's sale. The rich smoked chiefly 'Canton opium' imported from India and blended with the home-grown product; the middle classes could only afford Chinese opium mixed with ashes of the drug already once smoked; the poor, such as Isabella's crew, sucked ashes of the second smoking, adulterated, perhaps, with ground pigskin, and the real down-and-outs made do 'with eating or drinking the ashes of the third burning' that were sometimes mixed with treacle.

Well, for rich and poor alike it was New Year in Kuei Fu, smokers reached for their pipe-dreams, river junks cavorted with bunting and coloured lanterns, shops blossomed with huge red and gold paper flowers, and every tree, well, statue, fence, plough, lintel, coffin was plastered with an appropriate prayer. 'May I know the affairs of the world for six thousand years' a scholar might plead; a shopkeeper, less ambitious, might ask that his profits 'be like the morning sun rising on the clouds'. Everyone wore their New Year's best, women had flowers in their hair, toddlers had new toys, and rich men, snuggled in sedan chairs, dashed about with card-cases. Firecrackers sputtered, temple gongs and cymbals banged through clouds of godly incense, and one small foreign lady, dressed soberly, not part of the festivities, pottered busily about her little cabin in the houseboat, moored among hundreds of others on the bank. 'I had Baber's incomparable papers on Far Western China to study and enjoy, a journal to "write up", much mending and even making to accomplish, and, above all, there were photographic negatives to develop and print, and prints to tone, and the difficulties enhanced the zest of these processes and made me think, with a feeling of complacent superiority, of the amateurs who need "dark rooms", sinks, water "laid on", tables and other luxuries. Night supplied me with a dark room; the majestic Yangtze was "laid on"; a box served for a table; all else can be dispensed with.

'I lined my "stall" with muslin curtains and newspapers, and finding that the light of the opium lamps still came in through the chinks, I tacked up my blankets and slept in my clothes and fur coat. With "water water everywhere", water was the great difficulty. The Yangtze holds any amount of fine mud in suspension, which for drinking purposes is usually precipitated with alum, and unless filtered, deposits a fine, even veil on the negative. I had only a pocket filter, which produced about three quarts of water a day, of which Be-dien invariably abstracted some for making tea, leaving me with only enough for a final wash, not always quite effectual, as the critic will see from some of the illustrations.

'I found that the most successful method of washing out "hypo" was to lean out over the gunwale and hold the negative in the wash of the Great River, rapid even at the mooring place, and give it some final washes in the filtered water. . . . Printing was a great difficulty, and I only overcame it by hanging the printing-frames over the side. When all these rough arrangements were successful, each print was a joy and a triumph, nor was there any disgrace in failure'. Knowing the procedure, it is pleasant to observe that the plate that follows her description in the first edition (and is reproduced here as plate 35,) entitled 'The Author's Trackers at Dinner,' is faintly speckled with flecks of real Yangtze mud.

II

A few days after these festivities, Isabella's river journey ended at Wan, the stately Myriad City, its temples, pagodas, ornamented gateways splotched with oriental colours that looked resplendent at a distance, garish on closer view. The Yangtze drops away to the south-west at Wan, and as Isabella wanted to continue due west for three hundred miles to the city of Paoning Fu, she had perforce to leave the boat. Travelling by road put her entirely at the mercy of the country. There was no cabin into which she could retreat from manifestations of local xenophobia – and this, as she discovered, was a considerable drawback.

In order, as she hoped, to neutralise hostility by conforming to native custom, she travelled in an open chair and wore Chinese dress. At least, she wore loose Chinese robes (the sort of over-all mantle with capacious, quaintly-filled pockets that Mr Walshe described) and straw shoes, but she injudiciously topped the *ensemble* with a large bowl-shaped wicker hat of Japanese design, 'the perfect travelling hat' in her estimation. Neither did she go to the lengths of Dr Morrison who sported a pigtail attached to a skull-cap. Perhaps she should have done, for the peasants appreciated a bit of hamming. Once, when surrounded by an unfriendly crowd, Morrison removed his cap and scratched his head and 'when they saw the spurious pigtail they began to smile, and when I flicked the dust off a table with it, they laughed hilariously'. It was in any case, of course, impossible to conceal all signs of racial differences, which sometimes aroused the people to fury or revulsion. 'What ugly eyes and straight eyebrows', 'Why is her hair like wool?' were two of the more printable comments on Isabella's appearance, and, most commonly, 'What nasty big feet she has!' By western standards her feet were very small, but those of her female detractors were deliberately deformed to a length of about three inches, dreadful crippled stumps in foreign eyes, but 'golden lilies' to their male admirers.

This barbarous custom was almost universal in Western China (except among the Manchus) and as Isabella watched the peasant women tripping and toppling over the stony tracks, she wondered again at the deeply rooted conservatism of these people. When the first railway lines had been laid at Shanghai, the Chinese had torn them up in rage, saying the spirits of the earth would be disturbed; when the first telegraph wires were stretched across the paddies, they cut down the posts because the rusty liquid that accumulated on the wires was undoubtedly poisonous, blood of the offended spirits of the air; when foreigners began deep-cast mining in the interior there were riots, because the *feng-shui* of the whole area was being dislocated. It took a long time for change to wreak its havoc and bring opportunity to China, and meanwhile people travelled by cart and junk as they always had and the women hobbled as custom bade them.

And yet, as in Korea, this very 'grooviness' liberated and challenged Isabella. The challenge of the Chinese inn was similar to that of the Korean, and on her first arrival at one she admitted 'a cowardly inclination to abbreviate' her journey. There was the same foul mud-hole of a yard with piles of human and animal excreta dumped near the well; the floor of her room was like a cesspool, its straw pallet crawled with vermin, and next door was a sty full of honking, smelly beasts. However, she girded her loins, told herself that she had 'degenerated into a Sybarite', set up her bed on the oiled sheet that effectively repelled frontal verminous attack, ate a bowl of curry and rice and prepared to rest. By eight, all was quiet, except for 'the slighter noises, such as pigs grunting, rats or mice gnawing, crickets chirping, beetles moving about in straw and other insect disturbances [which] made themselves very audible and informed me that I was surrounded by a world of busy and predatory life, loving darkness; but while I thought upon it and on the solitary plunge into China which was to be made on the morrow, I fell asleep, and never woke till Be-dien came to my door at seven the next morning with the information that there was no fire and he could not get me any breakfast! That was the first of five months of nights of solid sleep from 8 p.m. onwards. I only allowed myself half a candle per day, and after my journal letter was written there was no object in sitting up.' And in this fashion she soon 'came to enjoy' staying in dens which at first had seemed 'foul and hopeless'.

Though Chinese inns were little better than Korean, there was a pervasive air of activity and sufficiency abroad – a rasp of water-mills, a plod of ploughing buffalo, a creak of farm-carts – that made a pleasant contrast to the droopy Korean doldrums.

The tracks were bustling with baggage coolies laden with opium, rush-wicks, indigo and paper for the Yangtze junks, or bringing from them salt, utensils and the ubiquitous Japanese cottons. The fields blazed with the promise of crops – spring-green rice terraces stepping up the cliffs, flaring yellow rape, grown for its oil, black-purple blossom of the bean, and, laced here and there, groves of bamboo, 'a creation of exquisite grace, light and delicate with its stem as straight as an arrow'. The bamboo was a universal product: its slenderest twigs were used for writing-pencils, its shoots for food, its roots for carved images of birds and beasts, its arrow-straight stems for sail-ribs, wattle fences, house-joists, spear-shafts, carrying-poles, aqueduct tubes; its leaves were sewn upon cord for raincloaks, swept into heaps for manure, matted into roof-thatch, stuffed into mattresses; its branches were cut and splintered into forms innumerable – of chopsticks, screens and combs, of water-wheels, flutes and stools, of bellows, buckets and bird-cages. And in addition the bamboo was, as Isabella remarked, so very gracious – an ornament in every garden, a shade in every village street.

So the spring-time countryside pleased and interested Isabella, and though the rural folk were suspicious, they did not openly molest her. But then, unfortunately, she reached the city of Liang-shan Hsien and there endured what must have been one of the most unpleasant and frightening episodes in all her travelling days. Considering that she was utterly isolated from all outside help, she relates it coolly, without a hint of that rather coy playing of the plucky-heroine-in-dire-distress role that was often resorted to by her contemporary 'adventuresses'. Incidentally, this lack of special pleading on account of her vulnerable feminity often won her commendation. The *Spectator*, for instance, deplored the increasing numbers of 'Ladies Errant' who went into great detail about how their 'delicacy and womanliness' had been so nearly violated by the perils and crudities of foreign parts. 'Mrs Bishop,' the writer concluded, 'has never been deterred from any undertaking by its discomforts or dangers, and yet we do not remember ever having heard that she laid claim to or received any special consideration on account of her sex.' And so here, Isabella's nasty tale goes plainly, like this.

As she was carried in her open chair through the city gates, 'men began to pour into the roadway from every quarter, hooting, and some ran ahead – always a bad sign. I proposed to walk, but the chair-men said it was not safe. The open chair however, was equally an abomination. The crowd became dense and noisy; there was much hooting and yelling. I recognised many cries of "*Yang kwei-tze*" (foreign devil) and "Child-Eater!" swelling into a roar; the narrow street became almost impassable; my chair was struck repeatedly with sticks; mud and unsavoury missiles were thrown with excellent aim; a well-dressed man, bolder or more cowardly than the rest, hit me a smart whack across the chest, which left a weal; others from behind hit me across the shoulders; the howling was infernal; it was an angry Chinese mob. There was nothing for it but to sit up stolidly, and not to appear hurt, frightened or annoyed, though I was all three.

'Unluckily the bearers were shoved to one side, and stumbling over some wicker oil casks (empty however) knocked them over, when there was a scrimmage, in which they were nearly knocked down. One runner dived into an inn doorway, which the innkeeper closed in a fury, saying he would not admit a foreigner; but he shut the door on the chair, and I got out on the inside, bearers and porters squeezing in after me, one chair-pole being broken in the crush. I was hurried to the top of a large inn yard and shoved into a room, or rather a dark shed. The innkeeper tried, I was told, to shut and bar the street-door, but it was burst open and the whole of the planking torn down. The mob surged in 1500 or 2000 strong, led by some *literati*, as I could see through the chinks.

'There was then a riot in earnest; the men had armed themselves with pieces of the doorway, and were hammering at the door and wooden front of my room, surging against the door to break it down, howling and yelling. "*Yang-kwei-tze!*" had been abandoned as too mild and the yells, I learned afterwards, were such as "Beat her!" "Kill her!" "Burn her!" The last they tried to carry into effect. My den had a second wooden wall to another street, through which they inserted some lighted matches, which fell on some straw and lighted it. It was damp, and I easily trod it out, and dragged a board over the hole. The place was all but pitch-dark, and was full of casks, boards and chunks of wood. The door was secured by strong wooden bars. I sat down on

something in front of the door with my revolver, intending to
fire at the men's legs if they got in, tried the bars every now and
then, looked through the chinks, felt the position serious –
darkness, no possibility of escaping, nothing of humanity to
appeal to, no help, and a mob as pitiless as fiends. Indeed, the
phrase "hell let loose" applied to the howls and their inspiration.

'They brought joists up wherewith to break in the door, and
at every rush – and the rushes were made with a fiendish yell –
I expected it to give way. At last the upper bar yielded, and the
upper part of the door caved in a little. They doubled their
efforts, and the door in another minute would have fallen in,
when the joists were thrown down, and in the midst of a sudden
silence there was the rush, like the swirl of autumn leaves, of
many feet, and in a few minutes the yard was clear, and soldiers,
who remained for the night, took up positions there. One of my
men, after the riot had lasted for an hour, had run to the *yamen*
with the news that the people were "murdering a foreigner", and
the mandarin sent soldiers with orders for the tumult to cease,
which he might have sent two hours before, as it can hardly be
supposed that he did not know of it.'

Such an experience would have totally unnerved a lesser
woman; as Isabella says, it was generally agreed that 'no one
who has heard the howling of an angry Chinese mob can ever
forget it'. This horrendous yowl had echoed in the ears of many
a foreign consul and missionary during the past decade. Western
homes and offices at the Yangtze treaty ports were looted and
burned in the xenophobic riots of 1891; during the Sino-Japanese
war there were sporadic outbursts of violence against foreigners
who just 'looked on with their hands in their sleeves' while the
Chinese were being defeated; and, of course, the undercurrent
of hatred was swelling into the tumultous tragedy of the Boxer
Rebellion, which began about three years after Isabella finally left
the country. In the latter case, a plucky show of British unflappability was not to be enough; but it stood Isabella in good
stead, and she concludes her account of the Liang-shan Hsien
incident by saying that, though 'half-inclined to return to Wan',
she decided to continue her journey and was glad she did so.
Once set upon a course she had the stubborn courage of the
explorer and it took heaven and earth to deflect her.

The accusation of 'child-eater', incidentally, that was hurled at her during the riot resulted from a widespread belief that westerners had a taste for Chinese babies. The hated 'barbarians' were also accused of burying babies under railway sleepers to give the lines stability and of grinding infant eyes into a powder used in the manufacture of cameras. A rather sickening corollary of this, vouched for by the reliable Dr Morrison though not mentioned by Isabella, was that the people sometimes offered to sell live female babies to the foreigners for use as stew-meat or rail-ballast!

The morning after the disturbance, Liang-shan Hsien was sullenly silent, carpenters were repairing the broken doorway, a new pole had been fixed on her chair and she was carried away unmolested by her coolies. These good-natured fellows remained loyal to her throughout her pilgrimage, and she must have retained in her old age that frank and unassuming cordiality which, some thirty years before, had enabled her to jolly along the Scottish emigrants and still helped her to 'get the best' from servants of all kinds. The next incident provoking native choler was light relief by comparison, and occurred while she and the bearers were crossing a foot-wide dyke between two flooded paddies and met 'a portly man in a closed chair' travelling in the opposite direction. The coolies of each party yelled defiance and 'came straight on till our poles were nearly touching. The clamour was tremendous, my seven men and his two all shouting and screaming at once, as if in a perfect fury, while he sat in supercilious calm, I achieving the calm, but not the superciliousness. In the midst of the *fracas* his chair and its bearers went over into the water. The noise was indescribable and my bearers, whom I cannot acquit of having had something to do with the disaster, went off at a run with yells and peals of laughter, leaving the traveller floundering in the mire, not breathing, but roaring execrations.'

The upkeep of these 'roads', no more than elongated quagmires, devolved like much else upon the district mandarins. In Isabella's view, some of the mandarins (unlike the *yang-bans* of Korea) tried to do good, 'but the system under which they hold office has a strong tendency to make them bad'. The mandarins were allowed, indeed expected, to use various methods of peculation in order to supplement their modest official salaries, and so

'squeezes' were again clamped upon the peasantry. Many of the
mandarins worked hard, Isabella thought, and each represented
in his plump and padded person the whole gamut of local government – executive, fiscal, judicial. If there was a flood or famine
(and there often was) the mandarin had to organise relief; if
there was a disturbance he had to quell it; if there was crime
(tax evasion, robbery, murder) he had to judge it, and if there
was a disruptive foreigner nosing about he had to examine her
passport and arrange for a two-runner escort to the next district.
So Isabella spent hours waiting outside the various *yamens* (district
offices) and watching the bustle of pomp and circumstance in
their little courts: 'People came and went – men of all sorts,
many in chairs, but most on foot, and nearly all well dressed.
All carried papers and some big dossiers. Within, secretaries,
clerks and writers crossed and recrossed the courtyard rapidly
and ceaselessly and *chai-jen* or messengers, bearing papers, were
continually dispatched. . . . At last a very splendid person in
brocaded silks and satins came out and handed me my passport
and we were able to proceed.'

In the evenings, Isabella often chatted (through Be-dien) with
the village headmen to find out how this administrative system
worked at rice-roots level, and her conclusion was that, in
comparison with the peasants of Korea or Persia for instance, the
Chinese 'are very far from being an oppressed people'. Over a
cup of tea and a pipe, the villagers grew eloquent on such matters
as carriage charges for goods, litigation delays, the hilarious
habits of foreign missionaries (of which, unfortunately, she gives
no examples), the venality of some minor officials ('rats under the
altar' they were called), and how this mandarin was a fine fellow
who'd just built them a stone bridge across the river, and that
one was a rapacious swine who decided every lawsuit in favour
of the most liberal palm-greaser. Fluctuations in prices were a
burning topic everywhere, for the Chinese loved to talk about
money and goods, even when they didn't have much of either.

In the sparsely-populated agricultural areas further west she
found that the only markets operated on a sort of Mad Hatter's
tea-party pattern: 'In travelling along the roads one comes
quite unexpectedly upon a long, narrow street with closed shop
fronts, boarded-up restaurants, and deserted houses, and

possibly a forlorn family with its dog and pig the only inhabitants. The first thought is that the population has been exterminated by a pestilence, but on inquiry, the brief and simple explanation is given "It's not market day".

'A few miles further, and the roads are thronged with country people in their best, carrying agricultural productions and full and empty baskets. The whole country is on the move to another long, narrow street closely resembling the first, but that the shop fronts are open and full of Chinese and foreign goods; the tea-shops are crammed; every house is full of goods and people; from 2000 to 5000 or 6000 are assembled; blacksmiths, joiners, barbers, tinkers, traders of all kinds are busy; the shouting and the din of bargaining are tremendous, and between the goods and the buyers and sellers locomotion is slow and critical. Drug stores, in which "remedies for foreign smoke" are sold, occur everywhere.

'The shops in these streets are frequently owned by the neighbouring farmers, who let them to traders for the market days, which are fixed for the convenience of the district, and fall on the third or fifth or even seventh day, as the need may be. . . . It is much like a fair, but I never saw any rowdyism or drunkenness on the road afterwards, and I never met with any really rough treatment in a market, though the crowding and curiosity made me always glad when it was not "market day" .'

And so Isabella jogged happily on, past markets open and closed, past flat-bottomed barges loaded with coal and salt, past pools where buffaloes wallowed with only their horns and flesh-pink noses poking above the water, past village schools whence whined the dreary shout of boys repeating the ancient classics which, as yet, they did not in the least understand. And at last, in the distance of one sunny afternoon, appeared Paoning Fu, her immediate goal. 'Built on rich alluvium, surrounded on three sides by a bend of the river, with temple roofs and gate towers rising out of dense greenery and a pink mist of peach blossoms, with fair and fertile country rolling up to mountains in the north, dissolving in a blue haze, and with the peacock-green water of the Chia-ling for a foreground, the first view of this important city was truly attractive.

'In the distance appeared two Chinese gentlemen, one stout,

the other tall and slender, whose walk as they approached gave
me a suspicion that they were foreigners, and they proved to be
Bishop Cassels, our youngest and one of our latest consecrated
bishops, and his co-adjutor, Mr Williams, formerly vicar of
St Stephen's Leeds, who had come to welcome me.' The two men,
the first Europeans she had seen for about a month, conducted
her to the city's China Inland Mission, with 'some very humble
Chinese houses built round two compounds, in which two married
couples, three bachelors, and, in the bishop's house, two ladies
were living, and at some distance off there is a ladies' house, then
occupied by five ladies. There are several guest-halls for Chinese
visitors, class and school-rooms, porters' and servants' rooms.
The furniture is all Chinese and the whitewashed walls are
decorated with Chinese scrolls chiefly. I never saw houses so
destitute of privacy, or with such ceaseless coming and going.
Life there simply means work, and work spells happiness apparently, for the workers were all cheerful and even jolly. Studying Chinese, preaching, teaching, advising, helping, guiding,
arranging, receiving, sending forth, doctoring, nursing and be-
friending make the mission compounds absolute hives of industry.'

By thus approving of this type of mission, Isabella was taking
a deliberate stance in the evangelical arena. Her allegiance was
with those missionaries who lived entirely at the mercy of the
country, who conscientiously tried to conform to native custom,
etiquette and dress and by so doing rejected the common, tacit
assumption of western cultural superiority. (Religious superiority
was another matter, of course: they were still intent on bringing
the light of a higher creed to the benighted heathen.) These were
the guiding principles of that doughty, fanatical institution the
China Inland Mission, which had been established by Dr Hudson
Taylor in 1865. It was an undenominational body without fixed
places of worship; its members were affiliated to other Protestant
groups and its links with the Church Missionary Society were
strong. Thirty years after its foundation, nearly six hundred
missionaries were working under its auspices, living in remote
Chinese towns in the interior, cooped up in filthy attics, taking
the brunt of intermittent hostility, facing a long series of setbacks
and difficulties. As a modern commentator has remarked, 'Only
a man whose theology was like a rock could have long withstood

the ceaseless washing of that vast sea of Chinese indifference.

Many of the C.I.M. missionaries were exclusive to a fanatical degree in the matter of spiritual salvation and believed that oblivion was the best that the unconverted could hope for. 'There is a great Niagara of souls passing into darkness in China,' proclaimed Dr Taylor during a recruitment campaign, and added that those who had been offered redemption and spurned it were beyond all hope. Dr Morrison, casting a cold eye upon one of the C.I.M. missionaries he met, remarked that 'It was a curious study to observe the equanimity with which this good natured man contemplates the work he has done in China, when to obtain six dubious conversions, he has, on his own confession, sent some thousands of unoffending Chinese *en enfer brouillé éternellement.*'

Morrison went on, 'It is generally recognised that the most difficult of all mission fields – incomparably the most difficult – is China' and on that point at least he and the missionaries agreed. There were immense doctrinal difficulties, because those natives who were converted to the total spiritual allegiance that uncompromising Christianity demanded had, perforce, to reject the creed of ancestor-worship on which the structure of Chinese social life was based. This meant that converts refused to pay the communal taxes towards local 'idolatrous festivals' and took no part in familial ceremonies that enshrined the sacred concept of filial piety. Consequently, charges were often brought against native Christians in the local courts and less than justice was often meted out to them. In such cases, missionaries (Roman Catholics according to the Protestants and vice versa) sometimes took it upon themselves to intervene on their disciples' behalf and this aroused fresh dissension. However, in the view of some evangelists, dissension was itself a healthy sign of success, for Christianity was an intrusive, aggressive force; had not the Lord himself said 'I come not to send peace but a sword'?

The upshot of all this was that many converts became social as well as spiritual outcasts, and had to be generously supported by the missions where they worked as hospital cleaners, servants and bearers. In the layman's view, therefore, a considerable proportion of the scant missionary harvest was made up of 'rice Christians' – unskilled, layabout opportunists who were, to put it bluntly, in it for the perks. Certainly, most of Christianity's recruits were from among the meek and lowly who had little to lose; the vast majority of the mandarin class regarded this upstart and disruptive doctrine with suspicion and contempt. Nevertheless, some missionaries had become identified in the people's minds with the ruling upper class, because they had built grand 'Europeanised' houses for themselves inside walled compounds. The 1860 Treaty of Tientsin had granted missionaries extra-territorial rights to build or rent premises suitable for their labours, and a few missionaries had taken advantage of this right to commandeer temples or assembly halls, or raise their edifices upon sites that seriously disrupted the local *feng-shui*. In such cases, riots often ensued in which missionaries were attacked and their compounds looted. The victim-evangelists then sought the protection of their national governments and occasionally demanded that retribution, in the form of a heavy indemnity, be exacted from the people. This convinced many Chinese that missionaries were indeed political agents in disguise. Why else should their governments be expected to protect them?

In some areas, the Chinese showed their growing distrust and fear of missionaries by the circulation of scurrilous and obscenely-illustrated propaganda in which Jesus was represented as a crucified hog surrounded, says one reporter, 'by male and female worshippers indulging in licentious merriment'. Christianity was described as the 'pig-goat religion', its propagators were 'primary devils', its native converts 'secondary devils', its prayers 'the squeak of the celestial hog', and so on. The missionaries retaliated by disturbing quantities of biblical translations, widely used, said their detractors, as draught-excluders and sandal-soles by the ingenious Chinese. Still, much thought and controversy went into the preparation of these versatile effusions, as, for instance, over the so-called 'terminology question'. The Jesuit fathers, earlier proselytisers on the Chinese scene, had used the native word meaning 'Lord of Heaven' to describe their Christian God; the English Protestants, anxious to sharpen a distinction in the heathen mind between themselves and the Catholics, gave God a different name, meaning 'Supreme Ruler'; the American Presbyterians, whose common ground with the other two bodies was small, chose 'The True Spirit'; the Chinese, hearing that all these foreigners worshipped different deities, wondered why they could not be left in peace to do likewise. For it has been suggested that the greatest barrier of all to the spread of Christianity in the Far East was the intolerant 'monopolism' of both Protestants and Catholics; the Chinese, never themselves proselytisers, were by contrast of polytheistic – and indeed polydaemonistic – inclination.

Isolated by all these problems from the bulk of the populace, scorned by many of their lay compatriots, the successful missionaries must have survived, as Isabella suggests, by the creation of busy, godly little compounds where 'preaching, teaching, advising' and so on went on apace, and the workers seldom paused to remember that, as Morrison put it, 'their harvest may be described as amounting to a fraction more than two Chinamen per missionary per annum'. Bishop Cassels, who met Isabella at Paoning Fu, was probably the right sort of man to put heart into such a group. He was of the Church Missionary Society, recently consecrated 'Bishop of Western China', a former Cambridge athlete, burly, bold and jovial. Some of his converts had just presented him with the hat of a Master of Arts and high boots, which, Isabella says, gave him 'the picturesque aspect of one of the marauding prelates of the Middle Ages!'

After financing the establishment of a small 'Henrietta Bird Memorial Hospital' to help the Paoning Fu Mission, Isabella continued her westward journey-by-chair for another three hundred miles to the city of Mien-chow, where she stayed with the Reverend Heywood Horsburgh and his wife in a dilapidated, squalid house in a noisy thoroughfare. Horsburgh had nothing of Cassels's muscular Christian heartiness; he was a highly-strung, intense, prickly proselytiser through and through, a lean man with burning eyes, every ounce of bone and spirit dedicated to Christ's service. He sought a return to primitive, apostle-style "missioning", and would have none of churches, Anglican prayer books or white surplices such as Cassels sometimes sported with his M.A. hat. Cassels, in Horsburgh's view, was 'too churchy' for China, where more pastoral simplicity was required. But nor did Horsburgh approve of the nonconformists, with whom he fought a running battle over territorial rights. 'If one Mission,' he complained, 'after infinite labour and even suffering has at last succeeded in getting a foothold in a new city and been able to begin settled work – it is most unfair for another Mission which is working on altogether different lines, to take advantage of the efforts of the first Mission and come to that very city and, to a great extent, neutralise their work.' This excerpt, which refers to the intrusion of the Canadian Methodists upon his scene, is taken from Horsburgh's correspondence with his 'Parent Committee' in London, to whom he also states his opinions on Cassels, and to whom Cassels put *his* views on Horsburgh. Both called the other 'an admirable and worthy man', but while Horsburgh deplored Cassels' 'C. of E. style pomp', Cassels deplored Horsburgh's 'exclusiveness'. 'A most difficult case', Cassels concluded, and, let it be whispered, one who kept such a tight rein on expenses that he once asked a young lady missionary to provide full details of her annual expenditure on underclothes!

Isabella gives no hint of these internal squabbles, but as she stayed with both men, she must have heard something of them, and it was the sort of evangelical bickering that greatly depressed her. She had heard so much of it, since those days over twenty years before, when she sat on the verandah of Titus Coan's Hawaiian home and listened to his diatribes against the Roman Catholics and the plagues of Mormons. So much missionary discord was the same the world over, and neither mature experience nor the most ardent dedication seemed to alleviate it. Nevertheless, she rightly thought that there was a gradual lessening of interdenominational tension, a slow thaw from the old-fashioned dogmatism of the fire-and-brimstone boys. Early in the twentieth century, Christian effort in China was increasingly directed along broader humanitarian lines and missionaries were less contemptuously ignorant of the native culture – developments that Isabella would have welcomed.

Upon leaving the Mien-chow Mission, Isabella simply kept going westwards, until, one day in early April, she reached Kuan Hsien on the Chengtu plain. Again she stayed with missionaries and, looking out from the back of their house, she saw that 'the clear, sparkling Min, just released from its long imprisonment in the mountains, sweeps past with a windy rush, and the mountain views are magnificent, specially where the early sun tinges the snow-peaks with pink. Why should I not go on, I asked myself, and see Tibetans, yaks and aboriginal tribes, rope bridges, and colossal mountains, and break away from the narrow highways and the crowds and curiosity and oppressive grooviness of China proper?'

III

Why not indeed – and also why? There *were* no more missions to 'inspect' or generously endow, so she could no longer justify her travels on these impeccably worthy grounds; but there were those aboriginal tribes and a very remote region about which useful anthropological and geographical observations should be made. The essential particular was that, as she says, mountains, snow-peaked and pink in the sunrise, lie beyond the Chengtu Plain as the Rockies lie beyond the prairie, the high haunts of the Kurds beyond the Persian plains, the Himalayas beyond Srinagar. The mountains drew her to them; they always had. And, in the fastnesses of these mountains she might come again upon Tibet, with its amicable easy people, its pure clear air, its empty, untrammelled spaces. If she reached it, she would have been full circle. So she determined to follow that sparkling Min along its north-westerly Siao Ho branch into the mountains where the primitive tribes of the Mantze dwelt and then, perhaps, to strike for the Chinese-Tibetan frontier.

She hired five new porters who carried her chair, two bamboo baskets and camera, and she replenished her stock of loose native robes beneath which her ample body was pleasantly at ease and kindly camouflaged. She retained the services of the sulky, proud Be-dien, but as his brand of polite Chinese would be of little use in these uncouth parts, she also had the company of Mr Knipe, disguised as 'Mr Kay' in her book, a melancholy-looking young lay missionary who knew something of the local dialects. As soon as she left the plain, she found the sort of scenery she loved. Dramatic mountains soared skywards tipped with 'ghastly snow-cones', chasms of scrambled greenery gashed the valleys and the only sounds were of torrents crashing over rocks and the occasional clop of mule or man. 'There was a decided Tibetan influence in the air which I welcomed cordially. Red lamas passed us on pilgrimage to Omi Shan, and numbers of muleteers in sheepskins and rough woollen garb, their animals laden with Tibetan rugs and, better than these, some "hairy cows" (yaks), which had not yet lost the free air of their mountain pastures and executed many rampageous freaks on the narrow bridle-path. Lamas and muleteers were all frank and friendly, asked where we were going, how long we had been on the road, enlightened us on their own movements and cheerily wished us a good journey. Most of the mules had one or more prayer-flags standing up on their loads, for the Tibetans are one of the most externally religious peoples on earth.' The houses, like the people, were workaday, rough, shorn of the gaudy ornamentation beloved by most Chinese; the women strode big-footed like the men; village inns, hung high on wooded slopes, were marvellously secluded and empty, with that bare, chill, clean emptiness of the mountains.

Clearly the boundaries even of China were near, and when they came to Li-fan Ting, a town of five hundred people with one long clean grey street backed by one long clean blue torrent it looked like 'the final outpost of Chinese civilisation – the end of all things'. But Chinese officialdom, she discovered, did not end there, rather it expanded in several last gasps of wilful obstruction. Two runners from the local *yamen* were posted outside her inn-door and she was told that she could go no further. In the wild regions ahead, officials explained, savage tribes were fighting, there were no inns or roads, snow blocked the passes; in short it was no place for an elderly, defenceless foreign lady.

Next morning, when Isabella quietly prepared to depart – forward not backward – the 'veneer of politeness' disappeared, mounted guards appeared and she was more or less confined to her room. The following morning, however, 'I woke everybody at 4.30 and was ready to leave at 5.30; but it was not to be. The officials were already there frightening the coolies with stories, intimidating them and threatening to have them beaten for disobedience, and there was a violent altercation between them and Mr Kay, in which some very strong language was used on both sides which did not mend matters. When I came out they tried to shut me into my room; but I managed to get into my chair. They told the bearers not to carry me. I told them to move on. The officials then tried to shut us in by closing parts of the outer door of the inn; but Mr Knipe opened them, and held them open till the frightened porters and my bearers had passed through. It was but fifty yards to the city gate. I feared they would close it, but they contented themselves with following us there, crying out, "We wash our hands of you!" and hurling at us the epithet "Foreign dogs!" as a parting missile.'

Four hours after they left Li-fan Ting for the unknown beyond, they were overtaken by two officials, so Mr. Knipe hurried ahead in order to reach the next village of Tsa-ku-lao before them. Soon, another horseman appeared who evidently had orders to get ahead of Isabella and obstruct her onward passage. She thought this a very unworthy stratagem. So, 'I jumped out of the chair, and set up my tripod on the narrow road, which he could not pass, and after a long attempt at photography, baffled by the wind, told him . . . to keep behind me. The horseman kept trying to get in front, but as the path is very narrow and mostly on the edge of a precipice, I managed to dodge him the whole way by holding a large umbrella first on one side, then on the other!' Isabella's casual narration of this little incident strains credulity almost to breaking-point. That she, on foot, armed only with a camera and a large umbrella could keep a mounted guard at bay for miles along even the narrowest track, seems fantastic. Perhaps the guard was so fascinated by her masterly improvisations that he couldn't bear to bring the performance to a close!

Trouble boiled again at Tsa-ku-lao, but by now Isabella was 'fairly roused and quite determined to proceed at least as far as Somo'. So proceed she did, with a much-swollen bodyguard, presumably designed both to protect her and to defend the country from her invasion. Each quenched mandarin along the route sent some runners, and there were more chair bearers, for herself, for Be-dien and Mr Knipe, there was a muleteer with 'three strong, whole-backed, pleasant-faced red mules' and a young lama. 'Climbing the Peh-teo-shan spur by a long series of rocky, broken zigzags, cut on its side through a hazel wood, and reaching an altitude of about 9,270 feet in advance of my men, I felt the joy of a "born traveller" as I watched the mules with their picturesque Mantze muleteer, the eleven men no longer staggering under burdens, but jumping, laughing and singing, some of them with leaves of an artemisia stuffed into their nostrils to prevent the bleeding nose which had troubled them ... the two soldiers in their rags and myself the worst ragamuffin of all. There were many such Elysian moments in this grand "Beyond".'

And so, for the last time, during that ragamuffin-free journey from Tsa-ku-lao to Somo Isabella relived many of the most intense, sublime and dangerous joys that had formed the quintessence of her life's wanderings. Hillsides rioted in the lush colours she had once seen in the Sandwich Isles: 'A free-flowering, four-leaved white clematis, arching the road with its snowy clusters, looped the trees together, and a white daphne filled the air with its heavy fragrance. Large peonies gleamed in shady places. White and yellow jasmine and yellow roses entwined the trunks of trees. . . . Maples flaunted in crimson and purple, in pale green outlined in rose-red; the early fronds of the abundant hare's-foot fern crimson on the ground; there were scarlet, auburn and old-gold trees . . .' And the ground below them 'was starred with white and blue anemones, white and blue violets, yellow violas, primulas and lilies . . . and patches of dwarf blue irises.'

She stayed among the Mantze and described their congenial everyday clutter and clatter with enthusiastic interest as, in former days, she had written about the Ainu, the Kurds, the Koreans. While her men slept, she, invigorated and alert, stared out from a village granary over moonlit valleys and thought, as she had sometimes thought before in like circumstances, that 'Anything might happen afterwards, but for that one day I had breathed again the air of freedom and had obtained memories of beauty such as would be a lifelong possession.' At 10,000 feet altitude she came into her own as usual and bustled about while coolies collapsed around her and 'my umbrella split to pieces, shoes and other things cracked, screws fell out of my camera (one of Ross's best), my air-cushion collapsed, a horn cup went to pieces spontaneously, and celluloid films became electric and emitted sparks when they were separated!' Higher yet, at the Pass of Tsa-ku-shan, the eyes of mortal danger flashed at her. Owing to Mr Kay's considerable ineptitude they did not start to cross this pass until three o'clock on a cold afternoon, and they climbed 'to a considerable height by a number of well-engineered zigzags, meeting Mantze travellers armed with lances and short swords, and journeying in companies from dread of the notorious banditti. Some of my men had armed themselves with lances. As darkness came on the coolies were scared and begged me to have the mule bells taken off. They started at every rock and asked me to have my revolver ready! . . . When we got into mist and broken shale and snow, after stumbling and falling one after the other, they set the chair down, very reasonably I thought and no arguments of Mr Kay's addressed either to mind or body induced them to carry it another step.

'It was then 8.30 and very dark. A snowstorm came on, dense and blinding, with a strong wind. I was dragged rather than helped along, by two men who themselves frequently fell, for we were on a steep slope and the snow was drifting heavily. The guide constantly disappeared in darkness. Be-dien, who was helping me, staggered and eventually fell, nearly fainting – he said for want of food, but it was "Pass Poison" and he was revived by brandy. The men were groaning and falling in all directions, calling on their gods and making expensive vows, which were paid afterwards by burning cheap incense sticks, fear of the bandits having given way to fear for their lives – yet they had to be prevented from lying down in the snow to die.

'Several times I sank in drifts up to my throat, my soaked clothes froze on me, the snow deepened, whirled, drifted, stung like pin points. But the awfulness of that lonely mountain-side cannot be conveyed in words: the ghastly light which came on, the swirling, blinding snow-clouds, the benumbing cold, the moans all round, for with others, as with myself, every breath was a moan, and the certainty that if the wind continued to rise we should all perish for we were on the windward slope of the mountain. After three hours of this work, the moon, nearly at her full, rose, and revealed dimly through the driving snow-mist, the round, ghastly crest of the pass, which we reached and crossed soon after midnight when the snow ceased. I have fought through severe blizzards in the Zagros and Kurdistan mountains, but on a good horse and by daylight. . . . On the whole this was my worst experience of the kind.'

But it did not kill her. Travelling – even through snow blizzards over 12,000-foot-high passes when she was sixty-four years old – could not kill her. Life, it seemed, had yet more to demand and more to offer, and in this she acquiesced.

The offering was Somo, capital of the Mantze, golden as Malacca, enchanted as Hilo, remote as Leh, eccentric as Seoul – the last town out on Isabella's road. 'The first view of it sleeping in the soft sunshine of a May noon was one never to be forgotten. The valley is fully one mile wide, and nine miles long, and snow peaks apparently close its western extremity. All along the "Silver Water" there were wheat fields in the vivid green of spring; above were alpine lawns over which were sprinkled clumps of pine and birch, gradually thickening into forests which clothes skirts of mountains, snow-crested and broken up here and there into pinnacles of naked rock. At short distances all down the valley are villages with towers and lamaseries on heights – villages among the fair meadows by the bright swift river, with houses mounted on the tops of high towers, which they overhang, their windows from thirty to fifty feet from the ground – and stretching half-way across, a lofty, rock spur, then violet against a sky of gold, developed into a massive double-towered castle, the residence of the *Tu-tze* of Somo, the lord of this fair land. In the late afternoon it looked like an enchanted region –

> 'Where falls not hail or rain, or any snow,
> Nor ever wind blows loudly.

The warm spring sunshine blessed it, the river flashed through it in light, the sunset glory rolled down it in waves of gold, its beauty left nothing to be longed for.'

She could have died there, with nothing left to long for; 'I was much prostrated,' she confessed at last, 'and also suffering from my heart from the severities of the night on the Tsa-ku-shan pass'. But perhaps it would have been too easy an escape. As things were, she merely suffered, the coolies all came down with fevers, food supplies were low, the authorities were absolutely determined that she should go no farther. So she stayed about a week in Somo and learned what she could about the Mantze.

They were a semi-autonomous people who paid annual tribute to China; they were ardent Buddhists of the Tibetan variety; they had a refreshingly un-oriental belief in the absolute equality of the sexes; they were noisy and amiable, 'taking this life easily and enjoying it and trusting the next to the lamas'. The women were dark, large-eyed as Latins and with hair twisted into dozens of thin waxed plaits; the men, similarly dark and ruddy, shaved their head sand wore woollen caps, but in olden days used to coil their hair into a horn 'as long as a hand'. Both men and women were robust and walked with springy zest; but they never washed, and a corpse was termed 'a twice-washed', having received one post-natal and one post-mortem ablution. They were hospitable, amoral, quite blissfully ignorant. 'Their views are narrow, their ideas conservative, and their knowledge barely elementary. England is not a name to conjure with in their valleys. They know of China and Tibet, and have heard of Russian but never of Britain'.

Britain, that 'dim pale island' as she had long ago called it, unknown and unmissed by so many, still waited, though it did not beckon. It was the only place she could possibly call home, it was where her duty lay and God had spared her to return to it. And so, reluctantly, she turned her face away from the desirable Tibetan frontier and, with Mr Knipe, Be-dien, the bearers, porters and muleteers, wended her way down from the heights. When she reached the Chengtu plain it was sizzling in the summer heat, buzzing with sand-flies and mosquitoes, heaving with a million groovy, sweaty Chinese and buffaloes. 'She left Chengtu', says Anna Stoddart, 'on May 20th, with the mercury at 90°, in a small flat-bottomed *wupan*, with a partial matting cover, drawing four inches of water. This was the beginning of the last river journey of 2,000 miles, "back," as she says, "to bondage." '

CHAPTER XI

Bondage

In a letter written while on the Sea of Japan early in 1897, just before she left the Far East for the last time, Isabella told her publisher, 'The high pressure of life in all departments, whether of work or pleasure is tremendous. I dread returning to England, for though I shall try to keep out of the season and must do so from necessity, the mere rush of the movements about me will I fear be more than I could bear, and I shall have to leave home again.' Still, she would try to 'settle' in some nice 'old-fashioned cottage within an hour of London (*not* Waterloo or Liverpool Street) close to a purely agricultural village' where she hoped to rest for a while and see hardly anybody. But the prospect was unappealing: 'Indeed I am returning to England with a very bad grace. I am far more at home in Tokyo and Seoul than in any place in Britain except Tobermory, and I very much prefer life in the East to life at home . . .'

When she reached England a few months later, Mrs Bishop took rooms in London, worked hard at some articles on Korea, attended a Queen's Assembly, sat on the committees of several missionary societies, dined out constantly and delivered a lecture on West China to the Royal Geographical Society – the first woman ever to address that august, masculine body at such length. Tireless, unrelenting, she also spoke to audiences in Birkenhead, Winchester, Birmingham, Carlisle, Aberdeen, and Dublin on the need for medical missions, to the British Association on the Mantze tribes, to a Church Congress in Newcastle, to Chambers of Commerce in Southampton and York on spheres of influence in China, to the Royal Scottish Geographical Society on Tibet and Korea. 'I wish I *could* avoid undertaking too much,' she complained to her publisher, as she hurried from one engagement to the next, sometimes losing her own door keys in the rush and arriving unexpectedly at the Murrays' hospitable house in Albemarle Street for a night's shelter.

The book on Korea was a toil and tribulation also, and she made more work for herself by allowing it to reach quite inordinate lengths. John Murray protested, as sheaves of new material poured into his office, 'I believe I am correct in saying that 257 pages of your manuscript may be taken as two-fifths of the whole MS? If so, and as 141 pages of manuscript equals 156 pages of print, the whole book willl work out to 430 printed pages plus illustrations, index, contents etc. – in fact a volume of five hundred pages. Of course this is impossible.' So it eventually appeared in two volumes, for Isabella was reluctant to cut it, even though she considered that Korea was 'a dull, remote subject' that could only interest the few 'who do not read for amusement but for information'. Once again her forebodings were unwarranted: *Korea and Her Neighbours* was published on 10 January 1898 and within ten days a second impression was being printed. Over two thousand copies sold in the first year, and Isabella made a profit of about £550 from its sales. All the reviews were 'monotonously favourable' and praised the perspicacity of her observations and the 'magic' of her descriptive powers. 'No other book is so satisfying in its presentation of the facts of nature and man in Korea today,' applauded the *Nation*; and Isabella was 'amused' to find herself 'transplanted in to the ranks of political writers and quoted as an "authority on the political situation in the Far East" '. In fact, she told her publisher in confidence, 'the reviewers are so ignorant of the subject that they are afraid to commit themselves by fault-finding!'

But apart from this warm sense of well-earned achievement, financial and professional success as a writer had little to offer Isabella. She had no personal extravagances to indulge – *objets d'art*, elegant clothes, fine furnishing held no charms for one so incapable of 'settling'; she took no delight in the comfort or status of luxury hotels, aristocratic drawing-rooms or fashionable watering-places; her friends were, as they always had been, worthy, intelligent professional people – retired diplomats or missionaries, the remnants of her Scottish circle, friends of her youth – and she had no ambition to move in the sophisticated literary or artistic circles of the day (and in any case, her brand of slow-spoken, well-informed, earnest discourse was not to everyone's taste). So early in 1899 she determined to escape from the 'high pressure' of urban life that she had dreaded and retire to that 'old-fashioned cottage'. After much searching, she took the lease (she never bought a house in her life) of a large, damp, gloomy residence called Hartford Hurst on the banks of the River Ouse: 'It is a very unideal house in an unideal neighbourhood,' she wrote, 'but the next parish was my father's, and I spent there a happy youth from sixteen to twenty-seven [happier, perhaps, when gilded with a retrospective glow] and it is less trouble to go into a neighbourhood which I know intimately. . . . At all events, it is a *pied-à-terre* so long as I can move about and when I can't it may prove a haven. It is very odd to look at all things in the light of old age and I am trying resolutely to face it, thankful all the time that my best-beloved never knew it and that they had neither to live nor die alone.' Her description of Hartford Hurst suggests that it would prove, as it did, the final blunder in her series of home-making disasters. The isolation, the overpowering nostalgia, the flat damp of the area depressed her and she 'faddled away' most of the time she spent there.

Still seeking rest in the surroundings of the past, she returned again to Tobermory, but in vain. The passing years had not improved her reserves of patient equanimity or her capacity to minister for very long to the meek and lowly – much as she had prayed for these gifts. Now the islanders could do nothing right in her eyes. 'Tobermory is certainly four years worse,' she told a friend. 'Drink is ravaging it. Several young men are at this time dying of it and many of the older men have come to wreck with it since I was last here . . .' And further, 'The place does not improve. The people are so intellectually lazy and so spiritually dead and so contented merely to vegetate. . . . It is hard for me to love the Tobermory people, and without love one is useless.' It was a period grey with lovelessness, and without the bright compensations of absorbing interest or stimulating work. 'I have felt profoundly depressed during my last winter here,' she told the widowed Ella Blackie in December 1899, 'and the indifference of friends to my last book, my youngest child, child of my old age, has grieved me much.' The book, *The Yangtze Valley and*

Beyond had appeared the previous month and, as Isabella said, had received less than the usual critical accolade at first, mainly because everyone was preoccupied with the South African situation. It was dedicated to Lord Salisbury, whose brand of humanitarian, prudent, moral and somewhat aloof conservatism she had long admired. He wrote twice to express his appreciation of the work, but that was slender comfort and her prevailing mood remained an old woman's pet of self-pity, disillusion and melancholy. Early in 1900 she left the cottage 'shrine' at Tobermory for the last time, bearing the 'dear treasures of the beloved' away with her to bleak Hartford Hurst.

But by May her indomitable, enterprising spirit came bouncing back. 'I have begun French conversation lessons,' she told a friend, 'lessons in photography (developing, platinotyping, and lantern slide making by reduction) and am preparing to take a few cooking lessons. I am also ordering a tricycle in the hope of getting more exercise.' But the exercise she was preparing for was more strenuous than trips awheel around the lanes of Huntingdonshire – it was another journey, no less, since she 'felt quite able for modified travelling', such as a jaunt up the West River in China and then to 'To-chien-lu and up to Somo and Sieng-pon-ling and thence to Peking'. But this time, alas, the flesh was too weak and the doctors' reports on her health were so unremittingly grave, that she compromised by going only as far as Morocco, where she planned 'a rest for embroidery, photography and water-colours'.

New Year's Day of her seventieth year found her in Tangier, the details of the thousand-mile six-month-long Moroccan adventure that followed are sparse, and confined mainly to her published articles on the political and social chaos of the country. The few other glimpses of it, however, that emerge from private correspondence, tiptoe on the very verge of fantasy – a fantasy so glorious and grand because this mettlesome old woman actually made it fact. 'I left Tangier;' she begins, 'and had a severe two days' voyage to Mazagan, where the landing was so terrible and the sea so wild that the captain insisted on my being lowered into the boat by the ship's crane, in a coal basket. The officers and passengers cheered my pluck as the boat mounted a huge breaking surge on her landward adventure. No cargo could be landed. . . . Before leaving the steamer I had a return of fever; and when the only camping-ground turned out to be a soaked ploughed field with water standing in the furrows, and the tent was pitched in a storm of wind and rain, and many of the tent-pegs would not hold, and when the head of my bed went down into the slush when I lay down, I thought I should die there – but I had no more illness or fever!' Incredibly, travel had yet again proved an elixir and she thoroughly enjoyed the 126-mile journey to Marrakesh.

At Marrakesh, Isabella had 'a Moorish house to myself with a courtyard choked with orange-trees in blossom and fruit. I also have what is a terror to me, a powerful black charger, a huge fellow far too much for me, equipped with crimson trappings and a peaked crimson saddle, eighteen inches above his back. I have to carry a light ladder for getting on and off! I have been waiting for three days to get away and make an expedition into the Atlas range, whose glittering snows form a semi-circle round half the plain.'

So it was away from the plains and back to the snow-peaked mountains, where, perched atop her magnificent black charger, she was received 'well', if with some astonishment, by the Berber sheikhs in their castle strongholds. From one of these she wrote, 'This journey differs considerably from any other and it is as rough as the roughest. I never expected to do such travelling again. You would fail to recognise your infirm friend astride on a superb horse in full blue trousers and a short full skirt, with great brass spurs belonging to the generalissimo of the Moorish army, and riding down places awful even to think of, where a rolling stone or a slip would mean destruction. . . . It is evidently air and riding which do me good. I never realised this so vividly as now'. (She should surely have realised it by then – it had been the story of her life for thirty years. And if only she had, for once, turned her camera upon herself in that fantastic rig-out.)

Back at Marrakesh after the 'splendid journey', she told her friend, 'I had an interview with the Sultan. It was very interestng, but had to be secretly managed, for fear of the fanatical hatred to Christians. I wish it could have been photographed – the young Sultan on his throne on a high dais, in pure white; the minister of war, also in white, standing at the right below the steps of the throne . . .; I standing in front below the steps of the throne, bare-headed and in black silk, the only European woman who has ever seen an Emperor of Morocco! as I am the first who has ever entered the Atlas mountains and ever visited the fierce Berber tribes. When I wished the Sultan long life and happiness at parting, he said that he hoped when his hair was as white as mine, he might have as much energy as I have! So I am not quite shelved yet!' She was not; she rode another five hundred miles after that from Marrakesh to Tangier via Mogador, Saffii and Fez, and was chased almost to the outskirts of Tangier by a gang of armed Arab bandits. 'On the whole Mrs Bishop benefited by her long rides in Morocco,' commented the imperturbable Anna Stoddart. 'Tent life always suited her, and in spite of alarms she enjoyed the absolute novelty of her experiences. Without alarms and difficulties she would have probably accounted her venture a failure.' Indeed yes, and to what extraordinary lengths she went, at the age of seventy, for one last draught of unalloyed joy. 'I know this delightful return of vigour is temporary,' she explained, 'but it is marvellous while it lasts.'

She returned to England in the early autumn, reinvigorated and 'unshelved', and immediately undertook another punishingly arduous round of 'missionary addresses' – guilty recompense, fervent penitence, pious restitution for those days of pagan delight abroad. The sense of moral guilt and spiritual unworthiness rankled almost to the end, legacy of her environment and the nobler dead who had gone before. It was a guilt that kept her modest all her days, that brought her much anguish, spurred her charitable endeavours, eroded much of the satisfaction she could legitimately have taken in her considerable achievements. In the final two years of her life it was, perhaps, stilled at last and she was as near as she ever was to peace, accepting that she had truly done her best in accordance with the talents she had been given.

By this time, sales of the book on China had picked up, following the 1900 disturbances in that frequently disturbed country, and so even the 'child of her old age' was eventually a success. When Isabella's books are compared with those of her travel-writer contemporaries this success is quite explicable, for she retained to the last that rare ability to transport the reader to whatever outlandish spot she happened to be in, conjuring its characteristic denizens sights, sounds and smells through her individually apprehended experience of them. And in a pre-radio, pre-television age, such a gift was both valuable and popular – for how else could the stay-at-homes have their horizons broadened? Nevertheless, it is easy to fault Isabella's work: she had little artistic appreciation and her descriptions of native arts are usually trite, sometimes downright philistine; in her conscientious desire (shared by most of her contemporaries) to instruct rather than merely entertain, she crammed wedges of text-book plain facts into her later books that impede and dull their narrative flow; and her judgements on the political, moral and religious aspects of national life in the countries she knew, though often shrewd and sometimes tolerant, are seldom very far-sighted or progressive. Many of her attitudes – towards women's rights for instance, or Christian evangelism – were representative of the responsible, high-minded, essentially con-servative Victorian middle classes from which she sprang; but at least she was never smug, squeamish or sanctimonious about them.

Within a year of her return from Morocco her health finally broke down, doctors diagnosed a fibrous tumour, thrombosis, worsening heart disease. Hartford Hurst, the last domestic failure, hardly ever lived in, was given up and she went to Edinburgh to die. 'I learn that I am threatened with a serious and fatal malady,' she told an old friend. 'I am not distressed, though there are some things that I should like to see out.' She wrote that in May 1902, but her tough, thick, oft-besieged body was stubborn, her mind was clear and calm and it took her more than two years to see things out. Even then she kept moving, from one Edinburgh nursing-home to another, from one lodging to another, with most of her possessions in storage – and the trunks in London, packed ready for that last, unrealisable journey to China.

Devoted old friends surrounded her, sent books, pot plants, game pies, flowers to cheer her, and preserved their recollections of her, knowing the days were numbered. Her cousin, for instance, wrote to Anna Stoddart: 'She was so wonderfully cheerful and uncomplaining. When I said to her how trying it was for her to be lying there unable to move, she said: "I have never once thought it hard!" One day I remarked how patient she was, and she answered: "I am not patient, I would much rather be going about" . . . She said to me one day: "I never thought very much of myself." Then another day, "I should very much like to do something more for people but I can do nothing" .' In fact, her continuing lively interest in people and events during these bedridden years did quite a lot to help those around her and inspired several younger admirers, Scottish girls who had seldom ventured to set foot south of the border, but listened wide-eyed to her stories and yearned hopelessly to go where she had been.

Where she had been – her death-bed must have been rich with memories of that. Perhaps she remembered floating in a blue Hawaiian grotto with Mr and Mrs Luther Severance thirty years before and looking up at the golden balls of guava fruit swinging overhead, apricots swinging in the orchards of the Nubra valley and women pounding oil from their kernels, golden curls of Jim Nugent swinging under his smashed wide-awake and his one good eye glowing at her; eyes of tiger congealed and stiff in the mud of a jungle clearing while Chinese ripped out its liver and dried its blood in slabs in the sun; Chinamen jogging over the endless paddies with loads of salt, coal and vegetables or chanting as they heaved the creaking junks up the rapid; tattered sail of sampan creaking at anchorage in the sunset on the Han River, with fleas rustling in the pheasant-grass roof, and sunset sight of flush-pink Japanese children riding their fathers' shoulders down the village street; and she riding, feeling the springy curl of the yak's back, the ridgy backbone of the baggage pony, the sweaty side of the mule, the nuzzling nose of Boy begging for grapes, the jaunty prance of iron-legged Birdie. Birdie, the first beloved of many beloved horses, and she astride her with that up-to-anything, free-legged air, the two of them galloping away towards the empty mountain spaces.

She was bound now, she could not even reach the foothills, her weak hands unable to write down what she was remembering. She died on 7 October 1904. The obituaries said that she embarked 'on her last great journey' with fortitude, acceptance and a kind of joy. It was fitting that she should, for, as she always said, she was a 'born traveller' – she told her tales well, she seldom retraced her steps, she never outstayed her welcome.

Sources

(*Place of publication is London unless otherwise stated*)

General

Isabella L. Bird (Mrs Bishop): *An Englishwoman in America* by 'I.B.' (1856), *Six Months in the Sandwich Islands* (1875), *A Lady's Life in the Rocky Mountains* (1879), *Unbeaten Tracks in Japan* (1880), *The Golden Chersonese and the Way Thither* (1883), *Journeys in Persia and Kurdistan* (1891), *Korea and Her Neighbours* (1898), *The Yangtze Valley and Beyond* (1899) also *Among the Tibetans* (1894). Articles in *The Leisure Hour, St James' Gazette, The Monthly Review, The Family Treasury, Good Words*

Anna M. Stoddart: *The Life of Isabella Bird* (1906)

Dorothy Middleton: 'Isabella Bird' in *Victorian Lady Travellers* (1965)

Original letters and other documents in the possession of John Murray

Chapter I   The Sandwich Isles

Mark Twain's *Letters from Hawaii* (1866) gives a lively picture of the Islands at a slightly earlier period. Professor A. L. Korn wrote about several early English visitors to the Islands, including Isabella, in *Victorian Visitors* (Honolulu, 1958). For a good scholarly historical account of the period when Isabella was there, Ralph S. Kuykendall's *The Hawaiian Kingdom* vol. ii *Twenty Critical Years* 1854–74 (Honolulu, 1953) is invaluable.

Chapter II   The Rocky Mountains

Marshall Sprague's *A Gallery of Dudes* (Denver, 1967) includes a very entertaining, quite irreverent version of Isabella's meeting

with Jim Nugent. His *Newport in the Rockies* (Denver 1961) is
full of the flavour and atmosphere of the Colorado Springs area,
including the period when Isabella was there. George Kingsley's
Notes on Sport and Travel (1900) contains his version of Jim
Nugent's death. *South by West* by Rose Kingsley (1874) gives
her very personal account of the pioneer days in the Colorado
Springs area. Harold M. Dunning has written a pamphlet about
Jim Nugent for local tourist consumption; it is called 'In the
Evening Shadows of Colorado's Long's Peak'. Le Roy Hafen has
written extensively on many aspects of Colorado's pioneer
history. There is an intriguing contemporary history of Denver
by W. B. Vickers with lots of flavourful photographs, *History
of Denver* (Denver, 1880). I also obtained cuttings from *The
Rocky Mountain News* and *The Fort Collins Standard*. The
Western History Department of Denver Public Library gives
much useful information and help to all enquirers about Colorado's pioneering days.

Chapter III   Japan

The Rev. John Batchelor gives detailed accounts of Ainu
life at the period in *The Ainu of Japan* (1892) A. H. Landor
wrote his petulant, eccentric account of North Japan in *Alone
Among the Hairy Ainu* (1893). The only (lifeless) biography of
Sir Harry Parkes is by F. Dickins and S. Poole. Other personal,
entertaining accounts of Japan during the 1870s and 1880s are
found in William G. Dixon's *The Land of the Morning* (Edinburgh
1882), and Dr Henry Faulds's *Nine Years in Nippon* (1887).
There are many 'straight' histories of nineteenth-century Japan
including Malcolm D. Kennedy's *A Short History of Japan*
(1963) and W. G. Beasley's *The Modern History of Japan* (1963).
Sir George Sansom *The Western World and Japan* (1950) is
always invaluable. In my own books, *The Coming of the Barbarians* (1967) and *The Deer Cry Pavilion* (1968) I give an
account of westerners in Japan – including, in the latter, Isabella
Bird.

Chapter IV   Malaya

An idiosyncratic 'woman's view' of Perak and Selangor during
the 1870s appears in Emily Innes's *The Golden Chersonese with*

the Gilding Off (1885). Sir Frank Swettenham's *British Malaya* (1907) gives much fascinating material about events and personalities he knew in the Malay States during the period of Isabella's visit. There is a sympathetic and very readable account of Sir Hugh Low's personality in *Verandah* by James Pope-Hennessy (1964). Extracts from Hugh Low's journals appear in the *Journal of the Royal Asiatic Society, Malay Branch* for 1954. Among many very readable histories of the Native States at the time are John Kennedy's *A History of Malaya* (1962); *Nineteenth-Century Malaya* by Prof. C. D. Cowan (1961) and J. Gullick's *Malaya* (1964). I also consulted records in the Public Record Office, London for material on Low's administration and Douglas's misdemeanours.

Chapter VII   Kashmir and Tibet

William Carey's *Travel and Adventure in Tibet* (1902) is good on contemporary atmosphere, and for the atmosphere of a rather earlier time, the lively, charming, *Travels in Tartary, Thibet and China* by Abbé Huc (Trans: by W. Hazlitt, 1852). *Working and Waiting for Tibet* by H. G. Schneider (1891) is a pamphlet about the Moravian missionaries there. *Tibet the Mysterious,* Sir Thomas Holdich (1906) gives the background of western exploration there. There is a comprehensive modern history by H. E. Richardson, *Tibet and its History* (1962); and for what happened when Curzon focused his attention on Tibet, don't miss *Bayonets to Lhasa* by Peter Fleming (1961) which concerns the Younghusband expedition.

Chapter VIII   Persia and Kurdistan

Persia and the Persian Question by George N. Curzon (1892) tells all, but all, about the country at the time. A colourful contemporary account of the period is Dr C. J. Wills's *In the Land of the Lion and the Sun* (1883). Clara C. Rice published a small worthy memoir of Mary Bird, Isabella's cousin, *Mary Bird of Persia* (1922). For the political background of Russian-British rivalry, *Persia and the Defence of India*, Rose Greaves (1959), is invaluable and lucid. There is also the very scholarly *Russia and Britain in Persia* by F. Kazemzadeh (Yale, 1968).

Sources

Chapter IX Korea

The Korean Repository published during the 1890s by the missionaries in Seoul is full of out-of-the-way local colour. *The Story of Korea* by J. Longford (1911) is an old-fashioned history. *Korea and the Politics of Imperialism 1876–1910* by C. I. E. Kim and Han-Kyo Kim (1967) gives the modern view. George Curzon's *Problems of the Far East, Japan – Korea – China* (1894) includes a long section on his pessimistic view of Korea. For the opinions of a lively missionary on the spot at the time (whom Isabella met often) Rev. J. S. Gale's *Korean Sketches* (Chicago, 1898) and *Korea in Transition* (New York, 1909). Articles about Korea appear in the *Journal of the Royal Asiatic Society, Japan Branch*.

Chapter X China

Other travellers who went along Isabella's route were A. J. Little *Through the Yangtze Gorges* (1888); E. H. Parker, *Up the Yangtse* (1895). For a very secular view of the missionaries and the work, see George Morrison's *An Australian in China* (1895) and for a modern estimate of the missionary influence, Paul A. Varg *Missionaries, Chinese and Diplomats,* (1958). An enlightened missionary view by a popular writer of the period is *China in Convulsion* by Arthur H. Smith (1901); Lord Charles Beresford's *The Breakup of China* (1899) gives the contemporary commercial and political view. J. B. Eamess *The English in China* (1909) is interesting.

Index